THE LITERATURE OF THE
SPANISH PEOPLE

THE
LITERATURE OF THE
SPANISH PEOPLE

*From Roman Times to the
Present Day*

BY

GERALD BRENAN

CAMBRIDGE
AT THE UNIVERSITY PRESS
1965

PUBLISHED BY
THE SYNDICS OF THE CAMBRIDGE UNIVERSITY PRESS

Bentley House, 200 Euston Road, London, N.W. 1
American Branch: 32 East 57th Street, New York, N.Y. 10022
West African Office: P.O. Box 33, Ibadan, Nigeria

First Edition 1951
Second Edition 1953
Reprinted 1962
1965

Printed in Great Britain at the University Printing House, Cambridge
(Brooke Crutchley, University Printer)

TO
THE MEMORY OF
ROGER FRY

CONTENTS

PREFACE TO THE FIRST EDITION

THE scope and purpose of this book require a few words of explanation. This is the history of a literature. Unlike most such histories, however, it does not confine itself to books written in one language, but describes the literary productions of a people—in this case the Spanish people—in whatever language they may have been written, from the earliest times to the present day.

Let me show what in practice this amounts to. The first chapter treats of the Latin literature of the Peninsula, written during the Roman and Visigothic periods, but only in so far as it can be considered to be truly Spanish. That is to say, it attempts to show the native element in these writings emerging from the Roman and West Mediterranean. Even Prudentius, thoroughly Spanish in feeling and education though he is, has been examined solely from this angle.

The next chapter, which is longer, discusses the brilliant and sophisticated literature that was written in Arabic. Here there are really two subjects—the classical literature in prose and verse, in which it is not possible to distinguish any specifically Spanish element, and the popular poetry of what we may call the jongleurs. Of the first I should have had nothing to say, especially as I do not read Arabic, if it had not seemed to me that the kind of images and conceits found in this poetry deserved mention for the reason that later on, in the seventeenth century, much the same kind of imagery reappears in a Baroque context. One cannot see Góngora or the Andalusian poets who followed him in their proper perspective—nor, for that matter, Juan Ramón Jiménez or García Lorca—unless one realises that they were obeying a tendency peculiar to their race and environment.

With regard to the second kind of Spanish Arabic poetry—

that of the jongleurs—my obligation was clear. This poetry was written only in Spain, was derived from a popular poetry sung in Romance and had a long line of descent in Spanish literature. No effort of the imagination is required to see that Ibn Guzmán and the Archpriest of Hita belong to a similar school of jongleur-esque poetry, or that the popular *copla* that is sung in the streets of Seville today is descended from the *markaz* or *jarcha* of Spanish-Arab popular song. One of the most striking things in Spanish literature is the persistence of the native folk-song and the influence it has had upon even the most sophisticated poets.

In my third chapter I describe the appearance of the Castilian border epic—so comparable to that of the *romance* or ballad two centuries later—and then the sudden spate of Galician-Portuguese lyric poetry that followed it. Galicians and Portuguese shared at this time one culture and one language: the political division between them was less than that which divided the Duchy of Normandy from the Île de France. Moreover this poetry acquired such a prestige that Galician became for a time the recognized language for lyric verse throughout Castile, not only among the nobles but also to some extent among the people. Its influence in forming and giving music to the Castilian lyric of the fifteenth and sixteenth centuries was capital, all the more since it did not operate through direct imitation by the court poets, but welled up in a devious and unconscious way in popular song. For this reason no history of Castilian poetry could be written without some account of the Galician *cantigas de amigo*.

Round about the year 1500 there was a short period during which Portuguese poets wrote in Spanish as well as in their own language, just as in earlier times Castilians had written in Galician-Portuguese. I have therefore given a few pages to the greatest of these bilingual poets, Gil Vicente, though only as regards his Spanish works. After this Portuguese literature broke away from Spanish and took its own course. At about the same time Galician ceased to exist as a cultural language and sank to the position of a provincial dialect. In this it continued until the 1860's, when the Federal Movement brought a brief renaissance and a burst of poetry. It seemed only natural to discuss this, all the more since

Galician is a language or dialect that has not travelled so far from Spanish as has modern Portuguese.

Over the question of whether I should include Catalan literature I have had hesitations. Catalan is a branch of the *langue d'oc* or Provençal language and much less closely related to Spanish than are Portuguese or Galician. Moreover this literature—divided into two parts, a medieval and a modern—is extensive. I have therefore compromised. That is to say, I have given a brief sketch of medieval Catalan, concentrating on the figure of Auziàs March, a great and original poet who is almost totally unknown to modern readers, and have said nothing of the revival of Catalan literature in the nineteenth century. March was in any case not a Catalan but a Valencian, and he wrote according to the rules of Provençal prosody in a literary idiom which was greatly influenced by that used by the troubadours. If I can succeed in drawing to him the attention of those Englishmen who read Provençal, I shall not have misspent my time, for as a poet he towers above the other exponents of *lo Gay Saber*.

Finally I should say that I have brought this work to a close with the rise of the generation that was born after 1890, thus excluding García Lorca and the contemporary school of poetry.

Perhaps it is desirable that I should say something of the various objects I have had in mind in writing this book. The first has been to persuade English readers to sample the delights of Spanish literature. It is not so extensive a literature as English or French, but it is a very concentrated one, possessing a strong flavour and idiosyncrasy. Both history and geography have combined to give it a character unlike that of other European countries: history, through the Arab occupation, the religious idealism induced by the Counter-Reformation and the frequent periods of anarchy and civil war; geography, through the division of the country by high mountain ranges into separate regions each with its own culture, by the aridity of the soil and by the sharp changes of vegetation and climate. It is thus the literature of a people who have scarcely ever known security or comfort. As one reads it one cannot fail to be struck by the fact that from the Middle Ages to the eighteenth century the note of hunger runs persistently through the novels, or that such a large number of Spanish writers have either spent some part of their lives in prison or else been exiles. These things account for the tautness and alertness that characterize so much Spanish literature and for the background of melancholy and nostalgia (*soledad*) out of which even the gayest passages—and much Spanish literature is gay—have sprung. They also account for the realism.

Spanish prose can of course be read in translation, though with a considerable loss of quality, but the poetry has to be read in the original. Now Spanish lyric poetry has no rival in Europe except English. Since it has never had any influence outside its own country, it is virgin territory, and it invites discovery because there is so much in its forms and its imagery that accords with modern tendencies. Also, though melodious, it is austere—little given either to wordiness or to rhetoric. For these reasons I would like to urge not only poetry lovers but practising poets to sample it. To read prose with proper appreciation it is necessary to know a language well, but poetry can often be enjoyed after a comparatively slight acquaintance. This is particularly true in the case of Spanish poetry, because it is written in a strongly stressed language whose vocabulary is mainly Latin, and it makes little use of idiomatic expressions. Except in satirical verse, the gulf fixed between the language proper to poetry and that to daily speech is great. Anyone therefore who is prepared to give a few evenings to a Spanish grammar and to spend his holiday in Spain will be in a position to start reading it. As for Galician poetry, it is scarcely more difficult to a Spaniard than is Scots poetry to an Englishman. The person who can read Spanish will therefore easily master it.

Another purpose that this book is intended to serve is that of a history of the literature written by Spaniards. Literary history is, in one respect, merely a branch of a total history that includes in its various departments political history, social history and the history of art. With this in mind I have taken any opportunities that seemed to be offered for showing in what way Spanish literary works are to be regarded as an expression of the national spirit in successive ages and, incidentally, to use this for throwing light on the character of the Spanish people—supposing, that is, that peoples really have a continuous character. It is partly for this reason that I have included short chapters on the Roman and Arab periods. It may be thought that this is extending too far the scope of a critical study of literature. But what limits can be laid down? Literature comes out of and leads back into life, and we should read very narrowly indeed if we never allowed our thoughts to stray from the book before us to the character of the people and culture that produced it. Besides it is through its art and literature that the essential spirit of a country or age is most readily grasped.

However, the main object of a literary history must necessarily be to display and, if possible, account for the various tendencies, movements and revolutions of taste and sentiment that take place among the writers and poets of every successive age. These movements are governed partly by changes of feeling due to alterations in the social and political environment, and partly by technical considerations inherent in the literary medium itself. This second factor has received very little attention from English critics. We in our amateurish way tend to think of writers as solitary geniuses who appear for no particular reason, express themselves and their age and vanish again. All that we grudgingly allow to literary tradition is the fact that it provides 'influences'. Now this to my mind is a very perfunctory way of approaching any art. It pays no regard to the fact that the succession of works of literature in any country, arranged in their various forms and categories, has, except in periods of hesitation, a logic and unity of its own. We can see this more clearly if we look at the history of painting. From Giotto to Rafael and on through the Venetians to Rembrandt and Velazquez there is a steady and logical line of development, inherent in the nature of the art itself and only in part influenced by the ethos of the age and country in which the pictures were painted. The same is true from Constable and Delacroix down to the painters of today. This development, which exists in music too, may be less obvious in literature, but it is there all the same and I believe that the most important advance that could be made towards an objective understanding of the growth of literature would be to take some account of it.

For tradition ought not to be thought of simply in the light of influences coming down from the past. That is not, as a rule, how it affects the artist, who himself chooses from among his predecessors the few whose guidance he requires. The poet, novelist or painter feels himself rather in the position of an explorer or pioneer: behind him stretch the lands already discovered and settled—before him are the new regions he must enter and map. That is to say, he will always have a compelling sense of something to be done that has not been done before: not merely a sense of what he personally can do in the way of expressing and developing his special gift or vision (though this also has to be considered), but an intimation of what the art he practises calls for and of the line—to be regarded as something like the grain in wood—along which he must move if he is to make progress. This may lead him—as in the case of Cézanne or Hopkins or Góngora—to a position where his work is isolated and does not express in any important respect the spirit of the age he lives in. In other words, what a tradition gives is not so much a series of works to be absorbed and imitated, as a pressure, coming out of the nature of the art itself in the position in which it has been left by his predecessors, which forces him to cross a new frontier. In most ages the various types of literature find themselves in this predicament, and the great writer is simply the man whose superior energies enable him to carry out an advance, the general necessity and direction of which many lesser men may have perceived. In this book I have endeavoured, whenever the indications seemed clear, to show this pressure at work.

However, the main emphasis of this book is laid, not on this elusive question of the literary-historical process, but on a critical examination of the principal poets, dramatists and prose writers. For this reason I have given a considerable amount of space to the outstanding figures and have dealt more briefly with the others. A large number of minor figures have been omitted altogether, or awarded only the briefest mention, in order to avoid cluttering up the book with names and so distracting the reader.

I must explain what I believe to be the proper approach to literary criticism. The business of a critic is, as Baudelaire said, to approach every work with an open mind and in the greatest possible state of aesthetic receptivity. He should never for a moment forget that a poem, a novel or a painting can be anything—that is to say, can have any form or content—so long as it evokes feeling, and that only when he has humbly and passively submitted himself to the work of the writer or painter will he be free to stand back and make comparisons and judgments. One has, therefore, the right to ask of the critic that he should allow no bias or preconceived opinion to affect him in his initial state of in-taking, only bearing in mind that one cannot expect his receptive organs to be adequate on all occasions. In one place at least in this work—in the appreciation of Gracián's prose writings— I am aware of probable deficiencies in mine, and there must be other pages where, in the labour of reading a great many books, I have failed to register properly. Such lapses I regret. But since I believe that one of the principal functions of art and literature, second only to the immediate delight and elevation of mind they give, is the manner in which they display the range and diversity of mind and experience open to human nature—thus putting us into the skin of persons very remote and different from ourselves and so mitigating our chronic state of self-imprisonment—I have not attempted to lay down any laws or principles, aesthetic, moral or religious, by which poems or prose works should be judged. Works of art and literature are, in my opinion, to be valued by the depth and quality of the experience they convey, and by the immediacy and clarity with which they convey it, rather than by their moral or ideological rightness. Ethical considerations only come in when they affect that experience by extending it or diminishing it.

I emphasize this view, which I believe to be the only one permissible to a critic, because the tendency shown in recent years to look at literature through the glasses of an ideological preconception and to rate highest those authors whose attitude to life is most in harmony with that of the critic seems to me regrettable. When these views are expressed by a great and admired poet, when they are echoed and drawn out by the little senate who take their laws from him, when the tone adopted is narrow, smug and cantankerous, when these dogmatic assertions are meekly received by readers who do not accept the ideological premises that dictated them, who can help being saddened by the decline in intellectual standards that is thus displayed? Literary criticism has its ethics, and it is the business of those who dislike the growth of the totalitarian mentality to resist the subjection of art to dogma and to stand out for the free examination and enjoyment of the literary production of all races and ages. Art and literature are to be judged by broad humanist standards, or by none at all.

Above all one should beware of the poet or philosopher critic. Poets have things to say about their art that are of the highest value and which no one else but poets can say. But the very fact that they are engaged in writing poetry of a specific sort means that—unless, like Dryden, Goethe, or Baudelaire, they are men of great breadth of mind and sensitivity of reaction—they are likely to have narrow and partial views on literature. We do not consult Lenin or even Lloyd George for an objective view of the political history of their countries, and so I do not see why we should expect from poets in a revolutionary age—and most ages are revolutionary in poetry—any better or juster view. Certainly we do not get it. The history of criticism by poets is strewn with dogmatic statements of contempt for their great predecessors and of absurd over-estimations of others. It may well be that such a narrowness of view is often a necessary condition of their work, though painters are less prone to show it, but at all events those of us who are not of the trade ought not to allow ourselves to be imposed on. For literature is by no means the possession of a small group of writers, who inevitably have their own axes to grind, who are all more or less cannibal-minded, but of its lovers and appreciators, wherever they may live and whatever their professions or modes of life may be. They alone are the judges of finished work and for them alone, with rare exceptions, is something like impartiality and a wide range of receptivity possible.

The critic then, if I am right, has to take into account the historical setting in which the work was produced: he must consider the problem which faced the writer, the means that were at his disposal, his artistic canons and intentions. He should not, for example, disparage Milton and Góngora for having written in a Latinized idiom, or Joyce, Pound and Cummings for preferring a jargon of their own invention. Rather he should submit himself with humility to what a writer has to give, and only when he is certain that he is attuned to it proceed to interpret and give judgment. If there is enough of the true stuff of poetry or literature in any writer, his work will always be worth reading. Yet the critic should also remember that he is a man of modern sensibilities and feelings. Every age has its special tastes and interests, and these will inevitably reduce the attractiveness of certain authors and increase those of others. Without abandoning therefore his fundamental impartiality, it will be only reasonable if he gives particular attention to those writers who have most to say to his contemporaries. Indeed he will only show that he is qualified to address his own age if in a certain measure he shares its tastes and point of view himself.

A final word must be said about the stress I have felt obliged to lay on medieval verse forms. The reader will, I fear, grow somewhat tired of the words *cuaderna vía*, *arte mayor* and *cantigas de amigo* and still more of *zéjel*, *estribillo* and *villancico*. But in the Middle Ages the form and genre are the important thing and not the genius or personality of the author. Each verse form is sustained by a school—one might almost say a guild—of jongleurs and poets, who supply a particular social need in much the same way as any other craftsman. Even such an apparently vivid personality as the Archpriest of Hita was following closely a traditional pattern and much of his, at first sight, amazing originality must be assigned to this. Except where, as in Italy, the spirit of classical literature makes itself felt, medieval poetry is deeply immersed in the traditional and anonymous.

With regard to the spelling of early poetry, I have followed, with slight simplifications, the rule set by Sr Dámaso Alonso in his excellent Anthology. That is to say, I have modernized it, keeping the older form only when it indicated a difference in pronunciation. Over Arabic words I have adopted what seemed in each case to be the most useful compromise.

Preface

I would like to express my thanks to Don Juan Ramón Jiménez for his kind permission to quote the whole of one of his poems together with short extracts from four or five others. I would further like to express my thanks to Dr Arthur Waley for the help and encouragement he has given me over the early chapters, to Dr F. J. E. Raby for information about Mozarabic hymns, to Mrs Isobel Henderson for reading and criticizing the first chapter, to Professor J. B. Trend for his valuable suggestions, to Don Alberto Jiménez for information about modern writers, to Mr J. L. Gili for invaluable help with the bibliography, and to Mr C. J. Hope-Johnstone for reading the proofs. I am also indebted to my wife, Gamel Woolsey, for the help she has given me in many parts of this book and especially in translating poems. It is only fair to state that I set her an almost impossible task by insisting that they should, in almost every instance, be word for word translations of the original, because it is this original that I should like the reader, if he has any Spanish at all, to read. It was only within these limits that she was free to seek what is the natural goal of every translator—some equivalent in English of the form and spirit of the original poem. Here we both agreed that, if this could be obtained for a few lines, a certain lameness in the rest of the passage could be tolerated. In every translation much has to be sacrificed. Poems that could not be put into verse without some loss of literalness have been given in prose.

6 *February* 1951   GERALD BRENAN

PREFACE TO THE SECOND EDITION

IN this edition I have corrected the errors that had crept into the first edition, have added to the bibliography, and have done my best to bring the passages on Arabic poetry up to date. This last has not been easy. The book had been finished and was ready to go to press when Mr S. M. Stern made his dramatic discovery of eleventh-century Spanish lyrics embedded in Hebrew poems, and I added an appendix to record it. Since then he has made further additions to our knowledge. In the last number of *Al-Andalus*, for example, he has cleared up the precise differences between the verse forms of the *zéjel* and the *muwassaha*, which had puzzled previous Arabic scholars, and has reinterpreted certain technical terms, such as the *markaz*. I have emended the text as best I could to accord with this new information and have added a footnote.

But the subject is growing. Quite recently, Mr Stern tells me, twenty-four Arabic *muwassahas* containing *jarchas* or short stanzas in Romance have turned up in Morocco. These *jarchas* conform to the same type as those already discovered in Hebrew poems—that is to say they consist of verses put into the mouth of a girl of the lower classes and expressing her grief at being separated from her lover. Many of them, like the Galician *cantigas de amigo*, contain appeals to her mother. No doubt within a few years a whole anthology of these little lyrics will have been dug out of the Arabic and Hebrew strata in which they have been lying buried and then this chapter on the Arab period, which I regard as important for a proper understanding of Spanish literature, will need to be rewritten.

On looking through this book again I find a number of passages which I should like to rewrite. These mostly occur in chapters where I allowed myself to be influenced by the sense of hurry and urgency which from time to time comes over those who are engaged on long books. Thus I did not give enough space to the sixteenth century or to the drama of Lope de Vega, I dismissed too lightly the poetry of Quevedo and I dealt with Gracián, a writer whom I read with effort, in a perfunctory way. Perhaps also, as some reviewers said, I should have devoted more space to the twentieth century. Opinions will always differ upon where to bring a history of literature or an anthology to an end.

I have been criticized too by several people whose knowledge and judgment I respect for my interpretation of Calderon. If I have erred here, as I think I have, it has not been for lack of taking pains. I went to as much trouble to understand this playwright and to trace the way in which his work had developed as I did over any other writer. But I do not see how anyone can interpret his *comedias* in a satisfactory way while we remain in our present state of ignorance upon his intellectual background. The theological controversies of seventeenth-century Spain, the development of Jesuit casuistry, the influence of Jansenist ideas, the new attitude to pagan mythology are subjects that have never been adequately studied by scholars, and until this has been done very much in the intentions that lie behind Calderon's plays will remain unexplained. A young Hispanist scholar, Mr Pring-Mill, has suggested to me that the key to a great deal of what I found obscure lies in the Jesuit-Dominican controversy over free-will and predestination, and I think it probable that he is right.

Another reviewer has pointed out that in my preface I promised to 'display and, if possible, account for the various tendencies, movements and revolutions of taste and sentiment that take place among the writers and poets of every successive age', but that in fact I have carried this out very imperfectly. No doubt I promised too much. A book which fulfilled such a plan would need to examine in detail the work of a large number of minor writers and to probe into obscure origins, and this would give it a different and much more prolix character than I intended. But I think that I have made reasonably clear the main tendencies and revolutions of taste and that anyone who reads this book will get an impression of Spanish literature, not simply as a collection of separate writers of genius, but as an organic and continuous whole.

Certainly it is desirable to obtain this. Just as one must have a certain acquaintance with the total work of a poet before one can receive the full effect of any single poem written by him, so one must possess some general familiarity with a literature if one wishes to draw the greatest possible benefit from any particular writer who contributes to it. This is not only for the obvious reason that poets and novelists draw so much of their style and content from previous poets and prose writers, but because there may be—indeed often are—elements in books or poems that do not acquire their full amplitude of meaning until long after the death of their author. To take a famous example from French literature, the line from Racine's play *Bérénice*, *Dans l'orient désert quel devint mon ennui!* could not stand out as it does until after the time of Baudelaire. Every great poem or passage of poetry is a sort of machine which acts on the mind through its faculty for calling up and condensing round it in a vivid way a body of associations and if, with the passage of time, the number and emotive power of the associations available to it should happen to grow, its potency will be increased proportionally.

To conclude, I will say that my aim in writing this book has been a modest one. I wished to draw the attention of English and American readers to Spanish literature, to show them what was most worth reading in it and, when the occasion offered, to help them to a better appreciation of it. I make no claim to special knowledge and, though I have done my best to absorb the work of scholars in the field I covered, the point of view from which I have written has been that of the person who reads literature for pleasure. I wrote to teach myself as well as other people and I would like to think that the sense of discovery I often felt while working on this book may have helped to make it more stimulating to readers. All the efforts of critics are wasted unless they lead us back to an increased understanding and enjoyment of the originals.

I have been influenced too by another consideration. It is becoming more and more the custom today for literary critics to leave all discussion of the early periods of literature to specialists, who alone are supposed to have the qualifications necessary for writing upon them. I believe that this retreat to the narrowness of modern times is a mistake and must eventually end in a large tract of literature becoming fossilized. If it is the business of the specialist or academic person to provide information and guidance of a detailed and circumscribed kind, it is that of the general writer on literature—the man of letters or critic—to make use of that information to carry out his ordinary task. In this there is no one who can take his place. The business of turning over and airing past works of literature and rearranging them in the *musée imaginaire* of modern times demands the services of a professional writer, and it is no disparagement to the academic person (who may sometimes be such a writer too) to say that someone else can do this sort of work best. It is thus because I think that literary critics must be prepared to take risks and, after due preparation, exercise their pens freely on the early periods of literature that I, who am no scholar, have been encouraged to write this history. If my book has any merit, it may be, I think, because I have approached the subject from this angle.

12 *September* 1952   GERALD BRENAN

CHAPTER I

THE ROMAN AND VISIGOTHIC PERIODS

TOWARDS 1766 two Franciscan friars, Fray Pedro and Fray Rafael Mohedano, sat down to write the history of Spanish literature. It was the age of long books and the good friars wished to do the job thoroughly. When at last they died, after twenty-five years of continuous work, they had finished ten volumes, bringing their history down to the year A.D. 65.

With this warning I shall try to deal with the beginnings of literature in Spain expeditiously. In fact there is not much, I think, that need be said about the first centuries. We know from Strabo that the Iberians of Andalusia had a literature, including epic poems and books of metrical laws, but it has not come down to us. All we can say is that it probably helped them to absorb Roman culture more rapidly than they would otherwise have done. They certainly showed a remarkable susceptibility to it. By the time of Julius Caesar the cities of the Guadalquivir and Ebro valleys—that is to say, the regions where the Iberians and not the Celts had settled—had become great centres of Latin civilization. We can see the results of this in the literature of the first and second centuries. The Silver Age, as it is called, is crowded with Spanish orators, teachers of rhetoric and poets. The two Senecas and Lucan from Cordova, Quintilian and Martial from Aragon, Columella from Cadiz are only the leading figures among a host of minor literati whose names alone have come down to us. But can we say that there is anything specifically Spanish in their writings? These men were trained in the Latin schools of rhetoric, spent their lives at Rome and wrote for Italians, just as the Spanish American poet José-Maria de Heredia lived in Paris and wrote for the French. The Roman character too—grave, ceremonious, sententious, at once emotional and stoical, humane and quick to shed blood—resembled the Spanish character in many ways. We must be careful then not to make hasty generalisations.

Let us take the younger Seneca. Two distinguished Spanish writers, Angel Ganivet and Unamuno, have declared that his Stoic philosophy is typically Spanish and have founded a theory of the Spanish character upon this. More recently people in other countries have called attention to his Baroque style (so typical, they say, of Andalusia) and to that of his nephew Lucan with his, as Dr Johnson put it, 'glittering accumulations of unsightly ornaments'. But Stoicism was simply the fashionable Roman philosophy of the day and the peculiarly religious tone given it by Seneca comes from a Syrian writer, Posidonius, whose books were then popular. As to the style, we should remember that the cult of eloquence leads naturally to a search for finer and more dazzling expressions. Seneca's rhetoric is partly a literary fashion, partly a political attitude. But it will be said that the melodrama of Senecan tragedies and of Lucan's epic poem, with their fierce insistence on the details of bloodshed, call up a Spanish vein of feeling. That may be so, but do they not much more reflect the Roman amphitheatres and the bloodbaths of Claudius and Nero? Finally let us remember that though their family was of colonial Roman descent, Lucan had never lived in Spain, while Seneca's complex and ambiguous character has nothing especially Spanish about it. Like Bacon's, it is the product of a struggle between strong ambition and noble impulses, taking place in the dangerous environment of a despot's court.

We are on safer ground when we speak of the Aragonese character of Quintilian and Martial. Quintilian (*c.* 35-100) was the great educator of his age—*summus moderator juventae*, as Martial calls him—and the first man in Europe to receive a diploma and salary for teaching from the State. His influence has been immense. His *Institutions* were studied by the men who founded the French Cathedral Schools in the twelfth century and by the humanists in the sixteenth. In Luis Vives, the disciple of Erasmus, and in Francisco Giner de los Ríos, the educator of modern Spain, we find not only many of his ideas, but a real similarity of temperament. Now Quintilian's aim was to turn out not pedants or prodigies, but complete citizens: men of all-round talents, able to live agreeably in the world, to judge correctly of ordinary affairs and to take part effectively in public life. Since the art of speaking well had come to be the most important attainment for an educated Roman, his book takes the form of a treatise on oratory. He starts in childhood, where he anticipates the modern idea of kindergarten (incidentally he disapproved of corporal punishment) and ends with his famous and, within certain limits, admirable appreciations of literature. His dislike of exaggeration made him react against the Senecan rhetoric towards the more serious and reasoned style of Cicero. He is alive to the moral implications in literature and in his saying 'Schoolmasters are the parents of the mind' he expresses his very Spanish sense of the teacher's universal mission. In every part of his book one finds a preference for observation rather than for theory and a dry, sober, gentle common sense that strikes us as more Aragonese than Roman.

Martial, too, is Spanish. His character at first glance seems less attractive than Quintilian's. He earned his living, as all impecunious authors then had to do, by toadying to the rich and powerful. He was not above giving fulsome praise to the tyrant Domitian or, when his wit ran short, regaling his readers with copious pornography. But when we study him more closely we find certain admirable traits, which have made him, a light-weight poet, one of the most original and widely read of Latin authors.

For all his jibes he was a good-natured man, direct and frank, who took the world as he found it. What he hated most were shams, and in these he included the rhetorical exaggerations of his day and the mythological apparatus that poets thought necessary for their verses. He went direct to life for his material and that is why, when one reads his epigrams, one gets a picture of the Roman world that nothing else in classical literature, except Petronius' picaresque novel, gives us. He had the Spanish eye for vivid detail—one of those dry, hungry eyes that absorb what they see around them because there is no inner preoccupation to prevent them from seeing it—and he had a Spanish spontaneity: his verses, for all their terseness, give a most un-Latin impression of effortless composition. He also had the Spanish philosophy of man.

'*Hominem pagina nostra sapit*', he wrote, 'My pages tell you about men'; and the words *vita* and *homo*, life and man, recur continually through his poems. It is this tolerance that saves him from cynicism. It also justifies to a certain extent his pornography—since nothing must be left out of the picture—and spares us the moralising which makes Juvenal's dark pictures so suspect to us. Martial, when he was not touting for a present, had no axe to grind.

But let me quote from the delightful poems that he has written on his own country. After forty years of bachelor life in Rome, getting up early, as the custom was, to greet his rich patrons on their rising from bed and returning late to his garret to sleep, he retired to his native Aragon, to escape, as he said, 'the togas stinking of purple dye and the conversation of haughty widows'. The place he chose was a farm that had been given him near to Bilbilis, a little town standing on a bend of the River Jalón, out of whose stones the Arabs later built Calatayud. There life was cheaper than at Rome 'because the soil maintained one'.

In a verse letter to his friend Juvenal he describes his property—the poplar grove and meadow, the springs with their open conduits of water, the pot-herb in January, the rose trees and vine trellis, the tame eel in its tank, the whitewashed dovecot, the tepid river in which one could bathe.

'Here we live lazily and work pleasantly. I enjoy a vast unconscionable sleep which often lasts till ten and so make up for all I've lost these thirty years. You'll find no togas here; if you ask for one, they'll give you the nearest rug off a broken chair. When I get up I find a fire heaped with splendid logs from the oak forest, which the bailiff's wife has crowned with her pots and pans. [Around it squat a crowd of grubby youths.] Then my huntsman comes in, a lad you would love to take off to some quiet wood. The bailiff gives the young slaves their rations and asks leave to have his long hair cut. *Sic me vivere, sic me iuvat perire*... 'That's how I like to live, that's how I hope to die.'

But there were also disadvantages—no theatres or libraries or good conversation, and all the petty gossip and backbiting of a small place. Martial grew bored and found the stimulus to write lacking. Bilbilis in A.D. 102 must have been very like what a small town in Spain is today.

We have seen how the Aragonese writers who lived in Rome kept their national character better than the Andalusian ones. That is precisely what we should expect, for the Andalusians are a quick and versatile people and the Aragonese are hard-headed. Besides they had not come out of the Roman colonies of Baetica, with their Republican and latifundist traditions, but from *municipia* of native Spanish origin. Now we must examine another writer of the Ebro valley, the Christian poet Prudentius, whose work, by its combination of two conflicting elements, the popular and the erudite, and its dry unrhetorical style, is more Aragonese still.

Aurelius Clemens Prudentius was born, probably in Saragossa, in 348 and died shortly after 405. Except for a brief visit to Rome, he spent his whole life in Spain, where he followed the careers of lawyer and magistrate. His early verses, which no doubt reflected those licentious years of his youth of which he tells us, are lost. All we have of his are the religious poems he wrote late in middle life 'to make amends' he says 'for his past uselessness'.

Prudentius' best-known works are the *Cathemerinon Liber* and the *Peristephanon*. The first is a collection of twelve hymns written in a variety of metres and entitled 'for cock-crow', 'for the hour when lamps are lit', 'for bedtime', and so forth. The second is a series of fourteen long narrative hymns or poems celebrating the deaths of various martyrs. Besides these he wrote a number of didactic poems in hexameters.

The Latin language had been changing all through the fourth century and the classical tradition in literature was breaking down. In poetry stress was taking the place of quantity, in spite of the efforts of the poets to prevent it, and rhyme and assonance were beginning to creep in. In prose the popular diction and emphatic rhythms of St Jerome's Vulgate mark a change almost as revolutionary as that of James Joyce and Gertrude Stein in our time. This tendency was first carried through deliberately in the hymns. In the year 360 St Hilary of Poitiers brought back from the East the custom of singing verse hymns. The principal metre he employed was borrowed from the chanties of Greek sailors and artisans: it had a very marked rhythm (Tennyson uses it in *Locksley Hall*) and under the name of *versus popularis* it was already popular with the Roman legionaries. But the person to make hymn-singing general was St Ambrose, the great Bishop of Milan who was a contemporary of Prudentius. Since he was a Roman aristocrat, brought up in the classical tradition, he did not care to use the marching-song metre. But quantitative poetry is not suitable for singing. He compromised therefore on an eight-syllabled metre, the iambic dimeter, which had the advantage of allowing him to write verses that were quantitatively correct and at the same time true to the rules of the new accentual poetry. His hymns were written for antiphonal singing—a practice which he was the first to introduce into the Western Church.

Now Spain has always been a country in which popular poetry, made for singing to instruments and not for recitation, has forced its way up into cultural poetry and permeated it. It is just this fusion of two different social elements and two different conceptions of the poetic function that makes its literature so alive and so remarkable. One would therefore expect Prudentius' hymns to be affected by the new popular style of accentual poetry. But this is not so. Everything he wrote is strictly quantitative and belongs to the old tradition coming down from Lucretius and Horace. His hymns were odes, intended for recitation to circles of cultured people, or occasionally for liturgical readings at special ceremonies, and not for choral singing in church.

Where then is the Spanish element in his poems? It lies first of all in the subjects chosen. His *Peristephanon*, as we have said, is a collection of hymns describing the deaths of martyrs. This was not an altogether new subject for poetry because St Ambrose and Pope Damasus (who was also a Spaniard) had already touched on it. But the extraordinary way in which Prudentius develops it and the new form that he invents to express the new material are entirely original and Spanish.

The martyr was the great heroic figure of the third and fourth centuries. We can see how he was regarded from the many so-called 'Acts of the Martyrs' that have come down to us. He was a man of superhuman strength and fearlessness, who through a succession of tortures, which are usually minutely described, defied his tormentors and argued with the magistrate who had condemned him on the dogmas of the faith. The point of the performance lay in its being a supreme exhibition of the triumph of mind over matter, of spirit over earthly or daemonic power, which for Christians and pagans alike was the great issue of the day. To the circus-loving crowds these martyrs were a new sort of athlete. St John Chrysostom speaks of them as 'running on hot coals as if on roses, plunging into fires as if into streams of cool water and garlanding themselves with tortures as if they were not tortures but spring flowers'. And when the end came, their souls rose straight to heaven among choirs of angels and their tombs on earth became centres of yearly feasts and pilgrimages.

Many people were converted by these scenes. As Tertullian said, 'Everyone, at the sight of such prodigies of endurance, feels himself struck with a scruple and longs to know what is at the bottom of it'. And the newly converted masses found in the martyrs' legends something to replace the stories of the pagan heroes which the world was forgetting. But in Spain the interest, or excitement rather, in martyrdom seems to have been greater than anywhere else in the West, in spite of the small number who suffered there. It was therefore a proper subject for a Spanish poet who wanted to do something more than write pastiches of the old literature.

Prudentius' 'hymns' on the martyrs closely followed the texts of the semi-illiterate 'Acts'. Although he was for those times an exceptionally well-educated man, deeply read in Latin and Greek literature and versed in theology, he identified himself in this matter with the popular spirit of his day. The result is therefore something quite new in literature—lyric-epic poems made up of action and dramatic dialogue and written in short stanzas. I do not see why we should not call them ballads. If the form is familiar to us, we must remember that there is nothing else in classic literature to compare with them.

Take for example this passage from the Passion of St Vincent. It begins with the prefect Dacianus, seated in his box in the

amphitheatre, calling on Vincent to offer incense to the statue
of the emperor:

> Rex, inquit, orbis maximus,
> Qui sceptra gestat Romula,
> Servire sanxit omnia
> Priscis Deorum cultibus.

> Vos, Nazareni, assistite,
> Rudemque ritum spernite:
> Haec saxa, quae princeps colit,
> Placate fumo et victima.

> Exclamat hic Vincentius,
> Levita de tribu sacra,
> Minister altaris Dei,
> Septem ex columnis lacteis:[1]

> Tibi ista praesint numina,
> Tu saxa, tu lignum colas:
> Tu mortuorum mortuus
> Fias Deorum pontifex.

> Nos lucis auctorem Patrem,
> Ejusque Christum Filium,
> Qui solus ac verus Deus,
> Daciane, confitebimur. . . .

> 'The great king of the world
> Who holds the sceptre of Romulus,
> Has decreed that every man
> Pay the ancient rites to the Gods.

---

[1] This line means 'one of seven deacons'. Note the characteristic ballad style. Images in classical poetry were brought in in the form of similes and were usually introduced by words such as *as if* and *like*. But here there is no *like*, because the image is a symbol and not a similitude of the thing it represents. This symbolic use of imagery comes from the East and was brought into Europe with Christianity. A thousand years later we find that it has sunk into the popular consciousness and become the characteristic image-type of European balladry.

> '*What did you fall out about, my dear son tell me?*'
> '*About a little bit of bush that soon would have been a tree.*'

Modern Spanish *coplas* abound in such symbolic expressions, as do the *villancicos* of the sixteenth-century song-books.

You Nazarenes, draw near,
Cast off your crude faith:
These are the stones the Prince worships,
Offer them smoke and sacrifice.'

Then up and spoke Vincentius,
Levite of the sacred tribe,
Minister of God's altar,
One of seven milk-white columns:

'Let them rule over you, these idols!
Worship you your stone and wood!
Be you a dead high priest
Of these gods that are stone dead!

As for us, we confess the Father
Of Light and the Christ his son,
Who alone, Dacianus,
Is the true and living God.'

Then the prefect was stirred to anger:
'Wretch,' said he, 'do you dare
To profane with haughty words
This law of Gods and princes?

A law both civil and sacred,
By the whole human race obeyed!
Surely even your headlong youth
Will be checked by imminent danger.

Hear then this word of mine:
Either you salute with incense
This turf and altar, or else
You shall suffer a bloody death.'

To this the other made answer:
'Come on then and put forth
Your utmost strength and power.
Here before all I defy you.

Tortures, prison, instruments,
Tongs and hissing iron,
Death itself, their culmination,
To Christians are a mere game.'

9

The hymn continues in the same bare, dramatic style for 144 stanzas. The tortures succeed one another—no detail is spared—whilst Vincent incites these S.S. men of the day, the *alumni carceris*, whom he calls 'artists in their trade', to wreak their worst on him. For they can only act on the body: the intrinsic part, *liber, quietus, integer*, is out of their reach. And when the *momento de la verdad* is over, the fortunes of his body are followed till it is buried by the seashore.

Another hymn, celebrating in sapphic metre the passion of eighteen martyrs at Caesaraugusta (Saragossa), takes one straight into the Spanish world. It begins with a magnificent painting, in Byzantine style, of the Last Day:

> Cum Deus dextram quatiens coruscam
> Nube subnixus veniet rubente,
> Gentibus juxtam positurus aequo
> Pondere libram.

The Son appears in a crimson cloud with scales in his glittering right hand and the peoples of the earth pour out by cities to meet him, bearing with them precious gifts in baskets. What are these gifts? They are the relics of their martyrs, and then follows a list of the cities of Spain—happy Tarragona, wealthy Gerona, populous Mérida, the pavement of whose church is like a flowering meadow —that are lucky enough to possess martyrs to intercede for them. Last of all comes Prudentius' own city, *Caesaraugusta studiosa Christi*, bearing the relics of its eighteen athletes: Caesaraugusta which never failed to shed its blood under every hail of persecution, which seemed to have been built expressly to make saints and had more martyrs to its account than any city in the world except Rome or Carthage. Here was born St Vincent, who later shed his blood at Saguntum. Caesaraugusta celebrated his day, to the Caesaraugustans he belonged. 'He is ours', they cry out. 'He is ours even though he died in a foreign city and was buried by the seashore. He is ours, for he is our lad on the wrestling ground and it was through him that we learned how to tame the enemy.'

After this follow, like the palm-bearing frieze in S. Apollinare Nuovo at Ravenna, the eighteen martyrs buried at Saragossa, beginning with Engratia, whose tortures (amputated breasts, gangrened limbs, liver torn out and so forth) are described with all the veristic detail of a Baroque painter. These martyrs shed their benefits on the land as water flows from springs: their sacred blood keeps away all dark ghosts and envious daemons from the doors: those who have visited their tombs with tears return home smiling: on their birthdays (as the anniversaries of their deaths were called) the people hold a feast at their shrines. The poem ends with an adjuration: 'Prostrate yourselves with me, noble citizens, before these holy tombs: then you will all of you follow quickly those resurgent souls and limbs.'

I need not point out to anyone who knows Spain how typical this poem is of certain aspects of Spanish life. The local saint or Madonna is still the protector of her city and a figure of patriotic pride and devotion even to those who have ceased to be practising Catholics. Arguments as to which town has the best saints and holds the best processions are still to be heard in any café. Till recently processions of flagellants with bloodstained backs offered a milder version of the cruel scenes in the amphitheatre, whilst the bull-fight represents the eternal drama of the triumph of spirit over brute force. Saragossa, today the fane of the Virgin of the Pillar, is still the religious capital of the Peninsula.

Prudentius' other books are in hexameters. One of these, the *Psychomachia*, is an allegory which describes in epic style a war between the personified Virtues and Vices. Though tedious to us, in spite of some fine passages, it had an enormous success in the Middle Ages and set the fashion for a kind of composition that continued right down to the seventeenth century, where it ends magnificently in Calderon's *Autos*. It also had a great influence on medieval iconography. But if we want to see Prudentius at his grandest we must take one of the didactic poems, such as the *Apotheosis*. This poem contains passages that for their energy of style, passionate belief and power of lucid argument recall Lucretius. The subject on which he writes with most conviction is death:

I know that my body will rise up again in Christ. Why do you want me to despair? I shall follow on the same road by which He returned after triumphing over death. This is my belief. And I shall be just as I was: I shall have the same face and strength and colour that I have today: not a tooth nor a nail will be missing when the open tomb vomits me up again.

This passionate desire for the resurrection of the physical body after death is unique among the great Christian writers of the fourth century: it belongs to a different climate of feeling from the philosophic neo-platonism of St Augustine or the allegorical exegesis of St Jerome. We feel something popular, something almost pagan in this literalness and see once more how close, in spite of his theological and classical learning, Prudentius was to the feeling of the masses. If generally speaking one can say that it was the intellectuals who controlled the growth of dogma in early Christianity, the tone of belief was being increasingly dictated by popular importunity.

Yet, whatever may be thought today of these passages, which can be paralleled in Donne and in Unamuno, there can be no doubt that Prudentius was an uncommonly sane and cultured person with a broad, liberal outlook on the world. As a lyric poet he suggests Andrew Marvell: there is the same reserve and dryness, the same fear of rhetoric, the same concern for purity of style, the same poignant sense of the passage of time. There is a certain sinew too that suggests that behind the Christian poet lay an able man of affairs. There is even the same robust political outlook. We have already noted his love for his city and province, but his Roman patriotism was deeper still. He felt such pride in the empire that when writing of Julian the Apostate he could not avoid praising him.[1] In his poem against Symmachus, the leader of the pagan

---

[1] As an example both of magnificent poetry and of a generosity unequalled in the history of Christianity, Prudentius' epigram on Julian deserves quotation:

> Principibus tamen e cunctis non defuit unus,
> me puero, ut memini, ductor fortissimus armis,
> conditor et legum, celeberrimus ore manuque,
> consultor patriae, sed non consultor habendae
> religionis, amans ter centum millia divum.
> Perfidus ille Deo, quamvis non perfidus orbi. . . .

'However among all our princes there was one reigning, as I still remember, when I was a child—a great leader of armies, a lawgiver, renowned in word and deed, devoted to the interests of his country but not to the religion he should have served, a worshipper of three hundred thousand gods, faithless to the true God, but not faithless to the world.'

If one wished for an example of Spanish *nobleza*, one could scarcely find a better one than this.

party at Rome, he is full of respectful admiration for his eloquence. Similarly he regards the temples and statues of the Gods as works of art that ought to be preserved. His sense of the benefits Rome had given the world was so strong that when he speaks of the barbarians beyond the *limes*, he calls them 'animals'. And we are left with the conviction that in all this he is saying what the majority of educated Tarraconensians thought in his time: there is something about his poems that tells us that the opinions they express are representative.

Four years after Prudentius wrote his last poem, the Vandals, Suevi and Alans poured over the Pyrenees. The Visigoths followed them. Cities were sacked and burned, the schools of rhetoric were closed and for two hundred years poetry ceased to be written.

The popular arts, however, flourished. The theatres with their indecent mimes remained open, in spite of the efforts of the bishops to close them, and augurs, magicians and diviners of all kinds multiplied. In the villages the old pagan rites round cave and spring and tree continued to be paid. Songs and dances accompanied every ceremony, including Church services (St Isidore anathematized the *saltationes et turpia cantica* that disfigured these), and dirges called *threni* were sung at the tombs of the martyrs. To put an end to this the Church Councils ordered that proper hymns should be composed to take the place of these ribald and semi-pagan practices.

The chief reform took place in the seventh century, and its results are incorporated in the Mozarabic Breviary, which remained in use down to 1085. A few of these hymns have some merit, but what strikes one especially about the collection is the extraordinary number of long hymns devoted to the martyrs. They follow the general pattern of the hymns of Prudentius, except that the scenes described have become more stereotyped and the narrative further removed from reality by the intrusion of miracles— as a rule one after every torture. These miracles were intended, no doubt, to bring out the supernatural character of the contest and are in conformity with the movement that was turning naturalistic Roman art into hieratic Byzantine. However, literature requires life, and the result is boring and monotonous.[1]

The Visigoths were converted to Catholicism in 586 and the following century saw a revival of literature. St Isidore compiled his encyclopedia of classical learning at Seville, whilst Toledo and Saragossa became centres of poetry. We have the names of five kings and six or seven bishops who wrote verse, and a certain number of these productions have come down to us. Why only kings and bishops? We must remember that in those depressing times the higher clergy alone were educated and that the kings lived on the closest terms with them. Besides, had anyone else written poetry—and we hear of a priest called Justus who sang obscene songs and danced *vulgari ritu* at banquets—it would have been lost, since it is only in ecclesiastical libraries that manuscripts of this period have been preserved.

The only one of these poets to show real talent is Eugenius II, Archbishop of Toledo from 646 to 658. He was a Visigothic nobleman, who had entered the Church against the wishes of his family and become archdeacon to Braulio, Bishop of Saragossa, who also wrote verse. He was a man who suffered from bad health and was obsessed by the fear of death, and this and the nature of his times gives most of his poetry a deeply pessimistic tone. Here are a few lines from his lament on the brevity of life:

> Mundus, ecce, nutat aeger et ruinam nuntiat,
> tempora grata fugantur, ingeruntur pessima,
> omnia mala propinquant, et bona praetervolant.
> Eugeni, miselle, plora: languor instat improbus.
> Vita transit, finis urget, ira pendet caelitus,
> ianuam pulsat ut intret mortis, ecce, nuntius.

See how the sick world staggers and announces its ruin;
The happy times flee, the worst are heaped upon us.
Evils of all kinds draw near and the good pass over.
Weep then, poor wretch Eugenius—the vile languor is on you.
Life passes, the end presses, the anger of heaven
Hangs over you and, see, batters on the door
That the messenger of death may come in.

[1] The Mozarabic Breviary contains a group of three extremely interesting hymns, or poems rather, describing a flood, a drought and an invasion of barbarians by sea, in a

But his poem on the nightingale has real beauty in spite of its uncertain quantities.

> Vox, philomela, tua cantus edicere cogit,
> inde tui laudem rustica lingua canit.
> Vox, philomela, tua citharas in carmine vincit
> et superas miris musica flabra modis.
> Vox, philomela, tua curarum semina pellit,
> recreat et blandis anxia corda sonis. . . .
> Nulla tuos unquam cantus imitabitur ales,
> murmure namque tuo dulcia mella fluunt.
> Dic ergo tremulos lingua vibrante susurros
> et suavi liquidum gutture pange melos.
> Porrige dulcisonans attentis auribus escas;
> nolo tacere velis, nolo tacere velis.

> Your voice, nightingale, compels one to make songs,
> So my poor tongue begins to sing your praise.
> Your voice, nightingale, conquers the cithers in song,
> Rises with marvellous notes above the sounding winds.
> Your voice, nightingale, drives away seeds of care,
> Refreshes anxious hearts with its soft sounds. . . .
> No bird will ever imitate your songs,
> For in their murmur the sweet honey flows.
> Give out your trembling whispers with vibrating tongue
> And tune your liquid air with your soft throat.
> Spread your sweet feast of song for listening ears.
> I do not want you to stop. I do not want you to stop.

As Mr Raby says, there is here a new note, something more than a recollection of Vergil and Ovid. For the poets of the Dark Ages the nightingale's song was a voice from Eden, before the fall of man, before the sack of Rome, before the great calamities that had destroyed civilization. It had all the pathos of a past that seemed lost for ever, and yet it held out a ray of hope that better days might come. The birds that are first heard in St Ambrose's hymns on

highly stylized diction. Amador de los Ríos, who first noticed them, put them down to the period following the Arab invasion, but, as they are mentioned by Bede, this is impossible. Mr F. J. E. Raby has recently investigated them and found that they are not Spanish at all, but were written in Italy between 437 and 457. The barbarians referred to are the Vandals, raiding from Africa. See *Medium Aevum*, Vol. XVI, 1947.

cock-crow sing their way through poetry till the thirteenth century and, whilst they sing, their note changes, as the distance that separates their singing from the human world diminishes. One can almost date the poems by whether their songs evoke melancholy or joy.

This Visigothic poetry was much read in its own day. The poems of Eugenius and King Sisebut were taken to England (Atlantic sea routes were then more open than Mediterranean), where they delighted Bede and St. Aldhelm. Alcuin took them to the court of Charlemagne, where they were admired and imitated. But in Spain Latin poetry ceased to be written for many centuries.

One hymn from the Mozarabic Breviary, which dates from after the Arab conquest, may be mentioned. It is a marriage hymn. It is arranged so that every line, and usually every half line as well, ends in an unaccented *a*, the letter of joy because it suggests Alleluia. Ten musical instruments are mentioned in it. In the tenth century, when it was probably written, even Northern Spain was an oriental country and this hymn calls up vividly the noise and singing of an Eastern marriage procession and the sound of the small, jangling bells then used. Here are two stanzas from it:

> Pusilla copula, assume fistulam,
> Lyram et tibiam, praestrepe cantica,
> Voce organica carmen, melodia
> Gesta psalle Davidica.

> Cithara, iubila, cymbalum, concrepa,
> Cinara, resona, nablum, tripodia
> Excelso Domino, qui regit omnia
> Per cuncta semper saecula.

This is poor poetry, yet, like several of the other Mozarabic hymns, it is popular poetry and thus carries us back in some degree to the remote and unchronicled age that gave birth to it.

CHAPTER II

THE ARAB PERIOD

ARABIC poetry is the poetry of the Bedouin of the Arabian desert, which was carried by them into the various countries that they conquered. The earliest poems we have go back about a century before the Hegira. It is a quantitative poetry composed in many different metres and always rhymed, but not divided into stanzas. Ballads, satires and epigrams were all made, but the principal form was the *qasida*, a kind of elegy whose peculiarity was that, though its metre could vary, it had to follow a fixed order of subjects. Starting off with an account of the poet's discovery of an old camping ground recently occupied by his lady-love and of the various recollections which this called up, it went on to tell of his great love for her and of all the sufferings it had brought him. After that it described his travels through the desert, which gave opportunities for brilliant descriptions of animals and scenery as well as of his own horse or camel, and ended up abruptly with a panegyric to some distinguished person whom the poet hoped would reward him.

In reading these poems in translation we are struck by their freshness and originality. Most classical poetry comes out of other poetry and its descriptions are at second hand. A great Latin poet such as Vergil prefers to get his impressions through books rather than by looking at things for himself. But these Bedouin had eyes and, whilst their verses follow traditional forms, they make us see the desert and its various kinds of life as they saw it themselves. Some of them were also men of powerful imagination. Their metaphors are bold and striking and often so far-fetched as to suggest modern poetry. But they had no alphabet and so could not write: their verses were carried in the memories of professional reciters and committed to paper a century or more after the death of Mohammed.

The conquests of the Moslem armies scattered the tribes and Arabic poetry was carried into the cities. Here the old classical themes of the desert no longer suited the times. A new sophisticated poetry, influenced by Persian refinement, grew up in Baghdad. Its subjects were those offered by city life—parties of friends in gardens, flowers, vegetables, picnics, jewels and of course those eternal themes of Eastern poetry, love and wine. The Bedouin imagery degenerated into a firework of conceits, not unlike those of seventeenth-century Europe. The sense of purpose required for great poetry had been lost. Then in the tenth century a classical revival began. Mutanabbi—the great man of Arabic poetry—restored the *qasida*, using the style of conceits of his age, but giving it a new seriousness and purpose. Like Milton's it was a poetry of the ear, not suited for translation, but it conquered the Moslem world. It is at this moment that Arabic poetry began to be written in Spain.

The centre of this poetry was the court at Cordova. The Omayyad caliphs there were the rivals of the Abbasid caliphs at Baghdad and of the Fatimite dynasty in Africa, and poetry was an important instrument of prestige and propaganda, as the theatre and ballet are in Europe today. The two caliphs competed as to who could pay their poets best. Thus we read that Al-Hákam II (961-76)—himself a very erudite man—created a special office for paying poets according to their merits, whilst Almanzor, the great general of the succeeding reign, never took the field without at least forty poets to accompany him and sing his campaigns. Under the Taifa princes of the following century the zest for poetry became even greater. The princes themselves were as a rule highly cultivated men and their prestige depended upon the number of literati they maintained. We should remember too the old Bedouin rule by which the *qasida* ended in the panegyric of a distinguished person, who in return was expected to reward the poet. Other Bedouin poems had been satires, and these satires and panegyrics could make or mar the fortunes of a tribe as effectually as a camel raid or a battle for a well. This was also the case in the eleventh century. A successful poem could carry the name of a Spanish princeling as far afield as the borders of India or Turkestan. The poets had thus a political function similar to that of radio commentators today, and the princes recognized this by putting them on regular salaries and sometimes giving them important posts such as ambassadorships or vizirates.

We need not be surprised then at the immense number of poets who flourished in Spain at this time among all classes of the people, or at the fact that the three who are most interesting to us lived in the troubled period that succeeded the fall of the Caliphate, before the Taifa princedoms had been properly set up. The greatest of these, perhaps, was Ibn Zaydún of Cordova (1003-70), a poet of classical tendencies, especially famous for his love affair with the Princess Walláda. This lady was a daughter of the last Omayyad caliph, who on the death of her father had left the palace harem and set up a salon for poets. She seems to have been an exacting character, and the stormy life of her lover after she had quarrelled with him and the plaintive verses he continued to send her recall the biographies of the Provençal troubadours. His *qasida en nun*, addressed to her from prison, is the most famous of Spanish Arab poems: some of its force and passion come through in translation.

Another poet who has a special interest for us today is Ibn Hazm (994-1063). His life, too, was agitated, for his youth was given to love and politics and his middle age to religious controversies. His most interesting book is a treatise on love, interspersed with poems, which shows a psychological curiosity into the workings of the heart that recalls Stendhal's *De l'Amour*. Among the points it discusses are the various ways of falling in love suddenly —by a look, through a description, in a dream: the predicament of those who are caught by exterior beauty only to find that there is nothing in the mind to match it: the curious penchant some people have for falling in love with deformities: the timidity produced by love—how, for example, some men have been known to kill themselves because they did not dare to declare their passion: other 'martyrs of love': and such general matters as jealousy, correspondence by letters, glances and signals and the various means of procuring secrecy. The resemblance of all this to the Provençal cult of love in the following century is obvious. But Ibn Hazm had an analytical mind rather than an impressionable one and he blows the gaff on his own love poetry by telling us that, though poetic convention had obliged him to say that he wept when his lady rejected him, he had as a matter of fact never shed a tear since he grew up. In middle life he wrote a *Comparative History of Religion*, showing, it appears, much erudition and, in his chapters on the Bible, considerable skill in textual criticism. There is thus a good deal of the modern intellectual about him: his interest in science and his anti-clericalism announce the rationalistic movement of the twelfth century, whilst in his talk of a literature freed from the schools and more closely dependent on actual life he put his finger on the great defect of Arabic poetry.

The only other poet of this century whom we need mention is Mutámid, the prince of Seville who was deposed by the Almorávides. His amazing life story is told by Dozy. Under his rule Seville became a city of music, festivals and poetry, in which it seems that the whole population took part. But his best poems are not those that he wrote to his enchanting wife Rumaiquíya, nor to the many other ladies his impressionable nature allowed him, but those written from his prison at Agmat, near Marrakesh, where, loaded with fetters, he spent the last years of his life. What this accomplished Arabic poetry needed to make it move the reader was sincerity and strong feeling, and Mutámid's calamities gave him the incentive he needed.

Let us now come to the poetry itself. Spanish Arab poetry depends so much for its effect upon its formal qualities that little of it comes through in translation. But we may accept Sr García Gómez's statement that with few exceptions it is of a great intellectual poverty. The length of the lines and the fact that each line must be a unit of sense (there is no *enjambement*) make it move slowly. This helps to give it that air of voluptuousness or sensuality that is characteristic of all the arts of the East. But there is one thing that does come through in translation, and that is the imagery. Eastern art is an art of surfaces and so the surface of Arabic poetry tends to cover itself with a network of conceits, just as Arab interiors are covered with elaborate scrolls and patterns in which the eye loses itself. It is this that, at its best, gives the verse a tension that saves it from dissolving in a sea of musical language, as Italian poetry later tended to do. At its worst, it becomes a game like acrostics. Let me give a few examples from Sr García Gómez's excellent anthology.

Here, to begin with, is a two-lined poem called *The Lily* which recalls Rimbaud's prose-poem on the foxglove:

The hands of the spring have built, on the summit of its stalk, the castles of the lily.
Castles with battlements of silver, whose defenders, grouped round their prince, hold swords of gold.

Observe how this transposition of the lily into another plane of associations brings out its peculiar aloofness and its air of stillness and expectancy. It is the method of Rimbaud's *Illuminations*.

Then here are some lines from a poem on a blue river, which convey a Titian-like feeling of brilliant light and richness of surface:

At midday the shadow of great trees covers it, giving a colour of rust to the surface of the water.
And so you see it, blue, dressed in its brocade tunic, like a soldier stretched out in the shade of his banner.

Such a sensuous appreciation of nature inevitably takes our mind five hundred years on to the Italian Renaissance, where poetry was being written under very similar conditions and for much the same reasons, that is, to enhance the simple pleasures of living and looking. But in other Spanish Arab poems one finds images that, by a combination of wit and innocence, aim at the instantaneous capture of a fleeting impression. To find anything to compare to them we must come to quite modern times and read the *greguerías* of Ramón Gómez de la Serna, that brilliant forerunner of Surrealism. Here are a few examples:

The Brazier. It cut out for us warm cloaks under which the scorpions of the cold did not know where to find us.
The Storm Cloud. The air tries on the dresses of the clouds and chooses among them a heavy black cloak.
The Dawn. The south wind lifted up the shirt-tails of the hills, and the face of the sky looked like the surface of the river.

Insomnia. When the bird of sleep thought to make its nest in my eye, it saw the eye-lashes and took fright, thinking they were nets.

The Noria (the Egyptian *shaduf,* driven by a donkey, which lifts buckets of water on a long arm out of a river and makes a groaning sound as it does so). It is like the incurable lover in a *qasida,* returning incessantly to its old rendezvous, weeping and asking why she has gone.

We can see from these examples that much of Spanish Arab poetry is a sort of charade in which the objects are perpetually dressing up as other objects. Sometimes the result is merely tedious or feebly amusing, but at other times a current is set up between the two poles of the metaphor, and the reader gets a new poetic impression. One is reminded of the Italian poet Marini's remark that poetry must always surprise (*È del poeta el fin la maraviglia*), but we must also allow that these Arab poets were far better at surprising than the men of the seventeenth century. They had for one thing the advantage of not being obliged to describe the world through the hackneyed forms of classical mythology; except for an occasional allusion to a desert camp or a camel, they were free to invent their own comparisons. And then we must not forget the different economic postition of the Arab poet. He lived in a highly competitive world, for everyone who could wrote poetry, and to attract attention he had, like Martial, to produce something that pleased immediately. These images often had the repeatability of *bons mots.*

But there is, I think, a radical weakness in all this poetry, which was a fatal bar to its development. It is a poetry made to express, not life as a whole, but some ideal conception of the beautiful and desirable. It revolves therefore round a dream of perpetual idleness in gardens, with the birds always singing and the water flowing and the wine set out on the napkin and the dancing girl waiting to come on. In this it resembles a good deal of Italian poetry after Dante. But Italian poetry was a young poetry which had richer traditions to draw on and grew more slowly. It had also its links with popular life, which revitalized it (Lorenzo de Medici, for example), and the vogue for the *conte* allowed it to turn to narrative when nothing more could be done with lyrical forms. But in Arab poetry the narrative element, which also existed at first, failed to develop and a terrible stagnation set in. As no poetry concerned with action was possible—for the business of the arts was to enhance leisure, to convey the pleasure felt by the senses of the passive observer—poets were left to do the kind of thing that painters really do much better. This meant that after every refinement of description had been tried, the arts of surprise had to be drawn on to stimulate the faculties and prevent monotony. When this happened the dryness of the Arab imagination led them to rely too much on the ingenuities of their hardworked fancy. While therefore we must admire the wonderful development given to the life of the senses by the Spanish Arabs, and the unsurpassed gifts for refined and voluptuous enjoyment which their poems show, we must also recognize in their poetry—seen dimly through the veil of translation—a lack of passion and vitality.

Spanish Arab poetry, so far as its matter and manner go, produced no direct descendants. If many centuries later some of its characteristic features reappeared in Spain, that must be put down to the uncertain operations of race and environment. Yet, while it was still at the height of its course, Provençal poetry appeared fully grown in the south-west of France and out of it came all the other Romance literatures. Can we say, as some Spanish scholars have claimed, that the Spanish Arabs had a direct influence on the birth of modern European poetry?

A first glance makes it appear highly probable. Christian Europe in the eleventh century was a barbarous region, scarcely more civilized than Abyssinia today, living on its distant memories of Imperial Rome. Moslem Spain had one of the most cultured societies the world has ever seen. Moreover it was just in this century that communication between the two became easy and frequent. There can, for example, be no doubt that the silks, embroideries, glass, pottery, paper and sugar that the Taifa states were exporting to the north in considerable quantities were one of the principal factors in breaking up the stagnant economic life of the Dark Ages. There is also evidence for the appreciation of Arab dancing girls and singers in the south of France. Yet there is no resemblance between Provençal poetry and classical Arab poetry. The former is a lyric poetry of short lines and elaborate rhymes, broken up into stanzas and without images. The troubadour had too much difficulty in carrying out his complex rhyme patterns to allow himself any complexities in the sense. The search for the rhyme meant that the meaning had to be kept fluid. If therefore there are any affinities, they must lie in a different direction.

Let us take the economic situation of the poet first. If no one pays the poet, there cannot be any poetry. Now we have seen that in Eastern countries the poet had made for himself a highly important position in the state. He gave it prestige, and it is largely by prestige that civilized states live. In his struggle to maintain himself, he had developed two weapons, praise and satire. If his praise was not rewarded, he could transfer himself to the next state and avenge himself by a poem that might be as damaging as a raid by hostile cavalry. (We can see a similar development in Ireland, where the guilds of poets known as *filid* maintained themselves in luxury by the crudest blackmail.) Now if we read the lives of the Arab poets of the Taifa period we shall see that they practised these arts with great skill. They kept themselves mobile—this is the essence of the troubadour conception— so that if not appreciated by one ruler they could carry their pen to another. And what are the qualities they praise in their panegyrics: Generosity. Without generosity, they say, there can be no courage, no nobility, no princely virtue. Rulers must give presents, and wonderful tales of the gold and jewels given in reward for poems or epigrams spread through the whole East.

Now these are very much the conditions under which the poetry of the troubadours took root and flourished in the feudal courts of Southern France. The old custom of hoarding gold in chests and living on the produce of the land suddenly came to an end in the last quarter of the eleventh century. A fashion for ostentation and extravagance succeeded it, and this took the form of expenditure on fine clothes, armour and poetry. Writing *vers* and *canzos* became an essential part of the type of courtly life that was growing up in the south-west of France, and the troubadour, as distinct from the humble jongleur (or *jougleur*, as he is more properly called) made his appearance. For the first time since Augustus, European poetry had acquired an important social function. And we can hardly doubt the immense part played in this by the Spanish Moslems. It was their example that was being followed in a feudal ambience.

But there is another conception that lies at the root of Provençal poetry and is developed later by Dante and Petrarch, which also has a Moslem origin. This is the conception of ideal, platonic or courtly love: the notion that love is *obedience*, something one serves and suffers for rather than seizes and enjoys.

It may seem rather surprising that this conception should have grown up in the sensual atmosphere of Moslem life. The low level of Arabic studies in Europe has not prepared us for anything of the sort, though recent discoveries have shown that there can be no doubt about it. We read, for example, of a Cordovan poet who fell in love with a beautiful slave girl whom he had only seen for a few minutes. She made such an impression on him that she became the Muse who inspired all his verse. Ibn Hazm describes the platonic love he felt for a girl whom he had known as a boy and who haunted his thoughts and inspired his verse over many years. In his book on love, written in 1022, he treats of the theme, so popular in Arab poetry, of abject and submissive love. The lover is like the soldier on military service. He has no will of his own, he is there to obey. Complete submission to the wish and caprice of his mistress is his whole duty. And his mistress is expected to make him suffer and to torment him. Ibn al-Labbana, a poet of Denia, speaks of his beloved's glance as being like a naked sword that cuts through his hopes. 'But my heart', he goes on, 'is still full of sweetness towards her who maltreats me.' This masochistic vein is found everywhere in the eleventh century. The lover suffers so much from his mistress's tyranny and disdain that he becomes thin and feverish and may even die of it. And so we read of Ibn Sahl, a converted Jew who died in Seville in 1251, that he wrote good poetry 'because he combined the two humiliations of being a lover and a Jew'. And Ibn Zaydún writes to the Princess Wallada 'Load my heart with what anyone else would find insupportable, and I shall bear it. Order and I will obey. Be haughty and I will humble myself.'

Now behind this attitude to love there is not only the general example of the pre-Moslem Arab poets, who offer perhaps the first examples of romantic love poetry known to us, but a definite philosophy. In the tenth century a Baghdad theologian wrote a book which dealt with the advantages of platonic love over sensual love. A group of writers followed who celebrated this *udri* love, as it was called (after a tribe of Bedouin, the Beni Udra or Sons of Virginity, who were said to have practised it in Southern Arabia), and wrote poems to illustrate it. This group was connected with the great Sufi movement which was transforming the Mohammedan religion by its doctrine of universal love and by the institution of mendicant friars or fakirs who preached it. It is not difficult to see how this *udri* notion fitted in with the customs of a country where, though the harem system was less strict than it is today, the two sexes could not mix as freely as they did in Northern countries. Also it was well suited to the purposes of poetry. Love poetry is a form of courtship and ends with the attainment, or at least the stabilization, of sexual relations; if this attainment is put off, a state of tension is set up in the poet's mind that favours the writing of amatory verse. If it is put off indefinitely, the love feeling may be sublimated into religious or philosophical channels, as it was in the case of Dante and Petrarch. I think therefore that one must conclude that the notion of courtly or platonic love (*amor de lonh*, love at a distance, as one of the early troubadours called it), which was the driving force behind most lyric poetry down to the time of Donne, had an Eastern origin and in fact reached the feudal courts of Southern France from Moslem Spain. Laura and Beatrice, Angelica and Una first combed their hair on the banks of the Euphrates and the Guadalquivir.

There is, however, another type of Spanish Arab poetry of which we have not spoken. The author of a twelfth-century history of literature, Ibn Bassám of Santarem, records that a blind poet of Cabra near Cordova called Mocádem, who flourished about the year 900, was the first person to compose verses in the form of *muwassahas*. 'He wrote them carelessly', says Ibn Bassám, 'with little art, in the vulgar jargon of the day and using words in the Romance language.'

Now what are these *muwassahas*, or *zéjels*, as they are also called?[1] They were short, rhymed poems made up of a number of stanzas in hemistiches. (The line of classical Arab poetry was always very long.) They were in accentual metre instead of in quantitative, because they were intended for singing and not for reciting, though sometimes, like St Ambrose's hymns, they also conformed to the laws of classical metrics. And they had this further peculiarity. They started with a theme-stanza, known as a *matla*, of two or three lines that rhymed. The stanzas that followed had three or sometimes more lines in mono-rhyme and a fourth line that rhymed with the *matla*, thus *A A   b b b A   c c c A   d d d A   e e e A*, etc.[2]

Now this type of verse has been made familiar to us by the folk-lorists. It is the verse of a carole or choral ring dance. The leader gives the theme-stanza *A A*: the chorus repeats it: the dance leader then sings the first stanza *b b b A* and when he has finished the last line, the chorus comes in with the theme-stanza that rhymes with it. That is to say, the chorus sings the theme-stanza every time the dance leader gives the rhyme cue for it.

We can see from this that Mocádem could not have invented this type of verse. He is simply a jongleur who took up and popularised a folk-song. And the moment at which he did so is significant. Andalusia just then was in a state of revolution. A strong national movement had broken out against the Arab court at Cordova and in this movement Spanish Moslems fought on the same side as Christians. Moreover, we must remember that though Arabic was the language of the court, of the administration and of the cultured classes, Romance—that is, proto-Spanish—was the language of the people and there were even Moslems of importance at Cordova who spoke no other. The verses of the blind poet seem thus to be connected with a national reaction against the language

[1] There is a difference between these two terms which has only become clear since the completion of this book. The *muwassaha* was written in literary Arabic on traditional themes: the *zéjel* in vulgar Arabic on light themes. It was the *muwassaha* that Mocádem introduced while the *zéjel* did not come in before *c.* 1100. For further information see the additional note on page 470. For the sake of simplicity I have used throughout the current Spanish transcriptions of these Arabic words: the correct English ones are *zejel* and *muwashshaha*.

[2] For an example in Spanish see Juan Ruiz's 'Trova cazurra' in *The Oxford Book of Spanish Verse*. An imperfect example is given on page 120 of this book.

of the invaders, similar to that which had taken place half a century before in Persia, only more feebly and on a semi-popular level.

Mocádem of Cabra was not the only Moslem poet or jongleur to write verses in this Spanish measure. Although the accession of Abderrahman III in 912 and the foundation of the Caliphate made Arabic more than ever the dominating language, the little, lively folk-song with its colloquial possibilities had caught on. We hear of many poets in the tenth and eleventh centuries who composed *muwassahas* into which they introduced Romance or popular Arabic verses, while in the streets and market places jongleurs sang the similar but much more lively *zéjels*. Yet, whatever it had originally been, the *muwassaha* was by 1040—the date of the earliest examples that have come down to us—a grave and serious poem, composed in classical Arabic on traditional themes, though intended for singing rather than for recitation and ending with a verse, the *jarcha*, written in the popular idiom. (See on this the Appendix on pages 466 ff.) This made it suitable for religious services and so we find such men as Ibn al-Arabi, the great Sufi mystic, writing hymns in it. If we wish to see what popular poetry was like, we must look at the *zéjels*, which were taken up from the jongleurs by literary poets about the year 1100. Both these forms spread rapidly through the whole Arab-speaking world and in far-off Bokhara we hear of cultivated audiences being enchanted by the new, lively tunes, the racy language, the salacious subjects and even (it is expressly said) by the unintelligible Romance words that the Arab poet brought in. Today the *zéjel* is sung and danced as a folk-song by the Arab peasants and Bedouin of the Near East.

We are able to get a pretty fair idea of what this popular or semi-popular poetry was like because, by a piece of unusual luck, a whole *diwan* of 149 *zéjels* has come down to us. These were written by a Cordovan poet called Ibn Guzmán who was born *c.* 1078 and died in 1160. The date of his beginning to write should be noticed. He first appeared, if our sources are not mistaken, as a prodigy at the court of Al-Mutawákkil of Badajoz. But in 1094, Al-Mutawákkil was deposed and killed by Yúsuf ben Taxufín, the Almorávide emir, who had already conquered the other Taifa princedoms. This Yúsuf was an old man who had been brought up on the foothills of the Sahara and knew little Arabic. He was also a fanatical puritan. The story is told of him that, after listening to a recital by Arab poets, he remarked, 'I don't understand what they say, but I can see that they want money.' He was not the man to give it, and so the thousand and one troubadours of the Taifa courts were driven to earning their living by other means. Some emigrated, others composed anthologies, but the majority enrolled themselves in corporations and carried their art to the people. Ibn Guzmán was one of these: he gave up the classical metres in which he had written till then and took to composing *zéjels*.

These *zéjels* of his were not, however, written to be sung in the market-place like those of the lowest type of jongleurs. Though popular in style, they were intended for cultivated audiences. We must imagine them as sung at private parties in gardens and patios to an accompaniment of lutes, cithers, timbrels and castanets, and sometimes of dances. We are told that he lived chiefly in Seville; the *juerga* or drinking party with its *cantaores* and gipsy dancers continues the same tradition today.

What are the subjects of these songs? That is easily answered—love and wine. The love is of a scandalous kind; in many places the modest translator has been obliged to omit verses, for the general philosophy of the poet is that eating, drinking and love-making are the only good things in life and most of his poems are devoted to describing them. Yet the theme of unsatisfied love is frequent too. The poet declares himself as thin as a spider's web through love. 'Love and death are the same thing.' At moments he seems to enjoy his sufferings—'The cruelty of my blue-eyed boy is sweet to me'—whilst in another he declares that kissing is donkey's love and that it certainly cannot content him. But what is more peculiar is the autobiographic form of many of these songs. The poet professes to take the audience into his confidence and to relate the most scandalous love affairs in which he has been engaged with boys, girls and married women. The tone is buffoonish, many of these adventures end in his own discomfiture and there is a good deal of sly satire of religion. Then at the end of every song there is always the request for a present. 'Flour is very dear, the poet is so hungry that he has been dreaming of black bread and chick peas, it is ages since he last tasted chicken, his cloak is completely worn out.' These complaints are usually accompanied by exaggerated praise of the generosity of the person to whom he has dedicated the poem.

Now this style of writing is familiar to anyone who has any acquaintance with medieval literature. It is that of the goliardic poetry which was being written in Latin by Primas of Orleans and the Archpoet just at this period, and which was to have its imitators in the Romance languages. It was written by clerks who were generally in Holy Orders, and we may note that Ibn Guzmán too, after a life of debauchery and adventure, which included a spell in prison, ended as the imam of a mosque.

There are, however, other features which he shares with his contemporaries in Christian countries. The words *mayo* (May), *alba* (dawn) and *verbena* (the sacred plant of Midsummer Day) occur in Spanish in his *zéjels*. Those constant figures of Provençal poetry, the *lauzengiers* or mischief-makers, the *gilos* or jealous husbands, the *gardadors* or keepers, and the confidant all appear in Arab guise, as well as the *senhal* or secret sign concealing the identity of the lady. The lover falls in love in a flash, at first sight; he is the humble slave of his mistress and suffers gladly her tyranny and disdain. 'Be either kind or cruel', exclaims Ibn Guzmán. 'Sentence me like a judge, give me pleasure or pain.' The form of abasement is different, for the Arab lived in an autocratic regime and the troubadour in feudal society, but in both cases the duty of the lover was to submit absolutely to the wishes of his lady.

But what of the verse form of the *zéjel*? Can we find traces of that in Provençal poetry too? Let us take the first Provençal poet, Guillaume, Count of Poitiers and Duke of Aquitaine. He was the ruler of a powerful feudal state and his dates are 1071-1127. We are struck at once by the fact that he writes in the autobiographic, buffoonish style of Ibn Guzmán. One of his poems is as shameless as anything that the Arab poet ever wrote and displays the poet in an absurd and undignified light. Elsewhere he speaks, as all the Arab poets had done, of the delight he took in love and of the joy he found in humbling himself before his lady. But he does not write *zéjels*. The troubadours who follow him belong to the succeeding generation. Their tone is more refined and their verse forms more complex and they develop the theory of love or *obedienz* into a sort of religion. But though none of them uses the *zéjel*, we do observe one thing that reminds us of it and that is the persistence of a single rhyme linking together the last lines of every stanza. This is a general feature of all Provençal versification.

A more *zejelesque* kind of verse, however, is found in the anonymous Provençal *baladas*. These, unlike the cultured poems of the troubadours, are folk-songs; their dates may be anything from 1100 to 1150. And in the following century we find that the popular folk-song of Italy is the *zéjel* itself. The Franciscan poets took them up for religious purposes and Jacopone da Todi wrote his beautiful *laudes* in them, just as the Spanish mystic Ibn el Arabi had done half a century before.

Now what are we to make of all these similarities? Are we to suppose, as some Spanish scholars have done, that the whole of South European lyric poetry springs out of an Andalusian folk-song? That surely is a very extraordinary hypothesis. I believe that we shall see more clearly if we distinguish three different' elements—the primitive *zéjel* itself with its folklore associations, the use that the jongleurs made of it, and the ideas of platonic or submissive love that form an intimate part of troubadour poetry.

As to the first, I would suggest that the *zéjel* is one of the primitive folk-song types of the whole of the Western Mediterranean and that it was originally connected with the May ceremonies which, as we know, go back over all this region to the last centuries of the Roman Empire. For surely it is not conceivable that such a conservative thing as a folk-song could be imported from a Moslem country and take root among the peasants of southern France and Italy. They did not import the words *mayo*, *alba* and *verbena* which we find in Ibn Guzmán's poems, because these words and the customs they imply had long been indigenous among them. Why then should they have imported the popular song and dance that went with these customs? However, there is one thing that we can allow: the Spanish Arab poets were the first educated people to adopt folk-poetry to the purposes of polite entertainment.

Their example may therefore have influenced the poets of the North to do the same thing.

For if the Provençals did not take their verse forms from the Spanish Moslems, they certainly took other things. We have already shown that the conception of courtly love first arose on the Euphrates and reached the feudal states of Europe through Spain. We have also suggested that the troubadour and his peculiar role in society had, more or less, the same origin. That is to say, the prestige which the Arab poet had won for himself in the Taifa kingdoms prompted a similar development beyond the Pyrenees. But what of the jongleur who wrote verses of a more scurrilous kind? We know, of course, that from very early times there were jongleurs of a humble type in almost all parts of Europe. I would suggest that the rise in Moslem Spain of a jongleur or *zejelista* of a somewhat superior social status and of greater poetic skill led to results of a similar kind in Christian countries. We cannot say exactly how this happened because nearly all the popular poetry of the twelfth century has been lost, but we get in the Latin Goliardic poems of that time, which were surely (in part, at least) imitations of Romance originals, as well as in Guillaume de Poitiers, the proof that a finished type of juglaresque poetry similar to that of Ibn Guzmán was current in France. As to the means of transmission, we have only to suppose the existence of Spanish-speaking *zejelistas* alongside the Arab ones. Nothing in itself could be more probable because Moslem Spain was a bilingual country, and Spanish would have been easily understood in southern France. Indeed if we are to account for all the cultural transmissions that went on during the eleventh century between Moslem Spain and Christian Europe, we must, I think, postulate the existence of some sort of travelling entertainers to carry them.

We have gone at length into the question of the *zéjel* because it is of some importance. In the first place it holds one of the key positions in the mystery that surrounds the rise of European poetry. Europe got her scholastic philosophy from the Spanish Moslems—did she, as is claimed, learn the art of lyric poetry from them too? Then, as will be seen later, the *zéjel* has a history in Spanish folk-poetry that has lasted right down to the present day.

This, in any other country, would be a matter of minor interest. But one of the peculiarities of Spanish literature is the immense influence that the poetry of the people has had upon cultured poetry. If I were asked what was the factor that most distinguished the literature (or music) of Spain from that of other nations, I would say that it was the strength and persistence of the triple complex of folk lyric, tune and dance among the people, and the effects that this has had on cultured poetry and drama. One has to go to Japanese literature to find anything comparable to it.[1]

The Arabs were not the only Oriental people in Spain; there were also the Jews. The Visigothic Monarchy had persecuted them, but the Omayyads took them under their protection. The result was that the Jews prospered, learned Arabic and assimilated Arab culture. A renaissance of Jewish poetry and philosophy set in that had no parallel either in eastern or in western countries.

Some of this poetry was written in Arabic: we have already mentioned the Sevillian Jewish poet, Ibn Sahl. But religious poetry was necessarily written in Hebrew because it was intended for singing in the synagogues, and since this offers more interest—for Hebrew secular poetry is a close imitation of classical Arabic—we will say a few words upon it.

After the Dispersion, Hebrew religious poetry followed much the same line of development as the early Christian. In the first centuries A.D. liturgical hymns known as *piyut* (from the Greek *poietes*, poet) were composed in the style of the Psalms and included in the liturgy, like the Byzantine hymns in rhythmical prose and our own *Te Deum*. They were written mostly in Mesopotamia, brought to Spain with the plain-song they were set to and added to the Sephardic ritual. Then in the reign of the first Spanish caliph (912-61) a Jewish poet called Dunas ibn Labrat arrived from Baghdad with a new Hebrew poetry modelled on the Arabic. His profane verse was in the classical Arabic style and his religous poetry was in form a compromise between the *piyut* and the *qasida*.

[1] Since writing these pages a number of early Hebrew and Arabic *muwassahas* have been discovered which contain, as their *jarchas*, little verses or ditties in Romance. This discovery throws a flood of light upon the origins of Spanish lyric poetry. For an account of it, see the Appendix on pages 466 ff.

That is to say, he introduced rhyme, but broke up the long mono-rhymes of the Arabic metre into short mono-rhyming stanzas of four lines to conform to the strophe form of the Psalms. The language of his hymns, like that of all Hebrew religious poetry, was taken from the Bible.

After this, Hebrew poetry in Spain grew side by side with Arabic poetry and reached its highest point of development in the Taifa states of the eleventh century. Although liturgical hymns were sometimes written in the old style or in that chosen by Dunas ibn Labrat, the usual form came to be the *muwassaha*. The reason for this is obvious. The *muwassaha* had a stressed metre like Hebrew and it was designed for choral singing: its stanza form and even its refrain had analogies with Old Testament literature. But it was only in Spain that Hebrew poetry developed rhymes and only there that great poets made their appearance. Among these were such world-famous figures as Solomon ibn Gabirol, known in Christian countries as Avicebron, and Yehudá Halevi.

One of the interests of this Hebrew religious poetry lies in the way in which it developed the elementary rhyming system of these hymns. Over a hundred different rhyme combinations are known, and they show a striking analogy to the development of the Latin sequence or Missal hymn during the same period. As this poetry comes to be better studied, it may throw light upon the origins of the European lyric, which also moved in the course of a single century from very simple to very complex rhymes. It is an obscure yet intriguing subject. The discovery and development of the rhyme is comparable to that of the pointed arch and rib vault of Gothic architecture. It created European poetry.

But what influence, it may be asked, had this Hebrew poetry or, for that matter, philosophy upon Christian Spanish literature? In a direct sense, none at all. The poetry was not translated and the philosophy was passed on to the schoolmen of Northern Europe and Italy, who alone were able to assimilate it. But indirectly there was a strong Jewish influence on Spanish culture. When the Almorávides expelled the Jews from Southern Spain, they took refuge in the Christian states, where they were protected and looked on with favour. There they became the transmitters of the arts and sciences of Moslem civilization. They occupied positions at court, became administrators of estates, architects and doctors. They had especially close contacts with the nobility. And the ideas they passed on were those moral and didactic ones that one finds in the Hebrew Wisdom literature. It was more, perhaps, a tone or an atmosphere than anything concrete, but it was sufficient for one to be able to say that down to the middle of the sixteenth century there was a perceptible Jewish flavour in much Spanish literature.

Before we end this chapter let us take a last glimpse at Spanish Arabic poetry as it was when the Christian conquest of Andalusia overtook it. The Almorávides fell in 1150 and were replaced by the Almohádes, who favoured the poets and exiled their enemies, the *alfaquíes*. Classical verse became more recondite and obscure and, as a reaction to this, the *zéjel* flourished. The chief city in Spain both for wealth and poetry was now Seville. Its tall minaret, the Giralda, rose new and delicately pink above the flat roofs and cupolas, and from its summit one saw the villages of the Aljarafe 'gleaming like white stars in a sky of olives'. By night the *zejeleros* roamed the streets with their stringed instruments, drawing the women to the lattice-work windows to listen to their provocative songs. But the river was the chief centre for pleasures. Its wharves were crowded with ships and, where these ended, there were orange groves and gardens. From sunset to long after midnight parties of revellers sailed up and down it, singing and playing on instruments and drinking the wine that gave a double liberation because it was forbidden. When the great poet Ibn Sahl decided to end his life, he drowned himself in its waters so that, as he wrote with the arrogance of the poet of those times, 'the pearl might return to its native land'.

Such scenes were not to be seen again at Seville till the Siglo de Oro. Then the song to be heard in its streets was no longer the *zéjel*, but rather the little theme-stanza from which it had started, the four-lined *copla*. That is to say, the song that is still to be heard in its streets today.

CHAPTER III

THE EARLY MIDDLE AGES

EPIC POETRY

CASTILIAN literature begins with the epic poem or *cantar de gesta* known as the *Poema de Mio Cid*. It was written round about the year 1140 and is the first poem of any sort that has come down to us in a Peninsular language. Now, as it happens, the first literary work in the French language was also an epic poem and was written about forty years before this time. This is the *Chanson de Roland*. These two poems are both great works of imagination, highly characteristic of their respective nations, and what is more, they came to birth in a peculiar historical relation to one another. I think therefore that it may be useful if I draw a comparison between them. Such a comparison will illustrate better than anything else could do some of the outstanding differences between the two nations and literatures.

I will take the *Chanson de Roland* first. It is a story based on an incident that took place during an expedition made by Charlemagne against the Moors of Saragossa in the year 778. But the historical element in it is very slight: in reality it springs almost entirely out of the events and feelings of its own time. Let us see briefly what these were.

Almanzor, the scourge of the Spanish Christians, died in 1002 and the Arab Caliphate broke up soon after. This gave the Christian states of the North the chance to regain lost territory. But they were still weak and to strengthen themselves they called in to help them volunteers from across the Pyrenees. From 1018 onwards, therefore, armed bands were passing almost yearly from France into Spain to assist the Kings of Navarre, Aragon and Castile. For the most part these bands consisted of Normans and Burgundians, who were the most formidable fighters of the day as well as the most ambitious and restless of the feudal peoples. Thus it was the Normans who, with the help of the Duke of Aquitaine, twice took the key fortress of Barbastro in Aragon, and when Toledo fell in 1085 to the forces of Alfonso VI of Castile, it was the strong Burgundian contingent, led by its counts, who made this possible.

These men from the North were more passionately and romantically religious than the men who lived south of the Pyrenees. They therefore looked on these wars as holy wars undertaken against the enemies of Christ, whereas the Spaniards, who knew the Moslems and respected them, thought of them chiefly as wars for booty or for the reconquest of their land. And behind these expeditions was the growing power of the French Church. The greatest order in Christendom at this time was the Benedictine Order of Cluny, which had just reached the height of its power and influence. It was an order which held wide political views, as have the Jesuits today, and it was largely by its influence that the Papacy had been reformed and far-reaching claims of supremacy made for it. Now these Cluniacs took a special interest in Spanish affairs. From their headquarters in Burgundy they recruited the feudal forces, who were usually at war among themselves, and directed them upon Spain. They had acquired great influence at the courts of the Spanish Kings, especially at that of Castile, and were founding large and wealthy abbeys there. Yet they remained predominantly French in feeling. The attitude of the French monk or crusader beyond the Pyrenees seems to have been almost as nationalistic as that of the French soldiers in the time of Napoleon.

Another interest that the Cluniacs had in Spain was the pilgrimage to Compostella in Galicia. The shrine that held the relics of St James had been rebuilt in 1027-37 after its destruction by Almanzor. The Cluniacs took it under their protection and made it, after Rome, the principal place of pilgrimage in Europe. They organised the pilgrim road and built monasteries and inns along it, which were run by Frenchmen. Even today this road is known as the *camino francés*. By drawing large numbers of pilgrims to Spain, the shrine at Compostella helped to focus the eyes of Europe on the Moorish wars and brought recruits and money to the Spanish kings.

Thus we find that from the first quarter of the eleventh century onwards a continual stream of crusaders and pilgrims were passing from France into Spain. The road by which most of them crossed the Pyrenees was the pass of Roncesvalles, leading to Pamplona. It was in this way that the legends about Charlemagne and Roland grew up. The fact that Charlemagne's expedition to Saragossa had been a failure and that it was the Christian Basques, not the Moslems, who had destroyed his rearguard in the mountains, was forgotten. Charlemagne was thought of as the first crusader and the first pilgrim: it was believed that he had conquered the whole of Spain and discovered the relics of St James himself. The road the pilgrim travelled was his and, if confirmation of this were needed, he could point to the tomb of Roland at Blaye, at the foot of the Pyrenees, and to the cross on the summit of the pass which bore the name of the saintly emperor. It was in these circumstances, immediately after the return of the crusaders from the first Crusade to Jerusalem, that the *Chanson de Roland* was written. Its author was a clerk called Turold from the north of France and it is thought that it was intended to be recited at the religious festivals where the pilgrims collected.

A cursory glance at the poem is apt to be disappointing. One is shocked by the extraordinary demands it makes upon the credulity of its hearers. From beginning to end every incident is drawn out into the marvellous. This note is struck in the first lines, where we learn that Charlemagne was two hundred years old. Then the battle begins and we enter the realm of the fabulous. Roland with only sixty followers puts to flight an army of a hundred thousand paynims. Archbishop Turpin, when gravely wounded, kills four hundred with his own sword. Charlemagne prays for the sun to stand still in the heavens so that he may have time to overtake the enemy, and it does so. We become so accustomed to this piling up of impossibilities that when the Archangel Gabriel descends to take the glove which the dying Roland has offered to God in token of his fealty, we feel it to be a quite ordinary occurrence. The *Chanson de Roland*, in short, is hagiography of the crudest kind and supposes an audience of fanatical pilgrims or crusaders who are ready to believe anything.

And yet when we read this poem more attentively we see that its author has a standard of poetic truth of a strict kind. The characters, drawn in clear outlines, are consistent, and are just what the action requires. They are described and placed in relation to one another with extreme simplicity. Roland is *preux*, Oliver prudent, Ganelon treacherous—that is all we are told about them; and yet, if we listen to what they say, we find that they are developed within these limits with remarkable subtlety. Take Ganelon's defiance of the Moorish King Marsile to whom he is intending to betray Roland, or the dialogue of the two heroes on the battle-field. We see feelings suddenly pouring out that the characters who spoke them did not understand themselves. The author makes no comment and we, the readers, are left to put our own inter-pretation on them. The spirit of the great French dramatists, Corneille and Racine, seems to brood over these occasions.

The skill with which the poem is composed is no less remarkable. Every incident is arranged so as to produce a carefully thought out result. The artistic condensation—by which I mean the economy of means to end—is very great. Take as an example of this the use made of Roland's blowing the horn. His refusal to blow it when Oliver wishes him to do so defines for us the two characters. Oliver, though perfectly brave, is *sage*, but Roland is *preux* and in this word *preux* we are meant to see knightly valour carried to the point of sublimity. Roland is to Oliver what, in a different sphere, the saint is to the virtuous man. Then it is this same incident that leads to the touching dispute between the two friends which gives life and drama to the battle. Again, when Roland, seeing that defeat is imminent, does at length blow the horn, in spite of Oliver's ironic observations, a tremendous thing happens: ex-hausted by the fight and feeling the need to sound it so that Charlemagne, who is now far away, may hear, he blows so hard that his brain comes out through his ears. We realise that the Moors have no power to kill him—he has killed himself. Finally we are given a picture of the scene when Charlemagne hears the horn, of the discovery of the treachery and of the turning of the army back. I think it would be difficult to find anywhere else in literature an example of a single incident used to produce so many striking effects.

The style is just that required for a poem written, as this is, in a

39

consistently high key. It is stripped and terse, so that it is in the incidents rather than in the language that we find the great poetic effects. The key passages are repeated three times over in slightly different words, which helps to raise the picture above the world of actual occurrences and to emphasise, for a simple audience, the dramatic moments. Yet there is often beauty in the language too. Its power of conveying a great deal in a few unemphatic words recalls Racine. And then at intervals, placed as a kind of refrain, occur lines of haunting beauty and melancholy:

> Halt sunt li pui, e li val tenebrus,
> Les roches bises, les destreiz merveillus.

The natural background—landscape, or time of day, or weather —is brought in in brief flashes to throw its particular colour over what is happening. Finally, in the famous lament of Charlemagne over his dead peers, we get one of the great passages of French poetry. It is on a theme, very popular in medieval literature, which finds its highest expression in Villon's ballade *Mais où sont les neiges d'antan*. The poet of the *Chanson de Roland* took it from a Spanish-Latin source, Isidore of Seville's *Synonyms*.

The *Chanson de Roland*, then, is a poem of great art and concentration which is constructed not in the open form of a historical narrative, but drawn in round a central climax (the *passio* or passion of the warrior saint) to which every incident looks forward or back. Its aim is to present an ideal picture of the great vassal and crusader, perfectly loyal to his king and to his God. The religious and feudal ideas are fused in it: it is at the same time both the epic tale of a hero and the Acts of a martyr. Its greatness as a poem consists in the way in which its characters and action transcend human life and reach the sublime. In this sense we cannot compare it, or the other French *chansons de geste* that take after it, with anything else in medieval literature: to find a parallel one must go to the sculpture of the Biblical kings in the west porch of Chartres Cathedral or to its stained glass. And it has another quality too, peculiar to French art but never found in Spanish. It is not content with telling a story, it sets up a universal pattern or example. Already in this early period we can see the French mind at work, consciously and deliberately creating ideals and values for its age. The twelfth century, let us remember, was the period when the main lines of medieval culture were laid down by France.

Before we turn to the *Cid*, let us see what effect this crusading spirit of the French, accompanied as it was by a keen national feeling and by religious propaganda, had upon the Christian states of Spain. We notice at once a strong reaction. The Spanish world, politically divided, weak and passive, resented this powerful outside influence and yet was obliged to put up with it. Thus we find that a Spanish monk, writing in the Benedictine monastery of Silos, near Burgos, about the year 1100, shows a strong exasperation at the arrogance of the French claims. Delving into Einhard's *Life of Charlemagne*, he points out that the emperor, far from defeating the Moors, had allowed himself, *more Francorum auro corruptus*, to be bought off by them, and that in recrossing the Pyrenees he had been shamefully defeated by the Navarrese. Not long after, a *cantar de gesta* appeared whose hero was an imaginary Castilian paladin called Bernardo del Carpio. This Bernardo is represented as rousing the Castilians against their king, Alfonso the Chaste, because he had done fealty to Charlemagne, and as joining forces with the Moors of Saragossa to inflict a shameful defeat on the French at Roncesvalles. Elsewhere we read of the resistance of the peasants to the new feudal tenures which the French Cluniac monks were seeking to impose on them. And there is the famous story of the strong opposition made by the people and clergy to the introduction of the Roman rite. Perhaps we may be allowed a modern comparison. In the twelfth century the French Cluniac monks provided soldiers and weapons for the Spanish kings, but in return imposed themselves, their feudal customs and the uniform discipline of Rome upon the Spaniards; in the recent Civil War the Communist International intervened in what it regarded as a crusade against Fascism and brought upon itself the sullen resentment of large numbers of the workers whom it was helping. The contrast between Spain's political weakness and her national intransigence has made this the regular pattern of all the many foreign interventions in Spanish affairs.

The *Poema de Mio Cid* was written by a Spaniard who had read the *Chanson de Roland* and other French *chansons de geste* and decided to write something different. In doing so he had before him earlier Spanish epics, dealing with the origin and early struggles of Castile, which have only come down to us in prose, incorporated in the royal chronicles. It was from these that he took his general style and treatment. He was, it seems, a Mozárabe—that is, a Christian born under Moslem rule—and he came from the district of Medinaceli on the borders of Castile and the Arab state of Saragossa. That is to say, from a frontier region. His poem is a local poem in the sense that he is at his best when describing places that he knew and reporting stories of his hero that were current in his native town. He wrote round about the year 1140, forty years after the Cid's death. As a point of curiosity, we may note that his hero was a contemporary of Turold, the author of the *Chanson de Roland*, and that it is quite possible that they saw one another in 1085 at the siege of Tudela.

The *Cid* is a poem in four-accent lines of approximately fourteen syllables (that is, in what Hopkins called 'Sprung rhythm'), divided by a strong caesura and grouped like its French prototype in sections or *laisses* of varying length, all the lines in each *laisse* having the same assonance. Its subject is an episode in the life of a Castilian soldier and condottiere, Rodrigo Díaz de Vivar, known by the Arabic title of Sidi or the Cid. The poem begins with the exile of the Cid as a result of the slanders with which his enemy, Count García Ordóñez, has turned the King against him. He leaves his wife and two young daughters at a monastery and, as he does so, prays that he may live long enough to marry off these daughters and enjoy a few years of family peace and happiness. Then, with the money he has raised from two Jews of Burgos by a clever trick, he sets out with only 300 lances to gain his living among the small Moorish states of Aragon. Here he prospers, winning fortresses and booty from the Moors and defeating in battle the Christian Count of Barcelona. His *mesnada* or feudal band is swelled by more recruits from Castile, so that after a little he is able to capture the great city and plain of Valencia. He sends for his wife and daughters, defeats a Moorish army led by the

Almorávide emir, Yúsuf, and settles down to enjoy the wealth and fame that he has won.

His success has now given him back the king's favour. Alfonso offers to marry his daughters for him and chooses as bridegrooms the two Infantes of Carrión. These are relatives of his old enemy García Ordóñez and, besides, *ricoshombres* or noblemen, but they are ready to marry beneath their rank in order to acquire the magnificent marriage portions which a millionaire like the Cid can offer them. The weddings are celebrated at Valencia and the married couples settle down there.

However, the pride of the two Infantes has been wounded at having made so low a match and also because the cowardice they have shown during a battle with the Moors has brought them into contempt. They meditate revenge and with this idea set out for Carrión. On reaching the oak forest of Corpes, just inside Castile, they strip and beat their wives and, making off with their dowries, abandon them there. The Cid then appeals to Alfonso, who has made himself responsible for this affront by arranging the marriage.

The king summons a court at Toledo and the Cid appears before it. After stating his case, he claims the restoration of the two famous swords the Infantes have taken. The court grants this. Then he demands the restoration of his daughters' dowries. This is granted too. He thereupon makes a third demand—the right to avenge his honour, in accordance with the old Visigothic law, by fighting the two Infantes in single combat. Whilst the court is deliberating on this, two messengers arrive from the Kings of Navarre and Aragon requesting the hands of the Cid's two daughters for their sons. The king gives his permission, and, as the Infantes have meanwhile challenged the Cid's two nephews to single combat, he consents to this too. The poem ends with the duels in which the Infantes are ignominiously defeated and forced to admit their villainy.

Let us consider the story first. The great Spanish scholar, Sr Menéndez Pidal, has shown that it keeps close to historical events, simplifying them a good deal and adding a few details, but not, so far as can be seen, exaggerating them. It is true that the chronicles tell us nothing of the first marriage of the Cid's daughters or of the affront in the wood of Corpes, but the quarrel with García Ordóñez and his family is true and so are the second marriages. The dramatic episode of the first marriages to the Infantes may well, therefore, be founded on fact.

Turning to the poem itself, we note that there is no question, as in the French *chansons de geste*, of any crusade. The Cid's motive is to win *averes*, that is, lands and money. He is a good Christian and when he takes Valencia he sets up a French bishop, but he does not interfere with his subjects' religion. He has friends and allies among the Moors and in fact, though the poet glosses over this, when he fought the Christian Count of Barcelona, he was in the pay of the Arab Emir of Saragossa. But if the religious feeling displayed in the poem is moderate, the social feeling is strong. After the Cid's capture of Valencia it provides the main theme of the plot. The Cid came from the class of simple *caballeros*—men who possessed a *solar* or small manor and a good horse—and he had risen by his own exertions to being an *infanzón*, which was the name given to a leader who employed *caballeros* under him. In fact he had been the previous King's *Campeador* or Champion. He was thus the type of self-made man, and the point of the story is the triumph of this man with his natural courage and ability, first over circumstances and then over the hereditary nobles or *ricoshombres*, who are represented as proud, cowardly and treacherous. The poem, that is to say, is an expression of the strong democratic movement that was making Castile, and not Leon, the leader in the war of reconquest and ultimately the most powerful state in Spain. In this it is characteristic of all the *cantares de gesta*, which one may call the revolutionary literature of the Castilians. No other province in Spain produced any epic poetry.[1]

The whole tone of the poem is sober and realistic. The Cid is a man like any other, only more doughty and capable, and he acts from the natural human desire to make money, settle down with

---

[1] The lost epics that preceded the *Cid* had dealt with the wars by which Castile liberated herself from the Leonese kings. They were therefore hostile to Leon. The *Poema de Mio Cid* does not show this hostility because Castile was now the dominant partner in a dual kingdom, but it stresses all the more the hostility to the nobles, who stood for the aristocratic principles of Leon and who were now threatening to destroy the results obtained in the war of liberation.

his wife and marry his daughters well. One might say, like any modern business man. But money and position were in those days won not by trade, but by fighting, and therefore the Cid has the code of honour that is normally found in all countries among men who risk their lives. Yet this code is not exaggerated, as it was in feudal courts or, in later times, among noblemen who carried swords which they did not use. He has merely the natural and reasonable self-esteem which we may expect from any successful leader. And then, though his exile had made him an adventurer, he still kept a strong sense of social obligations. Thus the author of the poem lays great stress upon his respect for the laws of his country and for the king who had banished him unjustly. His Moorish subjects weep when he leaves and his vengeance on the Infantes has a most un-Germanic moderation. One has only to compare the Cid's conduct as shown in this poem to that of the lawless and unrestrained behaviour of the heroes of contemporary French *chansons de geste* (the *Guillaume d'Orange* cycle, for instance) to see that we are in a different world altogether. The French feudal system demanded strong personal loyalties, but was otherwise anarchic: the system that prevailed in Spain, even in a frontier state such as Castile, made for respect for the laws and institutions.[1] It is true that in these matters the poet idealises the Cid's character: in actual life he was certainly less humane and less ready to fulfil his loyal obligations than he is here shown. But the fact that the portrait takes this form is significant. It shows a social conscience at work among ordinary people—a thing that in France one finds only among a few churchmen. Nor is the idealization carried too far. No attempt is made to conceal the Cid's passion for money: we get a picture, not of a half supernatural figure such as Roland, but of a man of flesh and blood.

The style of the *Poema de Mio Cid* is terse and dry, without ornaments. Adjectives are few and are scarcely ever used to heighten the effect. The occasional 'poetical' lines, describing the

[1] The Castilians refused to accept the codified laws of the Visigoths known as *Fuero Juzgo* which prevailed in Leon, and went by their unwritten local customs. But these customs had a moral force behind them which old codes do not always have, and the Cid, who shows a considerable knowledge of legal affairs, was always careful to have the right on his side.

scenery or the time of day, are borrowed from the *Chanson de Roland*. The beauty of the poem—and the more one reads it the more this word beauty seems appropriate—lies in the sense it gives of truth and actuality. As we peruse the accounts of the small battles and sieges of the first *cantar*, the events rise before our eyes, although the poet makes no attempt at vividness, but merely describes briefly what was said and done. Our imaginations work all the more keenly precisely because so little effort is made to force or direct them. Nor is the interest all centred on the battle itself. The strategy to be used is described, the forces are numbered, the onset begins, and when the victory is won we are shown the Cid, his *almófar*, or hood of chain-mail, thrown back, his face streaming with sweat, his right arm soaked to the elbow in blood, riding up to congratulate his lieutenants. Then the great moment of the day arrives—the collection and distribution of the booty. This is given as much space as the battle itself. When we have finished reading we feel that we know exactly what a *corrida*, or a small siege or battle of those times, was like.

Here, for example, is a passage describing a charge:

> Embraçan los escudos   delant los coraçones,
> abaxan las lanças   abueltas de los pendones,
> enclinaron las caras   de suso de los arzones,
> íbanlos ferir   de fuertes coraçones.
> A grandes voces llama   el que en buen ora nació:
> '¡Feridlos, caballeros,   por amor del Criador!
> ¡Yo so Roy Díaz, el Cid   de Bivar Campeador!'

They grip their shields tightly in front of their hearts, lower their lances hung with pendons, bend their faces low over the saddlebows and get ready to strike with strong hearts. Then he who was born in a lucky hour cries out in a great voice: 'Strike, knights, for the love of your Creator! I am Ruy Díaz of Vivar, the Cid, the Campeador!'

How well these lines bring the scene before one! Without any rhetorical exaggeration or emphasis, they not only paint a picture of the charge, but they convey its excitement.

The *Poema* also shows a considerable sense for dramatic situations, though these are never worked up or intensified as in the

Chanson de Roland. The episode of the tricking of the Jews, for example, is delightful and in its good-humoured way gives the essence of all shady deals in which people who regard themselves as honourable condescend to swindle people whom they regard as without honour. The moral aspects of this transaction have an almost Henry James-like subtlety. The Cid's business agent has persuaded the two Jewish money-lenders to lend him six hundred marks on the security of a chest full of sand, which they, being very astute men, like the Spanish café politicians of today, believe to be full of gold that he has kept back from the king when collecting the royal tribute in Andalusia. We are shown the agent, Martín Antolínez, arranging the deal with many flattering expressions of esteem and friendship, and then we see the Cid, magnificent in his long beard, receiving the two partners when they call to fetch the chest. Smiling ironically ¡ *Ya, Don Raquel e Vidas,* he exclaims, *avédesme olvidado* ! 'I thought you had forgotten me !' Note that collective title of Don; it is by such small touches that the poet makes the scene come alive. And note too that the purpose of this incident, which is taken from an Eastern tale, is to show that the king's suspicions were unjust, in other words to vindicate the Cid's honesty.

Another scene that lingers in the mind is that in which the Cid, after welcoming his wife and daughters to Valencia, takes them proudly to the summit of the castle to show them the city and garden plain that he has won. A little later a Moorish army encamps under the walls and we get another picture of the great man, expressing his delight that now his wife and daughters will be able to see him fight. They must stand on the battlements and have no fear: then they will see with their eyes *como se gana el pan,* 'how his daily bread is earned', whilst his heart will swell as he deals blows, because he will know that they are watching him. And when the battle is over, he dismounts from his sweating horse and kneels at their feet, like a bullfighter after a *corrida,* to offer them (*brindarles*) the battle he has won.

Or take another scene from the last *cantar,* when he is preparing to attend the king's court and demand reparation of the Infantes. We watch him dressing and arming himself with care and prudently tucking his famous, never-trimmed beard into a net so that none of his enemies may be tempted to pull it. Then, when he has won his case and is therefore safe, he ostentatiously takes it out again, and everyone present understands the significance of the gesture.

The Cid, with his enterprise, his prudence, his majestic mien, his thirst for money and above all his great flowing beard, is the outstanding figure of the poem and the other characters are slight by comparison. Yet some of them come to life and even show comic tendencies. For example there is Pedro Bermúdez, one of the Cid's lieutenants, who is very silent, but when he once begins to speak cannot stop. And there are the two Infantes, ridiculous through their cowardice and pride, who sum up their case in one preposterous phrase:

> Nos de natura somos   de condes de Carrión;
> deviemos casar con fijas   de reyes o de emperadores.

We are sprung from the Counts of Carrión; by right we should marry daughters of kings or emperors.

We can imagine how the listeners in the market-place must have enjoyed this passage. And though the dozen or so other characters who appear are only briefly characterized, they help by their words and presence to give life and breadth to the narrative.

The *Poema de Mio Cid* is thus not only a perfect expression of the dry, bare, soberly realistic imagination of the peoples of the *meseta* and of the moral and juristic sense of the Castilians: it also foreshadows the picaresque novels and drama of the Siglo de Oro. Only one factor is lacking to give a complete picture of the Castilian sensibility—the lyrical sense. Yet this is adumbrated. In the famous account of the Cid's arrival at the monastery of San Pedro de Cardeña just as day is dawning—

> A priessa cantan los gallos   e quieren crebar albores . . .

Hurriedly crow the cocks and the day begins to break . . .

we get an impression that can only be called lyrical and that owes nothing to the French *chansons de geste*. It is too long to quote: I can only refer the reader to it and to the beautiful prayer by Doña Jimena that follows it. But this lyrical feeling is rare. It is only at intervals that one comes on even a single line that draws one's attention by its beauty. Here for example is one, taken from the duel with the Infantes at the end of the poem:

> Martín Antolínez   mano metió al espada,
> relumbra tod el campo,   tanto es limpia e clara.

Martín Antolínez put his hand to the sword; all the field lights up, so clean and clear it was.

The beauty and value of swords are often spoken of in the poem: they were the best kind of booty and this was the famous sword *Colada*, worth more than a thousand marks, which the Cid had won in battle from the Count of Barcelona. And so the line that describes it being drawn lights up the sober pages of the poem as the sword-flash lit up the flat field.

Let us now try to sum up the results of the comparison we have been making between the great French and Spanish epics. In all the *langue d'oïl* literature of this age we are deeply conscious of the French being a new people. There is a barbaric rawness underlying the prodigious explosion of creative energy that produced the Crusades, the cathedrals, the scholastic disputes and the new epic and lyric poetry. In Northern France there was as much Germanic blood as Celtic, and French art and literature of this time are therefore deeply impregnated with the German romantic imagination. Even in the refined psychological dialogue of French courtly poetry we often detect something false and sickly, as of a people without established social habits, which is anxious to acquire a culture quickly and therefore pretends to a refinement it has not got. The age too was a cruel and dangerous one and its unsolved conflicts and predicaments often led to mass neuroses. The poem of the *Cid*, on the other hand, shows us a society which is healthy and self-assured. It is rude, because it is the society of a frontier people engaged in continual warfare, but it possesses an old culture or habit of life whose roots go back uninterruptedly to Roman times. We see this in the sobriety and lack of emphasis of the description, but also in the prudence and self-restraint displayed by the principal actors. There is an adjustment of means to end shown by the Cid and his companions that is far from according with our idea of the Spanish—still less of the Castilian—character. No doubt we tend to think of Spain too much in terms of that century of marvellous but fatal intoxication known as the Golden Age and of the prostration that followed it.

One last contrast I wish to make concerns the different degree of social development. Castile, as we have said, was at this time in an expansive and democratic phase—by which I mean that larger numbers of people were every year acquiring political consciousness. This is reflected in the poem. Not only are its themes political, but the comments that the poet makes are mostly political too. Take the well-known line that sums up the injustice and folly of the king in letting himself be persuaded by the nobles to banish the Cid:

> ¡Dios qué buen vasallo,   si oviesse buen señor!

> God, what a good vassal, if only he had a good lord!

and contrast it with that famous speech of Roland's in which, after declaring that the only duty of a vassal is to suffer great heat and great cold for his lord, he ends with the pronouncement:

> Paien unt tort   e chrestiens unt dreit.

> Pagans are wrong and Christians are right.

A pronouncement which, of course, gives him a good conscience in killing them all.

In the first case we have a real political reflection and, what is more, a profound one. It opens up that long Spanish debate upon the relations of society to government which generally concludes with the judgment that the former is morally superior to the latter. In the second case we have one of those expressions of abject faith in the rulers which we have come to recognize as typically Germanic. I do not say that Roland's remark—which, granted the premises of the poem, strikes us as noble—is typical of French feeling in those times. It belongs to the crusaders' ideology. But it is the case that we may search French literature of the twelfth century in vain for any assured and responsible expression of political feeling that is at all comparable to what one finds in the *Cid*. And this is true, I think, of every other literature in Europe. Spaniards, though backward in material resources and decidedly inferior in intellectual and artistic creativeness to the French, were the first people in Western Europe to reach, within the framework of medieval life, some sort of social and political maturity. One of the reasons for this was that they were not taken up with the international question of the relations of the Church to the civil authorities that was engrossing the best political minds in other countries. They were therefore freer to work out their own affairs. But the principal reason, of course, was that the never ceasing warfare with the Moors led to a steady movement of social change and liberation, because, to obtain volunteers for those wars, the kings and nobles had to free slaves, grant land and offer liberal charters.

Lyric Poetry: Galician-Portuguese

The plain narrative tradition of the Castilian *cantares de gesta* was continued in the admirable prose chronicles of the following century and in the earliest of the *romances* or ballads. We shall speak of these later. At present we have to consider the rise of lyric poetry—or rather the appearance of the first examples of it that have come down to us.

There are, as has been shown by Sr Menéndez Pidal, two quite different traditions of lyric poetry in Spain, each deriving from the folk-song of a particular region. One is the Castilian-Andalusian, based on the *estribote* or *villancico*, which is the romance form of the *zéjel*. The other is the Galician-Portuguese of the *cantiga de amigo*. We will consider the latter first, because, together with forms imported from Provence, it dominated the cultured lyric poetry of the early Middle Ages, whereas the former lay dormant in the villages and, except for the purposes of religious verse, was only taken up by the cultured classes much later.

The European lyric begins with the poetry called, rather inaccurately, Provençal, which reached its highest point of development between 1150 and 1200 in the south of France. This was a poetry of small feudal courts, celebrating love for married women in *canzos,* and political feelings in *sirventes* or satires. It contained few ideas and still fewer images, but showed great technical skill. The art of the poet lay in the management of elaborate metrical and rhyming schemes and sometimes in the use of rare and difficult words and recondite allusions, which even contemporaries often found unintelligible. Some of this poetry still moves us by its cascade-like sparkle and exuberance, but most of it was meant less, perhaps, to move than to win praise for its virtuosity. The one important idea that ran through it and gave it its *raison d'être* was love—not the sensual love of the later Middle Ages but the kind of 'love in the head' which Shelley has expressed in the *Epipsychidion* and which could be safely felt for married women. Such love was not therefore an antisocial thing, leading to the break-up of families, but on the contrary a highly civilizing practice, built up into a sort of lay religion, round which the whole social life of the upper classes revolved. As Senhor Rodrigues Lapa has said, love was thought of as a 'fountain of moral education, by which people raised themselves to the highest good and beauty'. And poetry was the language, the propagandist organ, of this love cult.

Provençal poetry was carried to Galicia and from there to Portugal by the pilgrim route to Compostella in the second half of the twelfth century. French influence was at this time very strong in these countries. Galicia had a considerable French population and the kingdom of Portugal had been founded not long before by Henry of Burgundy. Imitations of Provençal poetry began therefore to be written in the Galician dialect, which at that time was identical with the Portuguese language.[1] But the social conditions in this region were very different from what they were in Southern France: life was more primitive, feudal courts and a commercial middle class scarcely existed and love for

[1] Why not then imitations of French poetry? The principal reason for this is that though the Northern French had at this time (the late twelfth century) a lyric poetry of their own—the *chansons de toile*—it was a poetry without prestige, for home consumption only: a poetry sung by women at their work. The superior artistry of the Provençal lyric and the fact that it was the vehicle for the new courtly way of life were making it an article for export through the whole of Southern Europe. Another reason is that the Limousin or Provençal language was more easily understood both in Galicia and in Castile than was French.

married women was not to be thought of. The forms of Provençal poetry could not therefore make a wide appeal: what they chiefly did was to stimulate an interest in the local peasant poetry—out of which Provençal poetry had itself in the main arisen—and to create a superior class of jongleurs (in Galician *jogral* or *segrel*, in Castilian *juglar*) who should work it up and refine it.[1]

One of the, no doubt, many types of folk-song current in these parts seems to have been the very primitive kind still found in Asturias and known there as *danza prima*. Here is an example of one of them:

> Ay, probe Xuana de cuerpo garrido,
> Ay, probe Xuana de cuerpo garrado,
> ¿Dónde le dejas al tu buen amigo?
> ¿Dónde le dejas al tu buen amado?
> Muerto le dejo a orillas del río,
> Muerto le dejo a orillas del vado.

Note three peculiarities in this verse: first the parallelism of the lines, secondly the fact that assonances in *i* are succeeded by assonances in *a*, and thirdly that it is a kind of ribbon form that could go on slowly unwinding for ever. Clearly the original purpose of such verse is that it should be sung either by two lines of dancers facing one another or by two concentric circles, one line or circle singing the *i* rhymes and the other those in *a*. And in fact we are told that in the eighteenth century the *danza prima* was sung in Asturias by two concentric circles of men and girls. Now the Galician lyrics of the twelfth century have all these three peculiarities and one other that has today been lost: they were love songs that purported to be sung by women. They are therefore known as *cantigas de amigo*.

Out of the primitive folk-songs of the *danza prima* had developed —at what period we cannot say—more elaborate forms and, working on these, the *juglares* produced the lyrics that have come

[1] As a matter of fact Galician poetry and music had had a certain reputation both in their own country and in Leon and Castile since the end of the eleventh century. Thus we hear of a Galician *juglar* at the court of Alfonso VII of Castile in 1136. As we shall see, the high degree of elaboration of the Galician lyric in the thirteenth century implies a long period of development. But it was the influence of the Provençal troubadours that led the upper classes to compose these poems themselves and to collect them in *cancioneros* that have come down to us.

down to us, which, though not exactly folk-poems, keep close (as Provençal poetry did not) to the spirit of the originals. The most characteristic and beautiful form to be developed was the *cossante*, a Castilian word meaning a round dance, that had no exact equivalent in Galician. In the *cossante* the lines are grouped in assonanced distiches or couplets, the odd couplets having an *i* assonance and the even an assonance in *a*. In between each couplet there is a single-lined refrain which does not change throughout the poem. Thus: *iix, aax, iix, aax*, etc. But the *cossante* has also a sense pattern, which conflicts with the rhyme pattern. According to this the even couplets repeat the sense of the odd couplets, whilst every odd couplet except the first begins by repeating the *second* line of the preceding odd couplet and then introduces a new line to rhyme with it. Omitting the refrain, the sense pattern runs as follows: AB, *AB*, BC, *BC*, CD, *CD*, DE, *DE*, etc., the italicised letters representing the assonances in *a*. By this device, known as the *leixa-pren* (*laisser prendre*), a term taken from the dance, a slow, gradually uncoiling movement is set up which is capable of giving effects of remarkable beauty. Here for example is an *alvorada* or aubade written by an obscure *juglar*, Nuno Fernandes Torneol, in the early thirteenth century:

> Levad', amigo que dormides as manhanas frias:
> toda-las aves do mundo d'amor dizian.
> Leda m' and' eu.
>
> Levad', amigo que dormides as frias manhanas:
> toda-las aves do mundo d'amor cantavan.
> Leda m' and' eu.
>
> Toda-las aves do mundo d'amor dizian,
> do meu amor e do voss' enmentarian.
> Leda m' and' eu.
>
> Toda-las aves do mundo d'amor cantavan,
> do meu amor e do voss'i enmentavan.
> Leda m' and' eu.
>
> Do meu amor e do voss' enmentarian,
> vos lhi tolhestes os ramos en que siian.
> Leda m' and' eu.

Do meu amor e do voss'i enmentavan,
vos lhi tolhestes os ramos en que pousavan.
Leda m' and' eu.

Vos lhi tolhestes os ramos en que siian,
e lhi secastes as fontes en que bevian.
Leda m' and' eu.

Vos lhi tolhestes os ramos en que pousavan,
e lhi secastes as fontes u se banhavan.
Leda m' and' eu.

Awake, friend sleeping in the chilly mornings:
All the birds in the world of love are discoursing.
Gladly I go my way.

Awake, friend sleeping in the chilly dusk:
All the birds in the world are singing of love.
Gladly I go my way.

All the birds in the world of love are discoursing:
It is my love and yours they are discussing.
Gladly I go my way.

All the birds in the world are singing of love:
It is my love and yours they are talking of.
Gladly I go my way.

It is my love and yours they are discussing:
You took away the branches on which they were sitting.
Gladly I go my way.

It is my love and yours they are talking of:
You took from them the branches on which they reposed.
Gladly I go my way.

You took away the branches on which they were sitting,
And dried up the fountains in which they were drinking.
Gladly I go my way.

You took from them the branches on which they reposed,
And dried up the fountains in which they bathed.
Gladly I go my way.

I think that this translation, failing though it does to preserve the contrast between the *i* and *a* assonances, may give some idea of the slow, unfolding movement of the verse, which so perfectly suggests the weaving motions of the dance and two choruses of bass and treble singers that accompanied it.[1]

Many of these songs (some five hundred of them have been preserved) have a rhythmical vitality that carries the reader away. In the *barcarolas*, for example, we seem to hear the very sound of the waves beating on the shore. With their slow, unfolding movement—at first sight they seem almost stationary—and their air of vagueness and nostalgia, they strike a note that is not heard anywhere else in the Middle Ages. We read them and feel that time has taken nothing from them: they affect us as immediately and as poignantly as a folk-tune. In part this is due to their very simple and moving themes. The speaker is a girl complaining of the absence or infidelity of her lover: there is usually a mother to whom she is subject and a sister who is her confidant. No stilted, courtly convention comes between us and the actors, and the incidents are as simple and symbolical as in a fairy tale. Thus the *amiga* lingers at the fountain, washes her clothes or her hair in the river, waits for her lover by the seashore, asks the flowers of the pine tree for news of him, dances with him under the hazel trees, tears her dress, bathes in the sea, sleeps by the shore of the lake. The birds sing in the cool of the morning, the deer trouble the water of the river, the waves beat ominously, the ship with the lover on board sails out to sea. Nothing could be more simple or spontaneous and one's first impression is that here one has the poetry of an Arcadian society of peasants, celebrating joyously the pains and pleasures of their life in their 'natural' language.

Such an impression, however, does not really bear examination. These songs are as full of conventions as any other poetry. Let us

---

[1] In a famous stanza describing the Bower of Bliss—'The joyous birds shrouded in cheerful shade,' etc. (*Faerie Queene*, book II, xii, st. 71)—Spenser employs *leixa-pren* as a rhetorical device. As W. L. Renwick says in his excellent book on Spenser, this represents a brilliant transference into words of the effect of polyphonic music. The entry of the different voices can be heard. What Spenser does in one stanza, the composer of *cossantes* undertakes to do in all. No other poetry has ever been written in which the form is so closely modelled on music.

consider this for a moment. Their parallelistic form and the alternation they show of *i* and *a* assonances has led some people to think that they grew out of religious services or processions in which verses of the Psalms are sung alternately by choirs of men and women. Galicia, which had remained more or less pagan through the Dark Ages, became a great religious centre in the ninth century and the theory is that these songs grew up at the *romerías*, or festivals at local shrines (in England they were called *wakes*), which from early times have been such a feature of Galician and Portuguese life. In fact many of these *cossantes* are *cantigas de romería* written by patriotic *jograles* to celebrate the popular shrine of their home district, and it can further be said that the Asturian *danzas primas* are believed by their learned collector, Sr Torner, to bear traces of having originally been sung on similar occasions. But without denying the possibility of some Christian liturgical influence, I would like to point out that the form of these folk-songs has certainly a very much earlier origin. The liturgy from which they derive is not a Catholic one, but that of the ancient vegetation rites, of which traces have come down to us in the May ceremonies. These were rites in which the courting of young people was magically associated with ceremonies for helping on the growth of fruit trees and plants, and they are found in much the same form wherever one has a primitive agricultural society. The association of flowers, birds, trees and fountains with the idea of love is not due to some poetical notion inherent in country people, but to a definite magical intention. This and the fact that the ceremonies were performed by circles of young men and girls who sang alternate verses led to the development of the parallelistic form, which is a common feature of folk poetry in primitive countries. The beautiful Lithuanian *dainos*, for example, have a strongly parallelistic form although they go back to pagan times. The same may be said of that famous Chinese collection, the *Book of Songs*, dating from 800-600 B.C., which has been so admirably translated by Dr Arthur Waley. In these poems, which, like the Portuguese *cossantes*, were written in feudal courts in imitation of the folk-songs sung in the spring ceremonies, the first half of each stanza contains a description of the growth of the flowers and trees, whilst the second half speaks of the feelings or situation of the young man or girl who is in love. No 'like' or 'as' connects the two halves: the analogy between the vegetable and the human world is left as it is, though the primitive magical association has given way to a poetical one.

The forms and sometimes the language then of these Galician lyrics have behind them a long tradition, leading back to the rites of primitive agricultural societies and to later cults that came in from the Near East before Christianity. However, they have undergone a strong process of rationalization before we meet with them. Many of the old ritual elements have been shed and 'naturalistic' situations have been introduced, illustrating in a poetical way the real life of the peasant girls.[1] We may take it that this is the result not of peasant realism, but of the sophisticated art of the *juglares*. Most of these men came, in the period we are considering, from the more or less knightly or aristocratic class, or else were clerics. Two of the best poets among them were a priest of Santiago and a King of Portugal. Another was an admiral of Castile who had been born in Galicia. Now in Galicia and Portugal there was a custom known as *amadigo* by which the children of the upper classes were farmed out with peasant nurses in the houses of *vilãoes* or villeins, and grew up almost to manhood with them. It would not be surprising, therefore, if in after-life they felt the *sabor* or charm of this peasant life, as Gil Vicente and Lope de Vega did in the sixteenth century, and rewrote the dance poems of the village girls to express their sentiments about it. No doubt they had love affairs with these girls in which their feelings really played a part, whereas in Provence the cult of love for married women led to an entirely different orientation of erotic feelings and consequently of subjects for poetry. At all events we may say that the apparent naïveté of the language in many Galician *cossantes* and the naturalness of the situations they describe are the result,

[1] Take for example, in a *cantiga* by Martin Codax, the ceremonial (midsummer morning?) bathing in the sea of the girls who have lovers. Or the *cantiga* by Pero Meogo in which the girl tears her dress at a dance and awaits beside the fountain the coming of the stag, who is also the *namorado*, or lover. Stags, water, birds, flowers, branches, bows and arrows all have a symbolic meaning in these poems, as they have in the Lithuanian *dainos*, though the naturalistic treatment of the themes by the *juglares* has partly obscured this.

not of imitating peasant songs, but of sophistication. It is precisely in the verses of King Dinis and of other well-born poets that this style of composition is most artistically developed.

An important step occurs when the *juglares* take the verse forms of the original folk-songs and elaborate them without too much regard to their complete setting. For the words of a folk-song are only one element in a triple complex of words, tune and dance. In primitive conditions they are the least important element. The tune and dance between them fix the metre and the shape of the stanza as well as the subject matter, which is one reason why the study of verse forms is so important in early poetry. What happened in the twelfth century was that the increasing interest shown in love poetry by the upper classes, due chiefly to the evolution by them of a cult of love, led to the words of folk-songs being taken out of their triple context and developed on their own account. For a time the accompaniment of dance and tune were kept—then dance was dropped and, much later, music. Thus while we can only guess what *cossantes* were danced and what were not, or whether new dance forms were invented to match the new verse forms, we can see that the value of the *cossante*, as opposed to the folk-song, was held to lie principally in its poetic form. If any proof of this were needed, the fact that they were carefully collected in anthologies without their musical setting shows this.

The freshness and lyrical purity of these Galician songs is due to the particular stage of development they had reached between the folk-songs sung and danced from time immemorial by women on the village threshing floors, or round sacred trees or springs, and the finished, dressed-up poetry of the courts. The extreme elaboration of the Provençal lyric, once its dance accompaniment was dropped and the tune subordinated to the words, carried it beyond the range of the feelings and associations that had given birth to it into a cascade of verbal fireworks where it became desiccated. This did not happen in Galicia and Portugal, because these countries were too far removed from the main currents of European life to feel the urge to experiment and because the social situation was different. Their *juglares* were driven to exploiting the local vein. They took to writing the poems which the village women had once made themselves to the native dance tunes. If in doing this they failed to create, as the Provençals had done, a literary language with a great variety of forms and a large vocabulary, they produced a purer poetry, perfect in itself and capable of giving us today an emotion different in quality to anything else in literature. They achieved the sort of effect aimed at by Verlaine in his *Romances sans Paroles*.

Let me give as an example of this an aubade which King Dinis, writing towards the end of the thirteenth century, had remodelled from an earlier song by a Galician *juglar*, Pero Meogo.

> Levantou-s'a velida,
> levantou-s' alva,
> e vai lavar camisas
> en o alto.
> Vai-las lavar alva.
>
> Levantou-s'a louçana,
> levantou-s' alva,
> e vai lavar delgadas
> en o alto.
> Vai-las lavar alva.
>
> E vai lavar camisas,
> levantou-s' alva,
> o vento lh'as desvia
> en o alto.
> Vai-las lavar alva.
>
> E vai lavar delgadas,
> levantou-s' alva,
> o vento lh'as levava
> en o alto.
> Vai-las lavar alva.
>
> O vento lh'as desvia,
> levantou-s' alva,
> meteu-s a alva en ira
> en o alto.
> Vai-las lavar alva.

O vento lh'as levava,
levantou-s' alva,
meteu-s'a alva en sanha
en o alto.
Vai-las lavar alva.

The translation can be given in two lines. 'The girl got up at dawn
and went to wash her shifts on the hill. The wind blew them
away, the girl was angry.' *Velida* and *louçana* are adjectives
meaning lovely and are the usual appellations for *girl* in these poems
because they provide the necessary *i* and *a* assonances. *Alva* means
dawn and in *alvoradas* or aubades the word is often brought into
the refrain, whether it fits the sense or not. But it also means white
and in the third lines of the last two stanzas it is used as another
appellation for girl.

I have chosen this poem for quotation because it provides a good
example of the very small amount of material needed to make one
of these lyrics. If one compares it with the earlier version by Pero
Meogo one will see that in remaking it King Dinis cut out everything that did not conduce to the single, static impression he was
aiming at—of a girl washing her clothes in the brook at daybreak
and the dawn wind blowing them away. In this he was carrying
to its furthest possible conclusions the general tendency of the
Galician-Portuguese school, which was to reduce the narrative and
descriptive elements to a minimum so as to seize and fix a single
lyrical moment. Such poetry exploits a very narrow vein of feeling: it does not stimulate the mind or open up the way to new
forms of expression, because it has neither intellectual nor rhetorical
content. But it is the result of a very refined art and it achieves
what it aims at doing perfectly. Perhaps I should add that the
writers of these wonderfully limpid poems had other forms in
which they could express the more active and analytical sides
of their natures: they wrote *cantigas de amor* or love songs addressed
to women in imitation of the Provençal and also *cantigas de
escarnho* or *maldizir*, that is, satires, which are often remarkable for
their scurrility and obscenity.

One other feature should be noted of these Galician-Portuguese
lyrics—their melancholy. It has been suggested that this is due to

the fact that the Portuguese were, like the Castilians, involved in constant warfare with the Moors across the Tagus and that the *cantigas de amigo* are the songs of women whose lovers were absent at the front. But almost all Portuguese and Galician poetry is melancholy. Their constant theme is *saudade* (Spanish, *soledad*), which one can interpret as a vague nostalgic longing—*desiderium*, blues. The popular Galician poetry of today (the *muiñeiras*) expresses the same feeling. No doubt the reason is climatic: the moist Atlantic winds affect the glands, as they do on the west coast of Ireland or in the Hebrides, where the Gaelic poetry too is vague and sad. We shall have occasion to note again this vague, melancholy, lyrical tendency of the west and north-west of the Peninsula, which contrasts so markedly with the energetic, optimistic tone of medieval Castile.

The vogue of the Portuguese-Galician lyric lasted from the latter half of the twelfth century to the first quarter of the fourteenth. With the death of King Dinis in 1325 it ceased to be cultivated by the educated classes and when in the fifteenth century we again meet with Portuguese *cancioneros* or song books we do not find a single *cossante* or parallelistic poem among them. But whilst it lasted, it was not confined to the west of the Peninsula only. Galician became the language for lyric poetry through the whole of Spain, excepting only Catalonia, which, since the *langue d'oc* was spoken there, naturally formed part of the Provençal region. There is evidence that even the popular classes in Castile listened to the songs of the Galician *juglares* and composed verses themselves in that language.

Then when, in the fourteenth century, Galician poetry fell off and withdrew behind its own frontiers, the influence of its musical rhythms remained behind in the lands it had overrun. Almost the last *cossante* that has come down to us (it is in the *Oxford Book of Spanish Verse*) was written in Spanish by a Castilian nobleman a little before the year 1400. This influence continued, working through popular forms (greatly aided no doubt by the attractiveness of Galician music) and contributed to the great flowering of lyric poetry that begins in the fifteenth century. As we shall see later, the first stage of the Castilian lyric is the result of a marriage between the musical folk-song of Galicia and the narrative, choral folk-song of Castile-Andalusia: between, that is, the *cossante* and the *zéjel*.

POETRY IN CASTILE

We have said that in the thirteenth century Galician became the language for lyric poetry throughout the Peninsula. The most striking example of this is the *Cantigas de Santa Maria*, a collection of songs made by the learned Castilian King Alfonso el Sabio. Alfonso—his dates are 1221 to 1284—was the founder of Castilian prose and of institutions where Arabic and Jewish books were translated into Castilian. Yet he chose Galician as the proper language in which to compose his four hundred songs, many of them of admirable beauty, celebrating the miracles of the Virgin. But the form or measure he employed was not the *cossante*, for that was not suited to narrative purposes, but rather the *zéjel*, or to give it its new Spanish name, the *estribote*. It will be remembered that this is a measure that begins with a theme-stanza of two, three or four lines known in Spanish as *estribillo*, which is then developed in a succession of stanzas, each one of which ends with a repetition or rhyme-echo of the original theme-stanza. This theme-stanza and its repetitions were meant to be sung by the chorus, and, when one reads it, this dual role of solo singer and chorus impress themselves on the intimate structure of the poem and give it a peculiar vitality. The essential feature, that distinguishes it from other songs with choruses, is the theme-stanza at the beginning. Now, as we have said, there is reason for thinking that this form, which we first come across in Spanish Arab poetry, was the original round-dance measure of Andalusia and of other Mediterranean countries. At this very time the Italian Franciscan poet, Jacopone da Todi, was using it for his popular religious verses. But we have no early secular examples of it in Italian or Spanish. The only popular poem we have in Castilian from this century is the watch song *Eya Velar*, quoted by Gonzalo de Berceo, which, not being a dance song, is in a different measure.

One other kind of poetry flourished in Castile at this time, the narrative verse known as *mester de clerecía*. As its name shows, it was a 'learned' poetry written by priests or clerks, and it was written in Castilian. We have three principal examples of it from the thirteenth century, the *Libro de Apolonio*, the *Libro de Alexandre* and the rhymed lives of various saints by Gonzalo de Berceo. The first two poems are romances on classical themes, drawn from thirteenth-century Latin originals; somewhat tedious as a whole, they contain vivid, coloured passages that illustrate contemporary life and particularly the performances of musicians and jongleurs. They had a wide vogue that lasted nearly two centuries. The poems of Berceo, on the other hand, were never known outside a little group of monasteries on the borders of Navarre and Castile where he lived. It is only in recent times that their merit has been recognized.

Gonzalo de Berceo was born between 1198 and 1200 and was still living in 1246. He was a priest attached to the Benedictine monastery of San Millán de la Cogolla in the Rioja. This was a community that had grown up round a famous sanctuary: the cave in which San Millán, a sixth-century hermit who fled from even the sight of human beings, had lived cut off from the world. In the twelfth and thirteenth centuries it was a popular place of pilgrimage. Here, among the rough oak scrub and woodland of the mountain side, Gonzalo spent his life, only a mile or two away from the village of Berceo where he was born.

His principal poems (he called them *prosas*) consist of the lives of three saints, Santo Domingo de Silos, San Millán and Santa Oria, all of whom were local figures, and of three pieces dedicated to the Virgin—her Praises, her Mourning and her *Milagros*, or Miraculous Appearances. There is nothing in themselves to attract us in these legends and miracles. Spanish hagiography is a stunted plant which has refused to grow and its heroes make a crude impression beside the glittering efflorescences of the *Flos Sanctorum*. Nor does the poet often let himself go: he was translating, not inventing, and it was a matter of conscience to him to follow his Latin prose original as closely as possible. But his verse—sweet, grave and monotonous, as Antonio Machado describes it—has a peculiar charm and freshness and reflects the naïve and child-like and at the same time matter-of-fact outlook of the people of that age in an agreeable manner.

His *Milagros de Nuestra Señora* begins with an introit or introduction which recalls the opening of *Piers Plowman*. The poet describes how one day, when going on a pilgrimage, he came on a meadow, green, full of sweet flowers, threaded by streams, set about with tall trees, on whose branches a multitude of birds were singing.

> Nuncua trobé en sieglo logar tan deleitoso,
> Nin sombra tan temprada, ni olor tan sabroso.
> Descargué mi ropiella por yacer más vicioso,
> Poséme a la sombra de un árbor fermoso.
>
> Yaciendo a la sombra perdí todos cuidados,
> Odí sonos de aves dulces e modulados:
> Nuncua udieron omnes órganos más temprados,
> Nin que formar pudiessen sones más acordados.

> Never in this world did I find such a pleasant place,
> such tempered shade nor such delightful smells.
> I took off my habit to lie more at my ease
> and stretched myself in the shade of a lovely tree.
>
> Lying thus in the shade I lost all my cares,
> I heard the songs of the birds modulated and sweet.
> Never did a man hear instruments more melodious
> nor any that could make such harmonious sounds.

The birds sang, not as ordinary birds do, confusedly, but in harmony like the various instruments of an orchestra—compared to which, as he remarks in his flat Spanish manner, other orchestras are not worth a farthing. But just as we seem to be reaching the climax of the ecstasy or vision (the point where in Chrestien de Troyes' *Yvain*, which he was imitating, the birds on the pine tree that grew beside the magic fountain break into tumultuous song and *de lor joie me resjoï*) we find ourselves being conducted step by step through the interpretation of a tedious allegory, according to which the meadow is the Immaculate Virginity, the streams are the four Gospels and the songs of the birds the sermons of St

Augustine and St Gregory and other long-bearded Fathers of the Church. The prosiness of the medieval mind comes down heavily on us.

But this prosiness or literalness is one of the qualities for which, in other passages, we most esteem Berceo. It is the mark of his poetic good faith and gives a welcome earthiness to what might otherwise—if treated in the apocalyptic style of the paintings of the Beato de Liebana—prove far-fetched and tedious. Take his *Life of Santo Domingo de Silos*. He starts off by telling us that he is going to make a *prosa en román paladino*, that is, a poem in plain Spanish, because he has not wit enough to make one in Latin.

> Bien valdrá, como creo, un vaso de bon vino.

> Anyhow it will be worth a glass of good wine.

Then he goes on to describe in his plain, realistic way the life of this eleventh-century monk who became a successful abbot. We see him as a young man, walking along with his eyes lowered 'so as not to see follies', his lips tightly closed 'so as not to speak evil,' his complexion yellow from his austerities and his hood pulled well over his head. We follow him to his hermitage, where he suffers *laçeríos* from the wind and hail, while he prays day and night that God should give the peoples

> pan e paz e verdat,
> temporales temprados, amor e caridat.

> Bread and peace and truth, rain showers in moderation, love and charity.

And then we see him defying the King of Navarre, who had been so sacrilegious as to try to tax his monastery (it was the same one to which Berceo belonged), taking refuge with the King of Castile and refounding with his aid the monastery of Silos. The rest of the poem—that is, some two-thirds of it—is devoted to a rather tedious account of the miraculous cures which this worthy abbot (*el que nasçió en bon punto*, 'who was born in a lucky moment') performed both during his life and after his death. What we enjoy in this *prosa* is thus very much what we enjoy in the *cantar de gesta* about his contemporary, the Cid—a realistic picture of what life at this time was like. We get a similar pattern in the *Life of San Millán*, but with more picturesque details, because San Millán was, even as hermits of the Dark Ages go, an extremist.

Berceo's last poem was, it would seem, his *Life of Santa Oria*. It is more tender than his other poems, as well as more coloured in its language. It is also shorter. It begins by describing the dreams of an obscure nun—how one morning, as she slept in her cell, three virgin martyrs appeared to her, holding in their raised hands a number of doves that were whiter than untrodden snow. They told her they had come to fetch her on a visit to heaven, and on that she saw a column with steps round it leading up into the sky. She followed them and, as she climbed, the column turned into a leafy tree, on the branches of which the three virgins were standing gaily with their doves in their hands. In the distance she could see piercing the sky the innumerable lighted windows of the Celestial City:

> Estando en el árbol estas dueñas contadas,
> Sus palomas en manos alegres e pagadas,
> Vieron en el cielo finiestras foradadas;
> Lumbres salían por ellas, de duro serían contadas.

Some angels carried her across the gulf to it and she found herself in a place where men in richly embroidered clothes and beautifully dressed maidens were walking to and fro and talking in a very genteel manner. They welcomed her and took her to see the jewelled seat reserved for her—at that time women generally sat on the ground—so that she could hardly bear to think that she must return to earth and leave this very pleasant place. The maidens were most anxious to keep her and appealed to the saints to intercede for her with God the Father. So she was brought to His presence, and there she heard His voice telling her that she must return for a short time to earth to complete her necessary spell of suffering. She went back and the story ends with a long account of her pious death.

It is a delicious poem, written with great simplicity and poetic feeling, and in its transparent style it tells us all we need to know of the humble priest who wrote it and of the tranquil, thoughtless religious faith of the times. But its form, and that of all the poems in *mester de clerecía*, is interesting. The metre is the Spanish alexandrine of fourteen syllables, which as a rule are carefully counted: this counting is a sign of culture and French influence. The type of stanza is that known as the *cuaderna vía*—that is to say, the lines are grouped in fours, each four having the same rhyme (*not* assonance). They were intended to be recited, not sung. Where then does this very un-Spanish measure come from? Not from French or Provençal poetry. Its model is the Latin goliardic verse that began to be written by clerics and schoolmen in England, France and Germany at the beginning of the twelfth century. This Latin influence might seem natural in a poetry composed by priests, yet in crossing the Pyrenees it has undergone a change of tone and subject matter, for there is nothing goliardic or satirical in any of the Spanish *mester de clerecía* poetry of this century. To find that we must go on to the fourteenth century and to the Archpriest of Hita.

CHAPTER IV

THE ARCHPRIEST OF HITA

WE HAVE now come to one of the greatest poets of the Middle
Ages, the equal of Chaucer and one of the most varied and interesting writers of that time. Also to one of the most representative
figures of Spanish literature. Juan Ruiz was born probably at
Alcalá de Henares, close to Madrid, soon after 1280. He became
Archpriest of Hita, a small place some thirty miles to the east of
Alcalá, and wrote verses for singing and reciting by *juglares*. In
1330 he seems to have collected what he had written into a book,
but, being imprisoned at Toledo in 1343 by the Archbishop for
reasons that are not known to us, he brought out in prison a second
recension of it with a new beginning and ending. Then he disappears from our sight and by 1351 was almost certainly dead.
That is all we know of the external features of Juan Ruiz's life, and
though in form, at least, he is one of the most autobiographical of
poets and though the impression we derive from his verse is intensely vivid and personal, he remains in the end a somewhat
enigmatic figure.

His poems have come down to us in a collection called by him
the *Libro de Buen Amor*, which we may translate as the 'Book of
True Love', or perhaps of 'Good Companionship'. It consists of
narrative poems of varying length in *cuaderna vía*, interspersed
with songs in lyrical metres. Among the latter one will find the
first examples of the *estribote* or *zéjel* in Castilian literature and
there is no trace whatever of Galician influence. The general
tone is gay, ironic, buffoonish or satirical, but love is treated
delicately as well as humorously and there are a certain number of
hymns to God and to Our Lady; in its mixture of comic and
serious, satirical and touching themes it is intensely juglaresque and
medieval. The most original feature, however, is the autobiographical thread which runs through it, holding together the moralizing

and satirical passages and the fables that are brought in as *enxiemplos* or illustrations. This consists in the description of a series of scandalous love affairs in which the Archpriest claims to have played successively the parts of rejected lover, seducer and victim. Yet on several occasions he insists that his book has a higher—that is, a religious or moral—purpose. No wonder that his modern commentators have been puzzled and have come to the most varied conclusions as to his intentions.

Let us look at this more closely. On the first page we find a verse prayer to God to deliver him from prison, which in its pathos reminds one of Villon's petition from another bishop's dungeons. After this comes the prose preface which explains in what sense the book is to be understood. There are, he declares, two kinds of love—*buen amor*, which comes from God, and *loco amor*, which is the worldly and sinful love of women. His book is written to show by its examples the dangers of this worldly love and how much the true love inspired by God is to be preferred to it; yet, he slyly adds, since it is in the nature of human beings to sin, those who, contrary to his advice, may wish to practise this *loco amor* will here find some useful ways of doing so.

Obviously this explanation of the Archpriest's intentions cannot be taken very seriously. The whole book rises up to protest that it was not written to discourage the pursuit of worldly love. One may regard it rather as the impish apology which a priest who is in trouble with his superiors has felt obliged to make for a book such as priests, even in a relaxed age, are not supposed to write. (In 1324 a Council at Toledo had expressed its regret at the attendance of clerics of the archdiocese at the performances of *juglares*.) Yet I do not think that these excuses are entirely disingenuous. Ruiz insists many times that his book must be judged by its intentions rather than by its matter and that it is more subtle than it seems. What does he mean by this? In the first place, that the art of writing verses well is a good thing in itself and that by giving *solaz* or entertainment of this kind the poet is saving people from sin, which is often the result of boredom. *Ca la mucha tristeza mucho pecado pon'*. He returns to this idea later when, with obvious seriousness, he speaks of *acedia* or boredom as being the worst of all the seven deadly sins. (The Middle Ages were, of course, the classic age of boredom.) Then, that the knowledge of the world, which is the *cosa sotil* he claims to communicate under the show of merely providing entertainment, is profitable both to saints and sinners. Even if his book does not lead many people to God, it will make everyone who hears it more cheerful, more charitable and more sensible. The Archpriest, one may say, is basing his claim for the propriety of his poems on a plea for the moral and humanizing value of literature.

Let us now look at the book itself. After a prayer to God for grace to write verses that would give pleasure to those that heard them and a couple of songs in honour of the Virgin (all performances by *juglares* began with such songs), he embarks on the main theme of his book, which is, of course, love. First of all he sets out its philosophy:

> Como dice Aristótiles, cosa es verdadera:
> El mundo por dos cosas trabaja: la primera,
> Por aver mantenencia; la otra cosa era
> Por aver juntamiento con fembra placentera.

As Aristotle said and said truly: The world lives for two things. The first is to have food and lodging and the other to procure union with a pleasing woman.

Men, birds, and animals, everything that walks and flies, desire by their nature a constant succession of new mates. Every sinful man is thinking continually and all the time of how he can accomplish this. And he himself, the Archpriest, had been especially inclined from youth upwards to love women: the stars (here a treatise on astrology is brought in) had given him that inclination.

After this somewhat Lucretian introduction, the poet describes two youthful love affairs he had had. In the first the lady had refused him: in the second a friend, whom he had sent to her with a letter, deceived him and won the lady himself. This is told in a punning *troba cazurra*, or song sung by the lowest class of *juglares*, beginning *Mis ojos no verán luz:* it is given in the *Oxford Book of Spanish Verse*.

With these examples to comment on, the Archpriest now resumes the exposition of his amatory philosophy. Love is delightful even when the lover's suit is unsuccessful. Although one may not be able to taste the pear, to sit in the shade of the pear tree is very sweet. It is also an education. It makes the lover gay, frank and eloquent. It refines the coarse man, teaches the dumb to talk and gives energy to the lazy. It keeps the young in their youth and makes the old lose much of their age. Above all it gives value to what in itself is not worth a fig. Thus the lover and his mistress may both of them be ugly, poor, base, and doltish, but to one another they will seem more beautiful and noble than anybody else. One may say that this passion has only one defect—that it is deceitful: *el amor siempre fabla mintroso.*

What a breath of warm, human air one feels on reading these pages! We are in a totally different world from the romantic, neurotic, springlike twelfth century with its air of clever children playing elaborate games. To the Provençals and their Arab teachers love had also been an education in the moral and aesthetic values. For them it was an institution that brought refinement through a religious-like striving after distant horizons, through a delicious sort of suffering. The French and the Italians had developed these theories—the former in the *Roman de la Rose*, the latter through Petrarch, who was just now receiving the poet's crown on the Capitol. Yet where among all these poet martyrs of love does one find the idea that base and ugly people could love one another or that anything was to be gained for human society by that? They would have rejected such an idea with scorn: the base and the ugly were precisely the people excluded from their paradise. The Archpriest, however, with his truthful plebeian eye saw deeper. Like them he wrote upon love, but, being a true Castilian, he wrote upon it as it was, not as he thought it ought to be. And he put it in the setting of that intensely human medieval democracy of which Spain and England, so far as literature is concerned, provide the best examples.

The Archpriest now describes a third unsuccessful love affair of his, in which he made the mistake of offering the lady *trobas* and *cantares* instead of jewels. Discouraged by his repeated failures, he breaks into a long invective on love, which with various fables and satires continues somewhat tediously for 242 stanzas. Love then appears in person and answers him. He has gone, he tells him, the wrong way about it. First of all he has not chosen the right kind of woman to approach, and here follows a minute description of the proper type—those who are *en la cama muy loca, en la casa muy cuerda,* 'prudent in the house, wild in the bed.' Then he must choose a good bawd to act as go-between. The best are those old women who hang about churches and convents, wearing many strings of beads round their necks and selling powders or cheap jewelry. They have the entry to all houses and are besides very experienced in these matters. Finally he must learn good customs, avoid drink and bad company, and assume an air of gaiety and discretion

> Sey como la paloma, limpio e mesurado,
> Sey como el pavón, loçano, sosegado,
> Sey cuerdo, non sanudo, nin triste nin airado:
> En esto se esmera él qu'es enamorado.

Be like a pigeon, sedate and well preened. Be like a peacock, gallant and assured. Be discreet, not violent, neither gloomy nor enraged. The lover must excel in courtesy.

As a result of this good advice the Archpriest resolves to pursue a young, rich and beautiful widow called Doña Endrina. But he still feels a certain lack of confidence in himself and so he calls on Doña Venus to help him. In a passage that again recalls Lucretius —*Ella es nuestra vida e ella es nuestra muerte*—she appears and tells him some things that will be useful to him. She lets him into the secret of women—what their real character is, what dangers they fear, how to help them to overcome their modesty, how to interpret their answers. His business will be not so much to get round them as to help them to get round themselves. And in doing this he must use art. Everything in the world has its art and the seduction of women most of all. So he must be gay, loving, forceful and deceitful and above all never take no for an answer. The successful lover is the one who persists to the end.

The stage is now set for the principal episode in the book—the wooing and seduction of Doña Endrina—in which the correct application of all this good advice will be seen. She appears and he falls in love. (I say *he* because, though on some occasions the narrator of this story is called Don Melón de la Huerta, on another he is called Ruiz). To carry on his suit he secures the services of Trotaconventos, an old hag of the type recommended, and the chase begins. The story is brilliantly told. Doña Endrina and Trotaconventos come to life as vividly as any characters in medieval literature and the Archpriest's hopes and fears are movingly portrayed. The most masterly part is the description of Trotaconventos' arts and wiles and the wonderful way in which she plays upon the feelings of the two lovers. Doña Endrina falls in love, but is held back by the fear of scandal and also by her need for securing a suitable husband for taking over the management of her property. The episode ends with the poor woman, who has finally decided to marry someone else, being enticed to Trotaconventos' house and seduced there by the Archpriest. The actual scene of the seduction has been cut by a prudish copyist, but enough is left for us to see that the end is conceived with a proper artistic detachment. The man satisfies his lust, Doña Endrina is ruined and the bawd offers the kind of stoical advice that people of that sort usually offer. A final verse describing the marriage of the lovers must be regarded as a tag added to disarm criticism.

This episode cannot be described as a *conte* or tale. The treatment is completely different from anything in Boccaccio or Chaucer. This is no doubt because the plot was taken from an obscure thirteenth-century Latin play, *De Amore* by 'Pamphilus', yet the story moves with such naturalness and realism that we find it hard to believe it was not drawn from actual life. The interest lies in the three characters and in their varying relations to one another and, though the seducer is not a villain but merely the *homme moyen sensuel*, the plot is precisely that of Richardson's *Clarissa*. One must therefore regard it as a novel and, as we shall see later, it was the direct ancestor and inspirer of one of the greatest of all novels, *La Celestina*.

The sentimental education of the Archpriest does not end with Doña Endrina. He embarks with every prospect of success on the seduction of a young girl. But in a fit of impatience he forgets the advice of Doña Venus to flatter his bawd and give her good words, and with typical Spanish pride Trotaconventos breaks with him and gives his schemes away. A reconciliation is effected in which the old woman tells him that so long as he calls her *buen amor* she will do anything for him, but meanwhile the girl has been lost and the Archpriest falls ill with disappointment. To recover, he sets out one March day to explore the sierra.

We have now come to the most original and fascinating part of the book. The Archpriest crosses the Guadarrama alone and on foot from the valley of Lozoya to Segovia, and returns by the direct road to Madrid. In the course of his walk he encounters four *serranas* or shepherdesses (actually cow-herds), each uglier than the last, and has adventures of various kinds with them. Each adventure is described first in *cuaderna vía* for recitation and then in a *cantica de serrana*, or pastoral lyric, intended to be sung. Many of the Archpriest's love adventures were recorded twice over in this way, but in most cases the *canticas* or songs have been lost. We must remember that the copies that have come down to us have been expurgated.

The first encounter takes place on the summit of the pass of Malangosto in a snow storm. A woman who is guarding cows leaps out on him and demands passage money. She is ugly, snub-nosed, pock-marked and she carries a crook, a sling and a *dardo pedrero*, or flint-tipped dart, like a hunter of the Stone Age. On his asking her name she tells him *Yo só la Chata recia que a los omes ata*, 'I am Snubnose the Tough who ties up men. Pay me the toll or you'll see how straw is threshed.' And she draws back her sling and aims it at him.

> Facíe niev', granizava.
> Díxome la Chata luego,
> Hascas que m'amenazava:
> "¡Págam', sinon, verás juego!"
> Díxel' yo: "Por Dios, fermosa,
> Decirvos he una cosa:
> Más querí' estar al fuego."

"Yo te levaré a cassa
  E mostrart' he el camino,
Facert' he fuego e brasa,
  Dart' he del pan e del vino:
¡Alahé! prometem' algo
  E tenert' he por fidalgo.
¡Buena mañana te vino!"

Yo con miedo, arrecido,
  Prometil' una garnacha
E mandel' para'l vestido
  Una bronch' e una prancha;
Ella diz': "¡Doy más, amigo!
¡And' acá! Vente conmigo:
  Non ayas mied' al escarcha."

Tomóm' recio por la mano
  En su pescueço me puso
Como a çurrón liviano,
  Levóme la cuest' ayusso:
"¡Hadeduro! Non t'espantes,
  Que bien te daré que yantes,
  Como es de sierra uso."

Pússome mucho aina
  En su venta con enhoto,
Dióme foguera d'encina,
  Mucho conejo de soto,
Buenas perdices asadas,
Hogaças mal amassadas,
  E buena carne de choto.

De buen vino un quartero,
  Manteca de vacas mucha,
Mucho queso assadero,
  Leche, natas, una trucha;
E dijo: "¡Hadeduro!
Comamos deste pan duro:
  Después faremos la lucha."

Desque fué poco estando,
Fuime desatiriciendo;
Como m'iba calentando
Así m'iba sonreyendo;
Oteóme la pastora,
Diz': "Ya, compañon, agora,
Creo que vo entendiendo."

La vaqueriza traviessa
Dixo: "Luchemos un rato,
Liévate dende apriesa,
Desvuélvete d'aques' hato."
Por la moñeca me priso,
Ov' a facer lo que quiso.
¡Creed que fiz' buen barato!

A translation of this that will convey something of the spirit of the original is beyond my powers: but here is a literal prose rendering which will help readers to follow the Spanish.

It was snowing and hailing. Then Snubnose began to threaten me. 'Pay up', said she, 'or there'll be trouble.' 'By God, my lovely', said I, 'I've something to say to you. But I must say it by a fire.'

'I'll take you to my house and show you your road. I'll make you a fire and a blaze. I'll give you bread and wine. Only promise me something and, by my faith, I'll hold you for a gentleman. This will be your lucky day.'

In fear and trembling I promised her a coat, and a brooch for her dress, and a medallion. 'I'll give you more than that, lad', she said. 'This way —come along with me. Don't be afraid of the ice.'

She seized my hand and threw me over her shoulder like a light sack, then set off up the hill. 'Poor creature', said she, 'don't you be afraid. I'll give you a good meal, such as we have in the sierra.'

She brought me safe and sound to her hut and lit a fire of holm oak. Then she set me a meal of rabbits from the copse, good roasted partridges, badly baked bread, and good kid's flesh.

A quart of good wine, plenty of cow's butter, plenty of smoked cheese, milk, cream, and a trout. Then she said to me; 'Come on, you poor creature. Let's eat this hard dry bread. After that we'll have a bout.'

When I'd sat there a bit I began to unfreeze. As I began to warm up,

I began to smile. The shepherdess gave me a look. 'Aha, lad', she said, 'now I think you're beginning to understand.'

Then that lewd cowgirl said: 'Come, let's get to work. Up quick and take off those clothes.' She seized me by the wrist; I had to do what she wanted. You may think I got off pretty cheaply.

After this alarming adventure the Archpriest reaches Segovia, where, like any tourist, he goes to look at the rib of the *serpiente groya*, a fabulous dragon or serpent. Then he sets off to recross the mountains, but before reaching them he loses his way in the pine-woods of the Riofrio, close to La Granja. Here he meets another *serrana* called Gadea, who aims a stone at him with her sling and hits him behind the ear. She takes him to her hut and suggests 'having a bout' with him whilst her man is away. As she threatens him, he is obliged to do what she wishes.

Next morning he sets out to climb the pass. Before he has gone far he meets a *serrana* who is cutting firewood. She is one of the silly kind and asks him to marry her. He agrees and she gives him a long list of the wedding presents she will expect. He promises to give them; then, telling her to get everything ready for the ceremony and to invite her family, he goes off, as he says, to fetch them.

He now reaches the summit of the pass. It is snowing and freezing hard and an icy wind is blowing: in great fear he runs down the further slope. Then, at a spot not far from where the chalet of the Club Alpino now stands, he meets with the most terrible figure of a woman he has ever seen. A giantess, monstrously ugly, with a huge nose and ears, dark hairy skin, bloodshot eyes, asses' teeth, and half-naked breasts hanging to her waist. Even in St John's Apocalypse there was nothing to match her. As he is half dead with cold, he begs her to give him shelter and she leads him to her *choza* or hut, which is close to La Tablada.

The sequel, he tells us, he put into three *canticas*, but only one of these, an *estribote*, has come down to us. In this he begins, in an ironical pastiche of the pastoral style, by describing the *serrana*— Alda is her name—as *fermosa, loçana e bien colorada*—that is, as beautiful: the truth about her appearance only emerges later. They reach the hut, where she informs him that anyone who spends the night in it must marry her and give her a present. He replies that he already has a wife in Ferreros, but promises money. On that she sets before him a meal of black rye-bread, sour wine, and salted meat. Then she gives him, in the usual *serrana* style, a list of the presents she expects in payment for her hospitality. He promises to bring them on his return, but she refuses to trust him. The *cantica* here breaks off and we are left to guess how the matter ended. The last passage in this series describes the Archpriest's visit to the shrine of Santa Maria del Vado, where he keeps an all-night vigil in gratitude for his escape from the dangers of the sierra.

Now what are we to make of these poems on *serranas*? The *serranilla* or *pastourelle* had been introduced by the Provençal troubadours and French jongleurs to Galicia, where it had suffered a lyrical change and lost some of its narrative elements. It seems to have been introduced into Castile too both in its Provençal and in its Galician forms: at all events we find it there later. In these *serranillas* the story is always the same: the poet meets a shepherdess or cowherd of remarkable beauty and makes love to her. Here the Galician *pastourelle* usually stops, with a glimpse of the shepherdess singing, but in the Provençal form he persists in his suit and she refuses to have anything to do with him.[1] The intention of the Archpriest in writing these *canticas* seems therefore quite obvious. He is debunking the conventional or courtly *serranilla* and showing what sort of creatures cowgirls in fact were and how little likely to refuse any advances made to them. He is also following his usual, though, as we have seen, not invariable, practice of displaying himself as a lover in an absurd, unsuccessful or even buffoonish light. Yet this is not the whole story. As Sr Menéndez Pidal has shown, there existed from early times in Castile a popular type of *serranilla*, in which an uncouth cowgirl leaped out upon travellers and plundered them. Usually she took them to her hut and demanded that they satisfy her lusts as well. A number of these *serranillas* have come down to us from the fifteenth and

[1] One may draw a line across Western Europe such that in nearly all the *pastourelles* written to the north of it the shepherdess says *yes*, and in nearly all those written to the south of it she says *no*. This line follows the boundary between the *langue d'oil* and *langue d'oc* regions and separates two zones of different sexual habits. In the West it corresponds to the division between German-occupied and Vichy France.

sixteenth centuries, sometimes in ballad form, and we can be sure that they were not derived from the *Libro de Buen Amor* because there is also a thirteenth-century Portuguese example. The Archpriest was therefore not so much satirizing a courtly poem as writing in a very old juglaresque and popular genre indigenous to the Peninsula.[1]

The rest of the *Libro de Buen Amor* must be described more briefly. The adventures in the sierra are followed by a Carnival fantasia, in which Don Carnal, representing feasting, has a battle with Doña Quaresma, who is, of course, Lent. It reads like a chapter from Rabelais. On the one side are assembled all the various birds and animals which are good to eat, arrayed like knights in armour in the utensils they are cooked and served in: on the other are the fishes and vegetables similarly accoutred. The lines of battle are drawn up and Don Carnal, a *muy rico emperador*, whose rule extends over the whole world, sits feasting on his raised platform and listening to his jongleurs, whilst his cupbearer blows a wine-jar as trumpet and the cocks crow because he has eaten their wives. Then night falls over the sleeping host. Doña Quaresma's army attacks and after a fierce fight, described like the battles of the day as a series of separate duels, defeats the army of Don Carnal and takes him prisoner. The satire on knightly prowess is obvious.

The battle, however, does not decide the matter: Don Carnal escapes. Travelling through the countryside, he collects his forces of sheep, cattle, and goats and sends a letter of defiance to his rival. She submits (Lent is now over) and, uniting their forces, the two great emperors, Don Carnal and Don Amor, make a triumphant entry into Toledo. Herds of bleating and lowing animals follow

---

[1] There is a parallel to these *serranillas* in the ugly and boastful lady who appears in Arthurian tales and in Scottish ballads such as *King Henry*. But Guillaume de Poitiers' amusing and obscene *vers* on the two women he met in Auvergne and their cat is a much earlier example of this kind of poem (it dates from *c.* 1100), though in this case the women are neither ugly nor shepherdesses. These stories evidently belong to an early and widely diffused genre. If, as some people think, the origin of the pastoral encounter lies in stories of water or hill spirits who carry the traveller off to their dwelling, like the fairy lady in the ballad of *Thomas the Rhymer*, then the ugly and boastful shepherdess will derive from an especially Christian or monkish version of the occurrence. But if, on the other hand, they are poetisations of fertility rites of a licentious kind, then the ugly shepherdess will be harder to account for.

the former to the slaughter house, whilst Don Amor is met by birds, flowers, trees and by men and women playing on all kinds of musical instruments. After them comes a procession of priests, monks, abbots, and nuns chanting *Te, Amorem, laudamus* and *Benedictus qui venit*. A sacred image of Venus is carried past and the knights and clerics have an altercation as to which shall have the honour of lodging the hero. The scene ends with a beautiful description of the Tent of Love and of the allegories of the Twelve Seasons represented in it: a word-painting of the illuminations in a medieval Book of Hours, taken either from the *Roman de la Rose* or from the *Libro de Alexandre*.

Here then we have a full-dress satire on the corruption of the Church and on the general relaxation of customs that followed the great wave of piety of the thirteenth century. It is all the more convincing because it is written without indignation. The Archpriest was not, as the earlier satirists would have been, in the following of Doña Quaresma. On the contrary he goes out of his way to show us his stout jovial figure and small penetrating eye among the intimate companions of Don Amor.

The apotheosis of Love is followed by a new episode in the poet's *vie amoureuse*. On the advice of Trotaconventos he woos a nun. This proves to be a difficult affair because the nun is virtuous, and the negotiations between her and the bawd become protracted. They take the form of a poetic debate, in which each tries to convince the other by reciting to her an appropriate fable. The matter is decided when Trotaconventos, having worn down the nun's resistance, gives her a minute account of the Archpriest's appearance. The nun then agrees to receive his suit, but on the condition that her chastity is respected. So, till her death a few months later, the Archpriest serves her with *limpio amor*, platonic love—a relationship on which, and on nuns in general, he has some acid comments to make. He would have agreed with the remarks of his predecessor Ibn Guzmán on finding himself in a similar plight, that kissing by itself is donkey's love.

The last *amorío* we are treated to is with a Moorish girl: it is unsuccessful like most of the others, but affords the Archpriest an opportunity of airing his knowledge of colloquial Arabic and

Moorish music. Then Trotaconventos dies. This provokes a long
and impassioned arraignment of Death, in the style of the Dances
of Death of the following century, ending in an *endecha*, or lament,
in which we are told, with penetrating irony, that on account of
her sufferings in this world she is now sitting in heaven side by side
with the Martyrs. Her epitaph follows. The book is now coming
to an end. We are given the portrait of Don Furón, the Archpriest's rascally servant, and then we come to the envoi. Since this
book is about *buen amor*, he says, no one must sell it or hire it, but
must pass it round freely. He leaves it open, so that anyone who
can rhyme well may change it to suit his taste, or add to it. Seven
songs in honour of Our Lady bring it to an end. Three more *canticas*
follow as a postscript.

The extraordinary richness of this book will be clear even from
the brief summary I have given of it. As Menéndez y Pelayo said,
it is the *Comédie Humaine* of the Middle Ages. Let us therefore see
how it compares with the *Canterbury Tales*, which also sets before
us a broad picture of its time. At first sight the range of the Archpriest's book appears to be much more restricted: it lacks the
immense portrait gallery of the English poet: Chaucer resembles
a twentieth-century novelist in his comprehensiveness. On the
other hand it is far more compressed. The Spanish poet deals as
much with ideas and modes of conduct as with actual men. In his
work the two interact and illuminate one another, and it is this
mixture of the abstract and the concrete—so eminently suited to a
poetic style—that helps to give the verse tension and compression.
The Archpriest's diction too is more vivid and racy: his natural
quickness of mind was assisted by a keen eye and a sharp ear and he
diversifies the generally monotonous metre of the *cuaderna vía* with
phrases and rhythms lifted from actual speech. Proverbs or *refranes*
abound and great use is made of that ironic *double entendre* which
is still such a regular feature of Spanish conversation. In short this
poetry is the product of a more alert and mature society than that
depicted by the English poet: one in which the eye and the mind
lived in close association with one another and in which there was
little room for the naïve and the innocent.

One has of course to remember the special position of the

Archpriest. He was a cleric of a certain standing, but he wrote for
iuglares and lived a good deal in their company. The society of
iuglares—there is no English term—resembled in many ways that
of actors or journalists today. They travelled a great deal and mixed
with people of every rank and occupation; they were cheerful and
gregarious and knew life well from its seamier side. Only, of
course, they were poorer. Some of them were very poor indeed
—mere street pedlars—but the Archpriest wrote for them too,
just as (he tells us) he wrote for blind men, for begging scholars,
for Jews and Moors and wise women and serenading lovers, though
most of the *cantigas* he made for these have been lost. Now an
educated man who frequented such company must have known
everything there was to know about the society of his time, and he
must have seen it from inside and from a satirical, not to say cynical,
angle. Chaucer, on the other hand, looked at the society he has
depicted from above: he was a courtier and a fine gentleman.

The subject of the Archpriest's book is love, but its loose structure
allowed him to treat of many other questions. Indeed there is
scarcely any matter of interest to the people of his time on which
he has not something to say. For example there is a satire on the
courts of justice, in the form of a law-suit in which a wolf sues a
fox for stealing a hen, a discourse on the properties of money
'which makes lies true and truth lies', and another on astrology.
Then take this stanza on poverty:

> El pobre con buen seso e con cara pagada
> Encubre su pobreza e su vida lazrada,
> Coge sus muchas lágrimas en su boca cerrada:
> Más val', que facerse pobre, a quien no l'darán nada.

The poor man hides his poverty and his wretched life under a quick
wit and a contented air and catches his many tears in his clenched teeth.
That is better than showing a poor mouth to those who won't give him
anything.

My translation fails to show the raciness of the language, but anyone who has lived in Spain will recognize that the observation is
as true today as it was then.

Three qualities stand out in the *Libro de Buen Amor*—the dryness, the sense for style, and the irony. Dryness is the characteristic of all Castilian poetry till it is impregnated by the melancholy lyrical feeling of Galicia, the musical sense of the Italians and the rhetoric of Andalusia. It remains the salient characteristic of Spanish prose down to modern times. We certainly feel it as a limitation in the Archpriest's book, which, with all its variety of subject and feeling, keeps too much to one plane. One misses the warmth and charm that Chaucer threw over his narrative. However, this is to a certain extent made up for by the poet's incomparable sense for style, which enables him to fit the tone of actual speech into his metrical pattern and on occasion to give verbal beauty to the most ordinary statements. But he never allows himself to heighten a passage, as the Italian poets were doing, by letting it expand into a pool of poetic language. Delicate though his treatment of love can be, his style remains tight, rapid, dry and without a trace of lyrical feeling. Where he bores us it is by his sententiousness. Medieval writers had an unlimited appetite for moralizing—the 'sentence' or aphorism with them did the work of the rhetorical metaphor of later poets —and when the Archpriest starts on his task he sometimes goes on for too long.

His irony is felt from one end of his book to the other: it is omnipresent, all-pervasive, but, unlike that of Chaucer, it is not directed simply at particular characters or situations. It embraces himself (that is, the narrator) as much as other people; it takes in in its complex webs and folds all the features of society and of human life. This helps to make him a subtle writer, whose meaning we can never be entirely sure we have caught, but it also blunts the edge of his satire, because it is only too evident that he is not capable of feeling real indignation. He took the lax and worldly age he lived in for granted, and his satire is really his expression of the immense amusement that its shams and hypocrisies gave him and of his feeling that, after all, this sinful world is not such a bad place. One purpose of virtue, he seems to say, is to give a spice to life by showing how what ought to be differs from what is, so that, if one cannot be good, one can at least enjoy the spectacle this contrast offers. Yet he is very far from being a frivolous or heartless writer: the sharpness with which he observed poverty and suffering and his constant harping on them show that he was well aware of the darker side of life—only he found in irony the best remedy. There is a melancholy undercurrent in his book—the medieval man's fear of loneliness, old age and death—and it helped to drive him on to laughter and joviality.

But sometimes his humour seems to show a lack of sensitivity. The fourteenth century, we must remember, was the age of exuberance and gusto. It had, much more than the Renaissance, the qualities that one associates with Rabelais. Although, therefore, the Archpriest keeps a certain Spanish restraint and prefers a sly comment to an open guffaw, one sometimes finds that the fine point one expected has been dissolved in a burst of laughter. It is laughter without malice, laughter for the sake of laughter, like the puns in *Finnegans Wake*. The satires on the Church are usually of this kind: there is no barb in their arrow: they are offered us for our wholehearted enjoyment.

Menéndez y Pelayo observed very well that the *Libro de Buen Amor* is 'at once the most personal and the most exterior book possible'. The Archpriest is the most self-aware of all the writers of the Middle Ages and he put the whole of himself into it. This raises the much discussed question of how far the adventures he describes in the first person can be said to be true autobiography. He lays considerable stress, let us note, on their having happened to himself, Juan Ruiz, Archpriest of Hita. Yet in some cases we know that they have a different source. The episode of Doña Endrina, for example, was lifted from a twelfth-century Latin play by a man who called himself Pamphilus. So far as we can tell, he rarely invented stories, but drew them from medieval Latin poems (he did not know the classics), from Spanish tales and romances, and from French *fabliaux*.

The episode of the *Clérigos de Talavera* will perhaps throw some light on his method. In this he describes how he was sent to Talavera by his Archbishop to tell the clerics there that they must put away their concubines; their indignant reply makes it one of the most entertaining pieces in his book. Now there are excellent reasons for thinking that something like what he describes really happened—had it not, he would scarcely have dared to write it—

and it has been conjectured that it was this poem (it forms a post-script to his book) that led to his imprisonment. Yet it can be shown that he was imitating a satire written in England in the twelfth century in the Latin goliardic metre. That is to say, in practically the same metre as the *cuaderna vía*.

I think we shall get a better understanding of this question if we look at it in its historical perspective. The first Spanish poet to write for *juglares* whose work has come down to us was Ibn Guzmán. In its autobiographical form, in its attitude to love, in its shameless confessions and buffoonish tone his *diwan* has a great resemblance to the Archpriest's book. Then we find Guzmán's contemporary, Guillaume de Poitiers, writing in a similar vein and manner, and a generation later two goliardic poets, Primas of Orleans and the Archpoet employing the same shameless, autobiographic tone in the Latin goliardic measure. These resemblances can scarcely be accidental. There was evidently in the early Middle Ages a definite juglaresque genre, analogous to a certain type of music-hall patter today, in which the performer spoke in the first person and described all kinds of disgraceful and igno-minious adventures which he claimed had happened to him. Just as the courtly *juglares* or jongleurs had their verses written for them by troubadours, so the more plebeian kinds would often have theirs written by clerics. Spain being the last home of forms that had vanished elsewhere, it would be natural for a juglaresque poetry of this type, and in the goliardic metre, to have flourished there a century and more after it had died out in France.

If this is so, we can accept the Archpriest's autobiographical style and scurrilous confessions as a convention which would have been perfectly understood by his contemporaries. It explains the double-edged nature of the irony, verging on buffoonery: how, for example, in a book that professes to teach the art of love, only one out of twelve examples given of the author's confessed love affairs is successful. It explains too how a cleric who had consider-able administrative functions in the archdiocese could appear to expose his own weaknesses. Under his mask the Archpriest could allow himself all kinds of licences. Yet had the mask not in some intimate way suited the poet, we should scarcely have had a work of such outstanding genius as the *Libro de Buen Amor*. We may say that it gave him the liberty to reveal himself to an extent that was not approached by any other writer of the Middle Ages. The complex nature of his irony is due to his sense of his shifting relations to it.[1]

If then we wish to arrive at some notion of what the Archpriest's actual life was, we must discount the things he tells us about it, yet remember that these things are projections of himself. Reading his book in this way, we see a cleric who as a young man courted women, yet never took a *barragana* or concubine: who liked conviviality, but not drunkenness: and who, but for his love of *juglaría*, might have passed, by the lax standard of those times, as a model cleric. But people who write as he did about their own profession are apt to get into trouble with their superiors, as we know that the Archpriest of Hita did. From his time on, it was to become almost a rule that Spanish writers must spend part of their life either in exile or in prison.

---

[1] There is a surprising parallel to the Archpriest's book in an Italian novel called *Zeno*, by Italo Svevo, which came out in 1923. This is a work of remarkable originality and penetration which is too little known today, in spite of its having been excellently translated into English.

CHAPTER V

THE LATE MIDDLE AGES

POETRY

THE Archpriest's book corresponds to a great efflorescence of the *juglar's* art in Castile, in a society permeated with Moors and Jews but free of Galician influence. It lights up for us the lives of the ordinary men and women of the fourteenth century. Then after his death the curtain falls and we hear little or nothing of his successors. When it rises again, it is on a very different kind of poetry.

Pedro the Cruel was stabbed to death in 1368 on the Campo de Montiel and his bastard brother, Henry of Trastamara, succeeded him. The new dynasty, born of fratricide, was weak, like the Lancastrian in England, and the nobles usurped a large part of the royal power. The result was an intermittent state of barons' wars and anarchy which lasted until the accession of Isabella and Ferdinand in 1474-9. During this period we know nothing of juglaresque verse except that it declined and died, but a large quantity of court poetry has come down to us.

The verse of the first two generations of these court poets is contained in a vast anthology, the *Cancionero de Baena*, made c. 1445 for King Juan II by a certain Juan Alfonso de Baena. It is a book of remarkable dullness and conventionality, containing few poems that can be read with pleasure today. The best are by that prince of Spanish *trovadores*, Alfonso Álvarez de Villasandino, a Castilian from Burgos who lived between 1345 and 1425. He had an extraordinary reputation in his time, the anthologist Baena speaking of him as 'the light and crown and mirror and monarch of all poets and *trovadores*, and master and patron of the poetic art'. Today that light has burned very low, yet the ease and naturalness of his verse and a certain buoyancy reminiscent of Lope de Vega often make him triumph over the conventionality of his themes and write lyrics that are full of life and colour. The most striking of these is a *cantiga* in praise of Seville, of which he wrote one every Christmas for the municipality of that city in return for a fee of a hundred gold crowns.[1]

The poets of Villasandino's generation who are represented in the *Cancionero de Baena* continue in Spanish (and sometimes in Galician) the troubadour tradition of the Provençal-Galician school, but without any trace of the popular forms that make the Galician *Cancioneros* so delightful.[2] Their measures are either the usual lyric ones of this school (but without the *cossante*) or, for longer poems, a twelve-syllabled metre arranged in stanzas of eight lines and known as *arte mayor*. The *cuaderna vía*, never a courtly form, vanishes and the French-imported alexandrine along with it. But what is curious is that the subject of these poems is scarcely ever the poet's love for his lady. When one of these *trovadores*, round about 1390, writes a Farewell to *Amor*, or Love, whom he pictures as departing with his company of beautiful damsels from the mountains of Castile in the manner of the fairies deserting countries where they have been insulted, he is expressing the situation of a whole generation. These poets, in fact, were mercenary men who wrote their verses to commission: the game of courtly love, which had never really taken root in Spain, was weakening and politics were beginning to take its place; and this change is reflected in the subjects of the poems, which from now on are either panegyrics or satires, or else verse contests, debates and *recuestas* upon the kind of moral and social questions that are today discussed by 'brains trusts'. Another novelty was that this poetry, even when written in lyric measures, was recited, not sung: the term *juglar* fell out of use and the *menestril*, or musician, made his appearance. This separation of poetry and music did not help the former, as it should

---

[1] I have omitted two minor poets who belong to a transition period: the Jew Sem Tob, rabbi of Carrión de los Condes, whose delicate gnomic verses, written in short stanzas, were dedicated to Pedro the Cruel, and the Chancellor Pero López de Ayala (1332-1407). This important political figure is best known in literature for his prose Chronicles, but he also wrote poetry. Imprisoned in Portugal after the battle of Aljubarrota in 1385, he composed a long didactic poem called *El Rimado de Palacio*, written mostly in *cuaderna vía*, but with passages in the new measure known as *arte mayor*. On the whole a rather dull poem, it contains occasional songs and satirical episodes that can be read with pleasure.

[2] The famous *cossante* to the may tree by Diego Furtado de Mendoza, though written at this time, was not included in the *Cancionero de Baena*.

have done, but it led to a great development of the latter: the guitar and the *vihuela* became the fashionable instruments and the concert of strings a usual form of court entertainment. The music played was the *ars nova* of the Florence motets.

A reaction against this frivolous verse set in in Andalusia. Micer Francisco Imperial, the son of a Genoese jeweller who had set up his shop in Seville, took to imitating—perhaps translating would be the better word—the allegorical style and metaphorical imagery of Dante and Petrarch. He was followed in the next generation by Juan de Mena (1411-56), the son of a *regidor* of Cordova, who became the leader of a new school of humanist poets. He is a rhetorical poet, like so many of the Andalusians, with a love of fine and pompous phrases, and his dry and laboured verse is encrusted with neologisms and pedantic reminiscences. But his importance is not to be measured by the quality of his poems as they appear to us today, but by the fact that he was the first Spaniard to feel what Matthew Arnold calls the 'high seriousness' of poetry and of the poet's vocation. He visited Italy and on his return set himself the task of broadening the Spanish poetic style and enriching its syntax by imitating the Italians (chiefly Dante) and the Latin classics (chiefly Lucan). This was an absolutely indispensable thing if Spain was to leave the narrow idiom of its juglaresque verse and Provençal imitations and to produce a great European poetry. Yet the absorption of the Italian style and the creation of a suitable prosodic instrument was to take the continual efforts of a succession of able poets, lasting over a century. Why did it prove so arduous?

The reason lay in the difficulty of educating the Spanish ear, accustomed to a rapidly moving verse of strong and too regularly placed accents, to a poetry which had learned or inherited from Latin some of the melodic qualities that are given by quantitative metres. The Spanish alexandrine of the *cuaderna vía* runs with a kind of canter, which even the art of the Archpriest of Hita could not entirely disguise. But the new measure chosen by the Andalusian school, the dodecasyllable of the *arte mayor*, is decidedly worse. Its four beats, with a caesura dividing it half-way, come down on the reader in an implacable manner:

Con dós quarenténas   e más de milláres
le vímos de géntes   armádas a púnto,
sin ótro mas puéblo   inérme alli júnto
entrár por la véga   talándo oliváres.

As W. P. Ker has pointed out,[1] this is the old 'tumbling verse' of English poetry, used by Gray in his *Amatory Lines:*

With beauty, with pleasure surrounded, to languish,
To weep without knowing the cause of my anguish.

Though more epic-sounding in Spanish than in eighteenth-century English, it is clearly not a metre suited to a long narrative poem, because it is very monotonous. Seeing this, Juan de Mena sought to vary it by mixing in hendecasyllables. Now the hendecasyllable is the classic metre of Italian poetry, as it was developed by Dante and still more by Petrarch, but its quality is not decided so much by the number of its syllables as by the placing and strength of its accents. Thus the Italian hendecasyllable, which is lightly accented either on the sixth and tenth or on the fourth and eighth syllables, is an entirely different metre from the anapaestic hendecasyllable of the French and Provençals (usually known to them as a decasyllable because its endings are masculine), which is heavily accented on the fourth and seventh syllables and has besides a strong caesura after the fourth. The Galicians had taken this Provençal hendecasyllable, but fumbled about with its accents and caesura in the endeavour to make it suit their local dance tunes, and their indecision was passed on to the Castilians. What happened then was that it became caught up in the galloping rhythm of the *arte mayor*. Thus Juan de Mena's hendecasyllables are merely dodecasyllables with the first syllable left out, and the name given to them, *verso de gaita gallega* or bagpipe verse, suggests the instrument and the kind of air to which they were suited. In the following century they were sung to lively dances such as the *zarabanda* and the *tárraga*.

Now the Provençal and the Italian hendecasyllables had both of

---

[1] *Form and Style in Poetry* (1928). It contains an interesting comparison of English and Spanish metres. But the *locus classicus* for these questions is Menéndez y Pelayo's *Poetas Líricos*, vol. x.

them been evolved in the course of the Dark Ages out of classical Latin metres, but the Italians had kept a sense of their old quantitative poetry and Petrarch had refined on this, producing a metre that was *piano*—that is, lightly stressed, variable and slow. Francisco Imperial, being half an Italian, had written a few stanzas of Italian hendecasyllables, but his experiment was not followed up. Juan de Mena does not seem to have understood the importance for his purpose of acclimatizing the Italian metre: his temperament inclined him to an emphatic style rather than to a lyrical one and his Spanish ear may have been unable to assimilate the subtle and sensuous movement of Petrarch's verse. He preferred Dante, where the *piano* quality is not so marked, or Boccaccio's *Teseide*, where he imitated the pseudo-epic style and the *ottava rima*, but neglected the metrical means to the effect. Moreover—in imitation perhaps of a new Italian fashion—he wrote his long epic-didactic poem, the *Laberinto de Fortuna*, to be sung. The tune is given by Salinas in his *De musica*, published in 1577: it is in triple time and suggests that the chief reason for Juan de Mena's rejection of the Italian metre was musical. An ear accustomed to associate verse with dance tunes could not assimilate a poetry that, like Latin, did not require a musical accompaniment because it had learned to make its own verbal music. A whole century had therefore to pass before a poet of genius, Garcilaso de la Vega, successfully naturalized the Italian metre and opened for Spanish poetry the broad channel which it has followed ever since.

I have devoted some space to this rather technical matter because the change from a poetry that depends on a popular musical accompaniment to one that does not (juglaresque narrative poetry was probably recited in a singsong) is the greatest and most difficult that the poetry of any country can make. It was particularly difficult in a strongly stressed language such as Spanish, where the tradition of singing to lively dance tunes was vigorous. Yet, till Renaissance poetry could be written, the Renaissance sensibility, with all that that has meant for life and literature, could not come into existence. It is the poets, even more than the painters and musicians, who shape the finer texture of the mind and show us in each age how we are to feel.

The efforts of Juan de Mena and the Andalusian school to produce a more serious poetry strongly affected their contemporaries
and successors. The frivolous court verse of the *Cancionero de
Baena* came to an end and was succeeded by a poetry of *grands
seigneurs*, members of the great noble families of Castile. Their
verse continued the same metrical tradition of the *Cancionero*, but
it was more serious in tone and shows an Italian influence. One
delightful lyric poet and one great poem, also in a lyric measure,
stand out. Let us take the former first.

Iñigo López de Mendoza, Marqués de Santillana, was born in
1398 at Carrión de los Condes near Burgos and died in 1458. He
belonged to one of the greatest families in Castile and one pre-
eminent, to a quite extraordinary degree, for its literary gifts. His
father was Admiral of Castile and a poet of charm—it was he who
wrote the *cossante* I have spoken of on the may tree (p. 89, n. 2);
one of his uncles was Pérez de Guzmán, author of the most distinguished prose work of his time, whilst another was the Chancellor
López de Ayala, the great statesman, historian and man of letters of
the preceding age. There seem to have been scarcely any members
of his family who did not write poetry, and his nephew and great
nephew, as we shall presently see, were as gifted as himself. But he
was a man of action before he was a poet. His father had died
when he was a few years old and his youth was a long struggle to
secure his inheritance. With the help of a remarkable mother he
succeeded in doing this; then, on reaching his majority, he threw
himself into politics and became one of the leaders of the party of
the nobles in their struggle against the king and his great constable,
Álvaro de Luna. The final success of that party, achieved after a
long though sporadic civil war, left him the most powerful man
in the country.

Santillana's devotion to poetry is, however, more important to ✓
us than his passion for politics. He was a great patron of literature.
In his palace of Guadalajara he collected the best library in Spain
and put it at the disposal of any man of letters who wished to use
it. He himself read French, Italian, Galician, Catalan and a little
Latin; and he has left us, in a *Prohemio* or Introduction to his own
poems, addressed to the Constable of Portugal, a valuable account

of the rise of Spanish poetry and of his reasons for studying the French and Italian poets so assiduously. He put the Italians first, but praised the French for their *guardar del arte*, by which he meant their metrical exactness. For the same reason he thought little of popular poetry.

A considerable quantity of the Marqués de Santillana's verse has come down to us. There are long didactic and allegorical poems, mostly in octosyllabic metre: short poems, generally on love, in the courtly style of the period: a few sonnets. But the poems of his that we read with delight today cover only a few pages; they comprise ten *serranillas* and half a dozen or so other brief lyrics.

The *serranillas* were written at different periods of the Marquis' life, during his military campaigns in Andalusia and Aragon and on hawking expeditions over his estates in New Castile and La Montaña, which is the name given to the green, hilly country behind Santander. Conventional though their language is—for he kept closely to the style of either the French or the Galician *pastourelles*—they have the charm and freshness of something that has been really seen and felt. The pastoral encounter is an eternal theme in literature (one of the most beautiful comes in *A la Recherche du Temps Perdu*, where the narrator, looking out of a railway carriage at dawn, sees a girl carrying a bucket of water), and Santillana, with his head full of Galician and French lyrics, rediscovered its meaning when he saw a *vaquera* of La Finojosa or a *mozuela* of Bores standing among the flowering broom and wild roses. The form or measure in which he wrote his *serranillas* was the *estribote*, or, as it was now called, the *villancico*. This seems to have been the traditional Castilian form for poems of this kind, which dealt with the love not of court ladies but of village girls; and, as we have seen, the Archpriest of Hita had used it for a similar purpose. But the link with Galician poetry, which he had read as a boy in a large *Cancionero* in his grandmother's house, is also evident: some of his *serranillas* break off in the Galician way, whilst others are carried through to a finish in the French manner. All this poetry, if not exactly popular, had popular affinities.

Santillana's cowgirls are so delightful and the Archpriest's so uncouth and terrifying that it is usually supposed that there is no connection between them. In fact there is a very close one. The Marquis took from his predecessor not only the form of his *serranillas*, but also the admirable device of using the names of real places. This gives the encounter an actuality which most earlier poems of this kind lack. He borrowed too the descriptions of the dresses the *vaqueras* wore and of the presents they asked for, as well as the *dardo pedrero* or flint-tipped dart which they carried. Two of them appear to be of the familiar *bandolero* type, but the Marquis, who travelled well armed, was not a good subject for their depredations, so we read of one of them taking him to her hut and offering food, whilst the other asked for a *lucha* or 'bout'. All this plainly derives from the Archpriest, but where he describes the whole scene, Santillana, true to his Galician originals, breaks off or contents himself with a brief allusion. It is this combination of actuality and evasiveness that gives his *serranillas* their peculiar charm and delicacy.

But there is also a geographical connection between the two poets that deserves to be noticed. Santillana was lord of Hita, Buitrago and Real de Manzanares. These were his three *mayorazgos*, or family estates, and at Hita he had his principal castle. Now Hita was the Archpriest's residence, whilst Buitrago and Real de Manzanares, which are some thirty-five miles away, were precisely the starting and finishing points of his famous walking tour over the Guadarrama. The Marquis placed two of his *serranillas* here, so that the lovely girls he described guarded their cattle on the very same hill slopes as those prodigious creatures of the Archpriest's first and last adventures. With delicious irony Santillana showed his *serrana* of Lozoyuela as wearing the *garnacha de oro* and *broncha dorada* which the Archpriest had promised to bring on his return journey to her ancestor Snubnose. With the other, who very properly was of the tough kind, he had a *lucha* on the thyme-covered mountain-side.

The most notable of the Marquis's poems, however, is not called a pastoral, though it is very like one. It describes how he saw three beautiful ladies singing in a garden. Approaching them stealthily through the bushes, he discovered that they were singing about their lovers, and he quotes the first lines of their songs. Then he revealed himself, and they told him it was not him they were looking for. Sadly he sang a song himself:

> Sospirando iba la niña
> e non por mí,
> que yo bien se lo entendí.
>
> Sighing went the girl,
> and not for me,
> too well I knew.

Now these three ladies, we are told in the title, were the Marquis' daughters. The pathos of the poem lies in the feelings of a father when he discovers that his daughters' thoughts are about young men rather than about him.

The form of this poem is interesting. Each stanza ends with the *estribillo* or theme-stanza of a popular *villancico* which one of the four characters sings. This is a form found in French *chansons* of the early thirteenth century, but, as it happens, Santillana was here borrowing from a Galician *pastorela* by Airas Nunez. The Galician poem ends with two *estribillos*, the second of which is almost the same as that sung by the Marquis' second daughter:

> La niña que amores ha,
> sola ¿cómo dormirá?
>
> How shall a girl who is in love
> sleep alone?

Yet this *estribillo* was also the theme-stanza of a popular Castilian *villancico* of the fifteenth century. We see, what will become clearer later on, that the Galician lyrical genius affected Spanish poetry, not so much directly through the Castilian court poets, as through popular poetry.

The Marqués de Santillana wrote another poem in this form, the *Querella de Amor*. Here is the first stanza of it:

> Ya la gran noche passava
> e la luna s'escondía;
> la clara lumbre del dia
> radiante se mostrava;

al tiempo que reposava
de mis trabajos e pena,
oí triste cantilena
que tal cuito pronunciava;
   Amor cruel e brioso,
   mal aya la tu alteza,
   pues no faces igualeza,
   seyendo tan poderoso.

There is nothing popular about this, but you will see how Galician and Italian influences combine to produce a slow, sensuous, musical poetry of the Renaissance kind. This was easier to achieve in lyrical measures than in poems with longer lines, and in any case Santillana was by temperament better attuned to Italian poetry than was Juan de Mena. In his court poetry of *canciones* and *decires* Santillana generally writes in the thinner, more anaemic manner of the French poets. Some of these call to mind the nonchalant, melancholy tone of his contemporary Charles d'Orléans, whom, however, he seems never to have read. In his sonnets—he was the first poet to write sonnets in Spanish—he was moderately successful in introducing the Italian hendecasyllable.

We have one other poem to consider in this century—the *Coplas* of Jorge Manrique. Manrique belonged, like most of the poets and writers of this century, to one of the great Castilian families. His great-uncle was the Marqués de Santillana and one of his uncles was Gómez Manrique, a poet of distinction. But his father was a famous soldier, *Maestre* of the military order of Santiago, and unfortunately Jorge took after him in his love of war. He was killed in 1479 at the age of thirty-nine, fighting for Queen Isabella against her rival claimant to the throne, La Beltraneja.

Jorge Manrique is the classic example of a minor poet, who, by a combination of what are to us lucky circumstances, was able to write a poem that sums up the accumulated feelings of an entire age. The rest of his verse is trite and conventional—the sort of thing that every young man of parts was then doing. But his verses on the death of his father are the most famous and popular in the Spanish language.

The *Coplas* are an elegiac poem of forty stanzas, written in an octosyllabic measure broken by half-lines and known therefore as *pié quebrado* or 'limping verse'. The elegiac note is rare in Spanish poetry, which tends to avoid all intimate themes except love and treats even that in a somewhat impersonal manner. But this poem is much more than an expression of personal grief: his father's death appears rather as a call to seriousness than as a loss: it awakens in him reflections on the brevity of life and on the vanity of human desires and actions, and these reflections are the real matter of the poem. It is a meditation on the theme of Ecclesiastes, but in a Christian setting.

There is nothing new or original in either the thoughts or the images of this poem. Like Gray's *Elegy*, it consists of a string of commonplaces. The rhetorical forms and phrases he uses have come echoing down the Middle Ages in sermons and didactic poems from their original sources in the Wisdom Literature of the Bible, Boethius and the early Fathers: the anthologies of the fifteenth century are filled with them, so that one may say that there is literally nothing in these *Coplas* that had not already taken shape in the verses of Jorge Manrique's contemporaries and immediate predecessors. His uncle, Gómez Manrique, who was a more considerable but less lucky poet than he was, provided a good deal of the material: more was provided by one Ferrant Sánchez Talavera, or Calavera. Why then are these *Coplas* so good? The answer is simple—because under the stress of a strong emotion they condensed a great deal of floating sentiment and rhetoric into impeccable verse. About death there is nothing new to be said, and the poet who can revive in himself what has often been said and felt before is likely to find that his poem will have a wider appeal than most poetry. The very fact that Jorge Manrique was a man of little originality helped him to do this: the thoughts, metre, idiom, turns of phrase had already been fixed by others, as they are for ballad writers: all he needed was a strong emotion to bring it all together and an artist's sense for his medium.

The most beautiful stanzas are those in which the great kings and beautiful ladies of bygone days are brought before us and the rhetorical question is asked: What has become of them?

¿Qué se fizo el rey don Juan?
Los infantes de Aragón
  ¿qué se fizieron?
¿Qué fué de tanto galán?
¿Qué fué de tanta invención,
  como truxieron?
Las justas y los torneos,
paramentos, bordaduras,
  y cimeras,
¿fueron sino devaneos?
¿Qué fueron sino verduras
  de las eras?

¿Qué se fizieron las damas,
sus tocados, sus vestidos,
  sus olores?
¿Qué se fizieron las llamas
de los fuegos encendidos
  de amadores?
¿Qué se fizo aquel trobar,
las músicas acordadas
  que tañían?
¿Qué se fizo aquel dançar,
aquellas ropas chapadas
  que traían?

What became of the king, Don Juan?
And the Infantes of Aragón,
what became of them?
What became of the gallants all?
What became of the feats and deeds
that were done by them?
The jousts and the tournaments,
the trappings, the broideries
and the plumes,
were they vanity alone,
no more than springtime leaves
Of the gardens?

What became of the ladies,
their combs and veils and dresses
and sweet odours?
What became of the flames
of the fires that were lit
by their lovers?
What became of that singing,
and the burden
the music bore?
What became of that dancing
and the gold-worked garments
they wore?

This is one of the oldest and most well-worn themes of the Middle Ages. We have seen it in the *Chanson de Roland*. It occurs in several Spanish poems of the fifteenth century and it is of course the theme of Villon's famous *Ballade des Dames du Temps jadis*, which had been written only some fifteen years earlier. The two poets were condensing into final imperishable form a whole series of tentative efforts. But the tone of the *Coplas* and of the *Ballade* are as different as the characters of their two nations. Villon's poem has a poignancy that takes one on to Baudelaire and the personal poetry of the twentieth century: Manrique's is resigned and sententious: the brevity of life shows the folly of attaching too much importance to it. That is the characteristic stoic note of Spanish popular philosophy.

Jorge Manrique is the last poet of the Spanish Middle Ages and in his impersonality and dependence upon other poetry he is one of the most representative. For the medieval poet did not aim at expressing a personal vision of the world, but on doing a certain kind of thing, whose form had already been laid down, more perfectly than his contemporaries and predecessors. Such poetry is the product of an age where the individual did not stand out against society, but drew his strength from conforming to it, and when the idea of writing for posterity had not turned the poet into a kind of monk, distilling his essence into precious pages that would secure him a future immortality. But since we have now finished with medieval poetry, what of the prose? To consider this we must go back two centuries.

PROSE LITERATURE

The slow and painful war of reconquest had given Spaniards an interest in their own history. This was especially true in Castile, for it was the Castilians who had taken the lead in driving back the Moors and creating a Spanish Christian federation. The conquest of Seville, therefore, in 1258 was followed by a historical enterprise which was unique in Europe. Alfonso X, surnamed El Sabio, set up what we should today call an Institute for Historical Studies, whose chief task was to write the history of Spain from the earliest times. The result of this undertaking was the *Crónica General*, which was the first history of any European nation, other than the Anglo-Saxon, to be written in a modern language. What made it especially remarkable was the fact that great trouble was taken to make use of every available source: not only classical authors and Latin chroniclers of the Dark Ages were consulted, but Arabic histories and *cantares de gesta*. These were weighed and checked against one another. The King himself supervised the text and saw that it was in good Spanish.

These chronicles were continued in other reigns. At the end of the fourteenth century the great Chancellor Pero López de Ayala (1332-1407) wrote the history of the period during which he had lived, in a style broadened and enriched by the study of Livy. His picture of those cruel and stormy times is often vivid and graphic and shows a true historian's objectivity. Then, in the following century, a great nobleman, Fernán Pérez de Guzmán, spent his enforced retirement from public affairs in writing biographical sketches of the principal men of his age. Hernando del Pulgar followed him. In all these books one may say there is a seriousness of approach and a ripeness of judgment that are not to be found in the contemporary historical literature of other countries, except Italy.

But what of their style? Till the art of manipulating prose rhythms has been learned and a suitable vocabulary, especially of conjunctions, acquired, history and biography can only be crude affairs. The *Crónica General*, therefore, is rather stiff: though it can tell a story well, the finer shades of meaning are not registered. But in the continuer of Alfonso the Learned's great work, his nephew the Infante Don Juan Manuel, we have a prose writer who was an artist in narration. Limited though his scope is, he must rank as one of the best writers and most distinct and subtle personalities of the Spanish Middle Ages.

Don Juan Manuel (1282-1349) was a great prince and nobleman who had fought as a young man against the Moors, and during the king's minority acted as Regent of Castile. It was a time of troubles and civil wars and the part he played in these was that usually played by the great noblemen of the day. He abused his position, rebelled against the king and intrigued with foreign princes. When the king's party became too strong, he saw the danger and made good terms with him. But war and politics did not take up all his energies. He had a habit of retiring from time to time to his castles and estates, and it was during these retreats that he wrote his books. Most of them are works of information—treatises on falconry, chivalry, poetry and so forth—and a compendium of his uncle's Chronicle. But he also wrote a collection of moral tales and fables that goes under the name of *El Conde Lucanor*, and it is chiefly for this that we read him today.

It was the age of fables and tales, strung together in the manner of the *Arabian Nights*. Boccaccio's *Decamerone* came out a few years later and the Archpriest of Hita was busy tagging on fables to his pseudo-autobiography. But Don Juan Manuel's tales are as different as possible from either of these. In the first place they do not treat of love, for that is a subject he rarely mentions. Then their tone is thoroughly oriental: they breathe the spirit of Jewish and, to a lesser extent, Moslem Wisdom Literature.

The framework they are set in bears out this impression: a young nobleman asks advice of his steward and is answered with a story. This is the form of the Buddhist *Questions of King Milinda* and of much Sufi literature. As regards style, the language is necessarily stiffer and more antique than it is in Boccaccio: there is a certain tedious habit of repetition, but within these limits the art of the narrator could scarcely be carried further. We get, as we read, that sense of deliberation and choice in the flow of the sentence that one gets only from finished and self-conscious artists. And there is an artistic restraint too. The charm of most of these stories lies in their humour and irony, but these are laid on with such a delicate hand that without an attentive reading they escape notice.

We feel a marked yet ambiguous personality concealing itself behind these pages. There is an aristocratic aloofness and irony, there is a sort of narcissistic refinement, but there is also a great deal of distrust and uneasiness. Don Juan Manuel is only sure of himself as an artist. There, however, he had achieved an extraordinary self-confidence. It leads him among other things to display a very unmedieval anxiety for the survival of his books and for the correctness of their texts. Thus in his introduction to the *Conde Lucanor* he gives us a list of the books he had written and tells us that he had deposited the originals in the monastery of Peñafiel (one of the most impregnable castles in Spain), where they could be consulted by anyone who found errors of style or meaning in his own copy. Here then is a man who, without any classical or Italian culture, had developed the self-estimation of a Renaissance artist.

In the fifteenth century the interest in prose style increased with the study of the classical Latin authors. Cicero and Seneca became the rage and many of the books of this period are choked with pedantic forms and Latinisms. Juan de Mena's prose, for example, is quite insufferable. But these were growing pains and by the middle of the following century an excellent prose has emerged, well balanced, pliant and direct, and far in advance of anything achieved in England until much later.[1]

---

[1] One other prose work of this period deserves mention. This is *Corbacho o reprobación del amor mundano*, written in 1438 by Alfonso Martínez de Toledo, Archpriest of Talavera, when he was forty years of age. It is a moralising work, containing realistic and satirical pictures of the vices it reprobates. In conception it is an imitation of Boccaccio's *Il Corbaccio*, but it has been influenced by Catalan literature. Some of its sketches of contemporary life have a vivacity and brilliance that are very remarkable, and the characters that appear in it as 'examples' express themselves in monologues that would do credit to any play. Historically one may say that it forms a link between the Archpriest of Hita and *La Celestina*.

CATALAN LITERATURE

It will have been noted that the poets and writers we have been discussing in this and the last two chapters have, with the exception of the Portuguese-Galician song-writers, almost all been Castilians. In the fifteenth century the Andalusians made a characteristic contribution, but Leon and Asturias produced nothing. They were the old-fashioned, unadventurous regions of Spain. But what of the kingdom of Aragon? There were some Aragonese poets who wrote at Naples at the Renaissance court of Alfonso V, but their work is of secondary interest. An important literature had, however, grown up in those provinces of the Aragonese crown where Catalan was spoken—that is to say, in the Balearic Islands, Valencia and Catalonia. I will say something of this literature because, though historically and linguistically it is a special development of the *langue d'oc* or Provençal literature and grew up in isolation from the rest of the Peninsula, it is nevertheless geographically Spanish.

In the twelfth century Catalonia was culturally an outlying province of Southern France, speaking a dialect of the same language and contributing in a modest way to troubadour poetry. But after the Albigensian Crusade of 1209 this poetry declined and the Catalans, under their Aragonese kings, spread to Valencia, the Balearic Islands and Sicily, and finally to the far end of the Mediterranean. Since literature follows political power, a Catalan literature became inevitable. The Chronicle of Jaume the Conqueror, undertaken at the same time as that of Alfonso the Learned of Castile, was its first monument and this was followed by the writings, mostly in prose, of the Majorcan Ramon Llull (*c.* 1233-1315).

Llull, or Lully, as he is sometimes called, was a very extraordinary man, restless, visionary, chimerical, with something of the prophet of a new dispensation about him and much of the poet. The aim of his many activities was the conversion of the Moors in Africa. Since methods of conquest had failed—the last two Crusades had ended in disaster—more attention had begun to be paid to methods of persuasion. Llull was convinced that missionary work in Africa would only succeed if it was assisted by a simpler and more rational exposition of the truths of the Christian faith. He therefore sat down to write a new philosophy. Starting from premises which were accepted by all civilized human beings, he claimed to be able to demonstrate by rational argument everything that was necessary. The originality of this system lay in the set of tables and movable discs by which he combined the various principles and drew the correct deductions from them. But, amazing though it must seem, he knew at the time very little Latin, and his isolated position and mind untrained to philosophic discussion led him to underrate the difficulties of the task he had set himself. His *Ars Magna* was therefore received badly by the schoolmen and it was not till the Renaissance that he found any appreciators. Then Giordano Bruno saw in him a kindred spirit and Leibniz a man who had to some extent anticipated his logical methods.

But it is as a poet and above all as a writer of poetical prose that we must consider him here. His long romance *Blanquerna* (which has been admirably translated into English by Professor Allison Peers) is a remarkable book. It is an interpretation into religious terms of the novel of chivalry—the story of a young man who sets out through the forest with the aim of righting wrongs and converting everyone he meets to the love of God. He has adventures, rescues a damsel from a man who is carrying her off, challenges a knight-errant whom he finds singing by a fountain, saves a shepherd from despair, reconciles an adulterous woman to her husband; and all this he does, not in the manner of Sir Galahad with swords and lances, but using only reason and argument. Finally he attaches himself to a monastery and we follow his career as a reformer of ecclesiastical institutions. He is so successful in this that he is elected abbot, bishop, cardinal and, to crown all, Pope: then, after re-organizing the College of Cardinals, he lays down the tiara and ends his life as an anchorite on a mountain top.

The story is told in very simple language and with great charm. It is filled out with fables and discussions and fragments of folk-lore, which, with the various incidents and adventures, give one a wonderful though idealized picture of medieval life. Some of the didactic passages are boring, but the accounts of the hero's reforming plans and projects are interesting because they show an ingenious and original mind at work. Llull's personality, indeed, colours the whole book. We see a rather naïve and simple man who had an active and unconventional mind and a complete faith in the power of reason to convince those who were in error. He had a strong feeling for nature—like St John of the Cross, the sight of trees and stars and moonlight moved him to contemplation—and his general disposition was eager and optimistic. Of all medieval writers he is the one who is nearest in spirit to St Francis, and in fact, though he started in the Dominican camp, he became towards the end of his life a Friar Minor. I think we may sum up *Blanquerna* as a sort of day-dream picture of what Llull would have liked to achieve himself—the reform of the Church by good government, persuasion and example from above. It belongs to a type—the novel of compensation—that is all too common in our time; but it has the interest of being the first example.

Ramon Llull was a man who never stopped writing: his first book, which he composed in Arabic and then translated into Catalan, contained a million words. There is only one other of these, however, that we need to mention—the short mystical prose poem entitled *The Book of the Lover and the Beloved*. In form it is made up of a series of short unconnected paragraphs which refer to four characters—the Lover, the Beloved, Love and the Fool. Written in very simple language, in a prose that is sometimes rhymed, it has a strange and penetrating quality. Here are two examples:

The birds sang the dawn, and the Beloved, who is the dawn, awoke. And the birds ended their song, and the Lover died for his Beloved, in the dawn.

They asked the Lover: 'Who is thy Beloved?' He answered: 'He who makes me to love, long, pine, weep, sigh, suffer—and die.'

At first sight it is difficult to place the altogether new note that this book strikes: the musical quality of the imagery evokes Galician poetry: the simplicity suggests the *Flowers of St Francis*

But there is a peculiar overtone. One will see, I think, where this comes from if one opens the *diwan* of Jalalu'ddin Rumi, the great Persian Sufi poet, who lived in the same century. Ramon Llull knew Arabic much better than he knew Latin and was well versed in Sufi philosophers such as the Murcian, Ibn al-Arabi: he often speaks with admiration of their devotional practices and indeed he tells us that he wrote this book 'in the Sufi manner'.[1] Its coloured, allusive style, tender mode of feeling and pantheistic mysticism all breathe the spirit of the Persian East. This will appear less surprising if we remember that the Franciscan movement with its message of freedom and love (a new thing in Christianity at the time: since the beginning of the Dark Ages Christ had been thought of chiefly as the terrible Judge who would appear and condemn the wicked on the Last Day) was really a Christian form of the Sufi doctrine of brotherhood which during the past few centuries had been making its way westwards from India and Persia. If we knew more of the relations of the Moslem and Christian worlds during the early Middle Ages, we should probably find that this ability to combine admiration for Sufi practices with Christian piety was far from uncommon.

Llull's life was a very adventurous one: beginning as a courtier and libertine, he was later a hermit, a philosopher, a missionary, a man of visions and ecstasies who suffered also from periods of depression. He argued with Duns Scotus in Paris and with the Pope in Rome and three times visited Africa to preach the Gospel. On the third time—at the age of eighty-three—he was stoned to death. Those who are curious to learn more can consult Professor Allison Peers' biography. But the outstanding thing about him is a certain obstinate originality. He conformed to no prescribed

---

[1] The recently discovered *diwan* of the Sufi poet, Shushtari, who was born in Guadix c. 1212 and died in Damietta in 1269, offers a good example of this sort of poetry. Shushtari, after beginning as a jongleur of the type of Ibn Guzmán, took vows of poverty and sang his *muwassahas* in the market-place to the lowest classes of the people. These verses, though written in the same bawdy style and to the same exciting airs as those of the other jongleurs, were directed to religious ends. Their boldness is remarkable, for in them the poet plays the passive role of the prostitute and God that of the lover, and no details of their intercourse are left out. Llull twice refers to this sort of poetry as having influenced him (*Blanquerna*, trans. Peers, pages 375 and 410), and it is certain that he had read or heard Shushtari. See the article by Louis Massignon with translations of some of the poems in *Al-Andalus*, vol. XIV, Fasc. I, 1949.

rules, but followed his inspiration wherever it might lead him. It is just this uncompromising individuality that marks him out as a Catalan. By comparison the Spaniards of the interior are a dogmatic and conventional people with an aversion for anything new in intellectual or religious matters. Their churchmen breathe the spirit of tradition and conformity. One cannot imagine any one of them having the plasticity of mind or the adventurousness of spirit to absorb the mysticism of the East as Llull did, or to combine it with a reckless rationalism. Only a Catalan could do this, because he was entirely a European.

The fourteenth century in Catalan literature is mainly an age of prose: it offers us a number of works of interest, of which the most readable today is perhaps Ramon Muntaner's *Chronicle*, describing the adventures of the Catalan crusaders in Greece; and the most mature and perfect, Bernat Metge's *Lo Somni*. The strong trading and commercial proclivities of the Catalans seem to have inclined them more to painting, architecture and prose literature than to poetry: in this respect one may compare them to the Genoese and the Venetians, though they showed an interest in moral and educational questions which the citizens of those hard-headed cities lacked. But in the fifteenth century an important school of poetry sprang up at Valencia, which, in spite of the foundation of a consistory of *Gay Saber* in Barcelona in imitation of that at Toulouse, became the literary capital of the *Lemosi* language.[1] This movement produced one really great poet in Auziàs March.

March is not an easy poet to read, even for those who know Catalan better than I do. The great obscurity of many of his poems and the difficulty of nearly all of them, added to the fact that the only edition in which the text is not corrupt is expensive and difficult to obtain, have tended to confine the appreciation of his poetry—even in Valencia and Catalonia—to a small circle of scholars. Nor has any effort been made to present him to the

---

[1] *Lemosi* or Limousin, the language spoken in Limoges, was the dialect of *langue d'oc* in which the troubadours composed their poetry and which today we call Provençal. March and the other Valencian and Catalan poets of his time wrote in an artificial idiom which they called *Lemosi*, but which was really an adaptation of this language to Catalan and Valencian usage.

world in the form of a prose translation facing the original text (the only way in which the poetry of the learnable languages should be presented: verse translations are a deception). Yet he is a poet who should particularly appeal to us today because he is a psychological poet whose subject is *Angst*.

Auziàs March was born in 1397 in the little white-walled town of Gandía in the *vega* of Valencia. That is to say, in a landscape of orange trees and date palms, with the blue Mediterranean beating close by on a flat beach and the rose and violet mountains cutting the horizon in the distance. His father was the feudal lord of a village and estate worked by Moslems and in his time had been a successful soldier and a poet of distinction. But he was past sixty when Auziàs was born and his wife had been childless for eighteen years. The only other child by that marriage was a deaf mute. However, if this had any bearing on the poet's chronic melancholia, it does not seem to have affected his physical health. As a young man he followed Alfonso V of Aragon in his war with the Genoese and took part in an expedition against the Moors on the island of Djerba in the gulf of Gabes. After that he became the manager of the king's falconry establishment on the lagoon of the Albufera. Then in 1429, as a result, it seems, of a scandal over a girl, he gave up the king's service and retired to his estate. Here, or at his town house in Valencia, he remained till his death thirty years later.

March's life after his retirement was divided between hawking, love-making and writing poetry. He was a passionate hunter and a man of very sensual disposition. He married twice, in 1437 and 1443, and also kept a number of concubines, by whom he left four children. His wives were heiresses and, as he was skilful at managing his sugar plantations, he died a rich man. Yet his nature was at war with his disposition. His poems are the expression of an intense and agonised search for pure and spiritual love in the person of an actual woman. He frequently praises poverty. He was obsessed by death. And his stark, concentrated, violent poetry lacks as a rule all sensuous and aural qualities. Three centuries before, the Arab, Ibn Jafacha, living in the same delicious, flower-scented region, had written his famous poems on gardens. March never mentions Nature except in her sinister aspects, just as he never describes the appearance of his lady. His puritanism, no doubt, was offended by its too pagan beauty.

The subject of Auziàs March's poems is love. He had a lady, Dona Teresa—a married woman—and his platonic love for her provides him with his principal theme. Most of his *Cants de Amor* are addressed to her. It is a poetry of a very original kind—psychological, introspective, perversely tormented—so that one finds it hard to believe that it was written in the Middle Ages—still less by a man who belonged to that most unintrospective of peoples, the Spaniards. March craved a pure and ideal love without any taint of sensual feeling and yet his own nature and that of his lady were continually drawing them towards what he wished to avoid. Thus many of his poems to her are bitter reproaches that she has allowed herself to succumb to his sensual advances. He hates her on that account—an unusual interpretation of Catullus' *odi et amo*—whilst in other poems we find him wishing that she could be both pure and impure at the same time. This insoluble predicament whets his love: the poet has created in his own mind the conflict needed to perpetuate the tension and has not left it, as other poets do, to the hazard of his mistress's caprices. In any case the pleasure he seeks in love is the pleasure of suffering. *Riure james no'm plach tant com est plor*, he declares. 'Laughter never pleased me so well as tears.' For since the human mind is endowed with a greater capacity for painful sensations than for agreeable ones, suffering offers a depth and richness of feeling that pleasure can never give.

> Aprés lo mal, qui sent de bé sabor
> no pot ser dit de tot malahuyrat:
> lo past d'amor no ha tant' amargor
> que sus tot dolç no sia estimat.

> After affliction, he who can savour comfort
> cannot be called altogether unfortunate:
> the food of love has not so much bitterness
> that it should not be priced above all sweets.

But March's conception of love has really a metaphysical basis. The pain it gives, he says, is caused by a realization of the happiness we lack. Without such pain there can be no clear apprehension of man's position—cast out from the paradise that was once his and bound, if he wishes to taste the plenitude of human life, to keep his heart and mind set on returning. Suffering is thus the mark of having understood the human situation and March uses an earthly love as the symbol of a divine one. But not in the purely intellectual sense in which Dante uses Beatrice. His love for Teresa is an exercise ground on which his struggle for the ideal can be daily tried out and practised. It is the hair shirt and the demon-filled waste of the anchorite. And it is more positive than that, because the spiritual being to be loved and the demon to be resisted have both their dwelling in the same body. The secular and the religious implications of *amor de lonh* coalesce in a single synthesis.

March was strongly obsessed by death like so many other people in his century. He brooded over its more macabre aspects and extracted from them a special charm. Then, after sixteen or more years of this love, Teresa died. He was present at her death-bed and longed to die too, but 'Death does not take anyone who desires her.'

> Enquer està que vida no finí,
> com prop la Mort yo la viu acostar,
> dient, plorant: 'No vullau mi lexar:
> hajau dolor de la dolor de mi!

> And so it was that my life did not end
> when I saw her lying close to Death,
> when I said weeping: 'Do not leave me,
> take pity on this sorrow of mine!'

And then a new anxiety came over him—was she in paradise, or in hell, or in purgatory? His prayers to be allowed to know this were not answered.

Yet it is possible that after her death he took a new lady. One of his *Cants* describes the beginning of another love affair and the *senhal*, or secret sign, which, in troubadour fashion, he always gives in the *tornada* of his love poems, changes. Teresa had been *Lir entre carts*, Lily among thorns, or else *Plena de seny*, full of intelligence. The new *senhal* is either *Amor, Amor* or *Mon derrer bé*, my last good.

The difficulty of dating his poems makes it impossible to say when this episode occurred. Can it have been during Teresa's life time?

Auziàs March was a deliberate and self-concious artist. He set out, he tells us, to explain the secrets of love and give its mysteries to the world in a new Apocalypse. Explain is the word. He is never content with describing a feeling, but seeks always to analyse it and draw out its full psychological and metaphysical implications. It is this that makes him obscure. He is an intellectual poet and the things he wants to say are not easily said, especially in the condensed idiom he uses. He had too a precedent for writing obscurely in the Provençal style known as *trobar clus*. His own style is arid and abstract with bursts of clear, passionate expression and long passages of dialectic, which are the drier for being difficult or even impossible to understand. He concedes nothing to ornament and rarely paints a picture. But the force and immediacy of his lines is at times astonishing. One feels in his poetry the struggle of an artist to organize and express the violent and contradictory feelings that possessed him, but one also, I think, recognizes his deliberate choice of a life which should wring the last drop of poetry out of him. Being in love and writing verse were for him two complementary parts of one thing—the experiencing of the real meaning of life through suffering. They were at once his vocation and his *via crucis*.

March has often been compared to Petrarch. I agree with his biographer, Amadée Pagès, that this comparison is inept. Nothing could be further from his manner than Petrarch's rich and coloured language and Vergilian melancholy. In form, and often in idea too, March came out of Provençal poetry. He wrote in troubadour metres, using octaves of *coblas croadas* or *coblas encadenadas* (crossed and chained rhymes) with a *tornada* or envoi at the end: his hende-casyllable was the Provençal one, with a caesura after the fourth syllable and masculine endings. For his didactic poems he used the unrhymed stanzas called *estramps*. Like the other Catalan poets of his time he adhered closely to the rules of versification drawn up by the Catalan troubadour, Ramon Vidal, a little before 1200. The Provençal poet he most admired and whose obscure way of writing influenced him was Arnaut Daniel, whom Dante praised so highly, but whose dry word-patterns seem tedious and empty to us today. But of course there is in March a complexity of thought and a depth of feeling that one does not find among the troubadours. Yet such a complexity was really implicit in the troubadour themes: they did not develop it because poetry in their day was not intellectual: instead they expended their ingenuity in the elaboration of difficult measures and rhymes. But March, living in an age when poetry was expected to express ideas, took up the old themes and, using simpler measures, gave them a new content. He showed what could be done in an unhappy age with *lo Gay Saber*.

He was of course only able to do this because he came under other influences. The chief of these was Dante. March was perhaps the only medieval poet who was able to learn something useful from the great Italian, whose influence on his successors was as disastrous as Milton's: he took from him his stark and concentrated style and his way of introducing similes, with the image preceding the idea. After Dante, the philosophers seem to have been his chief reading. He knew Boethius and Aristotle's *Nicomachean Ethics* and above all St Thomas Aquinas. Except Calderon, no Spanish poet has drawn so deeply on Thomist philosophy. He read too everything he could find on love, including the Arthurian romances, but it does not appear that he cared for the great Latins. His tastes were gothic and metaphysical rather than classical.

The poet to whom, I think, one can best compare Auziàs March is Baudelaire. His poetry lacks the marvellous resonance of Baudelaire's lines: it lacks too the charm and childlike appeal of the poet of *Le Balcon*. There is something unpleasantly hard and egoistic in March's character, as there was in Donne's, that makes it difficult for us to feel in complete sympathy as we read him. But there is a great similarity, not so much in their actual philosophies—for Baudelaire had lost his Catholic faith—as in the manner in which they felt the tragedy of the human situation. Both had the same way of conceiving their own erotic experiences as condensed examples of that situation. Both believed that the way to redemption lay in suffering and poetry—or rather in suffering that justified itself by producing poetry. And, in spite of the great difference between the ages in which they lived and the styles they wrote in, March's images and turns of phrase do in fact sometimes suggest Baudelaire. Here, for example, is one of his rare descriptive passages:

> Lo jorn ha por de perdre sa claror,
> com ve la nit qu' espandeix ses tenebres.
> Pochs animals no cloen les palpebres
> e los malalts crexen de llur dolor.
> Los malfactors volgren tot l'any duràs
> per que llurs mals haguessen cobriment,
> mas yo visch menys de part en mon turment
> e sens mal fer, volgra que tost passàs.

> The day is now afraid to lose its light,
> as the night comes and scatters out its shades.
> There are few beasts that do not close their eyelids
> and the sick feel an increase of their pain.
> Evil-doers wish it could last all year
> that their ill deeds might be hidden,
> but I live less alone in my torment
> and, doing no ill, wish it may pass quickly.

No poet except Baudelaire has expressed so well the sense of solitude and deprivation which is the reverse side of love, still less has drawn it out of that supposed bliss, returned love, for the reason that that love suggested a yet higher love and an even more impossible impossibility.

Two other Valencian poets of this period may be mentioned. One was Jaume Roig, whose *Llibre de les dones* is a brilliant and lively satire on women, purporting to be an autobiography. The other was Jordi de Sant Jordi, a Petrarchist, who wrote a small number of exquisite poems. Then the crowns of Aragon and Castile were united and the Valencians ceased to use their language for poetry and wrote in Castilian. Although the Catalans, who alone had a national feeling about their language, resisted longer, they too in the end were compelled to yield to the force of history. But the change cost them dear and during the following three centuries they contributed few names to Spanish literature.

Before closing this chapter there is one feature of the Peninsular literature of the fourteenth and fifteenth centuries that I should like to draw attention to—its preoccupation with moral instruction. In fact nearly all the poetry and prose of this period either was or claimed to be didactic. That was not of course peculiar to Spanish literature: after its first emergence as the language of courtly love, medieval poetry had taken a more and more moralizing turn, and prose, outside the light vein of romances, never had any other aims. But in Spain this tendency was carried further than elsewhere. There can be no doubt that this was due in part to the Jewish influence which till the pogroms of 1391 was very strong, especially among the nobility. As a concrete example of this we have the gnomic verses of the Rabbi Sem Tob, a Castilian Jew who came from the same town as the Marqués de Santillana. Many of them are delicious and call to mind the popular *coplas* of the twentieth century. Without much exaggeration we might say that all the best literature of this century had been spun round *refranes*, or proverbs.

In the fifteenth century classical Latin influences took the place of oriental ones: the didactic tone of the aristocratic writers of this period was stoic, strongly impregnated, of course, with Christian feeling. The popular influence in polite literature declined, but so great was the importance attached to wisdom of all kinds that the Marqués de Santillana overcame the disdain he felt for popular art and at the king's request made a collection of the *refranes*, or proverbs 'that old women say *tras el huego*, behind the fire'. And in the sixteenth and seventeenth centuries the didactic current continued to flow more strongly than ever, taking gradually a more Catholic and theological form. It was responsible both for making and for marring much good literature.

Richard Ford, commenting on the constant use by Spaniards of the *refrán*, declared that it gave them their 'sententious, dogmatical admixture of humour, truism, twaddle and common sense'. Certainly sententiousness is one of the most marked of Spanish qualities. It goes, one might say, with a certain dryness of the imagination. The Spanish mind is riveted by its keen senses to the actual world and leaves it with pain and difficulty. Moralizing is a sort of ointment laid on to soothe the too sharp impressions. But it is also a consequence of the very deep and strong social sense of the Spaniards, as well of their feeling that, to overcome certain aggressive tendencies in themselves that work in the opposite direction, this sense ought to be stronger still. In English literature on the other hand the great quality is imagination. The English poet, sitting alone in his room, allows his mind to soar and wander from the world he is contemplating into new and miraculous regions. The French writer too allows his intellect to choose its own free course. But the Spanish writer never loses a sense of social obligation. Not for him the exploration of new worlds of being! He must write of the actual scene around him and of the day-to-day lives of the people who inhabit it. He must see them as they are, bound together in a close social framework (far closer and more intimate, in spite of their continual revolt against it, than anything we are accustomed to in England) and what he says about them must be useful or profitable.

I must be careful not to exaggerate here, for what I am trying to define is merely a tendency, and there are exceptions to it. But I think it is generally true to say that the average Spanish writer has always thought of himself as the guardian or physician of society, whereas the Italian humanist or French intellectual has regarded himself as a missionary of culture. That is one reason why Spanish literature has travelled so little beyond its frontiers: if merit were the deciding factor, it would be placed on a level with Italian. But it has been too exclusively written for the home audience, and its strong national character does not easily stand a change of climate.

Yet for those of us who are prepared to be interested in a foreign country, this pungent national flavour will be one of its chief charms. It takes us out of our Anglo-Saxon skins as neither Italian nor French literature do. Behind every book we read, we feel not so much a new author as the pulse of a strange and peculiar society. For of all European literatures Spanish is the most homogeneous. The popular poetry of the villages, still being made and sung today, drifts like smoke into the brains of the cultured writers. And these cultured writers, what else are they doing but re-affirming the social pattern? In the intervals of their creative passages we hear their voices guiding, warning, scolding, satirizing, or dogmatizing in a homely, somewhat pompous way. We may often feel we have reason to complain of this, yet in the long run a moral attitude to society is more productive of good literature than the art for the sake of refinement of the Italian Renaissance, or the art for art's sake of later times. In French and Italian literature the accent falls on the individual, but a social literature such as Spanish needs to be fed with the moral ideas and passions of social life.

CHAPTER VI

THE PERIOD OF THE CATHOLIC KINGS

THE period from the accession of the Catholic Kings, Ferdinand and Isabella, in 1479 to the election of their grandson Charles to the Imperial throne in 1519 marks a transition from the Middle Ages to the Renaissance. Events of immense importance took place during these years—the conquest of Granada from the Moors, the discovery of America, the expulsion of the Jews from Spain, the setting up of the Inquisition, as well as other less dramatic ones that had a special influence on literature—the introduction of printing in 1473 and the publication of the first Spanish grammar in 1492 by the great humanist Nebrija. The foundation by Cardinal Ximenes in 1508 of the new university of Alcalá de Henares to encourage the study of Latin, Greek and Hebrew was also to have an important though delayed influence.

One effect of these changes was to break the rule of the great noble houses, which had almost monopolized literature during the previous century, and to bring to the front writers and poets who, though attached to the court, belonged to the class of the smaller gentry. Technically speaking, their verse is less perfect than that of the great magnates, probably because the influence of French poetry had declined, but it is more varied and spontaneous. Popular influences were much stronger and one of the principal measures used was the *villancico*. There was also a considerable increase of religious poetry, written often by monks and in a much more devotional and popular tone than the stoic-religious verse of the previous century. Fray Ambrosio Montesino, a Franciscan who was chaplain to Queen Isabella, is the best of these poets: he had been influenced by the Italian Fra Jacopone da Todi and his *romances* and *villancicos*, which were written to popular airs, have a charm and tenderness that one does not often find in Spanish secular poetry. Tenderness in Spanish literature is as a rule given only to the Virgin and the *Crucificado*. The love poetry of this period shows the influence of the Books of Chivalry; when not gay, it has often an unpleasantly lachrymose tone. This was an age of sensibility and tears.

The Anonymous 'Villancicos'

The most interesting poetry of this period consists, however, of the anonymous *villancicos* of the song books. Chamber music had been developing rapidly through the last century. The contrapuntal influence had declined and the favourite instrument at court was now the *vihuela*, which is a kind of guitar, though the organ, lute and clavichord were also in use. Queen Isabella, like her brother Henry IV, was fond of music and kept an establishment of forty singers for her own use. Now the *vihuelistas* had discovered that the kind of verse best suited to their music was the popular *villancico*, which consisted, as we have said before, of a short theme-stanza closely associated with a particular air and of a narrative development in several stanzas.[1] A good example of one of these songs is the *Three Moorish Girls of Jaen*, which I give below in Sr Menéndez Pidal's arrangement. It differs from the primitive *zéjel* form in having alternate assonances in *i* and *a*, and in omitting the rhyme to the theme -stanza at the end of every tristich. That is to say, it has undergone a Galician influence. As to its subject matter, it is a rendering of an ancient Arabic song, once popular through the whole of the East, that related in very indecent language a scandal that had taken place in the harem of Harun al-Raschid, the caliph who was a contemporary of Charlemagne. It is quite possible that the rest of the Spanish version, which has not come down to us, was indecent too.

[1] The term *villancico* was also applied to the *estribillo* or theme-stanza alone, without its development. For this *estribillo* was in reality the essential part—a little seed of folk-song that was blown about the streets and fields, containing within itself the capacity for various sorts of development. To understand how a little snatch of folk-song only two or three lines long could have an individuality of its own that enabled it to persist for centuries (many *estribillos* are written in a language more archaic than that of the rest of the poem) one must read the description of the modern *copla* on pages 365-376. Towards the end of the sixteenth century the *estribillo* tended to lose its popular character and to become merely the introductory stanza of a poem.

Tres morillas me enamoran
    en Jaén:
Axa, Fátima y Marién.

Tres morillas tan garridas
iban a coger olivas
y fallábanlas cogidas
    en Jaén:
Axa, Fátima y Marién.

Tres morillas tan lozanas
iban a coger manzanas
y cogidas las fallaban
    en Jaén:
Axa, Fátima y Marién.

Y fallábanlas cogidas
y tornaban desmaídas
y las colores perdidas
    en Jaén:
Axa, Fátima y Marién.

Three Moorish girls have won my love
    in Jaen:
Axa, Fatima and Marien.

Three Moorish girls so gay
went to pick olives
and found them plucked away
    in Jaen:
Axa, Fatima and Marien.

Three Moorish girls so fair
went to pick apples
and found none there
    in Jaen:
Axa, Fatima and Marien.

And found them plucked away
and turned back in dismay,
their colour all flown
    in Jaen:
Axa, Fatima and Marien.

Songs of this sort were clearly meant for the open air. When brought into a room and sung to chamber music, the narrative development and the chorus were no longer wanted: they were therefore cut, so that the final result was often a lyric of from six to twelve lines. There was also a strong Galician-Portuguese influence, which came in perhaps because the airs had been brought from those countries. It was a popular influence—that of the old *cantigas de amigo*—and shows itself in the fact that many of these songs are addressed by a girl to her mother (this form of address is taken over by men's songs too), whilst others have the familiar alternation of *i* and *a* assonances. This is all the more curious because the Portuguese poetry we have from this period shows very little trace of such features.

Here are a few examples of these tiny lyrics:

> Malferida iba la garza
> enamorada:
> sola va y gritos daba.
>
> Donde la garza hace su nido,
> ribericas de aquel río,
> sola va y gritos daba.

> Badly wounded flies the heron,
> struck with love;
> alone it goes, uttering its cries.
>
> Where the heron makes its nest
> on the shores of that river,
> alone it goes, uttering its cries.

> Alta estaba la peña,
> nace la malva en ella.
>
> Alta estaba la peña,
> riberas del río;
> nace la malva en ella
> y el trébol florido.

High was the rock,
the mallow grows on it.

High was the rock,
on the shores of the river;
the mallow grows on it
and the flowering clover.

The mallow is, of course, the girl looking out from her inaccessible
upper window: the clover may be taken as her young sister.

Ay, luna que reluces,
toda la noche m'alumbres.

Ay, luna tan bella,
alúmbresme a la sierra,
por do vaya y venga.
Ay luna que reluces
toda la noche m'alumbres.

O moon that is shining,
all night may you light me.

O moon so beautiful,
may you light me to the mountains,
wherever I go and come.
O moon that is shining,
all night may you light me.

Vi los barcos, madre,
vilos y no me valen.

Madre, tres mozuelas,
no de aquesta villa,
en agua corriente
lavan sus camisas:
sus camisas, madre,
vilas y no me valen.

I saw the ships, mother,
I saw them, but they mean nothing to me.

Mother, three girls,
none of them from this town,
in running water
are washing their shirts—
their shirts, mother;
I saw them and they mean nothing to me.

De los álamos vengo, madre,
de ver cómo los menea el aire.

De los álamos de Sevilla,
de ver a mi linda amiga.

De los álamos vengo, madre,
de ver cómo los menea el aire.

I come from the poplars, mother,
from watching how they move in the air.

From the poplars of Seville,
from seeing my charming girl.

I come from the poplars, mother,
from watching how they move in the air.

> Aquellas sierras, madre,
> altas son de subir:
> corrían los caños,
> daban en un toronjil.
>
> Madre, aquellas sierras
> llenas son de flores:
> encima de ellas
> tengo mis amores.
>
> Those mountains, mother,
> are high to climb:
> the running streams
> end in a balsam plant.
>
> Mother, those mountains
> are full of flowers:
> on their summit
> I have my love.

Toronjil is *melissa officinalis*, or wild balsam. Like the sweet basil and other herbs it is used in popular poetry as the symbol (originally perhaps sexual, like *perejil*, parsley) of a girl.

> Al alba venid, buen amigo,
> al alba venid.
>
> Amigo el que yo más quería,
> venid al alba del día.
> Amigo el que yo más amaba,
> venid a la luz del alba.
> Venid a la luz del día
> non trayáis compañía.
> Venid a la luz del alba,
> non traigáis gran compaña.
>
> Come at daybreak, sweet friend,
> come at daybreak.
>
> Friend whom I love the best,
> come at the dawn of day.
> Friend whom I love above all,
> come at the break of dawn.
> Come at the break of day,
> but bring no company.
> Come at the dawn of day,
> bring little company.

This is of course a *cossante*, though I have failed to convey its chained assonances in my translation.

I have given seven of these poems because of their great beauty and interest. They are unlike anything else in European poetry. Of popular origin—what are called today folk-songs—they have been cut and arranged with exquisite taste by cultured but unknown poets to suit the music. The Galician-Portuguese influence reveals itself in the selection of the lyrical moment, whilst the influence of Castile is seen chiefly in the condensation. These little poems have thus an actuality and precision which the diffuse Portuguese lyrics lack. The need for condensation has also led to many things being left out that are usually said. Take, for example, *Vi los barcos, madre*. We are not told the precise significance of the ships or of the girls from another village: all we see is that the love-sick girl used to find pleasure in these things, but no longer does so. In cutting down these poems to suit the music, the authors have discovered the great poetic possibilities of suggestion.

Another feature to be noticed is the allusive or allegorical imagery. A mallow plant or a heron is the symbol of a girl: the poplars suggest her graceful figure, but no 'like' or 'as if' connects them. This has come to be thought of as typical of popular or folk-poetry, yet we have here its first appearance in Spanish. We get this type of imagery in the Chinese *Book of Songs* of the sixth century B.C., in Jewish poetry of the Old Testament, in Greek medieval distiches, but not in West European poetry before this date. Then it spreads everywhere: English and Scottish ballads are full of it and it permeates the Spanish *copla* of the twentieth century, which, as we shall see later, is to a great extent the descendant of these abbreviated *villancicos*. Is it an Eastern importation or a popular derivation from medieval allegory?

THE 'ROMANCES'

We have now arrived at a suitable moment for speaking of the *romances*, or ballads, which reached their highest point of development at this time, though they had begun to be composed much earlier. The first of them date from the period of civil war in the second half of the fourteenth century, when Henry of Trastamara rose against his half-brother Pedro the Cruel. As we have seen, this was a period of change in Castilian poetry. Not only was the juglaresque verse of the type represented by the Archpriest of Hita dying out, but the *cantares de gesta*, which were recited to a stringed accompaniment by a different type of *juglar*, were coming to an end as well. Although no examples of these late epics have been preserved, we know that they continued to be recited until this time, in spite of the fact that the form was moribund and that new poems had long ceased to be invented. Presumably they died out because more refined kinds of entertainment had come in and the country nobility, who had up to now supported this serious type of *juglar*, grew tired of listening to them.

It is at this moment that the *romances*, or ballads, first appear. They began in the small towns and villages, among the artisans, soldiers and manual labourers. Although they were sometimes recited by *juglares* (a few of the very long ones, such as *Conde Dirlos* with 683 lines and *Conde Claros* with 206, could not have been made public in any other way), they were essentially what Sr Menéndez Pidal calls traditional poetry—that is to say, they were intended to be sung and danced to by the people themselves. Someone, of course, made them up: probably, too, some sort of *juglar* carried them round; but they were then taken over by the people at large and transmitted orally with such changes and omissions as one would expect. They represent therefore an active role on the part of the people in epic-like poetry as against the old passive one.

We can only guess at the reasons—social, musical and so forth—which led the people to dance to *romances* on their festive occasions, when before that they had danced to *villancicos*, but perhaps an active interest in the drama of the civil war between two brothers had something to do with it. The first *romances* that can be dated with certainty are those of the Don Pedro cycle: they were written by the party of Henry of Trastamara and at the time must have had something of the effect of political pamphlets. They were succeeded by the ballads of the Moorish wars, the *romances fronterizos*, which form a continuous series from 1407 to the sixteenth century. (One of them, describing a Moorish assault on Baeza, dates from 1368.) They were composed on the spot and had the sort of function that newspapers have today: thus we hear of Henry IV ordering one to be written in 1462 to celebrate a foray he had made on Moorish territory. Another early type comprises the *romances* of the heroes of Old Castile—Bernardo del Carpio, the Infantes de Lara, the Cid and so forth. The material for these was drawn from the old *cantares de gesta*, but only one or two of them can be dated earlier than the fifteenth century. Finally there are the *romances* on subjects taken from the Books of Chivalry—the Round Table and Carolingian cycles. These, which are later in date, can only have been written by men of education. But by the middle of the fifteenth century the *romances* were becoming popular among all classes and nothing is more likely than that some of the court poets whose lyrics figure in the *Cancioneros* may have written in popular forms as well.

The metre of the earlier *romances* is a sixteen-syllabled line with a strong caesura in the middle. Later they came to be written down in octosyllabic lines. This happened because there are really two metres here which coalesced: an old epic metre of sixteen syllables which is probably indigenous, and an octosyllabic lyric metre that came from Galicia and was 'courtly'. The only difference between them is that in the old metre the sense continues through the line but breaks off at the end of it, whereas in the lyric metre there can be a break after any eight syllables. The most striking feature of the *romance*, however, is its single assonance, which may amount to a full rhyme, running through the poem from beginning to end. It corresponds, of course, to the old epic *laisse*, but it produces an effect of reiteration, not noticeable in the more irregular *cantares de gesta*, that is strange to English ears. Although this is countered to some extent by the variability of the stress accents and the vivacity of the action, there often remains a certain incantatory effect that—to me at least—suggests the twangling dance music of a guitar, with its mixture of excitement and monotony.

As regards diction, the style of the *romances* is more clipped and condensed than that of the *cantares de gesta:* there is a tendency to omit the narrative passages and concentrate on the dramatic ones, which generally means on dialogue. This is of course the case with all genuine ballad poetry: it is something that happens naturally in every part of the world when narrative poems are sung and transmitted orally. So long as this kind of poetry is alive, every transmission tends to leave out what is superfluous and to tighten up the key passages. This is the meaning of that much misunderstood dictum—that 'ballads are written by the people collectively'.

The historical and frontier ballads contain some of the grandest poetry in Spanish literature. Their diction is bare, stark and almost as matter-of-fact as it is in the *Cid*, though the tension is greater. There are few adjectives and little comment, yet with an extraordinary economy of words they convey a sense of truth and drama that, in their best examples, can scarcely be equalled anywhere.

The cycle of six *romances* on the *Infantes de Lara* reaches the highest point of tragic intensity. It is the story of an old blood feud, taken from the *cantares de gesta* and dated in the tenth century. The plot is developed with great dramatic feeling, whilst the scene in which Don Gonzalo Gustios recognizes the heads of his seven sons, washes the blood from their faces and speaks to each of them in turn has a force and pathos that take one's breath away. All the passion of the cruel and bloodthirsty civil wars of the fourteenth century has been poured into it. The frontier ballads, on the other hand, are more subdued: they deal with war, not vengeance: their tone is realistic and the sense of tragedy inseparable from ballad themes is given by taking one to the Moorish camp and associating one sympathetically with their losses. This is an old device of Semitic poetry—the ballad of Deborah and Barak, with its picture of Sisera's mother awaiting the homecoming of her son, is an example—but the Spanish *romances* do not jeer at the enemy, as the Hebrew and early Arab ballads do, but with an impartiality that is not far removed from sympathy allow us to see how bitter is the taste of defeat. The generosity of mind of the Castilian *caballero* and the secret feeling that binds him to his traditional enemy are well shown in these ballads, of which the most famous is that on the capture of Alhama, the key fortress to Granada, that so impressed Byron. It has a refrain, *Ay de mi Alhama*!

A few of the *romances* show lyrical feeling. The best known of these—*Rosa Fresca, Fonte Frida* and the *Conde Arnaldos*—date in their present form from the middle of the sixteenth century. They are to be accounted for by the same process of shortening and lyrification that we have seen at work in the case of the *villancicos*. Take the *Conde Arnaldos*, for example. It is one of the most beautiful of all ballads, and its beauty depends upon its air of strangeness and mystery. Here it is:

> ¡Quién hubiese tal ventura   sobre las aguas de mar,
> como hubo el Conde Arnaldos   la mañana de San Juan!
> Con un falcón en la mano   la caza iba a cazar,
> vió venir una galera   que a tierra quiere llegar.
> Las velas traía de seda,   la ejercia de un cendal,
> marinero que la manda   diciendo viene un cantar

corrido
without refrain
lyric romances
unhappy love

que la mar facía en calma,   los vientos hace amainar,
los peces que andan n'el hondo   arriba los hace andar,
las aves que andan volando   n'el mástel las face posar.
Allí fabló el Conde Arnaldos,   bien oiréis lo que dirá:
'Por Dios te ruego, marinero,   dígasme ora ese cantar.'
Respondióle el marinero,   tal respuesta le fué a dar:
'Yo no digo esta canción   sino a quien conmigo va.'

Its matter can be abbreviated as follows. On the morning of St John's Day Count Arnaldos goes hunting with his falcon by the seashore. There he sees a galley putting into land. The sails of the galley are of silk, its rigging of samite and the sailor who commands it is singing a song. It is a magic song, for the sea as he sings it becomes calm, the winds drop, the fishes in the deep come to the surface and the birds in the air perch on the mast. Seeing this, Count Arnaldos asks the sailor to tell him the song. But the sailor replies: 'I will only tell that song to him who sails with me.'

On that note of suspense and mystery the *romance* ends, and its tone is so unlike anything that we are accustomed to think of as Spanish that at one time it was believed that it must be a translation from the Portuguese. Now, however, its history has been explained. The *romance*, as we know it, was first published in or about 1545, but quite recently a much earlier version of it has come to light among the Spanish Jews in Morocco, who have preserved it intact, together with many other ballads, since their expulsion in 1492. This version turns out to be a long ballad of adventures by sea of the ordinary novelesque kind, with nothing particularly striking or beautiful about it. The brief *romance* we know is simply the first part of this, with certain significant alterations. With the aid of two other intermediate versions, Sr Menéndez Pidal has been able to show what happened.

First, all the latter part of the ballad was dropped, either because it had been forgotten or in obedience to the prevailing lyrical tendency to keep only the most striking and beautiful passages. Then three lines were inserted from another ballad, the *Conde Niño*, describing the magical effects of the song, which in the first version had not been magical at all. This too corresponds to a general tendency in all ballad poetry. Finally the words of the song, which in the earlier versions had been given, were omitted and the *romance* was brought to an end with the sailor's refusal to repeat them. This last emendation may have been due to the anonymous poet who published the *romance* in the famous Antwerp *Cancionero* of *c.* 1545. Thus we see how, in obedience to certain general tendencies, a very ordinary ballad was transformed into one of the most beautiful and evocative ever written.

I am told that the sense for omission, for the unsaid, of which this ballad is so striking an example, is common in Chinese poetry and that it has been deliberately cultivated as an aesthetic principle by the Zen school of poets in Japan. In Spain it was of course instinctive, brought about by the demands of music and by a lyrical influence that came from Galicia. It is a sign of how little cultivated poets really understand their own business that this sense for allusion, for suggesting rather than saying, so surprisingly discovered by the sixteenth-century song-writers, was never taken up by them and developed deliberately. Of later poets Góngora alone had any inkling of it. No doubt it was uncongenial to the definite, concrete Castilian temperament.

The *romances* began to be popular among the upper classes in the second half of the fifteenth century,[1] and from the time of Ferdinand and Isabella the whole nation from the queen downwards was enjoying them and singing them at their dances. They were written down and soon collections began to be published. The most famous was that which we have already mentioned as being brought out by the Plantin Press at Antwerp in or about the year 1545. Other collections followed, and it is no exaggeration to say that their influence on Spanish poetry and drama during the Golden Age was as great as that of Percy's *Reliques* in England after 1765. They spread too all over the Peninsula. Originally a Castilian form, like the *cantar de gesta*, they were now written in Portuguese and Catalan.

One may ask how the Spanish *romances* compare with English and Scottish ballads. As a body they are far more impressive. One

---

[1] And not only in Spain. The Cordovan traveller, Pero Tafur, visiting Constantinople in 1437, found that the Spanish interpreter of the Emperor John Palaeologus had obtained his post because he could sing Castilian *romances* to the lute. The Emperor enjoyed listening to them.

reason for this is that they were written down whilst ballad-making was still flourishing and not left to be picked up in the age of their decay from the lips of old women and pedlars. The British turned a blind eye on their popular literature till the antiquarians of the eighteenth century and the romantics who followed them drew their attention to it. The best Southern English ballad—*The Unquiet Grave*—was not discovered till 1868. But I agree with Southey that the Spanish ballads lack an imaginative quality that the finest English and Scottish ballads possess. The supernatural element in the *romances* is rare, and where it is found it does not spring out of deep-seated popular beliefs, but is a semi-cultured foreign element introduced with the novels of Chivalry. Contrary to general credence, there is no country in Europe that is poorer in superstitious beliefs or fragments of ancient mythologies than Spain. Those that exist are found in the north and west, in the mountains of Galicia and Asturias. Whatever vestiges of such beliefs had existed in the centre and south of Spain in early times, were wiped out by the Moorish invasion and by the Reconquista. For this reason one will look in vain for anything in Spanish balladry to compare with *Thomas the Rhymer*, *Clerk Saunders* or the *Wife of Usher's Well*. Except when under the influence of Galician lyricism or foreign novels, the Spanish ballad is severely realistic.

'La Celestina'

The greatest work of the period we are discussing is not a poem but a novel. In 1499 a book entitled the *Comedia de Calisto y Melibea* was published anonymously at Burgos. It was written in dialogue form like a play and divided into acts. The 1499 edition contained sixteen acts, but an edition that appeared at Seville in 1502 (entitled *Tragicomedia*) was expanded into twenty-one. From its principal character, this book is generally known as *La Celestina*.[1]

The author was, it appears, a converted Jew called Fernando de Rojas. We know nothing of him except that he was born round about 1465, was alive in 1525 and spent most of his life at Talavera,

---

[1] There is an excellent English translation, first published in 1631 and often reprinted, by James Mabbe.

where he practised as a lawyer and rose to be mayor. His wife too was a convert and his father-in-law was prosecuted by the Inquisition for indifference to religion. There is some doubt whether he was responsible for all the additions to the later edition, which in many cases detract from the merit of the book.

The plot is very simple. A young nobleman called Calisto falls suddenly and violently in love with a girl of high rank called Melibea, whom he has met through an accident. Since, by the custom of the age, she is secluded and never leaves her house, he calls in the services of a bawd called Celestina to help him to press his suit. Celestina is successful, Melibea falls in love and agrees to meet Calisto by night in the garden of her house. The tryst takes place, but on a subsequent occasion there is an alarm and in his hurry to descend the ladder, Calisto falls and is killed. Melibea in despair throws herself off a tower and dies also. Her parents are left to weep and moralize.

This simple lover's tale, so like that of Romeo and Juliet, is not, however, the part of the book that most holds our attention. The person who dominates the scene is Celestina. She is a woman with a multiplicity of professions. From her little ruined house by the river bank outside the town she has a finger in every shady and libidinous transaction. To cover these activities and to have the entry into the houses of the well-to-do, she peddles various small objects such as thread and face-powders, kohl for the eyebrows and hair-nets, besides practising as midwife and quack doctor. But she is also a witch who sells charms and love philtres, who arranges clandestine love affairs and mends broken virginities; and a procuress who keeps what we should today call a *maison de passe*. At the time of her portrayal in this book she is old, full of knowledge and experience of the world and wonderfully alive and intelligent.

The plot is woven through the medium of Calisto's two servants, Sempronio and Pármeno, and two prostitutes, Elicia and Areusa, protégées of Celestina, with whom the men are in love. These four persons are carefully drawn and characterized, and by their jealousies, quarrels, friendships and mutual suspicions they not only set the scene for Celestina and give her a material to manipulate, but keep a continual stir and movement going through the book. This movement, however, is never forced or artificial, and when the two lackeys in a fit of rage kill Celestina because she has refused them the share of the reward she had promised them, one feels not only that this is the inevitable tragic destiny working itself out, but also that it is what would probably have happened in real life.

Celestina herself is one of the most vivid and splendid creations of all literature. She talks her way through the book in the raciest conversation ever written by a Spaniard, elliptical, witty, stuffed with proverbs and quick sayings like all popular talk, and rich in wisdom and experience. We are given her philosophy of life, her reminiscences of her youth, the detail of her daily habits, her soliloquies: we see her scheming, persuading, flattering, boasting, standing up for her dignity and, in a lachrymose and sentimental mood, after many pulls at the wine jar, lamenting her old age and the days of her past prosperity—those palmy days when, at that very table, nine girls of the choicest looks, the oldest of them but eighteen, would sit down to dinner with her, every one of whom loved her, every one of whom honoured her and obeyed her; whilst the men, up to the very nobles and bishops and clergy, would doff their hats when they saw her in the street and address her as Señora, Sweetheart, Respected dame. And, as we read, we forget the old wretch's villainies and sympathize with her, because she is so human and talks so frankly and intelligently.

Celestina's philosophy is that of the person who lives for and by sexual love. Everything erotic charms her: the approaches, the intrigues, the confidences, the deception, the singing and dancing and feasting, the act itself. For her, love-making takes precedence over all things, and though she is now old and can no longer indulge in it herself, she still gets pleasure from purveying it to other people. Thus she enjoys watching Areusa undress, and when she puts Pármeno into the bed beside her, she sweeps away the girl's protests and insists on remaining in the room while he does his act. Shame to her is a vice because it stands in the way of pleasure, and if one could speak, as one very nearly can, of her having a mission in life, it would be that of doing away with chastity and married fidelity and spreading a universal promiscuity.

There is indeed at times an air of conviction and authority about her that suggests that she is a survival of a pagan love cult. But she also needs money; like everyone else she has to live and 'maintain her honour'. The least suggestion therefore that she has not earned honestly what she has received puts her on her dignity. Her services to the world, she feels, deserve an adequate remuneration.

So this marvellously vivid old woman passes through the book, enjoying her life to the full, drowning her depressions in wine and above all rejoicing in her own sharp intelligence and in her great arts of manipulating others. Wicked and unscrupulous she of course is by any modern European standard, but we must in fairness grant her two virtues: one, that all her acts are undertaken in the service of a hedonistic philosophy, which excludes the ideas of envy, hatred and violence; the other, that her volubility, wit and frankness are a high expression of social life, only to be found in a world where people live close together and have constant need of one another. Her first instincts are generous: she likes to see happy faces around her.

Celestina has been compared to various Shakespeare characters, among them Falstaff; the comparison has a certain utility because it draws our attention to the fundamental difference of being that exists between the persons in Shakespeare's plays and those represented in this book. We feel of Falstaff that he is a great dramatic creation, yet, like Lear, so much larger than life that we suffer a certain diminution of belief when we see him acted on the stage. But when we think of Celestina, we forget the book that presents her and believe in her as in an actual person we have met. This illustrates the great difference there is between the Spanish method of creating character and the Elizabethan. The Spaniards, when they are not just improvising, as is too often the case with their dramatists, seek by some ascetic process to intensify the reality of the persons and situations they are depicting: they work into their models, as Goya did into his, to extract the last ounce of truth and significant actuality from them. The English, on the other hand, call in the untrammelled imagination with all its resources of expansion and amplification and create a figure that can only live in its own world. It is the distinction between an expressionist art, thrown up from inside, and one that almost painfully reflects the shocks produced on it from without. The Englishman, perhaps because his life is more sheltered, has chambers and recesses in his mind that the Spaniard has not dreamed of, but his eye has a film over it that the Southern eye lacks. The Spaniard, on the other hand, who lives in the street, with his sword by his side, with the sense of being surrounded by enemies, has his eyes skinned. Except by passion and its hallucinations, he cannot easily escape the pressure of reality.

The two lovers, Calisto and Melibea, are not drawn as characters, but as figures in whom all personal traits have been swallowed up and submerged by their passion. They have only to appear for us to feel that they are in the grip of a catastrophic force that is stronger than themselves. Calisto is out of his senses from the first moment of his seeing Melibea. The frenzy of his behaviour suggests Don Quixote, just as the language in which he speaks of his mistress—elevated, *altisonante* and stiff with Latin inversions—calls up the Knight of the Doleful Countenance's declamations. Melibea too falls under the spell, and all her training and education are insufficient to restrain her from yielding immediately. But there is none of the charm and sweetness in their relations that one feels in Romeo and Juliet. Their passion has an inhuman violence which makes it completely transcend the nature and identity of the person loved. Thus scarcely has Calisto found himself in the garden with his 'precious pearl' and 'angelical image' than he puts his hand under her skirts and demands, as he might of a servant girl, the immediate surrender of her virginity. One does not have to be English to feel one's sensibilities shocked by this hurried and one-sided insistence on the usual trophy. To some extent it must be put down to the crudeness of the age and to the peculiar interpretation it assigned to the traditional Spanish conception of love as a war without truce or pity between the sexes; for Calisto's urgency is due to *amour propre* and not to lust. But it is also a symptom of the violent, compulsory nature with which the passion of love is here depicted. Calisto and Melibea are not puppets, but they are human beings driven to act as puppets, because they are under the sway of a force that has deprived them of their reason.

This book is, in the purest Aristotelian sense of the word, a tragedy. It purges by pity and terror. All those who have any part in the central drama lose their lives. In the case of Calisto and Melibea, it was the ordinary course of their love that brought this about: there was never any other end or outlet for them but death. Celestina, on the other hand, is the victim of a lapse in her own good sense. The immensity of the reward she has obtained from Calisto goes to her head and she fails to see the danger of refusing to share it with the two lackeys. That is to say, the vortex of the lovers' passion throws out an eddy that involves even her, and she pays the price of a lifelong meddling in dangerous matters. Pármeno and Sempronio are killed by the police after their equally mad act of stabbing her. Thus we see the daemonic power of love bringing destruction on everyone connected with it.

But what enormously enhances the tragic beauty of this book is that the two lovers, although they occupy the centre of the scene and are the sole objects presented to our pity, are not the most interesting of the protagonists. Around them and set in a much more vivid light are the worldly figures who compass their ruin and incidentally their own as well. This contrast has the effect of placing the reader at a greater distance from the point where his feelings would naturally be expected to concentrate. Thus he is not distracted by any merely human emotion of sympathy from the god-like state of contemplative pity which tragedy is expected to evoke. The fate of Calisto and Melibea has to be viewed against a wider panorama of human life and of the storms to which it is exposed. It is surprising that this formula for a tragic novel or play, so classic in its lines and yet so susceptible to modern treatment, has never been adopted by later writers.

The *Tragicomedia de Calisto y Melibea* did not spring suddenly out of the ground: it had parents. By far the most important of these was the Archpriest of Hita, whose tale of the seduction of Doña Endrina provided the initial theme. Celestina herself is an expanded version of Trotaconventos. If her second incarnation is even more alive and vivid than her first, that is because Celestinas abounded in Spain (there are still plenty of them about today) and, once the merits of the type had been discovered, could be drawn from life. We may remember that the Archpriest's tale was taken from a play—a twelfth-century literary exercise modelled on Terence and Plautus: here then we see it returning to its original dialogued form. *Celestina* is the first European novel, and it owes its condensed, centralized plot to its dramatic origin.

There was another Archpriest who had a hand in the making of the book. This was the Archpriest of Talavera (the home town of the author of *Celestina*), whose racy prose satire on women, imitated from Boccaccio's *Corbaccio* and written in 1438, laid down the lines to be followed in low-life conversation. But we must not suppose that Fernando de Rojas knew only Spanish. He was a humanist, well read in the Latin classics and in Greek philosophy, and conscious of vying with the great authors of antiquity. If sometimes we find traces of pedantry in his mythological allusions, we must remember that it was precisely his strong feeling for classical literature that enabled him to portray so admirably contemporary life. There is nothing like a study of the masterpieces of the past for crystallizing the present, and realism more than any other technique requires the control of classical form.

A last point must concern Fernando de Rojas' Jewish origin. His book may have been written for a little circle of humanists and *conversos*, who met together to read it aloud and perhaps made suggestions for improving it. Now it is a common tendency for Jews to exaggerate the characteristics of the nation they belong to. Intensely Spanish and Castilian as this book is, I believe that in the uncompromising tone of its language, the crudeness of many of its scenes and the unflinching way in which the tragedy is carried through to its final consequences, there is something one may call Hispano-Semitic. It was written at the height of the persecution of the *conversos* and we know from the records of the Inquisition that Rojas' family was imprisoned and that he himself was regarded as a suspect. This has led Ramiro de Maeztu to suggest that this book was the result of a religious crisis. Although I should have thought it was simpler to suppose that it came out of an unhappy love affair, it is certainly true that there are no signs in it of Rojas' having had any religious belief. The burnings and torturings of Torquemada can hardly have seemed to a man of his race a good argument for the divine authority of the Catholic Church, yet to lack faith in the Spain of those days must have led to a painful sense of isolation. The other great dramatic work of this period, Machiavelli's *Mandragola*, was also written by a man who had lost his faith, but in the serener climate of Italy this was not a matter to cause undue disturbance.

BUCOLIC AND RELIGIOUS DRAMA

The last works of this period that we have to consider come from a school of poets who, following the example of the Italians, found a way of combining the vogue for popular poetry and drama with humanist culture. Starting from imitations of Latin bucolic poems, they produced short dramatic pieces that were acted at court. Scattered through these were songs of a popular or semi-popular kind and, since the authors were also musicians, they wrote the music for these songs themselves. The two chief names in this class of production are Juan del Encina and Gil Vicente.

Juan del Encina (1469-1529) was born near Salamanca and studied there under the great Spanish humanist, Nebrija. His first work was a translation of Vergil's *Eclogues*, written when he was twenty-one. Other eclogues of his own fabrication followed: they consisted of dialogues between peasants and shepherds, made to be acted at the houses of the nobility. They were written in the metre so popular in the fifteenth century and known as *pié quebrado*, or 'limping verse'.

Encina entered the Church, obtained rapid preferment and went to live at Rome, at the court of Alexander VI and Leo X—that is say, in a purely Renaissance atmosphere. Here he developed his new genre of bucolic drama, increasing the action and making the dialogue more realistic. But his plays—if that is the word to call them—remained flat and insipid. They lack life, and the sham dialect in which the shepherds are made to speak (suggested probably by Quintilian's remarks on the Doric dialect used by Theocritus) and the false naïveté of their tone make a somewhat disagreeable impression. But many of the songs, although they too are tinged with this affectation, have charm. Encina was not a great poet, but he had the temperament of an artist and a certain lyric sense. The music to which he set his *villancicos* is delightful, and it is with this music that they should, if possible, be heard.

He had imitators. A professor of music at Salamanca, Lucas Fernández (*c.* 1474-1542), wrote pastoral eclogues and *autos* which were performed in church. His beautiful *Auto de la Pasión* anticipates that pitiful and insistent dwelling on the details of the Crucifixion which one finds later in Spanish Baroque art: here the influence is that of Flemish painting and of German devotional books such as Landolph of Saxony's *Vita Christi*, which Fray Ambrosio Montesino had translated into Spanish. It is to be noted how early this vein of feeling began.

A more influential figure was the Extremaduran, Torres Naharro, who lived in Rome and knew Juan del Encina there. Beginning with imitations of his eclogues, he went on to write farces and *comedias* that were much closer to the theatre than anything that Encina had done. They may be said to anticipate the *comedias de capa y espada* of the following century. He too was a humanist: the Renaissance had many streams and currents and one of the most interesting of them was that which led students of Latin literature to imitate contemporary dance lyrics and to experiment with popular dramatic forms. If we sometimes feel impatient with the pastoral convention which these writers employed, we should remember that its object was to provide a disguise through which they could dramatize their own feelings and sensibilities. Just as the cave artist who can paint buffaloes is unable to portray men except in some symbolic form or in the disguise of animals, so the writer has in all ages had great difficulty in representing the ethos and mode of life of the cultured group to which he belonged.

The great figure in this genre of lyric drama was not, however, Juan del Encina, but a Portuguese, Gil Vicente. Portuguese poetry had come to an end with the death of King Dinis in 1325. When it began to be written again it was completely under the influence of Castilian court verse. It was, moreover, bad. The large *Cancionero* published in 1516 by Garcia de Resende contains scarcely a single poem of merit. But the discovery by Vasco de Gama of the sea-route to India was making Portugal the greatest maritime country in Europe, and the new sense of national importance this gave required some expression in literature. Gil Vicente was the first poet to accomplish this. We mention him here because he wrote in Spanish as well as in Portuguese. The two Peninsular nations were at this time in closer relations than they have ever been before or since, and it was expected that their crowns would soon be united by marriage, as those of Castile and Aragon had recently been. Most of the Portuguese poets were therefore bilingual.

Scarcely anything is known of Gil Vicente's life. He was born round about 1465 and his last play is dated 1536. His first known piece, a verse dialogue, was written in 1502, when he was nearly forty, and his work did not reach maturity till he was over fifty. From his plays it has been conjectured that he was brought up in the country, that he was largely self-taught and that he became very fat. He may or may not have been a certain famous goldsmith. Our ignorance is the more extraordinary because he lived at court and all his work was produced at the royal command.

Gil Vicente's first plays were imitations of Juan del Encina's eclogues. But, unlike Encina, he knew the country well: his peasants are real peasants, his impoverished nobles and greedy friars and crooked *corregidores* are taken from life and completely convincing. He had too a delicious comic sense and an exquisite lyric talent. His brief *villancicos* (of the kind we have already examined), his *cossantes* and *romances* are among the most lovely in Spanish and Portuguese literature. He was, moreover, a man of curious and observant mind: he read much and was in sympathy with the humanist tendencies of his age, coming especially under the influence of Erasmus. But there is never the least touch of pedantry in his writings: everything that he got from books has been transmuted by his imagination, firmly placed on Portuguese soil and made alive.

Gil Vicente's plays—he called them farces, *autos*, comedies and tragi-comedies—are very lightly constructed. They consist of a number of scenes strung together with scarcely any plot and no attempt at anything we call drama. Many of them are just humorous or satirical studies of contemporary life. Others, the *autos*, are religious pieces, where the poet built on medieval mimes and mysteries. What makes these works so delightful is first of all their freshness and spontaneity: we get, as we read, a picture of the whole life of this little country, with its vigorous peasant economy and its *nouveau riche* court, painted by a man who saw its defects and absurdities, but who loved it and can therefore make us love it. Gil Vicente belonged to the band of writers who, like La Fontaine and Stendhal, are life-enhancers. Then the fantasy and imagination shown in the invention of new episodes and situations is often remarkable. There is an Aristophanic quality about some of his *autos*—for example those entitled the *Barcas*. When we consider the exiguous basis from which he started and the fact that all his works were written as entertainments for the court and lacked therefore the stimulus of popular audiences, we find the freedom and vitality of these little dramatic pieces astonishing.

Gil Vicente's first pieces are in Spanish, which seems to have been the language usually spoken at court, but as he matured he came to write mostly in Portuguese. A few, however, of his finest works are in Castilian. Among these are two *autos*, written to be performed at Christmas, the *Auto dos Quatro Tempos* (1511?) and the *Auto da Sibila Cassandra* (1513?). The former gives a good idea of his eclectic methods, for it shows first the Archangels, Angels and Seraphim, then the Four Seasons and finally the pagan god Jupiter arriving to sing praises to the new born Infant. The song of the Angels is properly sublime and angelic, but the Seasons, who are disguised as shepherds, sing a *villancico* which develops from a little popular ditty:

> En la huerta nasce la rosa:
> quiérome ir allá
> por mirar al ruiseñor
> cómo cantabá.

> In the garden the rose is born.
> I want to go there
> to see how the nightingale is singing.

Then Jupiter appears and entones a magnificent *cantiga* in *pié quebrado* (the measure most commonly employed by Gil Vicente), in which he declares that he has come down from the heights to testify that all the pagan gods and goddesses, stars and planets, mountains and rivers, from the Ganges to Euphrates and Tigris, offer their obedience to the new-born Child. Such a fantasy could scarcely have been put forward after 1536, when the Inquisition was established at Lisbon.

The *Auto da Sibila Cassandra* is a still better work: indeed it is one of the most lovely and enchanting things in Spanish. Cassandra is a village girl who refuses to get married. Her admirer Solomon pleads with her in vain: then three of her aunts: then her uncles, Abraham, Isaiah and Moses. But nothing can shake her. To justify her refusal, she paints a lively picture of the married life of the Portuguese girls of the time—their subjection to their husbands, the continual quarrels and recriminations, the men's jealousies and infidelities. After this she gives her real reason—she knows that God will some day be incarnated in a virgin and feels that she deserves to be that lucky woman because she is superior to all others. With this the tone of the play changes: her three aunts, who are sibyls too, bring out their prophecies, and Isaiah, after reproving Cassandra for her conceit, adds his, declaring in a lovely passage that the woods and banks and flowers and snow are all heralds and prefigurations of this virgin's beauty. And now, declares the Erythraean sibyl, the time has come. When justice is perverted by malice, when faith is cold, when the Church is a captive to greed, when the poor are oppressed and all shame and reason lost, some great event is due to happen. On this a curtain is drawn aside and a cradle is seen with four angels standing round it and singing a lullaby. All the peasants—if we are still to call them that—worship the child and the play ends with a *villancico* of austere and simple beauty.

> Muy graciosa es la doncella,
> ¡cómo es bella y hermosa!
>
> Digas tú, el marinero
> que en las naves vivías,
> si la nave o la vela o la estrella
> es tan bella.

> Digas tú, el caballero
> que las armas vestías,
> si el caballo o las armas o la guerra
> es tan bella.
>
> Digas tú, el pastorcico
> que el ganadico guardas,
> si el ganado o los valles o la sierra
> es tan bella.

How charming the girl is! How lovely and beautiful!

Tell me, sailor, you who live in ships, if the ship or the sail or the star are as beautiful.

Tell me, knight, you who carry arms, if the horse or the arms or the war are as beautiful.

Tell me, shepherd, you who guard the flocks, if the flocks or the valleys or the mountains are as beautiful.

The play is, as we can see, a charade on the Incarnation. The idea of bringing in the sibyls was suggested by a line in the *Dies Irae*—*Teste David cum Sibylla*. All the characters, pagan and Old Testament, are prophets and Cassandra is besides a sort of comic prefiguration of the Virgin Mary—a preparation for her which did not come off. One might interpret this as meaning that although the whole tendency of pagan religion was to bring in Christianity, it was from Judaism that it actually sprang. But what makes the particular fascination of this play—and one can say the same of most of Gil Vicente's works—is the easy manner in which he slips from peasant scenes and humours to religious rhapsodies, love passages and sharp satire. He never dwells for long on any one theme: he never insists or underlines, or uses any but the lightest touch. And how exactly the style of the verse follows this change in the subject matter, in turns realistic, airy, tender, pungent and lyrical! The *letras para cantar*, or popular songs, with which he strewed his plays (and which were the signal for dances) add a peasant flavour that is fresh and precise without ever being, as Shakespeare's country scenes often are, boorish or crude.

Of Gil Vicente's other pieces in Spanish there is less to be said. One of them, the *Auto da Barca da Glória* (1519), is the third of a series of three *autos* on the medieval subject of the Dance of Death. The dead arrive at the shore of the river Styx and find Charon's boat, manned by devils, waiting to take them to the other side. Across the water they can see Hell with its wheels and lights and smoke, like a sort of sinister fun fair, and the play is made by their protests and prayers and indignation. The two Portuguese *Barcas* are full of Aristophanic humours and ironies, but the Spanish *Barca* is consistently solemn, because its characters are popes and emperors, kings and bishops, who are saved by a special intervention just at the moment when they are about to be carried off. The general intention of the three plays is, of course, to satirize the rulers of Christendom and the monks and clergy.

Gil Vicente also wrote two rather long tragi-comedies on subjects taken from the novels of Chivalry. These are *Amadís de Gaula* (1533) and *Dom Duardos* (1525?). They keep closely to the original theme —impossible and romantic love—and are without realism or humour. But they are worth reading for the charm and delicacy of their versification. Of his farces, only one, the *Farça das Ciganas*, is in Spanish: it is a slight but entertaining piece, portraying the gipsies who had recently arrived in the Peninsula and giving a little song about a dancing donkey. It is refreshingly free from the sentimentality shown by most gipsy fanciers, including Cervantes, and lets us see how little this enterprising people has changed in the course of the last four centuries.

We cannot leave this writer without pointing out how unlike the Portuguese atmosphere is to the Spanish. When we turn from Castilian literature to these plays by Gil Vicente we find ourselves in a different world: instead of the harshness and dryness, the cruel realism, the stoic resignation, the seriousness and dignity, we find an art that is humorous and tender, whimsical and tolerant, pious and sceptical, imaginative and free. It lacks only the greatness of scope to produce major works, and perhaps a certain driving force. Portugal is a rainy Atlantic country like England, and these farces and comedies belong to the same climate of feeling as Shakespeare's *Midsummer Night's Dream* and *Tempest*. They are also the most representative works to come out of Portugal. The great Portuguese poets who followed never attempted to set before us their own country: they were city dwellers, writing in the grand manner which had been brought in from Italy. We have to wait nearly a hundred years for Lope de Vega, to find in the Peninsula a writer who can be compared to Gil Vicente.

CHAPTER VII

THE *SIGLO DE ORO*.
CHARLES V AND PHILIP II

WE HAVE now reached the great period of Spanish literature known as the *Siglo de Oro*, which begins when Spain is at the height of her power and influence under the Emperor Charles V and ends when she is entering the last stages of decay and inanition. This period can be conveniently divided into two parts, each of which has very different characteristics. In the first Spain is a rising and growing power. The influences that move and inspire her come from two quarters: from Flanders—these are the deeper and more potent; and from Italy—these are the more cultured and artistic. One can sum them up as Reformation and Renaissance. In the second period, which begins towards the end of the sixteenth century, both these movements are exhausted. Spain follows Italy into a gradual decline, though at first it is only in economic matters that the descent is apparent. Indeed art and literature, which for obvious reasons lag behind their political and social stimuli, are for a time more brilliantly displayed than ever. But their style and temper have changed into that known by the rather vague term *baroque*.

It is sometimes said that baroque is the art type of the Counter-Reformation. In Spain, however, this is only partly true. The Counter-Reformation was in full swing by the time of the conclusion of the Council of Trent in 1563, but with the exception of El Greco, who was a Greek trained in Italy, there are few signs of anything one can call baroque before 1600. The literature of the reign of Philip II, when the religious current ran more strongly than at any other time, was built out of the elements of an earlier Spanish Reformation, which had grown up under the influence of Erasmus and of the German and Flemish humanists and devotional writers of the beginning of the century. It is true that many of

Erasmus' works were put on the Index in 1559, but by that time the seed had been sown and, though he himself was disowned, most of his ideas and those of the humanists in general continued to operate until the men who had absorbed them were dead. Even the mystical movement, which is so striking a feature of the second half of this reign, had its root in Erasmism and in the Flemish writers from whom Erasmus had sprung. This infusion of Northern seriousness helps to make the writers of this age easy to assimilate by Englishmen.

POETRY

So far as poetry is concerned, the *Siglo de Oro* began suddenly in 1543 with a book. This was the collected edition in one volume of two poets, Boscán and Garcilaso de la Vega. If one judges by effects, one must call it the most important book in Spanish literature, for by introducing Italian forms and metres it opened the way to a flood of new poetry. Let us see how this came about.

The story starts with a conversation between two people— Juan Boscán, a Catalan, and Andrea Navagiero, an Italian. Boscán was a poet who, though born in Barcelona, had been brought up in Castile at the court of Ferdinand. He was one of those serious, cultivated young men, steeped in humanist learning and yet polished in manners, who came to the front during the reign of Charles V. He had acted for a time as companion and tutor to a youth who later became famous—or notorious—as the Duke of Alba. Then he joined a military expedition against the Turks. But his tastes did not lie in this direction and on his return he gave up all ideas of court employment to devote himself to literature.

Navagiero was the Venetian ambassador. The Italian states often employed literary men upon such posts, and he was one of the most distinguished his country could provide. A brilliant Greek scholar, a writer of polished Latin verse, of the most exquisite taste in all the arts, with a particular *penchant* for scenery and gardens—such was the man the Signoria had selected for their difficult negotiations with the emperor. At this time—the year was 1526—he was accompanying the young Charles and his court on a state visit they were making to Southern Spain. He had not liked Toledo, but Seville had enchanted him. Now he had come to Granada and in the Alhambra and Generalife found buildings, gardens and scenery that enchanted him still more. Like many others of his nation he had formed a great respect for the Spanish Moors. Hard-working, refined and pleasure-loving, they reminded him of his own countrymen and were in every way a contrast to the idle and destructive Spaniards.

It is Boscán who tells us of his meeting and conversation with Navagero on the banks of the Darro.

He asked me [he said] why I did not try writing in Spanish sonnets and other forms used by good Italian authors: and he did not merely say this to me casually, but he pressed me to do it. A few days later I left for home and on the road, to while away the length and solitude of the journey, I turned over many times what he had said to me. That is how I came to try my hand at this kind of verse.

Boscán was not a Catalan for nothing. In his house in Barcelona, where he had now settled down, he set to work with determination to write verses in the Italian measures. The chief difficulty was the hendecasyllable. With his excellent good sense he mastered this and wrote lines which, if not exactly pleasing to the ear, are generally correct by Italian rules. In this metre he composed sonnets and *canzoni* as well as verses in *terza rima* and *ottava rima* and in what the Spaniards call *verso suelto*, or blank verse. All these forms were entirely new in Spain excepting the sonnets, but one may call this new too, since the Marqués de Santillana's experiments had remained in manuscript.

However, Boscán, though an excellent prose writer, was not endowed with the gift of poetry. His verse is flat and pedestrian and shows a lack of ear. All the same it is sometimes interesting: for example, his verses on his marriage—a very happy one—give a delightfully frank account of matters that are usually left in obscurity. But he never rises: one feels the hand of the man of letters, cultured, intelligent, able to please, but never the unpredictable touch of the poet. Boscán's real merit—and it is immense —lies in his having understood that the verse of his day moved in too narrow a field and seen what was to be done to remedy this: then in having had a young friend, Garcilaso de la Vega, who happened to be a poet of genius. One might compare the elder man's role in sixteenth-century Spain to that of Ezra Pound in the poetic revolution that took place in England thirty years ago.

Garcilaso de la Vega, who succeeded where so many others had failed, was born at Toledo, probably in 1501. He was one of those men who seemed to have come into the world to be happy and famous. His family was among the most distinguished in Castile, for his ancestors included both Pérez de Guzmán and the Marqués de Santillana. He was scarcely grown up when he obtained a post on the emperor's bodyguard, where he mixed with the inner circle of grandees at Charles V's court. Here his talents soon gave him influential friends. He had an astonishing facility for everything he put his hand to—whether it was tilting, or dancing, or playing on the viol and the harp, or composing Latin verses—while his charm of manner and gentleness of disposition softened the envy which such abilities would otherwise have brought on him. Altogether he seemed to be the perfect embodiment of the model courtier, as he is described in the most famous book of the day by Baldassare Castiglione. But his temperament was melancholy. Crossed in love for a Portuguese lady-in-waiting, Doña Isabel Freire, he vented his feelings not only in his poetry, but in the reckless daring that he showed on the battle-field. It was this daring that, after a near escape at Tunis, where he was badly wounded, cost him his life at the early age of thirty-five, whilst leading the assault on a tower held by some peasants close to Fréjus.

As we have said, it was by Boscán's advice that he had first begun to write poems in Italian metres. The two men were close friends. It would seem that Garcilaso's rather feminine temperament and congenital melancholy found a support in the robust character and solid good sense of his older companion. And when the young soldier died, the manuscript of his poems was sent to him. But Boscán died too in 1542, and it was his widow who brought out the volume of their combined verse in the following year.

Garcilaso's work consists of three long eclogues, some elegies and songs and a number of sonnets, all of them in Italian hendeca-syllables. The best are those written in the last two or three years of his life, when his style had reached maturity. Let us look at the most famous and characteristic of these, the *First Eclogue*, which was written in the shock caused by the death of his lady-love.[1]

It is a poem of about four hundred lines, beginning with a prologue and followed by complaints spoken by two shepherds. The measure used is the *canzone*. This, as is well known, consists in a mingling of eleven- and seven-syllabled lines in rather long stanzas, and from the praise given it by Dante and its great popularity since his time might be called the classic measure of Italian verse. It is not, however, one which it is easy to use well except in a fluid language such as Italian: its tendency, both in Spanish and English, is to become stiff and rhetorical. But in Garcilaso this does not happen. He is the least rhetorical of poets and his verse flows like the Spanish rivers he describes so well, the short lines providing a curb and pause and allowing the long lines that follow them to roll out to their full length.

The subject of this eclogue is given in the first three lines: it is the 'sweet lamenting' of the two shepherds, Salicio and Nemoroso. There is no dialogue: each bewails his dead or faithless love in a long *canzone*, and the poem ends. As in the other eclogues, the pastoral convention is worn lightly. There is no attempt, as with Juan del Encina, to make the characters talk like real shepherds. They are people of education and refinement: indeed, under a thin disguise of pastoral make-believe, one can hear plainly enough the voice of the poet himself, expressing his feelings on things that were very close to his heart. He was a young man deeply disappointed in love and it is this situation that, transfusing itself through the pores of his verse, gives to many of his poems their peculiar, sonorous melancholy.

We must not forget that Garcilaso was a man steeped in the Italian Renaissance. He spent the last years of his life at Naples, mixing in the society of its famous poets and humanists. For this reason he gave up imitating Petrarch, and, with his head full of

---

[1] In point of time it was his second eclogue, the so-called *Second* having been written about a year earlier, in 1532–3.

Horace and Vergil, chose as his models the Italian poets of the last generation such as Politian and Sannazaro, and even Bernardo Tasso, who was only a few years older than himself. Italian poetry at this time was reflecting in a rather lighthearted way the glow of the brilliant age and country that had given it birth. Half serious, half fanciful, delicately voluptuous, steeped in this life yet melting by mythological transitions and Platonic subterfuges into another, it aimed at conveying that idyllic, dream-like sense of being that is expressed by such painters as Giorgione. It did this by its coloured, harmonious imagery and by its musical sense for language. Indeed all through this century Italian poetry was leaning towards a more musical expression of life. Politian's *Orfeo* had already foreshadowed the opera. The current Platonism of the humanists naturally favoured this development, whilst classical mythology and pastoral settings were the mechanisms used to purify actual life from the dross of trivial circumstances that encumbered it and leave behind only what was poetically significant. Such were the models from which Garcilaso drew. We can see how completely he had been absorbed into this cultured Italian life when we note that, although the tone of his poetry is almost pensive and sad, there is not a single passage in which he speaks of religion. In a Spaniard of that age such an omission is remarkable.

Let us take a stanza of the *First Eclogue* and read it. I will choose one from the lament spoken by Salicio that ends with a refrain reminding one of Spenser's 'Sweete Themmes! runne softly, till I end my Song'.

> Con mi llorar las piedras enternecen
> su natural dureza y la quebrantan;
> los árboles parece que se inclinan;
> las aves que me escuchan, cuando cantan,
> con diferente voz se condolecen,
> y mi morir cantando me adivinan.
> Las fieras que reclinan
> su cuerpo fatigado,
> dejan el sosegado
> sueño por escuchar mi llanto triste.
> Tú sola contra mí te endureciste,

los ojos aun siquiera no volviendo
a lo que tú heciste.
Salid sin duelo, lágrimas, corriendo.

At my weeping the stones soften
their natural hardness till they melt it.
The trees seem to be inclining,
the birds to listen through their singing,
and with altered voice to pity me
while they prophesy my death.
Wild beasts that rest
their tired limbs
wake from their sleep
to listen to my complaining.
You alone harden your heart against me,
not even now your eyes upon me turning
to see what you have done.
Fall tears, fall, easily, softly flowing.

One will note, to begin with, what very musical poetry this is: almost everything Garcilaso wrote in the last years of his life is a delight to the ear, and the movement of these first seven lines, with their delicately combined verbal endings leading to a check that opens up a new direction, is a typical example of what he can do. Such things were only possible in the *arte nuevo*, or new poetry, with its weak and variable accentuation. But I would also like to call attention to the purity and elegance of the diction. The words chosen by the poet are a selection of those used in good conversation and they are brought in quietly and naturally without any trace of rhetorical flourish or emphasis. They move too in such close and intimate accord with the rhythm that their full quality, or rather as much of it as is required by the context, is drawn out of them. Although this is one of the chief functions of rhythm, it is here so delicately and soberly done and with such precise gradations that one has the feeling of reading not so much poetry—in the sense in which that word is generally understood, of something raised above the ordinary level of experience—as a purer kind of language, combining the plainness and sincerity of prose with a greater fineness and sensitivity. Garcilaso is a reminder that great poetry can be written without the help of a single unusual or vivid image or turn of phrase, provided that the fundamental thing, which is rhythm, has been mastered.

The obvious comparison to make is to Spenser, who did for English poetry very much what Garcilaso did for Spanish. Spenser had the same miraculous power of giving a flowing musical form to his verse—of driving in close harness the two horses of sense and melody which today have become so intolerant of one another. But there are great differences. Spenser's language is fresher and more coloured than Garcilaso's: his word-palette is deliberately richer: his images have a youthful fire and buoyancy that the other's sad and pensive verse entirely lacks. Yet how much more delicate and subtle the Spaniard can be, with his cult of sobriety and under-emphasis! Look for example at this passage from the elegy addressed to Boscán:

> Tú que en la patria entre quien bien te quiere
> la deleitosa playa estás mirando,
> y oyendo el son del mar que en ella hiere.

You who, at home among those who love you, are gazing at the delightful beach and hearing the sound of the sea that beats on it.

I think it will be agreed that these lines call up in the mind an image of unusual beauty and precision. Yet what language could be flatter or in the ordinary way less provocative to the eye or ear? Even *hiere*, the verb that clinches the picture, is weak in meaning and has a sound that does not at all suggest the action it stands for. We owe the pleasure we get from this passage solely to the power of musical evocation contained in the last line, which in some indescribable way recalls to us the familiar experience of watching the waves break on a southern beach and listening to their sound as they recede into the distance.

And now, to sharpen our perceptions by a comparison, let us look at this passage from Spenser. I have purposely chosen it for being as like as possible to that in Garcilaso. It is a description of the eyes of the wanton lady in the Bower of Bliss, which were:

> like starry light,
> Which, sparkling on the silent waves, does seem more bright.

Now this is also a beautiful and vivid image. Yet, subject apart, you will note a certain difference of kind. Spenser's image calls up an actual scene—starlight reflected on water—whereas Garcilaso's, if I am right, evokes rather the *feelings left in the mind by a scene*— in this case, the waves breaking—and only through those feelings a fleeting impression of the scene itself. That is to say, the emphasis in the Spanish passage lies rather on the feeling than on the thing that produced it, whilst a certain nostalgic aroma suggests the passage of time since the experience. This is the kind of impression one may expect to get when a poet seeks the equivalent of the state he wishes to convey in the musical effects of language, whilst refusing to admit any of those other effects of ingenuity, surprise, mixing like things with unlike, emphasis and so forth which are part of the common stock of poetry. It shows an advance in maturity and subtlety. It justifies us, I think, in comparing Garcilaso to the French classical poets, Racine and La Fontaine—the latter in, for example, his mythological poem, *Adonis*. Spenser, on the other hand, was intent on creating the poetry of a timeless world from which all taint of finer experience, of the twist given by the passing years, should be absent.

The musical element in Garcilaso's verse comes, as we have said, from Italy, but his grave manner and sober, unaffected diction are Spanish. They reflect the Erasmian tone of Charles V's court and of the Spanish circle of writers at Naples, their cult of restraint and measure, their dislike of all exaggerations of feeling, their love of truth and grammarian's care for the purity of the language. There is also a certain indefinable Platonism. The Platonic theory of ideas was bound to come up in the search for a poetic diction, which should exclude all words that did not, when drunk with the nectar of metre, rise and take their seats on a sort of Helicon of purified symbols. But Garcilaso did not go so far along this road as did some of his successors. His conception of a poetic diction was simpler—'to avoid affectation without falling into dryness and, with great purity of style, to use expressions that are elegant and accepted by good judges, and neither new nor fallen out of common use'. Such at least was his view of the qualities required in good prose, as he stated in his introduction to Boscán's translation of *Il Cortigiano*, and a reading of his poetry shows that he followed the same principles there also. Thus we may affirm that, though pastoral eclogue may seem to us today an artificial form, few poets have attached so high an importance to plainness and sincerity as Garcilaso de la Vega.

His last poems lack the personal feeling of those inspired by Isabel Freire, but they display an even greater mastery of the art of versification. Take the *canción* that begins *Si de mi baja lira*, written to help a friend in his courtship of a Neapolitan lady and often called from its dedication *La flor de Gnido*. It is in a lyric measure known as the *lira*, about which we shall have more to say later, that had been invented a few years before by Bernardo Tasso. In Garcilaso's hands it gives an effect of classic purity and distinction very different from that obtained in Italian. Read it, and one seems to hear a beautiful and unhurried voice speaking in the most perfect Castilian, for though this poem has a lyric form, it takes one back, like all this poet's verse, to the rhythms and cadences of actual speech. The rise, the buoyancy, the flash, the contrasts, the emphasis that seem almost the innate properties of poetry are subdued and pared down in this *lengua casi muda*. So it is in his two elegies in *terza rima*, composed in the autumn of 1535 after his return from Tunis. A little flat and uneven, but with passages of bare and melancholy writing scarcely to be matched even in this country of melancholy verse, they contain lines such as this:

> Mira la vanidad de los mortales,
> ciegos, errados en el aire escuro.

But the *Third Eclogue*, which is the last poem that Garcilaso wrote, makes a somewhat different impression. It is a mythological poem, written in octaves, and describing the nymphs of the Tagus and then two shepherds. The rhythm of the octave, so pervasive and insinuating—though also so lovely—imposes itself and weakens the particular music of the lines, but nowhere else does the poet show so fine a sense for the subtle cadences of the hendecasyllable. And then, after creating Spanish poetry in the short space of four years—years filled with war and official duties—he died.

The effect of the publication of Garcilaso's and Boscán's poems was immediate and prodigious. The younger generation felt that a new world of feeling and imagination had been opened to them. More than twenty editions came out within the next thirty years, and although one elderly though admirable poet, Cristóbal de Castillejo, protested against this invasion of foreign forms, it was becoming impossible to write verse except in the Italian manner. All the poets, therefore, of the reign of Philip II may be called disciples of Garcilaso.

The outstanding figure among these was Fray Luis de León (?1527-91). He was the son of a lawyer from Belmonte in La Mancha who had risen to being an *oidor*, or judge. Sent at the age of fourteen to the University of Salamanca, he entered the Augustinian convent there and two years later took vows. Here, in this far from quiet seat of learning, he was to spend the rest of his life.

Salamanca was just now at the height of its fame and activity. Religion was the master subject of the age and this was the place where dogma was discussed and refined. Eminent scholars and theologians competed for the applause of the students who thronged their lecture rooms, and there was particular rivalry for the chairs of scripture and theology between the Augustinians and the Dominicans. Fray Luis soon began to give proof of his outstanding talents and by the time that he was thirty had become the leading champion of his order in these fields. He was, it seems, a brilliant lecturer, direct, incisive and free from professorial pedantry, as well as a fine classical and Hebrew scholar, so that it is not surprising that he was able to rout his competitors in a succession of hard-fought elections and to carry off the most important chairs which the University could provide. However, he did not do this without making enemies. Impetuous and outspoken, easily roused to anger by injustice and with no patience at all for stupidity, he walked the dangerous minefield of academic and religious life as though it were an Oxford common-room. And he forgot one serious disability from which he suffered: his great-grandmother had been a converted Jewess who, sixty years before, had been reconciled in an *auto de fe*. This by itself was enough to cast doubts on his orthodoxy.

The consequence was that in 1572 Fray Luis was arrested by the

Inquisition on the secret denunciations of two rival professors. Shut up in a damp cell, completely isolated from the world, half starved and threatened with torture, he had to face the charges of having criticized the accuracy of the Vulgate edition of the Scriptures, and of having translated the Song of Songs into Spanish. Another monk who had been imprisoned with him died of ill-treatment, but he survived and, after five years spent in prison, was acquitted. A famous story has it that he began his next lecture with the words 'We were saying yesterday . . .'.

Luis de León belonged to the vanishing tribe of the humanists: more fervent and passionate than Sir Thomas More or Erasmus, with a mystical and platonic side to his nature which they lacked, he took after them in his robust intellect and scholarship. His range included both Hebrew and Greek, but his favourite authors after Plato and the Bible appear to have been Vergil and Horace. His love of Horace recalls that of Lucretius for Epicurus. It was an affinity of opposites—the craving of a restless, pugnacious, over-sensitive nature, continually at odds with the society around it, for the epicurean calm and moderation of the Roman poet. For this reason the most famous of Fray Luis' poems (written when he was a young man) is a passionate celebration of the charms of a retired life, such as Horace had led, far from the tumults and disappointments of the world. Here, however, he was indulging in one of the favourite day-dreams of his time. The men of that age suffered, as we do today, from a painful sense of the increasing speed and complexity of life, and were always playing with the idea of retiring from it. But Spain was not organized for country life, nor do Spaniards easily give up the fascinations of the town. The pleasures of solitude and rural scenes were rarely therefore put to a practical test, but remained a mere topic of literature.

Luis de León's admiration for the Roman poet also accounts no doubt for his writing so many of his poems in the beautiful lyric measure known as the *lira*. This was a form which had been invented by Bernardo Tasso in order to convey in a stressed language the feeling of Horace's *Odes*, and Garcilaso, as we have already said, had borrowed it for a famous song, *Si de mi baja lira*. Like the *canzone* it is a combination of seven- and eleven-syllabled lines, but its peculiar feature consists in the way in which the last long line of each stanza, coming as it does after two short ones, the second of which rhymes with it, rolls forward like the fringe of a wave to reach a new high-water mark. Here are two stanzas from a poem dedicated to D. Diego Olarte as an illustration:

> Cuando contemplo el cielo
> de innumerables luces adornado,
> y miro hacia el suelo
> de noche rodeado,
> en sueño y en olvido sepultado,
>
> El amor y la pena
> despiertan en mi pecho un ansia ardiente;
> despiden larga vena
> los ojos hechos fuente,
> Olarte, y digo al fin con voz doliente.

When I contemplate the sky, adorned with innumerable lights, then gaze towards the earth, shut in by darkness, buried in sleep and forgetfulness;

Love and pain awake a burning longing in my breast; my eyes become springs, releasing a long stream, and at length, Olarte, I speak in an anguished voice.

It may be thought that this is not very like Horace. But that is not the fault of the measure, which is well adopted for turning out lines, such as he often wrote, where music and language seem to fuse together into some marmoreal substance. If the verse of Luis de León strikes a different note, that is because their author was a Spaniard of the Counter-Reformation, restless, tormented, aspiring, inclined to mysticism and with nothing of the dreamy sensuousness of the Renaissance left in him. As he used it, the *lira*, with its pavane-like movement in seven and eleven steps, takes on a new character and acquires a facility for expressing those different levels of feeling, those longings, descents, *arrobamientos*, suspensions, ecstasies that are the life blood of mystical poetry. From now on it becomes the Catholic dithyramb.

> ¡O son! ¡O voz! ¡Siquiera
> pequeña parte alguna descendiese
> en mi sentido, y fuera
> de sí el alma pusiese,
> y toda en ti, o Amor, la convirtiese!

O sound, O voice! Would that some small portion of you could descend upon my senses and drive my soul beyond itself and convert all of it into Thee, O Love!

Luis de León wrote little poetry, but half a dozen of his lyrics, all in this measure, are among the most beautiful in Spanish. They are also, I believe, well adapted for pleasing the English mind. Perhaps that is because they recall Milton. The two men were considerably alike both in tastes and character and their poetic styles have a resemblance too: this comes from the fact that they have been more strongly affected by the weight and sonority of Latin poetry and by the sublimity of Hebrew than by the coloured language and rhetorical conceits and allegories of the Italians. That, and the influence of Plato, gives them the same sort of diction. If they differ so much in other respects, it is largely because Fray Luis did not regard himself as a professional poet, but wrote in the intervals snatched from his stormy University life to relieve his pent up feelings. His verse is therefore lyric in form and strikes an ejaculatory note of longing for rest and escape—to a garden in the country, to the contemplation through Nature or music of the eternal forms and patterns, to the full knowledge of them in the *campos verdaderos* of heaven. That is to say, it is personal poetry, which in the sixteenth century was not taken seriously. It is for this reason, no doubt, that he never published it, and that it did not see the light till 1637. He made his chief effort in his prose works, to which he gave all the thought and artistic deliberation he could command. It was typical of the age of Philip II that prose had a greater prestige than poetry.

A greater lyric poet than Luis de León—in fact (if quality alone is the test) one of the greatest poets of any country—was St John of the Cross, or to give him his Spanish name, San Juan de la Cruz (1542-91). Everything about him is extraordinary. Born in a village of Old Castile of humble family, he entered the Carmelite

Order and took his degree at Salamanca. Then he joined the very strict reform which had just been initiated by Santa Teresa. From now on he led a life of the most extreme asceticism, starving his body and spending his nights in prayer and contemplation, often by a stream, or under an olive tree, or in a cave looking out on the landscape—wherever he could steep his mind in the beauty of Nature. But reforming a religious order could in those days be a dangerous occupation. Fray Juan was kidnapped one December night of 1577 by the unreformed friars of his order and imprisoned at Toledo. Here he lay for nine months in great hardship and suffering, half starved and subjected to weekly whippings, till a vision of the Virgin inspired him to make his escape by a rope of blankets let down from a window. In his prison he had, apparently for the first time, begun to write poetry, and almost all the poems we have by him—they cover only a few pages—were written either there or within the few months following his escape. It was not till some years after this that he wrote his mystical works in the form of prose commentaries on three of them.

What are these poems? The two most famous are in the measure we have spoken of called the *lira* and describe the search of the Beloved, that is the Soul, for the Lover. The imagery is drawn either from Garcilaso's pastoral eclogues or from the Song of Songs. They are a little obscure, which is natural enough when one remembers that they are allegories of the mystical ascent of the soul to the state of union with God. But above all they are love poems, arranged in the form of a journey, a search and a finding, love poems of the most passionate, the most delicate, the most enchanting sort. Such poetry has never been written in Spain to women. Tenderness, abandon, delight were reserved for religious occasions. The strong sense of propriety of Spaniards has generally prevented them from expressing intimate feelings for human beings in print.

It is not possible to give in a short space any idea of the intoxicating effect these poems produce or of the manner by which this has been attained.[1] But the rocket-like soaring and bursting associated with

[1] Those who wish to know more of this extraordinary figure may care to read two articles I have written on his life and poetry in *Horizon*, May and June 1947.

the lyrical impulse, the sense of flight and thrill and ecstasy which Juan de la Cruz's two great poems display have never been equalled by anyone else. This mystic, at least, brought back from the stratosphere he visited something to show where he had been. Obviously such poetry cannot be written by sitting down to a table. It draws its potency from some enormous explosion of delight, as well as from many other attendant circumstances—one of which was in this case the poet's escape from prison into the beauty of an Andalusian spring and the solitude of a mountain hermitage. And so Juan de la Cruz's poetic phase was brief—briefer in fact than that of any other known poet. Although he wrote a few more verses after it had passed, with one exception they have no merit.

Luis de León and San Juan de la Cruz are for us the great poets of the reign of Philip II, but in their own day their verse was unknown outside a small circle of friends. To their contemporaries the great poet was Fernando de Herrera, who was called on that account *el Divino.* Herrera (1534-97) was a Sevillian who, as every true Sevillian prays to do, spent his whole life in his native city. Since his family was poor, he provided for his needs by taking minor orders and obtaining a small benefice: with his frugal habits, this enabled him to devote the whole of his time to study and writing. Thus he was spared those cruel money troubles and anxieties that wore down so many other writers of the day and choked their talent. He also talked well: a circle of poets, painters, ecclesiastics and doctors collected round him, so that for the first time in Spanish history we come across that famous institution, the literary cénacle or *tertulia.* A long, tedious and necessarily platonic love affair with a lady of high rank suited both his need for emotional stimulus and his timid character.

His poetry, however, does not please us quite so much as it pleased his contemporaries and successors. It is written in Italian measures—sonnets, *terza rima* and *canzoni*—but it is for the most part a rhetorical poetry, over-emphatic and inflated, with too little variety and too much crude energy. We feel our minds sagging as we read of seas that are always angry, suns fierce and mountains savage, yet we notice that he had a fine ear. Some of his Petrarchian sonnets are exquisitely phrased—half a dozen are among the best in Spanish—while three of his patriotic odes, written in a language influenced by the Old Testament, have an almost Miltonic grandeur. His poetry abounds in words expressing colour—purple, emerald, snowy, fiery, golden, red—and thus opens up a vein which all the Andalusian poets of the next century will follow and develop.

For this poetry, monotonous and over-forceful though it generally is, was the admiration of all the great writers of the seventeenth century; Góngora drew his particular conclusions from it and Calderon's style was deeply affected by its imagery. I believe the explanation of this to be that at certain periods rhetoric can play an important part in poetic development by its vigour and impersonality. The style of Garcilaso, with all its merits, was of too sensitive and delicate a texture to breed a strong line of poets without the admixture of a tougher, more energetic versification. This Herrera gave. With the change of religious climate that came in about the time of his death the age had begun to move from a poetry that had deep roots in the personal life towards a more general and decorative style that, like that of Pope or Dryden, was completely depersonalized. The simple rhetoric of Herrera formed therefore a bridge leading to that more subtle and decorative sort of rhetoric known as Baroque.

With his abstemious diet, his midnight studies and the terrible zest he put into his verse, Herrera calls up that other Andalusian poet, Juan de Mena. But the ages they wrote in provide a difference. For the medieval poet the writing of good poetry was the most important thing in the world. All his studies were designed to that end. He had the great Italian writers as examples and a road leading upwards. But Herrera, with the Renaissance behind him, lived in an age when poetry seemed to be losing its hold. Humanism was almost dead. The new relation that art must have to life and conduct had not been determined. And so, at the age of forty-eight, with his great love affair put finally behind him, he abandoned verse and sat down to celebrate the glories of Spain in a prose history. But before doing this he published his *Commentary on Garcilaso*, a critical work which Menéndez y Pelayo called the *Ars Poetica* of the century. We shall have occasion to speak of it later.

The minor poets do not in general come into the scope of this book, but there is one about whom I must say a few words—Baltasar del Alcázar (1530-1606). He was a Sevillian who, after spending some years as a soldier, became steward to one of the big Andalusian magnates. I mention him because, of all the very numerous poets of Seville, he is the only one whose work contains any of the *gracia* (a word combining the meanings of wit and charm) for which that city is famous. His output was not large, but his best poems are very delightful and convey so well the spirit of this easygoing city of taverns and bull fights and pleasant conversation that everyone who cares for Spanish things should read him. His light tone and the fact that he generally used the traditional measures rather than the Italian ones should not lead one to suppose that he was uncultivated. He knew Latin and Italian well, was a lover of music who himself composed and a connoisseur of painting who drew landscapes. We are even told—incredible though this must seem in a Spaniard—that he had a taste for natural history. The delicious gaiety of his poems and their subtly buffoonish tone give one some idea of the social arts of this society of poets, wits and painters who during the reign of Philip II made Seville the artistic capital of Spain. Since he has not been too well treated in anthologies, let me advise anyone who can to read his poem *Tres cosas me tienen preso* on the difficulty he had of deciding which he really loved best—his mistress Inés, Aracena ham, or aubergines fried in cheese: his *Cena Jocosa* (in the *Oxford Book of Spanish Verse*): the poem to Francisco Sarmiento describing his life in old age, and some of the epigrams imitated from Martial. He is one of the most original of Spanish poets, and since he had the good sense to choose a vein that suited him and to confine himself to it, his work has stood the test of time better than that of many poets who have been more ambitious.

PROSE

The prose literature of the sixteenth century is much richer and more varied than the poetry. We shall, however, deal rather briefly with it. The art of writing prose had reached its maturity in the reign of Charles V in Boscán's translation of *Il Cortigiano* and in the writings of the two brothers Alfonso and Juan de Valdés. They were both Erasmists. The air blowing from the North brought with it a certain severity of tone and diction that suited the natural stoicism of the Castilians. Among other things it led them to resist the taste prevailing in Italy for the more fluid style of Cicero and to cultivate a restrained sort of elegance. A different type of writer was Fray Antonio de Guevara (1480?-1545), whose mannered style and floods of imagery anticipate the Baroque writers of the following century. He left no descendants in Spain, but after his most famous book, *Relox de Príncipes*, had been translated by Lord Berners in 1535 and again by Sir Thomas North in 1557, he was taken up and imitated by John Lyly in *Euphues*.

When we come to the reign of Philip II we find that some of the best writers are the historians. Diego Hurtado de Mendoza, yet another descendant of the Marqués de Santillana and a friend of Garcilaso, wrote in his old age a history of the Moorish insurrection that broke out at Granada in 1568. The book towers above its subject: written in a style of great concision, influenced by those of Sallust and Tacitus, it compares favourably with anything of its kind at this time outside Italy. Then, at the end of the century, we get the great history of Spain by the Jesuit, Juan de Mariana. (1536-1624). It is not a critical history or one dictated by a new view of the subject: Mariana took his materials where he could find them and put them first into Latin and then into Spanish. And the Spanish is excellent—a clean, balanced style modelled on that of Livy and well suited to flow without resistance into the ear of the reader. A different sort of work is Bernal Díaz del Castillo's account of the conquest of Mexico, in which he took part as a common soldier. This is a book by an uneducated man, but containing scenes so vividly seized and put down that we really get the feeling of having been present. It is one of the great masterpieces of this sort of narration, and has been well translated into English, and better still into French by the poet José-Maria de Heredia.

Another vein of writing is provided by the homiletic literature. It is here as a rule that the arts of rhetoric are best displayed and languages put through such exercises of stretching and bending as they are capable of. But Spanish does not go to the extremes of English: it has no Donne's *Sermons* nor anything near them, either in force or genius or in the defiance offered to the receptive powers of the mind and to the habits of the spoken language. Nor has it, I think, anything of the intellectual calibre of Hooker's *Ecclesiastical Polity*. By common consent the best of these writers is Fray Luis de Granada (1504-88), who offers a rich oratorical style, full of Biblical echoes, but tending to diffuseness. A rather different type is Malón de Chaide, more popular, more picturesque, less intellectual. His one book, *La Conversión de la Magdalena* (c. 1580), can perhaps be compared to Jeremy Taylor's *Holy Dying* for the telling way in which it makes use of images drawn from ordinary life. However, the minute descriptions it contains of the tortures of the martyrs or of Christ on the Cross, which, in order to draw our pity, spare us no detail, are of a kind that could only be Spanish. They bring to our minds the anguished wood-carvings of Montañés and Pedro de Mena in the following century.

But the greatest prose writer of the sixteenth century is without question Luis de León. His two books, *Los Nombres de Cristo* and *La Perfecta Casada* (the former written in prison), are something more than homiletic literature: they are deliberate attempts to create in Spanish a prose style rivalling those of the great Latin masters in clarity, harmony of sound, and elevation. He wrote with care and deliberation, giving much thought to the art of composition and to what was proper to the genius of the language. In all literatures there are periods when the chief business of writers is to show the paces of the language, displaying it in its intrinsic powers and beauties, yet avoiding anything that might suggest strain or personal eccentricity. That is what Garcilaso had so superbly done in poetry: now Luis de León, crowning the efforts of the Erasmist generation, was to follow his lead in prose.

A writer who is in a class by herself is Santa Teresa of Avila (1515-82), the reformer of the Carmelite Order. The lay-minded reader should not allow himself to be deterred by the title of Saint or by the kind of subjects on which she wrote, for she is one of the most fascinating human beings who have ever lived. Her character

was a very complex one, full of paradoxes and contradictions, yet
bound together in action by her strong will. She was, of course,
a mystic—a word that frightens many people—but women's
mystical experiences are less abstract than men's and there is little
in hers that cannot be related to the feelings of a woman who is in
love with an absent person. This makes them humanly intelligible,
whatever they may be on the religious plane. She is also a quarry
of psychological materials and a standing temptation to biographers
in search of a subject and ready to embark on a huge theme. This
is because very few men or women have written so extensively
about the processes of their own minds. Her feelings and experiences
were a perpetual surprise to her and, with the instinct of a born
writer and the excuse of a person whose good faith has been
questioned, she took every opportunity for putting them down
and explaining them. She did this in a simple, straightforward
way without any trace of false modesty or egoism, and the result
is that we have a portrait of quite unusual psychological interest,
which entitles us to put her beside Montaigne as one of the earliest
explorers of the human personality. In a general way we may say
of the Spanish mystics of this age that they were the pioneers of the
deeper levels of psychology that border on the unconscious.

Santa Teresa's works comprise her autobiographies, her mystical
works which are really autobiographical too, a few poems and the
large collection of her letters. There is besides a certain amount of
information from other sources to supplement what she tells us
about herself. We can thus say that we know her more intimately
than we know any other human being in history before the
eighteenth century. Even Erasmus and Montaigne are less familiar, because, if they have a good deal to say about themselves,
there is also much that they are careful to keep from us. Santa
Teresa, on the other hand, wrote without reserve and with little
thought for the kind of effect she was producing. As for the style,
it is plain, simple and direct and in the language of everyday speech.
Her books show a certain care for the balance of the sentences, but
her letters have the roughness and spontaneity of pages written in
a hurry and never re-read. However, there is a real beauty about a
style so uncorrupted by the literary language, when it is written by

a person of her sincerity and feeling for life. It is a beauty of a rather homely kind, and yet it has dignity. In this it calls to mind the *Journal* of George Fox. If I may give my personal reaction, I would say that these books make an impression of great whiteness —the white of clean limewashed walls and scrubbed tables, the white of dust, the white of the granite boulders of her mountain city, the blinding white of the Spanish sunlight. And behind the hurriedly moving pen—a trifle garrulous, as those of elderly spinsters are apt to be—one feels at times a great emptiness and silence. I would recommend anyone who wished to know what Castile is really like to read through in Spanish the whole of this great woman's autobiographical writings and correspondence, with Mrs Cunninghame Graham's pleasantly diffuse biography as a general guide. The effort required will be great, but for those who have time to spare it will be rewarding.

FICTION

There remains to be considered imaginative fiction. This, in the period we are reviewing, consists of two quite distinct kinds—that which deals in an ideal way with high life and that which deals in a realistic way with low life. The first starts off with the *libros de caballería* or books of Chivalry—a class of literature that derived from the Arthurian romances of the early Middle Ages, but had a more popular and melodramatic appeal. Spain provides two readable examples—*Amadís de Gaula* (1508), which is thought by some to have a Portuguese origin, and *Tirant lo Blanch* (1460), which is Catalan. *Tirant* pleases by its mingling of adventures with realistic descriptions of contemporary life, but *Amadís* is a pure romance, full of marvellous incidents of the kind that happen only to knights-errant and in fact very like Malory's *Morte d'Arthur*. But it is not so good. It lacks the concreteness and air of actuality that delight us in Malory's narration and, being further removed from the early French sources and indeed not dealing with King Arthur's knights at all, it has lost all trace of that mysterious stuff, the *matière de Bretagne*, that gives even to the late Arthurian romances some root in poetry. *Amadís* really marks the end of the novel of feudal imagination and the beginnings of popular melodrama, and though there are fine incidents in it—the birth and infancy of the Child of the Sea, his love for Oriana, his retirement to an island hermitage when she sends him an angry letter, the many dreams—it will not quite stand comparison with the best romances of the Breton cycle. Written in admirable prose by its author or compiler, Garci Rodríguez de Montalbo, it has been translated into English by Southey.

Amadís had an enormous popularity in its own day and gave rise to a host of imitations. A craze for this sort of reading swept the Peninsula during the first half of the sixteenth century—that is to say, long after it had died out in the rest of Europe—(much as that for detective novels has swept the world in recent years), and slowly faded away during the reign of Philip II. Its place was taken, though in more restricted circles, by the pastoral novel. A Portuguese, Jorge de Montemayor, introduced this form from Italy to Spain in 1558 with his famous *Diana*. Another and perhaps better *Diana* followed, by the Valencian poet, Gaspar Gil Polo, and both Cervantes and Lope de Vega made their contributions.

Pastoral novels date even more quickly than novels of chivalry because they contain few adventures or surprises, but are simply books written to express the taste and sensibility of their time. Since the days of Ovid, one of the functions of literature has been to provide elegant models for love and courtship, and the pastoral novel represents the transference of this function from poetry to prose. But prose is an idiom that requires as its material the complexity and contrariness of actual experience, and though pastoral novels are generally *romans à clef*, relating in veiled and highly idealized language the love affairs of the author and his friends, they contain in fact no more life or experience than a mannequin parade. For this reason we find them too insipid to read today, in spite of their passages of fine writing and of our recognition that to be able to write 'finely' represents an advance in the art of novel writing. But they have all the same a psychological interest because they throw a light on the men of their time. The age of Philip II was a grave, sober, meditative age with a puritanical attitude to pleasure and a passion for religion. The pastoral theme,

which runs through so much of its prose and poetry, has a counterpart in the religious movement which was filling the wild places
of the Peninsula with anchorites and ascetics. Now all pastoral
implies an idealization of Nature, but the Nature of these books is
not the smiling Nature of Theocritus, Vergil and the Italians, but
a rather sombre and conventionalized affair of mountains, rocks
and evergreen oaks, where the presiding spirits are solitude and
silence. This is precisely what one would expect. Spaniards have
rarely looked at Nature for its own sake, as the lack of landscapes
in Spanish painting clearly shows. When they have described it,
it has been simply as a stage or background for human actions.
And those actions have not, as in Italy, been picnics or parties of
pleasure, but the musings of rejected lovers or the vigils of hermits.
In other words, Nature to the Spanish mind has the medieval
connotations of solitude and sadness. At its worst it is ominous
and dangerous. One has to go to a religious writer like San Juan
de la Cruz to find any real familiarity with its beauty.

The realistic fiction of the sixteenth century runs, as we have
said, along entirely different lines. At the beginning of the century
is *Celestina.* This was followed by that highly original genre, invented in Spain—the picaresque novel.

The first and best of these books is *La Vida de Lazarillo de Tormes,*
which appeared anonymously in 1554. It is an extremely short
book—what we should today call a long short-story—and it relates
in the form of autobiography a series of adventures in the life of a
boy who came from one of the lowest families in Salamanca. Its
three principal episodes describe his life as servant to a blind beggar,
to an impoverished and miserly priest and then to a squire in
Toledo who possessed nothing but the fine suit he walked about in.
In the case of the first two episodes, the point of the story lies in the
efforts of the famished boy to outwit his masters and obtain a proper
share of the food they have begged or otherwise obtained. The difficulties are great, both blind man and priest are astute because they are
hungry, and we follow with anxious delight the boy's schemes and
the ingenuity and craftiness he puts into them. The episode of the
priest is particularly good because, although he is never described,
he is brought so vividly before us by the few remarks he makes

that we seem to remember having known him in our own child-hood. In the third episode the boy's master is sympathetic: the irony consists in the fact that, although he looks like a gentleman, he lives even worse than a beggar, and we are left wondering what strange people these Spaniards are whose pretensions to gentility make them prefer starvation to the ignominy of working.

The thing that strikes us most about this book and about the other picaresque novels that followed it is their realism. What exactly does this word mean? The aim of the picaresque writers is to make us look at the world without our usual rose-tinted spectacles. They strip life of its pleasant coverings and show us the naked struggle that goes on underneath, just as the religious treatise shows the dust and bones in which everything ends. But the peculiar merit of *Lazarillo* is that it does not do this by broadening its view to include disagreeable and sordid details (as did the romantic realists of the twentieth century), but by concentrating it so as to get a greater penetration. And that perhaps is why this book is so stimulating. We quickly acclimatize ourselves to a world where bread is hard to come by and eating an exceptional event, and give ourselves up with a delight to a story that enlarges our imaginations, just because it is, we cannot exactly say why, truer than life. And then, after all, it is a success story: Lazarillo escapes and rises. By his good luck in marrying an archpriest's mistress, he reaches the dizzy height of town-crier. It is only on second thoughts that we realize that this book is a satire, and that the author has been painting the vices of his time. In fact he was almost certainly an Erasmist.

Lazarillo de Tormes was a great popular success and went into many editions, but no other picaresque novel followed it during the long reign of Philip. It was not till 1599, a year after that king's death, that a successor came out. This was *Guzmán de Alfarache*. Its author was the son of the prison doctor of Seville, one Mateo Alemán. Born in 1547 and given a university education, he had married a woman he did not like, and then, after sowing his wild oats with the money he got from her, had led a wandering, poverty-stricken, frustrated life, supporting himself by small posts in the Administration and frequently in prison for debt. It was precisely the life that Cervantes, who was born in the same year, had led after his return from Algiers, but the effect on the two men was very different. No misfortunes could depress for long the great writer's self-reliance and optimism, whereas Alemán's book is one of the most pessimistic ever written.

As a novel *Guzmán de Alfarache* is very unlike *Lazarillo*. It is ten times as long and contains a wide variety of adventures, not all of which belong to low life. It is humourless, shows no leanings to satire, and every incident is accompanied by a lengthy moral commentary. Indeed, there is often so much more commentary than narrative that one is inclined to protest that this is not a novel at all, but a religious tract.

Let us look at the story first. It begins with Guzmán, a boy accustomed to a soft life, running away from his home at Seville to Madrid. The first chapters describe the inns he passed through on the road and the terrible situation of finding oneself in the world without money. These are the most vivid in the book. Then comes a life of petty adventures in towns. He becomes assistant to a pastry cook, falls into bad ways and steals, poses as a young nobleman, makes his way to Italy, is made page to a cardinal and finally ,after spending half the book abroad, returns to Spain, where he marries for money, is deserted by his wife and, succumbing once more to the temptation to steal from his employer, is caught and condemned to the galleys. Such are the incidents, set down in a casual sequence with little art or invention and with no attempt either to make the characters live or the circumstances revealing. For Alemán is a writer who lacks the novelist's imagination, and in reading his book one is reminded not so much of other novels as of those flat, conventionalized memoirs of low life that came out in France in the late eighteenth century.

Yet *Guzmán de Alfarache* is all the same a remarkable book. Its merit lies precisely where one would least expect it—in the running commentary. For one thing, this is written in magnificent Spanish. Its short sentences, lean and whip-like, fluent and yet taut and compressed, register all the suffering and humiliation, the disgust and weariness which the narrative has failed to put over. They contain, we feel, the essential stuff of what the author wanted to say, and the story is there merely to give the cues for them. And what cues they are! Guzmán is Charlie Chaplin viewed by a sixteenth-century Calvinist minister. At every moment he is falling into some disgrace or humiliation, which the commentary then explains, no doubt correctly enough, as an inevitable consequence of our sinful human nature. We watch him stumbling and rising, rising and stumbling through sixty chapters—but we are not allowed to rejoice at his buoyancy. Since all pleasure is evil, and calamity in this world is the best road to bliss in the next, Guzmán's condemnation to the galleys has the effect of a happy ending because it leads to his conversion. How different from the views of that English writer of picaresque, Daniel Defoe, whose heroine, Moll Flanders, found that conversion led, in Old Testament style, to worldly prosperity!

Guzmán de Alfarache then is a cautionary novel, saturated through and through with a belief in the utter corruption of human nature. But its pessimism goes beyond that. Alemán is obsessed not only by the wickedness of man, but by the squalor and ugliness of life. Like Swift, he has a scatological mind. If in conduct the groundwork is sin, in tangible things it is excreta. And what goes into the body can be as disgusting as what comes out of it: his neurosis about food blossoms in a chapter of horrors, when an innkeeper serves to his guests horse-meat instead of calf. There are also his irrational hatreds. His hero hates the poor, though he is poor himself, because they are coarse, brutal and envious. He hates women and regards them as bitches and liars whose only thought is how to get money out of men for nothing: his own dealings with them always end in his discomfiture. Hatred and disgust for life well up so automatically that we end by being reminded of a modern book—Céline's *Voyage au bout de la Nuit*. But Alemán is saved from Céline's complete despair, which made him a Fascist, by his Catholic faith. The Church, unlike the Lutheran and Calvinist creeds of the time, provided in the practice of confession and absolution a cure for the fears and terrors it had called up. And so one may say that the moving power of this novel—and his contemporaries found it so moving that it became a best-seller—lies in the fact that it describes the slow, uncertain

and for a long time feeble effects of grace upon a person sunk in
sin and misery, until he is finally rescued by it.

Alemán's book then can be described as a dissertation upon
original sin. So deeply sunk are all men in this that the *pícaro* or
rogue is really little worse than the others and, because his sins are
more open and obvious, is well suited to figure in a novel as the
typical man. When the hero is a criminal, the battle of vice and
virtue, salvation and hell-burning will naturally appear more
dramatic. But one must note that Guzmán owes his final conversion to the fact that he had never given up regular attendance at
mass. In this he was true to type. The thief and murderer who
heard mass daily and was a devout Catholic was becoming one of
the characteristic features of Spanish life, and the Jesuits, by the
stress they laid upon faith (in its Catholic sense) rather than upon
works, were encouraging it. In fact the separation of these two
activities, which in a healthy state are indissoluble, correspond to
a phenomenon of divided personality, such as is liable to break out
in difficult and unhappy times. The Renaissance, which, by its
concepts of Reason and Nature, represented a deliberate effort to
integrate the human personality, had spent itself: the age that
followed it was one of acute economic distress: between the difficulties of making a living on the one hand and the terror of death
and hell on the other, the individual found himself too weak to
take the strains placed upon him. So we get, to quote Dr Enrique
Moreno, 'the conception of a devout *pícaro* who trembles to think
of the enormity of a crime at the very moment of committing it,
and weeps at the holiness of his own victim'.[1] But it is surely not
true that, as he goes on to assert, such a figure could scarcely occur
outside the Spain of the Baroque period. Italian *novelle* and memoirs
of the time are full of persons of this sort and in Webster's *Duchess
of Malfi* we have, in the character of Bosola, an even more extreme
development of the same spirit. Yet we may agree that Alemán's
masterpiece is the first Spanish example of the new style. If it
lacks the conceits of full Baroque, it has the short, hard sentences,

---

[1] I am greatly indebted to Dr Enrique Moreno for allowing me to read in MS. his
admirable study of *Guzmán de Alfarache*. It is a book that should be read not only by
Spanish scholars, but by everyone interested in the history and literature of this period.

the tight elliptic phrases—signs of a contracting age—that are equally characteristic of that period.

Guzmán de Alfarache set up a vogue for picaresque novels: within the next half-century a dozen or more came out. They all kept to the same form—a narrative with a moral commentary attached— though in most cases the story was the real thing and the commentary put in because it was the custom. The best of them, Vicente Espinel's *Vida del escudero Marcos de Obregón* (1618), is the least characteristic. Espinel was a poet and musician from Ronda and his book is really an account of his own life and adventures, heightened and romanticized a little. It does not deal with low life and is not painful. I shall have something to say of Quevedo's *Buscón* when we come to Quevedo.

The picaresque form had its root in social conditions. The ruin of the middle-income classes by inflation, the need so many people had of living by their wits, the hardships of the writer's life which threw him into low company were the things that prompted it. On the reader's side there was a new curiosity about the world and a sentimental attitude to crime. After all it was sin that gave drama to life in the seventeenth century: the day of fate and destiny was over. But there is one other aspect we should notice. These novels depict as a rule a child growing up under sordid conditions and making his way through the world where everything is hostile and dangerous. He has no arms but his mother wit: by using it he becomes a criminal, but essentially he is innocent and well-intentioned and it is the wickedness of the world that corrupts him. Conversion and submission to the Church will enable him at the end of the book to be saved, but meanwhile what holds the attention is the contrast between the solitary, struggling individual and the hostile world around him. I believe that the awareness of this contrast is one of the things most deeply ingrained in the Spanish character. The Spanish soul is a border castle, adapted for defence and offence in a hostile land: *soberbia*, or pride, and an eternal suspiciousness are its most ingrained qualities, together with a distrust of any but its own skill or weapons. But what the garrison feels all the time is loneliness.

CHAPTER VIII

CERVANTES

A CURIOUS thing about Spanish literature is that it travels badly. Whatever the reason may be, few Spanish books have gained general currency beyond their language frontiers. The one exception to this is Cervantes, who has been translated into more than fifty different languages and into English alone some eight or nine times. So well known is his great book in this country that I shall take a certain familiarity for granted and confine myself to aspects that seem less obvious than others. Otherwise I should merely be repeating what other writers with far greater authority than myself have already said.

Let us begin by seeing what sort of a man Miguel de Cervantes was. Born in 1547 near Madrid, the son of an apothecary surgeon with seven children, he had an early introduction to poverty with its harsh routine of pawnshop, money-lender and prison. In spite of this, however, he was able to obtain a fair education—first, it is thought, at Seville and then at the city school of Madrid. Here his master was one of the last of the old humanists and followers of Erasmus; we hear of the young man, just twenty-one, writing a poem which this master singled out for praise and have reason for thinking that his influence was an important one.

A desire to see the world now took him to Italy. At Naples he joined a Spanish regiment as a private soldier and fought in the great sea battle of Lepanto, where he lost the use of his left hand. Other engagements followed. Then, on his way back to Spain with letters recommending his promotion, he was captured by the Moors and taken to Algiers. Here he spent five years as a slave. When at length he was ransomed, his daring in planning escapes and in taking the blame for them when they failed had given him the sort of reputation reserved in our day for the heroes of the Resistance.

Back in Spain at the age of thirty-three, he suffered the common

175

experience of soldiers in peace time: his war services had been forgotten and no one was interested in his Moorish exploits. He decided to take up literature. With his usual energy he began at once to write a pastoral novel, a number of comedies for the Madrid stage and a quantity of verses. Let us consider these for a moment. Cervantes thought of literature as most great writers have done at the commencement of their careers—as something that expresses ideal states and desires rather than experiences. Moreover, this was the general opinion of that time in literary circles: the current was running strongly against realism. Writing a pastoral novel was the obvious and natural thing for a young man to do, especially if he was in love, and though we cannot read *La Galatea* today, we can see that he learned some of the balance and mellowness of his later style from it. His poetry is another matter. To the end of his life Cervantes wished more than anything else in the world to be recognized as a poet. He never was, and his steady output of fluent verses did little to help his literary reputation.

There was then the drama. This belonged to a category that had less prestige, because it was popular. But Cervantes had been deeply interested in it since he had watched the primitive performances of Lope de Rueda as a boy. Here again, however, 'literature' interfered. The Spanish drama was a new art waiting to be born: it needed a man who should combine a quick responsiveness to popular taste with a romantic imagination and some faculty for poetry to set it on its proper course. But Cervantes brought only a little Senecan rhetoric and a novelist's tempo: if his comedies held the stage, that was merely because, until Lope de Vega came along a few years later, there was nothing better to choose from.[1] The real trouble, however, about all these literary ventures was that they brought in no money. The reign of Philip II was a reign in which writers starved. Cervantes therefore gave up authorship towards 1585 and took a job at Seville, first as a commissary for requisitioning corn and oil for the Government and then as a tax collector. This move was the easier because his private life had

---

[1] Cervantes' *Entremeses*, or interludes, continuing the tradition of Lope de Rueda's *pasos*, are, however, brilliant. He wrote them late in life, after 1600.

just taken a new turn: a love affair which had given him an illegitimate daughter had been succeeded by a marriage to a girl of nineteen, who owned a house and a few acres of land not far from Madrid. But the marriage proved to be a failure and after a few months the couple separated. To all intents and purposes Cervantes, who seems to have had little power of pleasing women, was once more a bachelor.

The next twenty years find him leading a roving, harassed, impecunious life, mostly in Andalusia. Here, on long mule-back journeys, on the benches of crowded posadas, haggling over prices, he wore out the best years of his middle age. There were frequent money difficulties, for he was not paid regularly: there were lawsuits, for he was rash and unbusinesslike, and above all there was the terrible question of a deficit, in which, owing to a bank failure and to the fecklessness he may have inherited from a Micawberish father, he lost a large sum of Government money that had been entrusted to him. This led to a period of acute poverty and to at least one spell of imprisonment. One may judge his social position from the fact that, though his headquarters during most of this time was Seville, he does not seem to have known any of the distinguished group of writers and poets who lived there. Yet he never gave up. Elderly, shabby, obscure, disreputable, pursued by debts, with only a noisy tenement room to work in, he was still, in whatever spare time he could find, carrying on his unescapable vocation of literature. We owe *Don Quixote*, as we owe Joyce's *Ulysses*, to its author's having been a man of quite extraordinary persistence and optimism.

For Cervantes had never entirely stopped writing. The things he found it easiest to do were verse plays, and all through the nineties he was turning out *comedias* for the theatre at Seville. But Lope de Vega's new technique was making his pieces look stilted and old-fashioned. With more leisure now that he had lost his job, he took up again the art of novel writing and began to compose those short stories which he published later under the title of *Exemplary Novels*. They were of different sorts, some being romances in the Italian style, others pictures of criminal life at Seville, others again sketches of extraordinary events or characters, taken from actual life. One of the subjects that most interested him was madness. This was a taste of the time: the liking for calm and ideal scenes and generalized characters was giving place to a craving for the bizarre and extraordinary. The idea came to him—actually he seems to have taken it from an *entremés*, or one-act play—to write a short story about an amusing madman who imagined himself to be a knight-errant, carrying on the feats recorded in the novels of Chivalry, The date is thought to have been 1597, when Cervantes was fifty: the place, as he half-tells us himself, a prison—either that of Argamasilla de Alba or of Seville—and the title *Don Quixote de la Mancha*. Its first part, for it grew into a long book, came out in 1605.

Never, perhaps, before or since has a writer had such an extraordinary stroke of luck. The vein Cervantes had hit on was not only a wonderfully rich and productive one, leading to unexpected depths and possibilities, but it was one which he himself was peculiarly fitted to explore. So from the first chapter, with its plain and balanced portrait of the hero, we get a feeling of assurance: in the second, with Don Quixote's arrival at the inn and mistaking it for a castle and coming out with one of his magniloquent speeches, we begin to have some idea of the delicious consequences that could be drawn from his madness. But Cervantes had not yet hit on the device that would enable him to realize the full possibilities of his theme. The knight alone was not a sufficiently strong thread on which to string the incidents. It took a few chapters for him to discover this: then, bringing his hero home, he sent him out again with Sancho Panza. After that there are no more hesitations: master and man by their wonderful powers of conversation are sufficient to sustain the interest. It is this duality of heroes that turns what would otherwise be a short entertaining story into a long and very great book.

Don Quixote was conceived in prison at a low-water mark in Cervantes' life and he tells us that in writing it he 'gave play to his melancholy and disgruntled feelings'. Something more then than a skit on the novels of Chivalry must have been intended. I think, therefore, that we ought to take note of the fact that the famous knight had many features in common with his creator. We learn, for example, that Don Quixote was of the same age as Cervantes when he set out on his adventures and that he had the same physical appearance: we read of his wits being dry and sterile and his head turned by too much reading, just as we are told in the preface that his author's were. Moreover, he was the incorrigible optimist and idealist who set out to reform the world by force of arms and instead was beaten by it. Must not this, or something like it, have been Cervantes' view of his own history? It is true that these similarities are accompanied by even greater dissimilarities. But if the writer was in some sense 'putting himself' into his hero, that is precisely what we should expect. When novelists seek to create characters who will represent the deepest things in themselves, they start by delineating something very different. It is by wearing masks that one obtains freedom of self-expression. I suggest, therefore, that one of the sources of Don Quixote's power to move us comes from his being a projection of a discarded part of Cervantes himself: that is to say, of the noble intentions and failure of his life. It is for this reason that the irony in this most ironical of books has often the deep and searching quality of self-irony. It accounts too for that curious animosity against his hero which, as Sr Madariaga has pointed out, often seems to harden Cervantes' pen. When he thought of the harm his generous illusions had done him, he felt bitterly and took it out on the figure who represented them. But he was not the kind of man to remain embittered for long: his temperament was too buoyant, besides which the zest of such triumphant creation naturally made him well disposed to the most successful of his characters. The result is an ambivalence of attitude that runs through the book and adds to its complexity. Among other things it helps to determine what sort of life Don Quixote is to be allowed at each moment—whether the daemonic vitality of the puppet (that sure sign of his projection from great depths) or the wise and mature reflections that come direct from Cervantes' experience and reading. That is to say, in so far as Cervantes intended the figure of Don Quixote to stand for anything, it was quite simply for the man who ruins himself and others by his romantic and generous illusions and by his over-confidence in the goodness of human nature. If this conception is somewhat deepened in the second part, we must at least be careful not to read into the text, as some people have done, a political or social allegory on the Spain of Philip II.

But let us look at the book itself and forget the writer. We see then the knight and his squire wandering across Spain in search of adventures, the road they take picked out for them by the whim of Rozinante, the only horse in literature to have a character. As they go they talk—never was there book so full of discussion and argument—yet their conversation does not, as in most novels, appear to further the progress of the plot, but is concentrated round the great fantastical theme of knight-errantry. We watch the fluctuations of Don Quixote's far from robust faith, the wonderful crop of rationalizations by which he defends and preserves it, the effects of all this on Sancho, the constantly shifting relations of the pair to one another, and last, the gradual weakening of the knight's belief in himself, with his death when it fails and returns him to the empty state of sanity. This rake's progress of the believing man, passing from the wealth of total conviction to the bankruptcy of utter scepticism, with its deep pathos and sadness, has been so well brought out and analysed in Sr Madariaga's brilliant study that I shall not attempt to recapitulate it.[1] But *Don Quixote* is a complex and even a baffling book, presenting many different facets. Let us therefore try and approach it from some other angles.

We spoke just now of the felicity of the general theme. One of its merits is the way in which, in every incident that comes along, it stimulates the reader's interest. It does this by providing a series of fixed contrasts that set up between them a tension. For example, there is the contrast between the actual situation and what it appears to be to Don Quixote: there is that between his noble and exalted way of feeling and Sancho's peasant shrewdness and self-interest: and, if one likes, that between the knight's wise and sane ratiocinations and his violent fantasies whenever the subject of Chivalry enters his head. Every situation that turns up brings at least two of these into play and the reader is kept in suspense until he knows precisely how it will be decided. By this means the weakness inherent in the picaresque form—a chain of events loosely strung

[1] *Don Quixote: an Introductory Essay in Psychology*, by Salvador de Madariaga (1934).

together—is overcome and the greatest concentration brought to bear on each incident. Note too—a stylistic contrast—that this madness of the principal character has a language of its own: the archaic magniloquence of the books of Chivalry provides a sort of upper floor of pomp and imagery standing above the ordinary idiom of the book. This was a great discovery, made possible by the example of Ariosto in *Orlando Furioso*. For one feels not only the delicious irony of the knight-errantly speeches, but also the beauty of a stately feudal language rising out of the plain and habitable level of Cervantes' prose.

The point about which everything in the book revolves is of course Don Quixote's madness. Among other things it raises— and not simply in the obvious way—the question of the nature of Truth. At first we may say to ourselves that there is no real problem here: the Knight of the Doleful Countenance is mad, and that's that. But presently it dawns on us that his madness is confined to one thing—the belief, not itself irrational by the standards of that age, that the books of Chivalry were true histories. Once this is granted, it was no more mad for him to attempt to revive the profession of knight-errantry than it was for a monk to imitate the Fathers of the desert. Now the innkeeper, who was perfectly sane, also believed in the truth of the books of Chivalry, though since the things described in them had never fallen within his experience, he drew the (purely empirical) deduction that they had ceased to take place. What caused the two men to disagree was not therefore any greater degree of rationality on one side than on the other, but simply a difference of propensity or inclination. Don Quixote had a strong desire to play a noble and heroic part in life —to right wrongs and assist the unfortunate and by so doing become famous—whereas the innkeeper was content to take the world as he found it so long as he could go on cheating it. The knight's madness is thus the direct consequence of his nobility of character whilst the innkeeper's sanity is due to his being common-place.

We can explain Sancho's mixture of belief and disbelief in precisely the same way. When he is in the believing mood, it is because he is under the double influence of Don Quixote's superior rhetoric and of his own greed and ambition; and when he is sceptical it is because he lacks his master's sense of a high vocation as well as his years of browsing among the books of Chivalry. For once one grants the historical character of those books, the feats of enchanters in changing the appearance of things in order to thwart knights-errant become just as credible as those of the devils and witches in which, in theory at least, everyone believed. It is thus inexact to speak of Don Quixote as lacking in shrewdness or being gullible by nature. His delusion is the result of a long secretly sustained wish to rise above the dullness of his monotonous life, have adventures and distinguish himself. But Cervantes, in presenting to us his epistemological riddle, has gone further. For not only has he made his knight nobler and, for all his craving for renown, more disinterested than any of the persons who are shown to us as sane, but he has made him more intelligent. A good example of this will be found in those delicious passages where Don Quixote pours out a flood of subtle and convincing arguments to support a view that anyone can see is erroneous. His mind works more lucidly when it has a worse case to defend. If we stop to think a moment, we may well wonder where the author is taking us.

As we have said, the making of the novel lies in its having two contrasted heroes or principal characters—Don Quixote and Sancho. The best parts, those passages one reads again and again with never failing delight, are the conversations between them. One represents altruism, the other self-interest: one wisdom and learning, the other the practical intelligence: one is mad and the other is sane. And yet—this is an example of the subtle quality of Cervantes' observation—as the book progresses, they are constantly affecting and even invading one another. The simple contrast between them with which it started breaks down and we get what Sr Madariaga has called the sanchification of Don Quixote and the quixotification of Sancho. This leads to moments in which they almost appear to have changed places.

Such, it might be said, are the ordinary effects of living together. But the spell, the ideology, that binds them is important too. Whether one thinks of them as two partners of a firm dealing in futures, or as two members of a sect who must gather the rewards of their faith in this world (glory pure and simple for the one, wealth and power for the other) they march forward side by side, talking and arguing all the time, with their eyes fixed on the distance. This at least is the position in the second part, where Sancho's self-importance swells out till at moments he feels himself the equal, or superior even, of his master. It is then that one comes across those touches of mutual jealousy and rivalry—Don Quixote showing peevishness when Sancho is given his island, Sancho discovering for the first time the Quixotic pleasures of fame and glory—that make this book such a continually unfolding revelation of human nature. Once more one sees what treasures of subtlety and irony a theme based on simple contrasts can throw into the lap of a discerning novelist.

But perhaps the relationship between the pair may best after all be compared to that most intimate of partnerships, marriage. The long dialogue between them that takes up the principal part of the book suggests, in a more ceremonious key, the familiar dialogue of married couples. It is made up of the same inconclusive wranglings, the same recriminations and *tu quoques*, the same fixed recollections and examples dragged out again and again from the past to clinch an argument. Thus the fact that Sancho was tossed in a blanket early in their travels and that his master failed to rescue him and, to conceal his impotence, put the whole thing down to the work of enchanters, is brought up by the squire every time the question of enchantments is raised in the course of the book. It is one of the two rocks upon which his unbelief, when he is in the unbelieving mood, is founded. Just as in married life, every disagreement leads back to some classic precedent or 'You said so-and-so'.

And this has the effect of lacing together in an extraordinary way the various incidents. One of the most admirable things about this novel, which at first sight seems to be composed of a number of separate episodes, strung together like beads on a thread, is that few things in it are really finished with when they have occurred. On the contrary, they are taken up into the minds of the two protagonists and reappear later on as a part of their argument. This not only gives the plot a greater unity, but it makes it more subtle. Every striking event has, as it were, a succession of echoes and it is these echoes that make the book what it is. It would be hard to find a novel in which the psychological repercussions of happenings had a greater importance.

We have suggested that the relations of the knight to his squire have some resemblance to those of a married couple. And this comparison has perhaps more to it than might appear at first sight. In their peripatetic ménage, Don Quixote plays the part of the unmitigated male and Sancho that of the semi-dependent female. Hence the long story of Sancho's fidelities and infidelities, which is one of the most revealing things in the book. How true to life, too, it is that, as the spiritual potency of the male declines, the female should rise and spread herself and dominate! Through almost the whole of the second part it is Sancho who is the leading figure, and in the last chapters we see him, in spite of his touching devotion to his master, getting ready for a prosperous widowhood. The knight dies as all men die, when—sane, empty, deflated—he has fulfilled his role of impregnator. In this capacity one might say that Sancho symbolizes the passive and feminine world, which requires heroes and men of ideas to fertilize it.

But to return to the text—for the temptation to allegorical interpretation must be resisted—let us note how all the interest is deliberately concentrated upon these two. The outer world, in the form of innkeepers, muleteers, duchesses, distressed damsels and so forth, is brought in only to provide incentives, to put them through their paces.[1] In itself it is of no consequence: what alone matters is the performance of the preposterous couple and the discussion on the nature of reality and on the means of apprehending it that their mishaps invariably give rise to. It is not of course a purely philosophic discussion: rather it is a marvellous display of human prejudices, delusions, doubts, sagacity, stupidity, self-deception,

---

[1] Cervantes tells us that he often found the boredom of keeping the light focused on his two heroes intolerable. For this reason he introduced pastoral episodes, where they took a back seat. But his readers objected to this. In the second part, therefore, he allowed the plot gradually to lose all pretence of naturalness and to become a machine for producing situations that would extract every drop of humorous reaction from the pair. If this injures the unity of tone of the book, as the practical joking of the Duke and Duchess certainly does, it gives us in exchange a rich and complex development of the two principal characters such as the more cumbersome plot evolution of the naturalistic novel can rarely furnish.

shrewdness, arranged by a master of ironic perception to delight us by its contradictions and incompatibilities. We watch the give and take with all the amused superiority and detachment of people who see through the disputants' motives and know the real answers. And then, with a shock of surprise, we realize that, even though these particular answers may be known to us, we are looking on at a puppet show in which the puppets represent ourselves and that it is our own faith and doubt and certainty and ignorance that are being shown to us.

That is why we can speak of the profundity of this book: the *gracia* of some particular remark by Don Quixote or Sancho sets up a pulse of delight that goes echoing through our minds and drawing out our thoughts towards their frontiers. We scarcely need to ask how far the author intended this. It is in the nature of poets to say more than they know and Cervantes was carried by the current of the theme he had discovered far out of his depth. How could he have supposed that, in revealing the psychological mechanism of one particular faith, it was necessarily faith in general and even the possibility of knowledge that he was questioning? His book is one that will be reinterpreted by every age because it is continually suggesting very much more than it says.

And yet we cannot escape from this question of intention so easily. Here we have a writer, who in all his other works seems so limited in imagination, producing effects of a subtlety that make most other novelists appear crude. The natural properties of the theme are not in themselves enough to account for it: only an artist of abnormal fineness of perception could have made use of its powers of suggestion as he has done. But this seems to demand an illustration. I will take the adventure of Montesinos' Cave, which is one of the high-water marks of the book.

Montesinos is a knight who figures in a number of Spanish ballads that deal with the Carolingian legends. The most famous of these shows him following the blood-stained trail of his friend and cousin, the paladin Durandarte, as he flees from the field of Roncesvalles. After crossing the greater part of France at the gallop, he comes up with him near Paris. The paladin is lying mortally wounded *debajo una verde haya*, under a green beech tree, and with his last breath adjures him to cut out his heart with his dagger and to carry it to his lady Belerma, whom he had served for seven years without success. Montesinos does this, Belerma weeps tears of pure blood and faints—*vencida de un gran desmayo*.

The absurdity of the story and its great popularity had some time before tempted Góngora to write a parody of it. A cave by the ruined castle of Rocafrida in La Mancha was known as Montesinos' Cave. What could be more natural than that Cervantes should lead his hero to the place? And so in chapter XXII of the second part he does. The knight arrives, accompanied by Sancho and another person, and after an invocation of exquisite absurdity to Dulcinea (it suggests a parody of one to the Virgin) is lowered on a rope down the shaft and at the end of half an hour is pulled up again unconscious. His companions revive him, he sits up and asks for food. As soon as he has eaten he describes his experiences.

These really amount—as we can see, but he could not—to his having had an extraordinary dream. On reaching the bottom of the cave, so he tells us, he swooned and then, opening his eyes, found himself in a green meadow, at the end of which stood a castle whose walls seemed to be made of transparent crystal. As he looked at it, its gates opened and out of them came a venerable old man, clad in a long mulberry gown with a white beard that fell below his waist and—an absurd touch—a rosary whose every tenth bead was as large as a 'middle-sized ostrich egg'. Greeting Don Quixote by name, he told him that he and those who dwelt in these enchanted solitudes had long been awaiting his arrival, for it was to his invincible heart and prodigious spirit that the task of delivering them had been reserved. And he informed him that he was Montesinos.

A conversation followed in which Don Quixote questioned him about the events described in the ballad and Montesinos replied, correcting the text in one instance: in removing his cousin's heart from his body, he said, he had used a fine poignard and not a dagger. They then entered the palace and in a hall paved with alabaster came to a magnificent tomb. On the top of it lay the figure of a man made, not of bronze or marble, but of flesh and bone. 'This', declared Montesinos, 'is my friend Durandarte, flower and mirror of all the valiant knights and lovers of his day and kept here by the enchanter Merlin.' And he went on to relate once more the scene of his death, giving, as guides do, certain prosaic details, such as that his heart weighed at least two pounds. On this a surprising thing occurred: Durandarte in a loud voice, as if mechanically repeating a part, began to recite the actual words attributed to him by the ballad. On which his cousin knelt down and with streaming eyes assured him that his commands had been carried out, that his heart, carefully salted to preserve it, had been carried to his lady Belerma and that they all with their squires and attendants were waiting to be released from their enchantment. 'And now', he continued, 'I have news to tell you, for here you see that doughty Knight, Don Quixote de la Mancha, of whom so many things have been foretold, who has revived with greater glory than ever the forgotten order of knights-errant and by whose strength and valour it may well be that we shall be delivered from our enchantment.' To which Durandarte in a hollow voice replied, 'And even if this were not so, O Cousin, even if this were not so, patience, I say, and shuffle the cards.' And turning over, he relapsed into his former silence.

We are now shown in charade the last scene mentioned in the ballads—the procession of Belerma and her maidens, bearing Durandarte's heart and singing dirges. Their dress is strange and antiquated, for they wear black robes and white turbans, and Don Quixote with his matter-of-fact eye notes that Belerma is not the great beauty he had expected, but that she has a yellow colouring and lines under her eyes. Reading his thoughts, Montesinos explains that this is due, not, as might be supposed, to her montly periods—for it is many years since she last had them—but to her great grief. Otherwise one would see that even Dulcinea del Toboso scarcely equalled her in beauty.

After the tension caused by this *gaffe* has subsided—for Don Quixote was committed by his vows to maintaining in single combat that his lady excelled all other women in beauty—another dream charade begins. Dulcinea and her two maidens, dressed as common village girls, appear leaping and capering through the meadow like goats. This is a recollection of an incident that had occurred a few days previously, when Don Quixote and his squire had visited Toboso. Sancho, to conceal a previous deception of his, had pointed out three ugly village girls whom they had met riding on donkeys as being Dulcinea and her maidens, and had described their princess-like beauty and apparel. When the knight had protested that he saw only village girls, Sancho had assured him that that must be because he had been put under an enchantment. Rather unwillingly Don Quixote had accepted this explanation. It is for this reason that they appear in his dream in this form. They caper past, and Dulcinea turns her back rudely when he speaks to her. But now a very odd thing happens. No sooner have they gone than one of the maidens returns and approaches him. On behalf of her mistress she asks for a small loan—six *reals*, as security for which she offers a dimity petticoat. Don Quixote gives her all he has—four: the girl, instead of a curtsey, leaps six feet in the air and goes off. On this Montesinos offers some plausible reasons for their enchantment and the knight's account of his dream ends. During the three days and nights he has spent underground, he has seen and learned, he says, an infinite number of marvels, but he postpones their description to another occasion.

Let us now look at this adventure of the Cave a little more closely. At first sight it may seem to be just one more mock-heroic episode in the style of Ariosto. A chapter from a Grail-legend story, which, without losing all its poetic strangeness and beauty, has been brought down to earth and made ridiculous by a number of small touches. But how is it that these touches are given us by, of all people, Don Quixote? One explanation is that we have here the author's satirical humour breaking out through the mouth of his hero and making him parody himself. But this surely is to neglect Cervantes' perfectly clear statement that he was giving us Don Quixote's vision or dream. And in fact a dream atmosphere of wonderful verisimilitude envelops the whole chapter and gives to these absurd touches—which, if they were intrusions of the author's wit, would surely strike a false note—their peculiarly subtle flavour. Since this is, as we already know, a psychological novel, we must expect this dream to throw some new light upon Don Quixote's character. Let us see if it does so.

The magic castle, the enchanted Montesinos and his speech of welcome require no special interpretation: they are part of the knight's romantic fantasy and of his boundless self-esteem, and therefore already familiar to us. But note the realistic touches: the correction over the dagger, the weight of the heart, the speculation upon the yellowness of Belerma's skin, and so forth. These affect us not merely by their sudden reduction of high romance to the crudest reality: their comedy is finer than that, for it consists in their being indications of a fundamental dryness and prosaicness in the mind of this man who has set himself up against the prosaic scheme of things. It is a quality we have noted in him before, but which in the freer atmosphere of the dream takes on a greater latitude.

There is then that disconcerting remark of the recumbent Durandarte. Not only does he express doubt about the ability of Don Quixote to release him from his enchantment, but he puts his doubt into a popular proverb 'Patience and shuffle the cards', which startles us by its cynical inappropriateness. We are reminded of some of the remarks of the Red Queen in *Alice in Wonderland*.[1]

The incident of Dulcinea's maid asking for the loan of a few shillings is another example of the same enigmatic inconsequence. There is of course an insinuation under it. Many of the fair ladies of Madrid and Seville must have been in the habit of treating elderly gallants in just this way—only of course the 'loans' they asked for would have been considerably larger. But the incident has been caught up and absorbed into the dream, so that the insinuation is felt to be, not a satirical stroke of the author's, but a subversive whisper that has come from some small voice in Don Quixote himself. A whisper reminding the dreamer that, if any Dulcinea is ready to listen to his advances, it will be because she is mercenary.

We get then, through the device of a dream, an oblique yet penetrating glimpse into the deeper layer of Don Quixote's mind. We see that his knight-errantly fantasy, even in its moment of

---

[1] Durandarte had reasons that were not known to Cervantes for taking a cynical view of knight-errantry. He owed his own existence to a misunderstanding about Durendal, the name given in the French *Chansons de geste* to Roland's sword, which some Spanish jongleur had taken to be a person.

triumph, when freed by sleep from all the trammels of reality, has not achieved the conquest of every portion of his mind. There is a dry matter-of-factness that contrasts oddly with it and which one guesses may originally have led him, by its very dullness, to take this escape. And there is also the voice of common sense and reason, living on like a fifth column within him, disguised and in hiding, yet ready to seize every suitable opportunity for sabotage. One does not need to have read modern books of psychology to recognize the symptoms as they show themselves in the dream language, or the delicate exactness with which Cervantes has recorded their appearance.

There remains the question, how could a Spanish writer of the seventeenth century have such an understanding of the secret processes of the mind? The answer is, no doubt, that the instinct of a writer of genius may lead him a long way if he is prepared to trust himself to it freely. But a certain social climate is required if he is to be given the encouragement to do this. I believe that this climate existed in the peculiar kind of wit or humour for which Seville, and indeed most of Andalusia, is famous, and which is known as *gracia*. It is the humour of an imaginative people given over to the charms of social life in an easy climate, with the spectator's attitude to what goes on round them and little sense of responsibility. Description being impossible, I will only say that one of its features is a disinterested delight in the absurd (English and French humour have generally some moral implications), and another, an oriental love of double meanings, of suggestion rather than statement, of ambiguity and subtlety used for their own sake. And all expressed in that tone of slyness and ironic reserve known as *discreción*. It was on this humour, if I am right, that Cervantes drew what drafts he needed for his many-storied novel, just as Shakespeare drew many elements in his style from the witty jargon of courtiers, so that what to our minds seem far-reaching innuendoes, full of metaphysical or psychological import, were often in their original intention mere humorous contrasts and whimsicalities, intended for immediate delight yet all the more agreeable to their readers because they contained unexplored possibilities of interpretation. To an author who chose his theme well, this Andalusian *gracia* gave an unusual opportunity for working his conscious and unconscious faculties in harness, and on, as it were, two levels. Not in vain, we may say, had Cervantes spent so many years beside what an earlier poet had called *las aguas del rio sotil Sevillano*, 'the waters of the subtle Sevillian river'.

We have seen that *Don Quixote* grew out of Cervantes' long and painful experiences of frustration and failure. It thus deals with one of the classic themes of Spanish literature—disillusion. Spaniards, who commonly set their hopes too high and expect a miracle to fulfil them, often come to feel themselves deceived by life. Cervantes had also started off in a very optimistic frame of mind, but it had become too much a part of his nature to be given up. It will be remembered that we spoke of his having been educated by a schoolmaster who had Erasmist leanings. Now there is very much in his novel that calls up the humanistic spirit of Charles V's reign. There is the Renaissance notion of the perfection of Nature and of the supremacy of Reason: there is the optimistic attitude to life and the commonsense morality, without a trace of mysticism. Most significant of all is the absence of any sign of belief in original sin. This dogma, which expressed in theological terms the sense that there is a sort of inertia limiting the growth of reason and virtue in human beings, had lain dormant through the Middle Ages to burst up with terrifying force among the Lutherans and Calvinists. From them it had spread to Spain, carried in a modified form by the Jesuits. But in Cervantes we do not come across any trace of it. He remained what one might call a natural Liberal, living on in an age when the last spark of the Liberal spirit was dead. It is for this reason that he seems to have been regarded by his contemporaries as a man of old-fashioned views, half pedant and half, as we should say, Victorian, writing in a smooth, balanced style that had dated. And that, of course, is precisely one of the reasons why he is alive to us. We only partly understand the Southern Baroque writers, though we find them exciting. They lived in a tight, guilt-ridden world, turned in on itself and alternating between a superficial hedonism and a profound pessimism. Although in some respects it was like our own, it differed by having a certain stifling feeling in its air that was the result of the steady decrease of intellectual liberty. But Erasmus joins hands across a gulf with the eighteenth and nineteenth centuries. It is the background of his reasonableness and moderation that makes Cervantes a universal writer, as Calderon and Quevedo for all their genius could never be. Indeed it was in the countries north of the Pyrenees that his greatness was first recognized at a time when south of them his novel was still regarded as light literature.

One qualification: *Don Quixote*, as we have seen, came into the world like Montaigne's *Essays*, on the last wave of humanistic feeling and values. Yet it has seventeenth-century features. The hero himself belongs to the violent dream-world of Baroque hagiography. He is first cousin to the ecstatic saints of Zurbarán or Ribera, though painted without chiaroscuro and in comic guise. He is martyred under our eyes and by our laughter. The whole tendency of the book too, with its epistemological queries and its psychological subtleties, proclaims a more complex age than that of the Renaissance. We should remember this in speaking of Cervantes' dependence on the past.

Cervantes' powers of comic invention are bound up with his skill in using language to convey fine shades of feeling. One example of this is the tone of his narrative passages. He is the first prose-writer, I think, to understand that, in telling a story, one must gain the attention and confidence of the reader by one's manner. How he does this is more easily felt than described. But open *Don Quixote* almost anywhere and one will see how by the mere intonation, as it were, of his sentences he conveys a deliberation and assurance, a sense of being completely at ease with his audience that one does not find in earlier writers. Sometimes this is carried too far for modern taste, which does not like any trace of showmanship in its literary entertainers. But generally speaking the zest and enjoyment of the man, and his assumption that you are going to enjoy yourself too, give one an appetite to go on reading him. Then he is a master—and what a great one!—of the art of dialogue. It was only to be expected that he should have done this well, because one of the particular pleasures to be derived from his book comes from the continual victories we witness of words over facts. Some new situation arises which we know that Don

Quixote must interpret in accordance with his peculiar fantasy, and we wait to see how he will do it. Then, no sooner has his interpretation been given than the inevitable insurmountable objection is made by Sancho or some other person, and at once the question is how he will get round it. That he always does so, and far better than one could have hoped, and in quite unsuspected ways, is due not only to his ingenuity in argument, supported by the wide range of his mind and reading, but to his remarkable rhetorical powers. The knight, who loses every time he takes to the sword, wins a battle whenever he opens his mouth. But the battle won by Cervantes is greater still, because he must not only take care of his hero's dialectic, but also convey to us, the principal observers, something more, something finer about the unconscious motives of the actors. We are made to be deliciously 'in on' every episode.

Another thing to be particularly noted in Cervantes' style is the confident way in which he places his characters before us and makes them talk or perform some action, so that we really see them all the time and believe in them. There are no extraordinary flashes, no sudden revealing phrases, such as the Baroque writers favoured, but a steady even light. The speed too with which everything happens is just what it should be—an important thing in a novel, for it is this that keeps the attention stretched. In short we have in *Don Quixote* a classic model of novelist's style as it existed down to the nineteenth century. How remarkable an achievement that was will be seen if one looks at any of the novels, *contes* or romances, in any language whatever, before him, and notes the baldness with which they are written.

The English novel owes a great deal to Cervantes. Fielding, Smollett, Scott and Dickens came out of him. For more than two hundred years he has been more read and admired in this country than any other foreign writer. Yet today his stock is low. The ordinary reader of robust appetite may continue to enjoy him, but the intellectual, after a first youthful perusal, leaves him on the shelf. Now there are, I think, a number of reasons for this. In the first place it must be admitted that, like all very well written books, *Don Quixote* loses much of its savour in translation, and also that even in Spanish some parts of it are tedious. Then we are put off by the slapstick, though why we should refuse to accept from Cervantes what we gladly put up with from Charlie Chaplin, I do not know. However, there are some people who maintain that it is the author's evident enjoyment of the knight's drubbings that repels them. This seems to me to be based on too literal a reading: Don Quixote is a symbol before he is a man and his defeats are the defeats of the principle for which he stands. In a book whose subject is right thinking, the author must necessarily take sides with—to use Freudian language—the Reality Principle against the ragings of the Super-Ego. The significant thing about this novel—its claim to be twice over a tragedy—is that it not only shows us the defeat of the man of noble feelings by the second-rate and vulgar, but that it convinces us that that defeat was right.

But the chief reason for the neglect of *Don Quixote* today is, I think, that we allow the too simplified picture that the Victorians had of it, and which is confirmed by our first youthful reading, to stand between us and the original. This is a pity because it is really a book that has more to say to us than it had to them. Its subject is militant—which is as much as to say revolutionary—faith. It explains the psychology of the believing and half-believing man with a subtlety and penetration not approached by any other writer. If one wanted a modern equivalent, one could rename it the adventures of the party man and his fellow traveller. And where do its sympathies lie? The revolutionary is the hero of the book, yet its author has not only made him mad, but has cast doubts on the purity of his motives. Don Quixote may be inspired by a passion for justice, but he is also vain and egoistic and cut off by his obsession from an understanding of human life. The condemnation of his mission is expressed by his niece in the question, 'Would it not be better to stay peacefully at home than to go gadding about the world in search of *pan de trastrigo?*—which Shelton translates 'better bread than is made from wheat'. Yet we never doubt that Cervantes was a man of goodwill: he is emotionally on his knight's side, though he pronounces judgment against him. With all his failings, Don Quixote towers above the other characters as the one great and noble man in the book.

Lastly we may take this book on a metaphysical plane. Although in doing this we are going far beyond the author's intentions, the material for such an interpretation is there and there is pleasure to be got from the queries it raises about human certainties. If we cannot pin down this most elusive of writers to any definite attitude, we may at least say that he contrasts the biological need which man has for faith with the difficulty his intellect has in finding grounds for one. Don Quixote dies when he loses his illusion—a commentary on Baudelaire's *Il faut être ivre*—whilst Sancho, who has no intellect, lives on and flourishes. We may sum up Cervantes' contribution to philosophy by saying that, like Montaigne and Descartes, he set in motion a chain reaction of doubt.

Perhaps we have now reached a point when we can pull all these strands together and say what the author of *Don Quixote* was really like and how his book grew out of him. By temperament a positive, sanguine man with a strong will to live and high ambitions, he was secretly riddled, as one might expect from his early life and parentage, with uncertainty and self-doubt. At Lepanto and still more at Algiers he silenced these doubts by the means that are open in wartime to every man of spirit—that is, by reckless displays of gallantry. But back in Spain this comparatively easy way was no longer feasible. The chasm between what he was and what he wanted to be began to grow wider. A failure in love, a failure in literature, a failure even in the very ordinary job he had taken on, sinking deeper every day into shabbiness and disreputability and seeing round him a family even more disreputable than himself (his sisters had made their living out of rich men, just as his only daughter was soon to do), he yet found late in life the luck, the talent and the courage—for all were required—to face up to his predicament and express his tragic sense of it in a novel. And so we have *Don Quixote*, a book written, as a learned oriental critic has said, with the pen of doubt upon the paper of conviction, a profoundly human book, crude and tedious perhaps at times, but shot through with lights of marvellous subtlety and delicacy, and with this special characteristic—that it generates in the mind of everyone who reads it as it should be read new thoughts and reflections. It has the ambiguity, the faculty for being endlessly interpreted, of myths, so that one might almost say that the author wrote it in collaboration with his readers.

There is one last aspect I would like to touch on. The Russian novelists have accustomed us to expect that a great novel should portray in a broad way the life and character of the country where it was written. This is certainly done by *Don Quixote*. With the exception of the *Canterbury Tales*, there is no English book that conveys half as immediately or abundantly the flavour of England. Its scene of action lies for the most part on the roads and in the roadside inns or *ventas*. Along these roads there passed, generally on mules or asses and invariably at foot-pace, everyone who had any reason for travel, and this was an invitation to Cervantes to bring almost every well-known type or profession into his picture. A few episodes occur in more solitary places, among that inextricable tangle of hills and valleys that is known as the Sierra Morena. But, wherever we are, we feel the Spanish landscape with its treeless plains or poplar-fringed streams or valleys dotted with ilex trees— *toda la espaciosa y triste España*, as Luis de León called it—looking, as it were, over our shoulder. Though never described to us, it is always present.

There are then the two chief actors. I need not say that Sancho, with his strings of proverbs and his ready wit and his shrewdness and his obstinacy, is a national product. Starting off as the type of stage *gracioso*, he develops as the book goes on into the most complete and detailed portrait of a peasant or working man ever painted. (His appearances in the second part and those of his wife Teresa are especially delightful.) The knight too with his gravity and courtesy, and a certain plainness and bareness of mind that tells us that he also has been conditioned by the scenery, is made in the Spanish mould. And where else but in Spain could the friendship that unites master and man be found? In England or France it would, then or at any other time, have been unthinkable. It says worlds for the temper of Spanish society that such mutual loyalty and affection should have been able to transcend the barriers of rank and fortune. This was possible because the innate sense of dignity and self-esteem that are peculiar to Spaniards and to some of the Balkan peoples prevent them from thinking that any profession, however humble, can demean them. Even today, in out-of-the-way places, the servant who has eaten of his master's bread is a member of his family.

But, it will be asked, is not Don Quixote himself, with his delusions and his wisdom, his violence and his courtesy, his egoism and his moral fervour, in some sort the type and symbol of the Spanish character? That is what the Spaniards of today, moved by the insatiable passion for understanding and explaining themselves that has come over them since the turn of the century, have declared, and, so long as we are careful not to attribute this view to Cervantes, I do not see why we should not agree with them. For Don Quixote is the incarnation of the spirit of non-compromise. When the fit is on him, he believes in his own absolute rightness and virtue, and then nothing can deflect him from the course he has chosen. We call his moral passion and inflexibility noble because it appears to override self-interest, though modern psychologists have given a different interpretation of such states of mind. And we notice that whatever he does at such times ends in failure, because it takes no account of reality.

Now most people would agree that something of this sort is to be found among Spaniards. They hold their opinions, not merely obstinately and rigidly, but with a sort of *brio*, as though they held them for the express purpose of challenging other people. That is to say, they are often less interested in the truth of what they are maintaining than in the fact that it is they who are maintaining it. An opinion for them is much more than an estimate of probabilities; it is something you wear on your helmet when you want to give battle, something with which your honour, which is another word for your personality, is associated. You like to display it because you are proud of it, and you cannot compromise on it. Now this state of affairs leads to the Spaniards being a very frank people, but it also puts them in danger of being fanatical. No one who has read Spanish history since the time of the Catholic Kings can doubt that there is a strong tendency to fanaticism in Spanish life. But when they have not been roused and challenged, they display very different characteristics, such as tolerance, kindness, humanity, prudence and Oriental passivity. What, in my opinion, makes *Don Quixote* such a good allegory of the Spanish character is its demonstration of how the visionary, aggressive and fanatical element in Spaniards comes out of and recedes into the wise, patient and pacific one. No better example could be given of the faculty that some great writers have of creating scenes and characters that far transcend in depth and range anything that they may have consciously aimed at.

CHAPTER IX

LOPE DE VEGA AND THE NEW COMEDY

A REACTION against the poetry of the Italian Renaissance, which had been introduced by Garcilaso de la Vega and developed by Herrera, set in about the time of the Spanish Armada. It took the form of a return to Spanish measures. The hendecasyllable did not disappear, but remained the metre for poems of a grave and stately kind, as well as for sonnets. But for other purposes the octosyllables of the *romance* became the fashion. The cause of this change was the strong popular and romantic movement that was making its appearance in the large towns, in defiance of the economic difficulties through which the country was passing. It expressed itself in the new sentimental *romances* that were coming out in bulky collections, and still more in the *comedias*, or verse plays, that were written on the same subjects and very largely in the same metre. All the poets of this age show the influence of this popular romanticism.

Another tendency of the time was that towards *culteranismo*, which was the name given to the search for a more refined and stylized diction, influenced by Latin syntax. This met with a strong resistance from the purists. The names associated with these two schools were, respectively, Góngora and Lope de Vega, and their opposition led to a war of poets, which became more fierce and unrelenting when, in the following century, new writers appeared upon the scene. But there is one thing that all the poets and drama-tists of this generation, whatever school they belonged to, had in common—their insularity. Lope de Vega and Góngora were only fifteen years younger than Cervantes, but they lacked both his humanist background and his acquantance with foreign countries. This meant that they took the Spanish scene for granted and showed no trace of his critical and moral approach to life. If we except Quevedo and Gracián, who both saw further than their

contemporaries, we shall find that the literature of the next
130 years suffers from a steady and progressive contraction of the
horizon. The ostrich mood induced by the Inquisition and the
Jesuits was doing what was required of it.

Let us take Lope de Vega first. Lope Félix de Vega Carpio, to
give his full name, was born in 1562 in Madrid. His father was a
small artisan from Santander, an impulsive, unstable sort of man
who combined erotic susceptibility with great religious fervour
and the habit of writing verse—three things in which his son took
after him. From his earliest years the boy showed extraordinary
precocity: we hear of him dictating verse before the age of five
and writing plays at ten, and it was this no doubt that got him a
good education at the Jesuit college and after that at Alcalá University. But his impulsive temperament was not long in showing
itself: at twelve he ran away from school, walking as far as
Astorga and then returning again: at seventeen he fell violently in
love with the wife of an actor, Elena Osorio, and was exiled for
several years from Madrid for libelling her parents: at twenty-six
he left the girl with whom he had just eloped in order to join the
Armada; and scarcely had he married again after her death than
he fell passionately in love with an actress, Micaela de Luján, who
became his mistress and bore him five children. In all, three major
love affairs, each conducted with the greatest possible amount of
frenzy and passion, many minor ones and two on the whole happy
marriages provide the background to his immensely productive life.
Indeed, when we read the poems he wrote to Micaela de Luján,
his '*Etna de Amor*', or to Marta de Nevares, the love of his old age,
we cannot help being reminded of those French romantic writers
of the nineteenth century for whom being in love was the aim and
crown of existence. But Lope had no theories: he was merely an
extremely impressionable man in whom feeling and action were
one: he neither calculated the pleasure nor counted the cost of
what he did. His attitude to women was really one of emotional
dependence on them: they alone gave the peace of mind and
stability his over-sensitive nature required and satisfied his longing
to pour out his feelings in love and adoration. So in his middle age
we find him settled down with his wife and son in his house in

Madrid to a life of model domesticity. His garden was his chief recreation: it was small, he tells us—had only two trees, ten flowers, two vines, with an orange tree and a musk rose for scent and for fountain two pails of water and two coloured stones. But he worked it with his own hands and it was a chill caught in irrigating it that caused his death.

Lope's later life was enveloped in tragedy. His second wife died in 1613 after a long illness: a few months earlier he had lost his adored son. Before these things happened he had been going through a religious crisis, and now—for he was as passionate in religion as in love—he took holy orders. But he had overestimated his strength. Scarcely had two years passed when he fell violently in love with a married woman and took her to live with him. It turned out badly. She went blind, then mad, and died. Lope was left to face old age with only his young daughter to look after him. When, by what he must have felt to be a fitting retribution, she was carried off from his house by a courtier who enjoyed the king's protection, his one remaining link with life was broken, and he left it. That was in 1635. Almost his last act was the publication of a novel in dialogue form, *La Dorotea*, which dramatized the love affair of his youth with Elena Osorio. He had begun it as a young man and rewrote it as an old one.

Lope de Vega started on his literary career as a poet. His first verses to attract attention were a series of *romances* in the new pastoral manner recounting the loves of Belardo and Filis—in other words, of himself and Elena. We shall have more to say about these productions later on. He began to write for the theatre towards 1587. But for some years he was forbidden to live in Madrid and it was not till well on in the nineties, under the no doubt increasing need for making money, that he turned his attention seriously to play-production. His period of dramatic creation thus corresponds with that of Shakespeare, though it lasted longer. But before speaking of his plays, let us take a brief look at the Spanish stage at this time.

In a previous chapter we described the beginnings of the Spanish drama in more or less learned imitations of Vergil's *Eclogues*. These were written for private performance at the houses of the nobility.

Then in the middle of the century a Sevillian actor-playwright, by name Lope de Rueda, laid the foundations of the popular theatre in Madrid and Seville. On an improvised stage raised on barrels, he gave his loosely strung verse *comedias*, interspersed with short sketches or *pasos*, as he called them, written in prose, in which stock comic characters—the doctor, the servant, the negress, the Basque and so forth—talked and explained themselves in racy Spanish. He had a special gift for portraying clowns, and these *pasos*, little read though they are, are among the more vigorous and racy things in Spanish literature. I warmly recommend them to lovers of the *commedia dell'arte*. Incidentally, in writing them he had invented the *género chico*, or interlude, which under various names was to become a permanent and characteristic feature of the Spanish stage.

The taste created among the people by Lope de Rueda's performances demanded more substantial food. The travelling companies gave place to *cofradías*, or guilds, which to earn money for charitable purposes gave theatrical performances in the principal towns on Sundays and feast days. At first these performances took place in *corrales*, or courtyards—then theatres were built; by 1584 there were three theatres in Madrid. Except that actresses took the female parts, the stage in Spain was very similar to that in England. But what were the plays given in these theatres? In the 'seventies and 'eighties a number of writers, among them Cervantes, had come forward to supply the demand. Full-length *comedias*[1] were written

---

[1] The word *comedia* simply means play. At first there was a distinction between the *comedia*, which dealt with plebeian life, and the *tragedia*, which dealt with high life. But the word *tragedia* soon went out of use. Instead one had the *comedias de capa y espada*, which were plays of ordinary contemporary life, without kings or high personages, and the *comedias de teatro*, *de ruido* or *de cuerpo*, which involved kings, princes, saints or mythological persons. They cost more to produce because they required elaborate scenery. Such were the entertainments in the large towns. But one should not forget that the whole nation was play-mad and that ambulatory actors toured the countryside in ones, twos and fours, giving performances and recitals in villages and farms in exchange for small sums of money or rations of food. The *bululú* (single actor), *ñaque* (pair of actors), *gangarilla* (troupe of four), *cambaleo* (five men and a woman) had taken the place of the *juglar* of medieval times. And above these, serving the small towns, were the travelling companies. The *cambaleo*, though it had lost its name, still existed in 1930, precisely as it had done in the days of Cervantes, and I have myself listened in a remote mountain village to the complaints of an actress who had been compelled to dress in a stable from which its usual occupant, a donkey, had not been removed.

with plots adequate to maintain the interest, the division into acts was made and the principle of polymetry, or writing in a variety of metres, was established. But the models tended to be Plautus and Seneca, the development too slow and uneven and the form altogether too literary, so that the result rarely satisfied the audience. It was left to Lope de Vega to create the exciting, quick-moving, romantic drama that the Spanish people wanted.

In a poem written in 1609 and addressed to the Academy of Madrid, Lope has described how he wrote his plays. He arranged them in three acts. In the first he presented the situation, in the second he complicated the action and not till the middle of the third did he allow anyone to guess the dénouement. For as soon as this was known the audience walked out. As for the verse forms in which the play was written, they should be selected, he said, to suit the subject. *Décimas* for complaints, sonnets for soliloquies, the octosyllables of the *romance* for development, *redondillas* for love, *terza rima* for gravity, octaves when a special effect was needed. The Spaniards had no metre to be compared to the Elizabethan blank verse and their *romance* measure had lost its former dignity: by this fact alone their drama was confined to the narrower limits of rapid action and lyricism.[1]

The style was another problem. Lope found that an equivocal way of speaking and an 'amphibological ambiguity' were popular with the gallery because every member of it thought that he alone was clever enough to understand what was being said. This observation throws a certain light upon the far greater rage for conceits in the Elizabethan drama. But Lope was determined to put the blame for everything in his plays that did not accord with the classical precepts upon the rabble. He wrote, he insisted, to please them, in their style and not according to the rules. Before sitting down to work he locked up Plautus and Terence, that their 'truthful voices' might not disturb him. And this was not because he did not know and admire the classics, but because the rabble and the women, who paid him, demanded that he should write *sin el arte*. And he complained bitterly of their tyranny, which made the

---

[1] Cervantes used blank verse in some of his plays and the effect is so promising that one cannot help regretting that his influence counted for little in the development of the drama.

practice of play-writing so difficult. 'The fury of a seated Spaniard', he declared, 'is not assuaged unless he is shown in the space of two hours everything from Genesis to the Last Judgement.'

What these protestations really mean is that Lope was the victim of the same conflict from which Cervantes had suffered, between the Italian ideals and classical precepts on the one hand and the native genius of his country on the other. It is what one might call the permanent conflict of the Spanish people, spreading far beyond literature into habits of thought and politics. How much can they take in from the rest of Europe without corrupting their inner nature? If they try to absorb too much, the surface will crack and leave the African or Iberian core to set up its separate, independent life. If too little, they will sink into lethargy and a narcissistic isolation. Lope solved his personal problem by writing long poems, which no one reads any longer, in the Italian manner and surrendering in his plays to the dictates of the gallery. He studied their tastes and requirements with deliberate care and, like a thriller writer today, set himself to meet them. The result is that magnificent efflorescence of quickly moving, lively, marvellously varied but rather too slick plays that he called the *flores silvestres*, or wild flowers of his garden.

Lope de Vega is the greatest literary improviser the world has ever seen. The speed with which he wrote was fabulous: some of his plays were thrown off in a couple of days and towards the end of his life he was regularly turning out two a week. The Madrid theatres, which rarely ran a play for more than a few days, could never have enough from him. The total quantity of his production is naturally staggering. By the time he was forty-seven he had written, by his own computation, 483 comedies, and towards the end of his life the number had become 1500. His biographer increases this and we may perhaps feel grateful that a mere five hundred have come down to us. When one adds to these plays a couple of novels and an output of poetry several times larger than that of Spenser[1] and remembers that Lope led an active, agitated life, was involved in business of all kinds, in passionate and complicated

---

[1] Nothing could stop him writing verses. During the voyage of the Spanish Armada he wrote a poem in octaves called *La Hermosura de Angélica* of 11,000 lines.

love affairs, kept at one time two *ménages*, was secretary to four noblemen, had a large correspondence, a great number of friends, travelled frequently, devoted much time to religious exercises, was assiduous in visiting hospitals, took part in the work of the Inquisition, one feels that he was indeed what Cervantes called him, a *monstruo de la naturaleza*, a portent of Nature.

But what are the plays that he produced with such ease and fluency really like? In the first place let us note the firm framework of organization on which his power to improvise depended. Lope took from his predecessors a drama that was clumsy, laboured and of restricted scope. By drawing up simple rules for the plot he taught it to move well and to hold the interest of the audience: then he created useful types (the *gracioso* who parodies the actions of the principal character was his discovery), made the dialogue lively, natural and pointed and, when required, threw over it the veil of poetry. As a result a large number of his plays act well and can be read with pleasure. Then we must note his immense range and variety. Lope was a man who had lived much and got to know every aspect of Spanish life. Although he had little depth of character, he had a sensibility that took in and reacted sympathetically to whatever it came in contact with. Like other Spaniards of his time he was a realist, who saw things as they were without going into them too deeply, but he was also a poet who threw himself with zest into everything he did and delighted in whatever could give delight. He is thus a great life-enhancer. Nothing that is ugly or sordid is allowed to protrude itself in his plays—though one sometimes feels such things in the background—and the pain and suffering that appear are shown in the pure tints of his poetic language and then, for he disliked tragic endings, resolved away in the course of the action.[1] One rises from one of his plays with a renewed sense of the charm and variety of life.

There is then his complete naturalness and lack of class feeling. He can make us feel the savour of peasant life without any of those false touches that embarrass us in Shakespeare. He is equally at

---

[1] The fine tragedy, *La Estrella de Sevilla*, that goes under his name was probably not written by him. But *El Caballero de Olmedo*, written round an old snatch of song and one of his best plays, ends tragically.

home among noblemen or artisans or monks, or in the anarchy or civil wars of the Middle Ages. And when he writes of love—and this, as one would expect, is his favourite subject—he does so without profundity, but with a freshness and enthusiasm that do not exclude a good deal of exact observation. No one, not even Shakespeare, has conveyed the intoxication of first love better. Take for example the wonderful opening of *El Remedio en la Desdicha*, where the lovers' dialogue as they walk in an Andalusian garden has a flowing musical quality that suggests opera. It is not great poetry—for when taken out of its context its colours fade—but it has a lightness and effortless movement that in its place are immensely effective.[1] Reading plays such as this, one is reminded at moments of a Mozart sonata: there is the same lyrical charm and unerring taste and continually varying sensibility, with underlying them a rigid convention which prescribes the limits of experience that must not be passed. Only one must admit that Lope is as a rule much more diffuse and careless.

As we just said, he excelled in plays that deal with peasant life. These are written for the most part in *romance* measure and their songs are modelled on *villancicos*. They have a matt, earthy tone like peasant pottery that makes a pleasant contrast to his lyrical-romantic style, and show a remarkable power, unknown outside Spanish or ancient Greek literature, of conveying the corporate life of a whole community. The classic example of this is *Fuenteove-juna*, which tells the story of a remote Estremaduran village that rose, as so many villages have risen in Spanish history, against its tyrant, the Comendador of the military order of Calatrava, and killed him. The officers failed to find the ringleaders, for the deed had been done by the whole village acting as one, and the king, finding its provocation great, pardoned it. This theme of the tyrannous feudal lord is a favourite one of Lope's and usually it is the king himself who punishes him. But far from expressing a revolutionary feeling, as has sometimes been suggested, it springs from Lope's gratitude to the Monarchy for having put down the extortions of those local tyrants who had flourished in such numbers

[1] Góngora said of Lope's theatrical verse that it was like fritters, that lost their taste as soon as they got cold and did not recover it even if they were put back in the frying-pan.

towards the end of the Middle Ages. Under the stern rule of the Catholic kings and their successors a new class of petty gentry, farmers and artisans, had come to the front and found, if not prosperity, at least liberty and dignity. For such men the Hapsburg kings were what Augustus had been to the Italians of his day, and Lope, who was himself a man of the people, followed Vergil and Horace in celebrating them.

Beside dramas in the sober ballad manner such as *Fuenteovejuna*, Lope wrote a number of comedies of a gayer kind on country life: these pieces, like Gil Vicente's, are rich in what is today called folk-lore and in snatches of country songs and dances. It was typical of the popular nature of his genius that he showed little interest in the moral qualities that differentiate people: his characters are built on the way of life or profession. That is to say, he does not give us misers, hypocrites, envious people, schemers, but peasants, soldiers, nobles, mayors, kings, who, according to the role cast for them, are either good or bad. And even his villains seem to be driven to their bad actions rather by some force outside themselves than by any inherent viciousness. Thus, though so fervent in religion, Lope is one of the most amoral of writers, not out of philosophic conviction but for the simple reason that he was too much in love with life—and perhaps too conscious of his own lapses—to find serious fault with any part of it. Where women are concerned he has, however, a special touchstone of character—their conduct in love. His heroines are nearly always well drawn and by no means mere subjects for provoking masculine ecstasy. If he looked at men with a superficial eye, he studied women attentively and with sympathy, and took note of their individual characteristics. And then, as I have said, whenever he comes to the subject of courtship and love, with their military arts of attack and defence, we feel his great experience. One of the chief attractions of his plays must have lain in the *gracia* of the men's compliments and women's repartees, which gave the audience models they might hope, if they were witty enough, to imitate.

With his quick eye and his keen powers of enjoyment, Lope had a special genius for seizing the life of a particular place, whether a village or town or merely a street. In his *Arenal de Sevilla*, for example, we are shown in the first act the life of the great river port of Seville, with its sailors and soldiers bound for the Indies, its galley slaves and mulattoes and picnic parties and bravos and thieves. It was in all probability a play written expressly for some Sevillian function and it contains one of those panegyrics of the city such as one finds so abundantly in modern *coplas*. Other plays show us other cities, towns and villages with their Midsummer and May Day festivals, their junketings and weddings, quarrels and municipal assemblies—everything, in fact, except their bull-fights, which he did not care for. However fantastic his plots may be, he is always exact in his social and geographical delineation. But the range of Lope de Vega's comedies is far too great for me to attempt, even if I had read enough of them, to give any adequate description. I will sum them up by saying that they constitute a vast panegyric in praise of Spain and the Spanish way of life, and in particular of the principal occupation of Spaniards at that time —love.

Lope de Vega's drama then, taken as a whole, is one of the most prodigious feats ever carried through by a human being. Yet his reputation has suffered because there is no play or group of plays that one can point to in which he has condensed his gifts. Although some are naturally better in various respects than others, the level is surprisingly even. And then there are many things that we are accustomed to expect from great writers which Lope does not give us. Thus, though the range is wide and the treatment varied, noth-ing is ever gone into deeply. The characters are alive, but all that one learns of them could be put in a few words. The plots produce surprises, but, except perhaps in the portrayal of love, no new light is ever thrown on human nature. There is a lack of social criticism, for Lope was a man who accepted even the worst features of his age with enthusiasm, and the dénouement is often puerile. The lyric atmosphere too that envelops so many, though not all, of the plays weakens the dramatic conflict. And though the versifi-cation frequently charms, one feels in too many scenes a thinness and monotony in the style and composition. Lope wrote quickly for audiences who wanted to be excited, flattered and enthralled. What they looked for beyond this was an occasional finely pointed phrase showing perhaps the triumph of the noble and generous instincts over the base ones, and these they would carry home and talk over as they do today the *suerte*, or gesture with the cape, of a bull-fighter. Such audiences would never have tolerated those heavily loaded plays with their complex imagery and introspective ruminations which Shakespeare put on in England. In other words, Spanish drama could never have been anything but what Lope made it—a rapid, improvised affair of action and lyric poetry.

Yet let us remember that Spanish plays, though not written by actors, were founded above everything else on stage sense. The dramatist did not attempt to monopolize the whole work, but left a proper share to the actor, who was expected to build a character out of a part that as a rule had been only lightly characterized. In suitable places there were songs and dances, but nothing else was allowed to impede the movement of the plot. Except in love scenes, the diction was usually terse. And this is why it has been the Spanish stage rather than the English one out of which modern drama has developed.

Lope de Vega was not only a playwright but a poet. The bulk of his non-dramatic work consists in long poems in octaves or other stanzaic measures written in imitation of Tasso and full of classical allusions. But his genius showed itself best in his occasional verse, thrown off under the stimulus of a particular emotion, and this alone need concern us.[1] One may divide it into the poems in Italian metres—that is, hendecasyllables and their derivatives—and those in Spanish. Lope was a master of both kinds, though it is when he is writing in Spanish forms that he has most to give us. The poems in Italian metres have the ease and virtuosity that one expects from him and are full of beauties. What they lack is the density and depth of feeling that mere emotion never gives. The language is thin. Again and again in reading them one is reminded of nineteenth-century romantic poetry—of Shelley, de Musset, Hugo and the Parnassians. This takes away, for a foreign reader, much of their interest. The sonnets, however, are an exception to this, for Lope wrote some of the best sonnets in Spanish. His

---

[1] There is an excellent selection of it in two volumes of the *Clásicos Castellanos* edition, and a shorter one in the *Colección Austral*.

life of moods and passions provided the kind of material that the sonneteer requires, and the form was a check to his exuberance.

The poems in Spanish measures comprise first of all the *romances*. One or two of these, included in plays and intended to be sung, are in the old ballad style. They are admirable, for Lope was a marvellous imitator of traditional poetry. Those, however, which he published in collections are in the sentimental manner of his day —autobiographical poems with pastoral settings, or picturesque poems with Moorish ones. Though not a very serious kind of poetry, a few of them are all the same delightful. One might pick out *Hortelano era Belardo* with its description of his garden at Valencia and its air of spontaneity and gaiety, or else the more artificial lyrics from his novel *La Dorotea*, which have delighted many generations of Spaniards by their brilliant versification and romantic melancholy.

In the middle years of Lope's life there was a period in which he wrote much religious poetry. Some of the more striking of these verses are the *romances* to the Passion collected in his *Rimas Sacras*. They are written with unusual terseness, and one of them, by its painful description of the details of the Crucifixion and by its bare, stark language, recalls the hymns on the martyrs by Prudentius. In Spanish religiosity there has always been a strong vein of this sort. But tenderness came more easily to Lope than cruelty. In *Los Pastores de Belén* there is a series of delicious verses in short metres, some with skilfully woven refrains, to the Virgin and Child. This is the kind of thing—simple, delicate and lyrical, in the spirit of folk poetry yet more refined—that he could do better than anyone else. And this brings us to the verses of Lope's that, rightly or wrongly, we value more than all his brilliantly coloured and torrential rhapsodies. Scattered through his plays (and especially through those he wrote in later life) are *letras para cantar*, or songs, in many measures—*villancicos, romances, seguidillas, cantares* and so forth—that cover the whole field of traditional poetry. Some of them are so close to the popular manner that we suspect that he merely took current songs and changed a word or two: others are clearly original inventions, written in a cultured idiom but in

more or less the same spirit. Here for example is a *maya* or May
poem which is entirely in Lope's style:

En las mañanicas	In the early mornings
del mes de mayo	of the month of May
cantan los ruiseñores,	the nightingales sing,
retumba el campo.	the fields re-echo.
En las mañanicas,	In the early mornings
como son frescas,	when the air is fresh,
cubren ruiseñores	the nightingales fill
las alamedas.	the poplar groves.
Ríense las fuentes,	Then the springs laugh,
tirando perlas	throwing their pearls
a las florecillas	to the little flowers
que están más cerca.	that grow on the edge.
Vístense las plantas	The plants put on
de varias sedas,	their various silks:
que sacar colores	it costs them little
poco les cuesta.	to dress in colours.
Los campos alegran	The fields are gay with
tapetes varios,	varied carpets:
cantan los ruiseñores,	the nightingales sing,
retumba el campo.	the fields re-echo.

Or here again is a *villancico* from one of his best plays, *Peribañez:*

Cogióme a tu puerta el toro,
linda casada;
no dijiste: Dios te valga.

El novillo de tu boda
a tu puerta me cogió;
de la vuelta que me dió
se rió la aldea toda,
y tú, grave y burladora,
linda casada,
no dijiste: Dios te valga.

The bull caught me by your door,
lovely bride:
you did not say, 'God help you.'

> The young bull at your wedding
> by your door caught me,
> and at the toss it gave me
> the whole village laughed,
> while you, grave and mocking,
> lovely bride,
> did not even say, 'God help you.'

You may notice the effect of those three words, *grave y burladora*, in stamping the scene upon the eye: slight though this touch seems, only a poet who had all his senses about him could have made it.

Finally here is a *seguidilla*, one of those tiny poems that came into vogue after 1600 with the dance and air of the same name:

> Río de Sevilla
> ¡cuán bien pareces,
> con galeras blancas
> y ramos verdes!

River of Seville, how fine you look—with your white-sailed boats and your green branches!

It would seem impossible to pack into four short lines a greater power of evocation, and though this poem was intended to be sung rather than recited, we can see as we read it the broad river of Seville with its boats decorated with green boughs and its parties of revellers, and can hear the twanging guitars and the voices raised in the quavering, nostalgic melody. But we cannot be sure that Lope himself wrote it.

One last point needs to be dealt with—his attitude to the new sort of poetic diction known as *culteranismo*, which was introduced by Góngora. Lope's formula for writing verse required a balance of various elements: there must be ideas neatly or subtly expressed, feeling, colour, sensibility, movement and above all a natural word-order and syntax. He did not object to conceits—indeed he used them all through his life—but they must conform to the standards of good taste and not be extravagant. *El arte exige templanza.* What he disliked about *culteranismo* was its Latinized word order and its obscurity. 'Poetry', he wrote, 'must cost great trouble to the poet, but little to the reader.' These opinions naturally brought him up against Góngora, who was not slow in replying. This was something Lope had a great dread of. Góngora's biting wit was a thing to be feared, and Lope, who had all his life been a man of peace, warding off envy and criticism by fulsome compliments, lived more uneasily than ever on the pinnacle his fame had brought him, with the pack of envious writers surging round. His compensation came from the theatre audiences. Rejected by the young poets and by the court, he got from the people an adoration only given today to film stars and bull-fighters. His picture hung on every wall, his plays drew full audiences. He could not go out in the streets without people doffing their hats and asking his blessing. A priest living in open adultery, yet whipping himself till his blood tinged the walls of his oratory, a man with an enormous faculty for life and an equal fear of death, a poet of good looks, charm and generosity but little moral backbone, he typified the ordinary people of his age and was therefore deeply loved by them.

Lope de Vega had created the Spanish drama, but he was not left alone to exploit his invention. Within the broad limits he had laid down, a host of other dramatists appeared and carved out their particular territories. Their plays, considered individually, are sometimes as good as Lope's, precisely because their field was smaller and they worked it better. Let us consider two of them, though more briefly than their merits deserve.

Tirso de Molina was the *nom de plume* of a Mercedarian friar called Gabriel Téllez. Born, it is now thought, in 1584, he lived most of his life at Toledo, dying in 1648 as prior of a monastery of his order. Recent discoveries have made it probable that he was an illegitimate son of the Duque de Osuna—a fact which, if it is true, would account for his frequently bitter and disillusioned comments on society. It is not known when he began to write for the stage, but he ceased production in 1625 in consequence of a rebuke administered to him by the Council of Castile on the frankness with which he represented vice in his *comedias*. So far as is known he wrote no plays during the remaining twenty-three years of his life.

Tirso was a man of very different temperament from Lope de Vega. His plays lack the facility, lightness of touch and infinite seduction of the great magician, but to compensate they have a concentration which was not to be expected of the other. They do not as a rule seem to spring out of the Spanish soil as Lope's do, nor give the same impression of life flowing all round, but on the other hand the principal characters are more fully developed. Like our Elizabethan dramatists, he often shows a liking for extreme or unusual types of character, though he does not develop them analytically but portrays them in action. Of all Spanish dramatists he is the most forceful and dynamic. Let us take as an example his great play *El Burlador de Sevilla*, in which he introduces for the first time the immortal figure of Don Juan.

Don Juan Tenorio is a young Andalusian blood who makes a profession of seducing women by a mixture of trickery and violence. When the curtain goes up we see him escaping from the bedroom of a duchess, whom he has seduced in the royal palace of Naples by pretending to be her future husband. Forced by the king's anger to fly from Italy, he is shipwrecked on the Catalan coast. His servant brings him in unconscious through the surf and hands him over to a beautiful fishergirl called Tisbea. Don Juan's first words on regaining consciousness are a declaration of love to her, after which he seduces her by a promise of marriage and deserts her. We next see him at the king's court at Seville, where his father is chancellor. His conduct at Naples has become known, but the king forgives him and settles the matter by declaring he is to marry the duchess. Before this can take place, however, he enters by trickery the house of a certain noble lady whom his friend, the Marqués de la Mota, has told him that he loves, and attempts to seduce her: she raises the alarm, her father, the Comendador of Calatrava, appears and Don Juan kills him. He now flies to Lebrija, a town close to Seville, where we see him inviting himself to the wedding of a peasant girl and, again by a promise of marriage, taking the place of the bridegroom that night.

But this vertiginous course cannot last for ever. Whilst his father is endeavouring to throw earth on—to use the Spanish expression —the Comendador's murder, and the duchess and Tisbea are travelling to Seville to complain to the king, Don Juan returns secretly to Seville and, coming by chance on the Comendador's tomb in the cathedral, in a mood of bravado seizes the beard of his stone effigy and invites him to dine with him. That night the ghost appears at his supper table 'in the form in which he was in the tomb', sits down and eats and, when he gets up to go, invites his host to dine with him the following evening in his chapel. Don Juan, for whom it is a point of honour never to shrink from anything, does so. After the meal, in which they are served with the horrid foods of the dead, the ghost dares him to take his hand. Don Juan takes it, the fires of hell pour through it into his body and he sinks down dead.

The *Burlador de Sevilla*—or, to give it its other name, the *Convidado de Piedra*—is a play that, though hastily and even roughly written, moves with a gradually accumulating force to its tremendous end. The figure who dominates it is naturally Don Juan Tenorio himself. We see him four separate times at work on his seductions and then facing the ordeal of the two suppers with the ghost. His valet Catalinon accompanies him much as Sancho accompanies Don Quixote (let us note again the great utility of this Spanish device, which the French and Italians copied) and provides the occasion for his various confidences. But what is Don Juan really like? One may say that he is conceived on two planes. On the first, that of realism, he is a case of arrested development. He thinks of himself as the *burlador*, the great practical joker. 'This is going to be the best joke of all', he says before each of his seductions. Now to seduce women by violence and trickery was not looked on very severely in that licentious age, for the relations of the sexes were thought of as a warfare in which it was the business of the woman to defend herself, with the assistance of her family, against the attacks of men. But Don Juan, by the deception he practised on his friend the Marqués de la Mota, made the war, as it were, totalitarian. This was contrary to the conception of honourable conduct of that time and, though Don Juan piques himself on his sense of honour, all that he means by that is his readiness to accept any challenge that may be offered him. I think, therefore, that we may see an element of satire on the young bloods of the nobility as being part of Tirso's intention.

Then what of Don Juan's sexual motive? *Esta noche he de gozarla*, he says of Tisbea: 'This night I have got to enjoy her.' But there is no luxuriousness in his disposition. His notion of enjoyment is much more that of a hawk enjoying its prey than of a man spending a night of love with a woman. He flatters his prospective victims, but not a word of tenderness or *caricia* escapes him. Why should it? His success depends upon the attraction women feel for energy, and he is not capable of being in love with anyone.

However, the greatness of this play depends upon the fact that it raises the figure of Don Juan Tenorio to a higher plane than that of realism. He is something more than a young nobleman with a turn for seducing women; he is a symbol of the vital powers of man breaking loose from the social organism and turned to destruction. And he is aware of this himself. When he appears by night in the bedroom of Aminta, the last of the victims, she exclaims, 'Heavens, I am lost. You in my room at these hours!' And he answers in a significant phrase *Estas son las horas mías*: 'These hours are my hours.' It is the reply of a man who feels that he possesses daemonic powers which put all women at his mercy.

Don Juan is a Spanish idealization of the Renaissance type so admired by Nietzsche—the man who possesses an inner force which drives him on, unhampered by moral scruples, to undertake the most difficult feats. His sphere of action is women, and by the role that he has voluntarily assumed he is obliged to undertake the seduction of every attractive woman who crosses his path, more especially if that seduction is difficult and dangerous. It is in this obligation that his sense of honour lies: he must be true to his inner voice and must further accept all the consequences, however fearful, which his obedience to it may bring upon him. Whether or not there is a foundation of excessive sexuality in his nature—and a modern psychologist might make a case for his being semi-impotent—the essence of his activity consists in his need for proving to himself and to others that in the sphere he has chosen he is invincible. One might call him the conquistador of an age which had lost its interest in foreign exploration and conquest. Or one might compare him to Caesar Borgia, that Spanish adolescent corrupted by the Italian Renaissance, whom Machiavelli so greatly admired. But there is one difference that should be noted: Tirso de Molina wrote his play in a country and age in which a romantic admiration for extreme types of character and states of mind was shading into a fondness for the miraculous and supernatural. For this reason Don Juan, though presented to us as a real man, has also an aura of mystery and daemonic possession that makes him, in a certain sense, the Spanish equivalent of Milton's Satan. He is the corrupter, the destroyer, and the key to his actions is pride, but he has one quality which will always charm human beings—his energy.

As Ramiro de Maeztu has pointed out, Tirso's Don Juan is a portrait painted with El Grecoesque elongation of a very Spanish type—the man who feels his ego to be so sacred that it gives him the right to trample on everyone else. All countries have their special forms of egoism, and the Spanish form is active and militant. But it would be a mistake to suppose from this that there have ever been many Don Juans in Spain. There is an insuperable obstacle to their appearance in the reserve and insusceptibility of Spanish women, who make marriage and children the aim of their lives and put sexual love very low in their scale of values. It is a delusion of northerners that Spain is the country of great passions or of easy seductions. We invent it to account for the visible hunger of the men, their continual prowling round street corners and barred windows, the devouring stares they turn on any women they see, their obvious obsession all through their lives with the question of sex, their expectation of an Arabian Nights' miracle that may at any moment happen to them, when what one ought to ask is how it is that so many male Spaniards appear to be unsatisfied in their love instincts and why they seem to find their women, except in the capacity of mothers, so disappointing. No, decidedly Spain is, after Greece, the worst country in the world for light love affairs, unless they are to be sought in a class that can be influenced by money, and figures like Don Juan Tenorio have their origin in adolescent day-dreams and belong to the world of the Red Rider and the Master Criminal.

This does not of course prevent the *Burlador de Sevilla* from being a great play. It is a far better one than Molière's *Don Juan*, in spite of the delicious humour and the easy and brilliant conversation which the great Frenchman pours into his rather ill-combined work. Molière's Don Juan is a portrait of the *esprit fort* of his time and the supernatural ending clashes with the realistic tone of the rest of the piece. But in Tirso's play there is no such incongruity. The tremendous dynamism of the plot, the rich symbolism of the principal character and the eerie horror of the last scenes make it, in my opinion, the greatest of all Spanish plays. It is surprising that it has never been put on the stage in England.

Tirso de Molina wrote a number of other admirable *comedias* besides the *Burlador de Sevilla*. In most of them we are shown the working out in action of some particular trait of character. Thus *La Prudencia en la Mujer*, a historical play whose heroine is Doña Maria de Molina, Queen and Regent of Castile during her son's minority, illustrates the merits of prudence in statecraft. Its plot, which consists in a series of panels, showing the queen in action and culminating in her final triumph, resembles that of the *Burlador*. Or one may take *El Vergonzoso en Palacio*, which shows us the courtship of a man who was too timid to declare himself and the desperate efforts his lady had to make to assist him: whilst, as a parallel to this, we see the same lady's sister falling in love with her own portrait in masculine dress. Tirso delighted in drawing women of outstanding character and boldness in their pursuit of love: by comparison his men are generally feeble characters, easily manipulated by the women who are in love with them. A delicious example of this is found in *Mari-Hernández*, where a Galician peasant woman wins a nobleman by her persistence. Or one may take *Marta la Piadosa*, a very entertaining play, in which the heroine is a liar and hypocrite. Tirso de Molina had a rich comic sense as well as a strong vein of malice and satire, which we may suspect did not increase his popularity with the authorities.

Although most of Tirso's plays are comedies representing love and jealousy, he also showed a liking for daring themes. His best known religious play, *La Venganza de Tamar*, for example, with a plot taken from the Old Testament, deals with incest. But he did not go to the lengths of Webster in squeezing out the last drops of horror from a situation. Such gloating arts, though practised by

Spanish painters and sculptors, were not often used on the stage, and the Italian novels that gave occasion for them had long gone out of fashion. Spanish dramatists, except in their religious plays, drew all their themes from their native chronicles and *romances*.

Tirso de Molina is a dramatist who has all the marks of greatness. A magnificent creator of character, a master of plain, incisive language, with a talent for inventing dynamic plots and a delicious comic sense, he had the makings, one feels, of being the first of Spanish dramatists. Yet his genius never came to a head. Perhaps the Spanish mania for turning out plays in a week or two was fatal to him, or else we should blame his religious profession which cut short his dramatic career when he was still young. Of what he was like himself we can form only a vague impression. We discern a strong, trenchant character, a man who had been through the mill of love and jealousy, but who was essentially a moralist. We have his portrait—it shows a severe, intelligent, bony face with a long nose and chin and heavy eyelids—and we know that he held a high position in his order. The rest eludes us.

The other playwright of this generation of whom I must speak is Juan Ruiz de Alarcón. He was born about 1581 in Mexico, where his father was a superintendent of mines. He came to Spain in 1600, studied at Salamanca, and in 1611 entered the household of a nobleman and began to write plays. In 1623 he obtained a post in the Council of the Indies and he died in 1639. Apart from these facts we know little about him except that he was a hunchback. In the war of wits that then made literature such a dangerous profession he was cruelly pilloried for his defect, but we gather that, though he made few friends among poets or dramatists, he was well thought of in Government circles. In one of his plays he paints a portrait of himself: we get an impression of a sensitive, retiring man, well liked by his friends but given to despondency and easily discouraged.

His plays show a very different temper from those of any other Spanish dramatist. In the first place they are carefully written: when we read them we understand why he wrote a mere thirty comedies, whereas the other playwrights of the time numbered their works in fifties or hundreds. He is not a poet in the usual sense of the word, for his language is generally dry and devoid of images, but his versification has a fine grain and polish which suggests— though the metre is so different—French classical drama. But he is never rhetorical. His genius lies in discrimination and subtlety: in the analysis of moral sentiments and above all in a comic observation directed towards the everyday things of life. There is something of La Bruyère in him and something of Molière. But he has far less vitality, and little satirical sense. Alarcón was a quiet man who, in spite of the cruel attacks made on him by other writers, lived at peace with his age.

Though he wrote on most of the usual subjects, he is only in his element in his comedies of contemporary life at Madrid. By far the best of these is *La Verdad Sospechosa*. This presents the story of a young man of good family, arriving at Madrid from the University and plunging into fashionable life. He has every agreeable quality except one—he cannot tell the truth. On the least provocation he rattles off a string of imaginary adventures that he has invented on the spot, with such conviction that even those who know his weakness are taken in by them. What increases the comedy is that his father, a splendid type of the Spanish Polonius, professes a particular horror of untruth, chiefly because it brings discredit when it is found out, and there is a delicious scene in which, after listening to a long sermon on the subject of lying from him, the son replies with a story that is almost impossibly romantic and far-fetched, but so circumstantially told that it takes the old man in completely. One of the merits of this delicious play is that the plot springs entirely out of the young man's lies, which produce all the complications necessary.

Alarcón is really an eighteenth-century dramatist writing in the seventeenth century. Most of what is peculiar to that period, the Baroque ornament, the melodramatic tone, the appeal to popular taste, the violent contrasts and the dynamism are absent from his plays. Only the emphasis on subtlety is characteristic. One must conclude, I think, that the fact that Alarcón was brought up in Mexico made him insensitive to the hot-house atmosphere of the Spanish Counter-Reformation, and for that reason more European.

To all intents and purposes he is the first writer of the New World.

There were other notable playwrights of this generation—Guillén de Castro, Pérez de Montalbán, Mira de Amescua, Vélez de Guevara, Quiñones de Benavente (the writer of *entremeses*), and so forth. The Spanish drama is a forest as rich and profuse and full of the sap of life as anything to be found in other languages and the person who sets out to explore it may, if he likes, spend several years of pleasant reading on the task. But essentially it is literature of a rather light sort, which only occasionally stimulates the mind or the taste for poetry. A Spanish play of this period gives very much the kind of enjoyment one expects from a good film—that is to say, entertainment and a heightened sense for life. However, there is a change in the next generation. By 1635 all the dramatists we have mentioned had either died or ceased production, and they were followed by the very different drama of Calderon.

CHAPTER X

GÓNGORA AND THE NEW POETRY

Luis de Góngora y Argote is the poet who brought together the two strands of Renaissance poetry and traditional or popular poetry and wove them into a new and highly sophisticated form. He was born at Cordova in 1561—that is to say, one year before Lope de Vega. He came of a cultured family—his father had one of the largest libraries in the city—which prided itself on its descent from the great clan of the Manriques and from other noble houses. We know little of his early life except that he was precocious. He learned to read Latin and Italian without much effort, returning home from Salamanca with a reputation for wit, gaiety and extravagance, but very little inclination to canon law and theology. Then for five years he led the life of a young man of good family, falling in love, writing verses to amuse his friends and spending money lavishly. It was this no doubt that brought him in 1585 to take deacon's orders and so to step into the post of prebendary of Cordova Cathedral, which had just become vacant by his uncle's retirement. Certainly it was not any sense of vocation, for he was by nature a man with little feeling for religion.

During the next twenty-six years he continued to enjoy the rents and to carry out the duties of prebendary in his native city. The duties consisted firstly of attendance at choir, at which he was not very assiduous. We hear of his being reprimanded for talking during the services and for his frequent absences. Then he took part in organizing the fiestas and processions—a kind of thing which his love of display and his appreciation of the fine arts must have made congenial. Finally his social gifts—he was a man of many friends—led to his being entrusted by the Chapter with diplomatic missions which took him all over the country. With his family connections, his brilliant wit and his great self-possession he was before long one of the leading figures in the city.

We must imagine Don Luis at this time as an extremely gay and sociable man, fond of music and horses and bull-fighting and passionately fond of cards. No poet has ever been a greater card addict: his gambling orgies ate into his nights and sent him home at dawn: they ended by dissipating most of his fortune and throwing a shade of sadness and indigence over his last years. But there were also love affairs. One which began towards 1585 lasted with various vicissitudes for over ten years: later there were others. They were none of them apparently with women of his own rank of life, and some were with what we now call demi-mondaines. The age he lived in demanded discretion rather than chastity of its cathedral clergy. But his gaiety had a dark lining: in an autobiographical poem written in his usual satirical vein, he speaks of it as 'paying a thousand pensions to melancholy'.

Since the age of twenty Góngora had been writing sonnets and *romances*. They were passed round among his friends and got him a local reputation as a poet and wit. Many of them were *vers d'occasion*, written to celebrate some now obscure event, and highly satirical. Others were love poems. But though twelve of his *romances* were published anonymously in a famous anthology, the *Flor de Varios Romances Nuevos*, that came out in 1589, he does not seem to have taken himself very seriously as a poet. Life was probably too agreeable. Then in 1593 he was in Salamanca, where he met and took a dislike to Lope de Vega, and in 1602 spent two years at the court at Valladolid. Here he got to know the leading figures of the day and found that poetry was a highly fashionable art and, when combined with good birth, an important aid to preferment. But it was almost as dangerous as politics: young writers made their reputations by attacking older men and Góngora was now famous enough to be a target for the lampoons of a prodigiously learned young poet called Quevedo, who had just come down from the University with his head full of Greek and Hebrew. So the long and famous quarrel over poetics that was to divide Spanish writers into two warring camps began. It may have been at this time, on his way through Toledo, that he first met El Greco. They had much in common: distinction, refinement, an aristocratic bearing in the arts they practised. The painter had an ear for poetry and the poet an eye for painting. If we cannot speak with certainty of their friendship, we know of Don Luis' admiration for the Greek, which he expressed in a sonnet on his tomb.

These visits to the court and the contacts he made with the great wits and artists of the age were an incitement to Góngora's somewhat diffident muse to rise to new artistic levels. His best *romances* date from this period. The slow foot-pace journeys across plains and hills (there was another to Galicia in 1609) stimulated his nostalgic sense for peasant life and landscape: we find allusions to them mixed with snatches of village dance-songs in his verses of this time, though the bulk of his impressions were stored up for the long descriptive poems that he began a few years later. Then, in 1611, he gave up in favour of his nephew his prebendaryship at Cordova cathedral. This was the critical moment of his life. Should he settle in Madrid, where the court had now taken up its residence? Or retire to the country to compose, as his friends urged, some great work in fine language and magnificence of style that could compare with those of the Italians? After some hesitation he took up his residence in a small country house, the Huerta de Don Marcos, a couple of miles from Cordova, and wrote there the *Fábula de Polifemo y Galatea* and the first part of the *Soledades*.[1]

The circulation of copies of these two poems in the literary academies of Madrid during the summer of 1613 produced the greatest storm ever known in the history of Spanish literature. Everyone took sides—some enthusiastic, some scandalized. The famous war between *culteranismo* and *conceptismo*, long simmering, had begun in earnest. Góngora himself seems to have been taken aback by the stir his poems had created. There was, one suspects, a good deal of timidity and diffidence concealed under the armour of his wit and pride, and it may be on this account that he left the second *Soledad* unfinished. But he needed a new sinecure to support him, so, urged by his court friends, he left his native city for

[1] The building, today used as a hen-house, still stands, though in ruinous condition. The traveller will find it just below a viaduct, built to carry the Sierra Morena railway. A narrow rocky valley with a stream: a spring of water and a small *huerta*: a mill, now demolished: ilexes and olive trees, sheep and a shepherd lad. Such was the place to which Góngora retired like one of the famous hermits of the Sierra, and its solitary situation explains the title of the poem he wrote there—the greatest and most ambitious poem ever written in Spanish.

Madrid in 1617, was ordained priest and took a royal chaplaincy.

It was an unfortunate decision. In the hurly-burly of Madrid Góngora felt old age come upon him suddenly. He did not get the preferment he had expected, his debts increased, his friends fell from favour, whilst court life with its endless waiting in ante-chambers and dancing attendance on great men did not suit him. His poetry dried up; he wrote little, and as a rule with less feeling. As he struggled with his financial difficulties, his mind went back more and more to his home city, where he had a house and a garden waiting for him when he chose to return to it. But, like a typical Andalusian, he was unwilling to do this until he had obtained sinecures for all his nephews. To meet his debts, he decided to publish his poems. He had not kept copies of them and was obliged to rely on collections made at second hand by other people. He was working on the edition when he had a stroke and lost his memory; returning a broken man to Cordova, he died there a few months later, in May 1627. When later in the same year his poems came out, that supreme organ of bureaucratic malice and in-eptitude, the Inquisition, suppressed them.

We cannot understand Góngora without remembering that he was an Andalusian from Cordova. Cordova at this time was a city of some 11,000 inhabitants (in the days of the Arab caliphs it had had a million), but among the ruins of its former streets and palaces it contained many town houses of the nobility and gentry and a large and richly endowed clergy. Its great history—it had been the home town of the Senecas and the capital of Arab Spain —gave its inhabitants a great civic pride. Góngora shared this fully. He had grown up among the noble families of the province, had shared their joyful, spendthrift life and was passionately de-voted to his native soil. The Guadalquivir—*gran rey de Andalucía*— had the same fascination for him that the Tagus and the Danube had for Garcilaso or the rivers of Old Castile for Santa Teresa, and one is tempted to feel the movement and glitter of its waters as it flows through the yellow, sun-baked plains—contrast of water and aridity, melancholy of sunsets and herds of cattle—pervading his verses.[1] There is so much of Arab poetry in his allusive, rapier-like

---

[1] Apart from this, the life of rivers from their source under a rock in the mountains, by

romances that one wonders whether natural environment may not play a greater part than is generally thought in poetic creation.

Góngora's temperament as a young man was, as we have seen, gay and pleasure-loving, with a melancholy undercurrent. But he was also malicious and satirical. His pride, which was immense, concealed a great sensitiveness and like Pope he developed his formidable wit and sarcasm to defend himself and keep the world at a distance. As he grew older and was drawn into the literary arena, his susceptibility increased. He became a tough, heavily defended, somewhat saturnine man whom no one slighted except at his peril.

To come to his poetry, from 1580 to 1612 all Góngora's verses that we need to consider were in the form of *romances, letrillas* and sonnets. The *romances,* which were the current form for poets at this time, were very different in spirit from the traditional ballads that had been collected and published earlier in the century. They were amatory poems, disguising real love affairs under pastoral or Moorish trappings. In poetry the Moor had become a noble and romantic figure just at a time when in practice he was treated as a despised slave and was about to be expelled from the country.[1] As we have seen, Lope de Vega had started his career by writing poems of this sort, and Góngora, giving his own very personal twist, made them the vehicle for much of his best verse.

The *letrilla* was a polite derivation of the *villancico*. That is to say, it was a lyric poem with an *estribillo* (sometimes omitted) at the beginning, and a refrain that repeated it. Góngora's method was to take his *estribillo* from the popular songs of the day or from one of the earlier song-books, and make his poem an ironic or satirical comment on it. However, his *romances* are often in the form of

meanders, poplar fringes and islets to their final entry into the sea, where they lose their riverine consciousness, was one of his favourite themes, to which he returns again and again in his poetry. Since the time of Jorge Manrique's *Coplas,* the river had been a common symbol for human life.

[1] The fact that the Moorish revolt in the mountains of Granada in 1568-71 had been attended by great atrocities and massacres, committed in cold blood by both sides, shows the utter unreality—to use no stronger word—of this kind of poetry. It marks the beginning of the Baroque retreat from life. The fashion came in towards 1580, but received its consecration in 1595 from Ginés Pérez de Hita's *Guerras Civiles de Granada,* which made the struggles of the Zegríes and Abencerrajes the romantic subject *par excellence* of Spanish literature.

villancicos too: the only real difference lies in the subject—the *romances*, however lyrical in tone, being narrative poems, whilst the *letrillas* comment in a general way on life.

The sonnets need no explanation. Góngora is the greatest of Spanish sonnet writers. He was already writing very beautiful ones in 1582, when he was only twenty, in the style of Petrarch, and though the drying up of his personal life soon afterwards tended to weaken the jet of feeling that is required for sonnet writing, some of those he wrote in his later manner are among his best.

Let us begin by considering the poems he wrote in Spanish measures, the *romances* and *letrillas*. The first examples we have of these, written in 1580 and 1581, are not only delicious in themselves, but highly original. We do not see Góngora struggling like other poets to free himself from his predecessors and create a style of his own: when he appears before us as an undergraduate, he is already fully formed and writing in the manner which he was to develop and elaborate during the next thirty years. Take for example this *romance:* I have only space for the first stanza, but the rest is given in the *Oxford Book of Spanish Verse.*

> La más bella niña
> de nuestro lugar,
> hoy viuda y sola
> y ayer por casar,
> viendo que sus ojos
> a la guerra van,
> a su madre dice
> que escucha su mal:
> *dejadme llorar*
> *orillas del mar.*

The loveliest girl in our town, today a widow and yesterday a bride, seeing that the light of her eyes is going to the war, says to her mother who is listening to her complaint: Let me weep on the shore of the sea.

The last two lines are the *estribillo* round which the poem is written: you will note the typical Gongoresque conceit of the fifth and sixth lines. The poem was written when he was nineteen, yet he has struck in it his characteristic note of tender irony: the girl's grief at the loss of her husband is seen from a long way off, as grown-ups see the grief of a child, and the conceits, by their deliberate artificiality, help to produce the sense of a toy-like calamity. But this is not the poem of a middle-aged man about a girl, but the recollection by a young man of the scenes that took place when he was a boy of seven and the levies were called up to meet the Moorish insurrection at Granada. This suggests something that will, I think, become more evident later: that Góngora had a very special attitude towards his childhood. He felt for it a nostalgia which he reconciled with the present by means of an ironical manner, and it was this perpetual drag back of the past that prevented the emotional and affective side of his nature from developing in a normal way. Realist though he was, his feelings were focused on a point that was beyond his daily orbit of experience.

Another delicious *romance* of the same year, *Hermana Marica*, plunges directly into the life of children in the streets of Cordova. It is written in a tone of complete realism, without conceits, in language suited to the child of twelve who is supposed to be speaking it. One is reminded of some of Rimbaud's early poems—for example *Les Effarés*.

Yet another *romance* of this period describes a love-lorn fisherman on the Guadalquivir who from his boat 'casts sighs and nets':

> suspiros y redes lanza,
> los suspiros por el cielo
> y las redes por el agua.

The last two lines of each stanza:

> Dejadme triste a solas
> dar viento al viento y olas a las olas

are a refrain in which we hear an echo of that nostalgic music never far away in Góngora's poems yet never appearing except in snatches.

One of his favourite veins was the burlesque poem or parody. Two of these bear the date 1582: one is a ballad on Belerma and Montesinos which may have suggested to Cervantes the famous episode of Montesinos' Cave in *Don Quixote*, and the other is a rather fierce burlesque of pastoral poetry which no doubt is a reflection of one of his own love affairs. The shepherd Galayo is neglected by his Teresona, but does not feel her disdain so much as 'the terrible absence that ate away half his side'.

> No siente tanto el desdén
> con que della era tratado,
> cuanto la terrible ausencia
> le comía medio lado.

Another vein of his is the satirical self-portrait or autobiography (no poet ever made such fun of himself) and in two of these poems he tells us why he writes so much on frivolous subjects. It is because the world is in its dotage and would not listen to him if he wrote with greater seriousnesss. He pours scorn on people who discuss politics and the affairs of the world, what the Turkish fleet is doing and what the English, though it is true that a year later, caught by the general enthusiasm, he is inditing a patriotic ode on the sailing of the Armada. The truth is that long before the death of Philip II the Spanish sense of responsibility for the condition of the world was growing weak and all that the young men of the ruling class demanded was to stay at home and amuse themselves. The belief that Spain wore herself out in the religious struggle needs a good deal of qualification.

There are two poets in Góngora as there were in Heine: one a satirical poet, given to puns and scatological allusions and exercising his wit on the most trivial subjects, and the other a lyrical poet with a nostalgic sense for the fugitive and intangible. One might say of him, as of some modern poets, that his awareness of original sin, of the barrier that cuts off human beings from the enjoyment of the primitive Eden, took an aesthetic form. But his insights into the world of innocence were fleeting, and his lyrical vein was therefore short-winded and haunted by a sense of impermanence and unreality. He made up for this by his highly developed artistic sense, which taught him that his feeling for beauty and his feeling for reality must be brought together and either contrasted or harmonized. The poem in which he best succeeds in harmonizing them is his pastoral *romance* on Angelica and Medoro, written in 1602. Here are a few stanzas from it; the poem is given in full in the *Oxford Book of Spanish Verse*.

En un pastoral albergue
que la guerra entre unos robres
lo dejó por escondido
o le perdonó por pobre,

    do la paz viste pellico
y conduce entre pastores
ovejas del monte al llano
y cabras del llano al monte,

    mal herido y bien curado,
se alberga un dichoso joven,
que sin clavarle Amor flecha,
le coronó de favores.

    Las venas con poca sangre,
los ojos con mucha noche
le halló en el campo aquella
vida y muerte de los hombres.

    Del palafrén se derriba,
no porque al moro conoce,
sino por ver que la hierba
tanta sangre paga en flores.

    Límpiale el rostro, y la mano
siente al Amor que se esconde
tras las rosas, que la muerte
va violando sus colores. . .

    Todo es gala el Africano,
su vestido espira olores,
el lunado arco suspende,
y el corvo alfanje depone.

    Tórtolas enamoradas
son sus roncos atambores,
y los volantes de Venus
sus bien seguidos pendones.

    Desnuda el pecho anda ella,
vuela el cabello sin orden;
si le abrocha, es con claveles,
con jazmines si le coge.

El pie calza en lazos de oro,
porque la nieve se goce,
y no se vaya por pies
la hermosura del orbe.

Todo sirve a los amantes:
plumas les baten, veloces,
airecillos lisonjeros,
si no son murmuradores.

Los campos les dan alfombras,
los árboles pabellones,
la apacible fuente sueño,
música los ruiseñores.

In a pastoral lodging
among oaks
which the war had passed by as hidden
or spared as poor,

where peace is clad in sheepskin
and leads among the shepherds
sheep from the hill to the plain,
goats from the plain to the hill,

ill wounded and well cured,
a happy youth takes shelter,
one whom Love without piercing
has crowned with favours.

His veins—with little blood,
his eyes—with much night,
that life and death of men
found him thus in the field.

From her palfrey she alights,
not that she knows the Moor,
but seeing that the grass
repays his blood with flowers.

She wipes his face, her hand
feels the Love that is hidden
behind the roses, whose colours
death is already stealing. . . .

Gay and gallant is the African,
a sweet smell comes from his clothing;
he hangs up his crescent bow,
and takes off his curving scimitar.

Enamoured turtle-doves
are his purring drums
and the birds of Venus
his well followed banners.

With naked breast she goes,
her hair flies in disorder;
if she pins it, it is with pinks,
with jasmine, if she ties it.

Her feet are shod with golden
laces for their snow to delight in,
and that the beauty of the world
may not go barefoot.

Everything serves the lovers,
feathers strike them, rapid,
little breezes that flatter
when they are not murmuring.

The fields give them carpets
and the trees pavilions,
the gentle fountains sleep,
music the nightingales.

The subject of the poem is a famous episode in Ariosto's *Orlando Furioso*, describing the love of the Princess Angelica for the young Moor Medoro. It presents, as pastoral poetry should, the ideal and impossible situation, the love affair which has every conceivable feature that poetic lovers could wish for, and it does so with a caressing lightness and buoyancy and in a very stylized diction. It is this stylization that brings the story into focus with reality and gives it that flavour of nostalgic irony which we observed in *La más bella niña*. But how exuberant and joyful is that irony, how different from the self-pitying irony of Heine and the Romantics! Observe too the patterned nature of the language. Every stanza has a parallelism or an antithesis. This is a typical feature of Góngora's style. If one calls it baroque, one will have to say that both Pope's poetry and Voltaire's *Contes* are baroque as well. It gives the poem a tighter organization, all the more necessary since it is not rhymed but assonanced, and also a greater agility. As a rule it is only an agile art like music that is able to express a complex mood, half delight and half make-believe, such as is given by this *romance*, and that perhaps is why it evokes the music of lute and guitar, their liveliness, sweet harshness and clear articulation, better than anything else in Spanish poetry. No wonder that from the moment it appeared it became the most popular poem in the language, the perfect expression of its age and of its Andalusian birthplace.

Another poem written at the same time recalls a country dance which Góngora saw when on a journey to Cuenca:

> En los pinares de Xúcar
> vi bailar unas serranas,
> al son del agua en las piedras
> y al son del viento en las ramas. . . .
>
> ¡Qué bien bailan las serranas!
> ¡Qué bien bailan!
>
> In the pinewoods by the river
> I saw the girls weaving their dances,
> to the noise of water on the pebbles
> and to the sound of wind in the branches. . . .
>
> How well they dance, these village girls!
> How well they dance!

The melodic quality of the third and fourth lines, with their power of evocation which seems to overflow into the rest of the poem, is typical of Góngora, who is a poet for the ear even more than for the eye, but there is an example of his growing preciosity in the second stanza where he speaks of the country girls 'modestly raising the crystal of the column on its small base'—in other words lifting their legs. In another *romance* on Thisbe and Pyramus, written in the following year, we get a description of a girl which one might say was the starting point for García Lorca's imagery in his *Romancero Gitano*.

Era Thisbe una pintura
hecha en lámina de plata,
un brinco de oro y cristal
de un rubí y dos esmeraldas.

Su cabello eran sortijas,
memorias de oro y del alma;
su frente, el color bruñido
que da el sol hiriendo al nácar.

This Thisbe was a picture
made in silver foil,
a trinket of gold and crystal,
with a ruby and two emeralds.

Her hairs were ringlets,
memories of gold and of the soul;
her forehead, the burnished colour
which the sun strikes on mother-of-pearl.

And in his pastoral on the knight who ran off with the *colmenera*, or girl who tended bees (*Apeóse el Caballero*, written in 1610), we get an enchanting picture of the girl approaching from her hives, singing a song and beating time on an earthenware pitcher which she carries under her arm:

vió venir de un colmenar
muchos siglos de hermosura
en pocos años de edad.

He saw coming from her bee-hives
many centuries of beauty
in a few years of age,

In this *romance* Góngora reaches the climax of his experiments in working lyrical themes of popular origin into a framework of the most artificial kind, in such a way that each gives something to the other. *Apeóse el Caballero* has several such themes, one taken from a couple of ballads of the time and others from snatches of what we should today call music-hall songs. The whole poem overflows with a rich, honeyed, musical quality and is without a trace of irony.

Góngora's poetry during the period we are considering (*i.e.* down to 1612) shows a continual advance in complexity and stylization. The pattern of antitheses on which he built it has its origin in the old ballad style, but he elaborated it and gave it a sophisticated and *culto* tone. It is this pattern that gives his *romances* their clear articulation and vitality, just as a pattern of rather the same kind gives vitality and clarity to the prose of *Candide*. It is a style of wits, though Góngora uses it even when wit is not his object. But he is a poet with a great many resources. The texture of his verse is always fine—elaborate and recondite as the artist struggles with his medium, with every now and then passages of delicious melody that well up and die down again, or else sudden vivid phrases that get their effect by contrast with what has gone before. Even in his burlesques he strikes out lines that delight us, we cannot precisely say why. We feel a deep and complex mind and sensibility at work behind a poetry which, for reasons we can only guess at, refuses to be anything but gay and superficial.

So far we have been considering the verses that Góngora wrote in Spanish measures: we must now examine the longer poems he wrote in 1612-14 in hendecasyllables. These two kinds of verse are so different in character—one might say almost that they constitute two different poetic languages—that we must not be surprised to find many of the typical Gongoresque qualities to which we have accustomed ourselves—vitality, wit, lightness, irony, grace and so forth—disappear, or at least show themselves in a less obtrusive manner. But for the poet there was no sudden transition, since, as we have seen, he had been writing sonnets and occasional *canzoni* since he left the University.

The first of these major poems is the *Fable of Polyphemus and Galatea*. It is a poem of sixty-three stanzas in octaves and it tells the tale, given by Ovid in his *Metamorphoses*, of the love of the nymph Galatea for a faun called Acis and of how the giant Polyphemus was jealous of him and crushed him with a rock. But for Góngora the story has little importance; it serves him merely as a thread on which to string a number of rich and coloured descriptions. The diction is *culto*—we shall see what that means in a moment—but still fairly easy to understand. It differs chiefly from the other descriptive poems of the time—Tasso's *Aminta*, for example—in that none of its separate parts or even images stand out: the effect aimed at is not so much that of a series of poetic incidents as of a continuous atmosphere in which objects melt and fuse into one another. This atmosphere is that of summer, so that the impression one gets from reading it resembles a confused, half-sleepy recollection of the sun-drenched, light-soaked hills and plains of Sicily. For this reason it is not very easy to illustrate by quotation. Here, however, is one of those musical images with nostalgic overtones in which Góngora excelled:

¡Oh bella Galatea, más süave
que los claveles que tronchó la Aurora:
blanca más que las plumas de aquel ave
que dulce muere y en las aguas mora!

O lovely Galatea, softer far
than the carnations that the dawn destroyed,
whiter even than the plumage of that bird
that sweetly dies and in the water dwells![1]

Góngora made of this poem a texture of light, colour and sonorous language and we cannot help being reminded of Velazquez, an Andalusian too, for whom the painting of light and light-saturated surfaces took the place of the representation of distinct objects and of bodies in dynamic movement.

The other poem that we have to consider is his *Soledades*, or

[1] We get a glimpse of Góngora's method of composition when we see him experimenting with the musical effects of a line ending in *mora*. For example, in a sonnet written in 1602, we find:

Los montes mide y las campañas mora.

In 1603 we have three examples, among them:

del blanco cisne que en las aguas mora.

After this there is a dearth of *moras* for eight years, when the perfect solution—the binding together in contrast of *muere* and *mora* and the finding of the appropriate second rhyme in *ave*—is hit on. It is surely remarkable that a poet who, as his satires show, had such natural quickness and spontaneity should have been prepared to work slowly towards his objective in this way. It proves, I think, that in these poems in hendecasyllables he subordinated his inventive powers to the more passive operation of his musical sensibility, testing every line on his ear till it came up to his requirements. Góngora, we may say, killed the natural poet in him in order to make, with great labour, an artist.

Incidentally we may almost call this melody, with its dying fall, his signature tune. Its most personal expression occurs in the *Soledades*:

A cantar dulce, y a morirme luego.

olitudes. This was the production that caused such a tremendous
tir when it came out and which has been a cause of scandal to all
udges and critics of literature from the eighteenth century down
lmost to the present day. As we have it, it is a poem of some 2000
ines written in an irregular hendecasyllabic measure known as the
ilva. The choice of this measure freed the poet from the fixed
ecurrences of the octave and allowed him a greater liberty of
levelopment. It is divided into two parts, which it seems he had
ntended to call the 'Solitude of the Fields' and the 'Solitude of the
Sea Shore': two other parts, on the solitude of the woods and of
he heaths, were never written.

The plot is extremely simple. A young man, disdained by his
mistress, is shipwrecked and washed ashore on an unknown coast.
Received with kindness by some goat-herds, he passes the night
with them on the open ground. Continuing his journey on the
following day, he meets some peasants of the hill country on their
way to a wedding and is invited to join them. They entertain him
and we are given an account of the wedding dances and festivals,
whilst an old man tells a story of nautical exploration. Athletic
contests follow and the first part ends.

Part II begins with the youth's embarking at dawn in a boat
belonging to some fishermen. They sail down the estuary, dragging
a net as they go, and he sings a song of unhappy love to the accompaniment of the oars. They then land on a small island and are
entertained by an old fisherman who is the father of six beautiful
daughters. They are shown the sights of the island, a story of the
daughters' sea-fishing is told and, as night falls, two fisher-boys
serenade two of the girls from their boats. At daybreak they
embark again and watch from the boat a hawking expedition by a
troop of men who have come out of a castle. The poem suddenly
breaks off.

It will be seen that this is a pastoral or Arcadian poem, not
unlike in kind to those rather tedious prose interludes that Cervantes
introduced into *Don Quixote*. Its theme is the familiar one of praise
of simple country life, viewed under the ideal colours of the Golden
Age and contrasted with the vain and empty life of the court.
No subject could have been more hackneyed, yet it was felt. It

was indeed, if my interpretation is correct, felt all the more deeply by Góngora because it was conceived by him as an unattainable world of poetry and innocence from which the condition of man since the Fall (or to give the allegory its key, since his growing up and leaving childhood) cut him off. It is this attitude of his toward it that makes his Arcadia unlike any other. He paints an ideal world free of all taint of ugliness, but his picture has a richness of detail and an objectivity that distinguish it from the other pastoral poems and novels of the time, which are at bottom mere fancy dress representations of the love affairs of the author and his friends arranged in a conventional setting.

The most immediately striking thing, however, about the *Soledades* is the extreme artificiality of the language. Nature, though seen directly by the poet, is presented to us through a veil of mythological allusions drawn from Vergil and Ovid. There is a special poetic diction superficially resembling that of the French *précieux* and a highly Latinized word order. On top of this the reader has to push his way through an intricate jungle of metaphors. Although every one of these features had appeared before in Góngora's poetry, in the *Soledades* they reach a density that makes the poem difficult to read, and in a few places quite impenetrable. The person who wishes to make the attempt should endeavour to procure a copy of Sr Dámaso Alonso's prose commentary, or failing that, of Professor E. M. Wilson's excellent verse translation which simplifies the poem by straightening out the Latinized word order. The effort is well worth making by anyone who cares for poetry and knows a certain amount of Spanish, and most of the difficulties disappear when one has accustomed oneself to the poet's special diction.

The innovation for which the *Soledades* was most bitterly attacked was the liberty it took with word-order. Inversions are more easily allowed in Spanish than in English, but the systematic separation of the adjective from its noun was felt to be an intolerable abuse. *La dulce de las aves armonía* for 'the sweet harmony of the birds' is one of the simpler examples. But Góngora was not just indulging in a pedantic imitation of Latin. His procedure had, we may say, two objects. One was to allow him greater freedom in placing his words in the position in the line where they could give the maximum of sonority and musical effect, and the other, by breaking the normal syntactic order of the sentence, to enable him to cast his verse in a mould that should be less affected by the ordinary habits and rhythms of speech.

A problem that all the poets of the Renaissance felt themselves called on to grapple with was that of purifying their language from its daily contamination in speech and writing, and so giving back to words the gloss, or overtone of deeper associations and feelings, that utilitarian usage rubs off them. Normally this was effected by placing them in new contexts with other specially chosen words (all together forming a sort of poetic family) and then passing them through the rejuvenating current of a poetic rhythm. But Góngora was not satisfied with this. For him poetic composition meant the creation of an artificial world, as remote from actual life as Yeats' *Byzantium* (though coloured by a pathos derived, like things seen on a journey, by a sense of their unapproachability and fleetingness), and he sought therefore to elaborate a newer and 'purer' idiom that should be better suited to express what he was aiming at. This after all was what Spenser had done when he had flooded his poems with obsolete words and what his disciple Doughty was to do when he sought to convey his experience of a remote country such as Arabia. Góngora therefore was not content with revaluing the words he used by breaking their normal syntactic connections —he set about creating a new vocabulary.

Some remarks by the Sevillian poet Fernando de Herrera were probably the point from which he started. In his commentary on Garcilaso, Herrera had said that the first quality of style was *claridad*, or clarity, and had gone on to declare that in the interests of clarity each 'idea' should be exactly represented by a single word, and that if this word was lacking, it should be invented. Góngora interpreted this in his own more subtle way. He did not invent new words, but he replaced those that he regarded as insufficiently expressive by other words which were in some way connected with them. In particular he turned adjectives into substantives. *Oro*, gold, for example, became the synonym of a whole range of yellowish objects from corn to olive oil; *nieve*, snow, that of everything white. Thus *nieve hilada* (spun snow) means white linen table-cloths; *volante nieve* (flying snow) the feather of a white bird and, most extravagant of all, *nieve de colores mil vestida* (snow clad in a thousand colours) means peasant girls in their Sunday best. Nor is *nieve* the only word used to designate white objects: *lilios*, lilies, and *cristal*, crystal, are used as well. Thus we find sheep spoken of as *errantes lilios*, wandering lilies, and the arm of a girl drinking from a stream is described as 'an aqueduct carrying liquid crystal [water] to human crystal [her face]'. By an extension of this process a considerable part of Nature becomes a series of poetic labels— silver, marble, crystal, mother-of-pearl, gold, diamonds, rubies, roses, pinks and so forth.[1]

One may call the result a metaphorical idiom in which the first term of the metaphor has been omitted. But, if so, the metaphors are very mechanical: things are represented merely by that quality in them which the poet most wishes to emphasize—which is generally their colour. It is a proceeding very similar to that which one sees in the Impressionist painters: in place of a series of clearly defined objects we get a play of light and colour which ignores their separateness. Most of Góngora's more elaborate metaphors have the same purpose. He is greatly given to hyperbole, but his comparisons are intended rather to fuse together two different aspects of the world whose appearance he is describing than to throw light on the particular object in view at the moment. Let me give an example: T. S. Eliot's famous comparison of the evening sky to a patient lying etherized upon a table helps to bring home to us, in a witty way, a particular and well-known appearance of the sky. The wit consists in the fact that the second term of the metaphor, the patient, is so completely out of place and extraneous. But when Góngora compares a stream entering the sea to a 'crystal butterfly, with waves instead of wings, seeking its death in the lantern of Thetis', he is merely trying to enrich the texture of his

---

[1] One may see in Góngora's use of colours and jewels to designate objects the influence of Fernando de Herrera. Herrera's poetry abounds in adjectives, always of the most conventional kind, and some of his sonnets are a riot of words expressing colour—*blanco, oro, purpúreo, rosa, nieve, perlas, esmeraldas*. See in particular his beautiful sonnet, quoted by Valbuena, *Ahora que cubrió de blanco hielo*, where the word *blanco* is repeated nine times over. As Góngora's early sonnets show, it was to Herrera much more than to Garcilaso that he looked when he wrote in Italian measures.

poem by weaving together the two elements of air and water.

A considerable part of the *Soledades* is made up of long, involved metaphors of this sort. A pine tree, for example, is spoken of as 'treading clumsily underfoot a stream which, like a trodden snake, spitting liquid pearl instead of venom, hides in its twists (that are not complete circles) flowers which the fertile breeze gave in exuberant birth to the variegated bosom of the garden, among whose stems it leaves behind the silver scales it had put on'. Such an image is to be regarded as an arabesque in which the classical motives of stream, snake and flowers are playfully woven together. It lacks vividness, yet it does give in its Spanish original a flickering impression of water flowing in irrigation channels, flowers and shade, with the brilliant southern sun, which is not mentioned, pouring down on the landscape outside. Some of these metaphors are, as metaphors, pretty feeble, whilst others are too involved to be made out, but since it was the conjunction of words and images of different sorts that the poet was principally aiming at, the occasional failure of the meaning is not a matter of much importance. A rich, involved style, a twisting and interrupted surface is the effect to be achieved, so that in between the more elaborate images we get short conceits and flourishes, plays on words, antitheses and so forth, designed to prevent any breach in the texture. As examples of these, a road is said to be 'more tired than the person travelling on it,' sunset is 'the hour when Dawn permits the antipodes to greet the roses on her brow', and birds are either 'feathered cithers' or *esquilas dulces de sonora pluma*, 'sweet sheep-bells with sonorous plumes'. We may note the similarity of such a style to that of the Spanish Arab poets of the eleventh and twelfth centuries and also its analogy to Baroque façades and retablos.

Góngora, however, was something much more than a writer of decorative verse. Against a shimmering web of luminosity and colour and poetic symbols—broken and uncertain through the continual parentheses and metaphorical diversions and syntactic disturbances—he places a large number of concrete and often unusual objects. The *Soledades* is crowded with incidents, descriptions, observations and poetic rarities. Plants, fishes, grasses and birds appear that would not be mentioned in any other poem of that time and there is an underlying ground of exact observation that, though usually given obliquely in an adjective or an image, is occasionally revealed directly. Thus we are told that, when sleeping out with shepherds, the youth was kept awake by the dogs barking all night at the rustling of the dry oak leaves. Not every poet would have noticed that. Or when a shirt is put out to dry in the sun, we get a microscopic picture of its rays sucking the 'smallest drop from the smallest thread'. Or else we have a sudden, vivid image of a pair of hooded gerfalcons that brings them immediately before us:

> Quejándose venían sobre el guante
> los raudos torbellinos de Noruega.

> Complainingly they came, perched on the glove,
> the impetuous whirlwinds of Norroway.

But Góngora's exactness, it must be said, resides much more often in his catching some feeling or overtone which it is not at all easy to define. Most of his best images make use of the surprise of an extravagant metaphor to achieve this. Thus a holm-oak, lit up at night by the shepherds' fire, is a *mariposa en cenizas desatada*— 'huge butterfly in cinders there undone'. A flight of cranes is described as an arc 'waxing and waning like moons and writing winged characters on the diaphanous paper of the sky'. The chimneys of a distant village are watch-towers against the sunset. The Straits of Magellan are a hinge of fleeting silver, uniting two oceans. And when, after a bonfire has been lit, the music of a peasant dance strikes up, 'the greatest tree-trunk dances on the bank: there is no silence to which echo, whole voice once more, can reply: every ripple of the stream becomes a lantern, light the reflection, the water glass. And the fixed stars move across the hemisphere'.

Images such as these that seek to present not so much familiar objects as the state, nameless and evanescent, in which they have their being when they make their first impact on the senses, are what the eye chiefly looks for in Góngora's poem. He is like those animal photographers who do not pose their subjects, but seek to catch them unawares, leading their unrecorded lives in the virgin forests. But the *andaluz poeta*, as he called himself, is above all a poet who must be taken in by the ear. The *Soledades* could not affect us as an impressionist landscape with surrealist features, if it was not at the same time a musical composition. Should our ear fail us— and not all the rhythms of this poem sink in on a first reading— we may rely on the statement of Sr Dámaso Alonso that no Spanish poet has ever exploited so fully the varied possibilities of the hendecasyllable. Indeed I think we may say that, like Vergil before him and Milton after, Góngora transcends at moments the ordinary levels attainable in poetry and achieves something I can only describe as melody. Take, for example, lines of such deceptive simplicity as:

> Ella, la misma pompa de las flores.

Or:

> Donde el sol nace o donde muere el dia.

Or take this resonant line, of a river losing itself in the sea:

> Su orgullo pierde y su memoria esconde.

Or this, of a swan:

> A cantar dulce, y a morirme luego.

Or this, in which the repetition of the stressed *a*'s increases the sense of whiteness:

> En su volante carro blancas aves.

The power of evocation of such lines, reduced as it is by their being taken out of their context, must be obvious.

But longer extracts are necessary. Let us take then these stanzas from the traveller's song in the second *Soledad*. It is a song of solitude and discouragement in which the form of the stanza combines with the difficulty of the meaning to produce a musical effect of great subtlety. One seems to hear the lonely voice of the singer coming across the sea, now clear and now faint, as the gusts of wind catch it or let it pass.

'Si de aire articulado
no son dolientes lágrimas süaves
estas mis quejas graves,
voces de sangre, y sangre son del alma.
Fíelas de tu calma,
¡oh mar! quien otra vez las ha fiado
de tu fortuna aun más que de su hado.

¡Oh mar, oh tú, supremo
moderador piadoso de mis daños!
tuyos serán mis años,
en tabla redimidos poco fuerte
de la bebida muerte,
que ser quiso, en aquel peligro extremo,
ella el forzado y su guadaña el remo.

Regiones pise ajenas,
o clima propio, planta mía perdida,
tuya será mi vida,
si vida me ha dejado que sea tuya
quien me fuerza a que huya
de su prisión, dejando mis cadenas
rastro en tus ondas más que en tus arenas. . . .

Túmulo tanto debe
agradecido Amor a mi pie errante;
líquido, pues, diamante
calle mis huesos, y elevada cima
selle sí, mas no oprima,
esta que le fiaré ceniza breve,
si hay ondas mudas y si hay tierra leve.'

No es sordo el mar: la erudición engaña.
Bien que tal vez sañudo
no oya al piloto, o le responda fiero,
sereno disimula más orejas
que sembró dulces quejas
—canoro labrador—el forastero
en su undosa campaña.

'Though but articulate air,
no gentle grieving tears
are these, my grave complaints.
Voices of blood they are, blood of the soul.
He trusts them to thy calms,
O sea, as once before he them entrusted
more to thy fortune even than to his fate.

O sea, O thou, supreme
pitiful moderator of my griefs!
Thine shall be all my years,
redeemed by a frail plank
from draughts of Death,
who sought to be in that extremest danger
himself the galley slave, his scythe the oar.

Though I tread foreign lands
or my own country's, now, my footsteps lost,
thine shall be my life,
if any life is left me to be thine
by her who drives me as a fugitive
her prison forth, so that more marks my chains
have left upon thy waves than on thy sands....

A tomb like this does Love in gratitude
owe to my wandering feet;
let liquid diamond
muffle my bones, and the high crests
seal, yes, but not oppress
these few brief ashes with which I'll entrust them,
if there are silent waves and earth be light.'

The ocean is not deaf: learning deceives.
Though sometimes in its rage it will not hear
the pilot, or tempestuous answers him.
Serene, it simulates to have more ears
even than the soft complaints the stranger sows—
a singing labourer
on his wavy plains.

Or take again these three passages with their Vergilian pathos and melancholy:

> Comieron, pues, y rudamente dadas
> gracias el pescador a la divina
> próvida mano ¡'Oh bien vividos años!
> ¡Oh canas—dijo el huésped—no peinadas
> con boj dentado o con rayada espina,
> sino con verdaderos desengaños!'

> They ate their homely supper then, and rude
> thanks gave the fisherman to the divine
> and all-providing hand. 'Oh well-lived years!
> Oh white hairs!' said the guest, 'combed not
> with dented box-wood or the ray-like thorn,
> but undeceiving Truth!'

And this, which alludes to the stimulus that the invention of the compass gave to maritime exploration:

> En esta, pues, fiándose atractiva
> del Norte amante dura, alado roble,
> no hay tormentoso cabo que no doble
> ni isla hoy a su vuelo fugitiva.

> The winged oak, trusting to the faith
> of this hard lover of the North—
> there is no stormy cape it does not double,
> no island now that can elude its track.

And again this sonorous verse, which tells how the love of gold has driven so many sailors to their doom: the second line is an allusion to Charon.

> Tú, Codicia, tú, pues de las profundas
> estigias aguas torpe marinero,
> cuantos abre sepulchros el mar fiero
> a tus huesos, desdeñas.

> Thou, Covetousness, thou
> (the torpid sailor of the Stygian deeps),
> whom all the sepulchres the fierce sea keeps
> open to hold thy bones, do not dismay.

Góngora has much to say about the sea—its caves, its tombs, its wrecks, its fathomless abysses, and a deep resonant note comes into his verse when he speaks of it. But he is also a poet of the fields, the gardens and the flowers. Here, as a last example, is an unusually lucid passage on a nest of wild bees, which must have been suggested by the description of a bee-hive in the first book of the *Aeneid*. Vergil compares the workmen who are building Carthage to bees at work on their comb, whereas Góngora reverses the image and compares the queen bee to a winged Dido and at the same time, in a parallel metaphor, to the Queen of the Amazons.

> Cóncavo fresno. . . .
> Verde era pompa de un vallete oculto,
> cuando frondoso alcázar no, de aquella,
> que sin corona vuela y sin espada,
> susurrante amazona, Dido alada,
> de ejército más casto, de más bella
> república, ceñida, en vez de muros,
> de cortezas; en esta, pues, Cartago
> reina la abeja oro brillando vago,
> o el jugo beba de las aires puros,
> o el sudor de los cielos, cuando liba
> de las mudas estrellas la saliva.

> A hollow ash. . . .
> was the green glory of a hidden valley,
> if not the castle leafy
> of her who crownless flies, without a sword,
> a murmuring Amazon, a Dido winged,
> though of a chaster army, a more fair
> republic, girded, in the place of walls,
> with cork-bark; in this Carthage then, O see
> shining with wandering gold the reigning bee;
> either the juice she drinks of the pure airs
> or else the exudation of the skies,
> sipping the spittle from the silent stars.

But no amount of quotation from the *Soledades* can convey the effect of the poem as a whole or even the impression that the selected pieces make as one reads them in their context. For

Góngora's Arcadian epic never comes to a head, as other poems do, in any sustained passage that one can point to as containing the flower of his achievement. Either the elusiveness of his temperament, or his deliberate neglect of the ordinary resources of versification, or the broken, interrupted texture and rhythm prevent it from settling into those reaches of rhetorical or lyrical flow, where the current moves impetuously, that are the principal delight of poetry. Its returning on itself, inconclusive music (not unlike those meanders on a river which he describes as 'deviating in search of their own deviations',[1] or, a line or two later, as 'dividing to form islands which make leafy parentheses in the period of their current'), its metaphors that pass into one another like overlapping crystal feathers, tend to elude or disappoint when considered in detail. This perhaps, even more than their obscurity, is the reason for the neglect of his later poetry over so great a period.

But what, can one say, is the total impression that the *Soledades* makes on the modern reader who is prepared to take the trouble to saturate himself in it? Góngora's own words offer some clue. His most common adjectives, after those of colour, are *confuso, incierto, fugitivo, vacilante, breve, desigual, inconstante, inquieto*. He has too a way of describing objects in language that might well be applied to his own poem. Take this couplet on a fishing net:

> Fábrica escrupulosa, y aunque incierta,
> siempre murada, pero siempre abierta.

A scrupulous work though uncertain: always walled yet always open.

Or these lines describing the magic jewel carried on the forehead of some unspecified animal:

> Aun a pesar de las tinieblas bella,
> aun a pesar de las estrellas clara.

Even in spite of the darkness, beautiful; even in spite of the stars, clear.

Although these hints do not tell us much, they at least bear out

---

[1] Desvíase, y, buscando sus desvíos,
errores dulces, dulces desvaríos.
Lope de Vega called Góngora *el padre de los cultos desvaríos*.

the impression made on everyone who reads this poem attentively, that the poet was employing his new technique, not, as his imitators did, for its decorative effect, but in order to convey a particular mode of experiencing the world.

Can one in general terms say anything about this experience? I would put it somewhat like this. Góngora is the spokesman of an uncertain and scattered revelation. The structure of his poem reflects his view of the nature of things. The desired country, condition, state, which it is the aim of his poetry to reach, is not a splendour that can be seized whole in a moment of illumination, but something that leaks out in little glimpses, trickles, intuitions from behind a cloud of uncertain, shifting appearances. Therefore his poem must express this fugitiveness and piecemealness, and to do so must free itself from all trace of rhetorical flow and self-assertion. More than this: Góngora's sense of the confused complexity and interdependence of things as they are revealed to the senses demanded to be given expression in his work. Now writing is an art of one dimension: the chief difficulty of all descriptions is that the writer must find a means of organizing the three-dimensional world of appearances into one linear causal sequence. Obviously there are strict limits to the extent to which this can be done without impairing the chain of cause and effect which makes the sentences flow. But Góngora could not afford to recognize those limits if he was to convey all that he wished: he preferred to sacrifice immediate readability, and by means of continual parentheses and metaphors and mythological allusions to give to his verse the density that the subject required, but which was scarcely compatible with good writing. However, his method—that of a continuous metaphorical layer underlying the ordinary action of the poem—does provide what one might loosely call a second dimension, or more exactly perhaps, on the analogy of painting, a background and middle distance, to which the eye is continually being carried back. It is these continual shifts and movements of the inner eye—and of the ear and of the whole mind, as one reads the poem—that produce the special kind of beauty and the special view of the world that he desired. Wordsworth has described in a sonnet how the beauty of a view is much more powerfully brought home to one if one looks away from it to fix one's attention on a book or train of meditation, and then suddenly looks back at it again. Presumably it is in some such way that the peculiar resonant quality of so many of Góngora's lines makes itself felt. But, as I have said, this must not be regarded as a deliberately adopted poetic technique, but as something that has grown out of the poet's search to express his mode of feeling.

We find then, when we read the *Soledades*, that sort of organized experience of things which it has become usual to call 'a world'. It contains, like all great poetry, the germ of a metaphysic and an aesthetic which, though never formally expressed, can, if wished, be deduced more or less plausibly from it. I do not know if I am going too far when I say that it offers a sort of doctrine of aesthetic salvation. Out of a cloud of uncertainty and obscurity come imitations of something different—fleeting sensations that, though they linger in the memory, are difficult to give words to. We catch the flash of a bird's wing, the glint of sunlight on water, the sound of a voice trailing over the sea, the touch of air on the cheek, the red gash of a sunset, the barking of dogs, the flicker of a distant light, the shadow of a little bush. These images, if one can call them by so precise a term, rise between the interstices of the words like aromas, jostled by the sights and sounds of ordinary life and of ancient poetry, and haunt us, like things remembered between waking and sleep, with a sort of poignancy. We get the impression that these, and not the more coherent forms, are the important things and even perhaps that they have some special meaning for us. Though one hesitates to use the term Nature mysticism in the case of a poet who was guided only by his sensibility and who can have had no conscious thoughts upon this subject, it is in this direction that his poetry leads us. But his attitude to Nature was very different from that of Rousseau or Wordsworth. Far from supposing that union with it was possible (a view impossible to a Catholic), he regarded it as—or made it stand for—a lost region of poetry and delight, something perhaps possessed or shared in childhood, but of which adult man could only have glimpses at brief moments. We might say that it was partly for this reason that he raised between it and the reader the barricades of the artificial.

And then in the background there is always Vergil. Góngora is the only poet I know to reproduce, in his different way, those poignant overtones, those tender and melancholy cadences, that sense of universal beauty and doubtful human destiny that move us in the great Mantuan. But it is no more than a distillation, a few drops on the handkerchief of the Vergilian magic that he gives us. For Góngora lacked the wide views, the genial sympathies and the philosophy of divine immanence that paganism, but not Christianity, can give. In his dealings with other men he showed too often the hard, bitter mind, the prickly siege mentality of the Spaniard of his age, brought up to live in a state of perpetual civil war with his fellow men and in an atmosphere of religious and nationalistic intransigence. It is only in his solitudes and when dealing with a dim race of Arcadians that he can allow the tender and nostalgic feelings that occupied the secret parts of his being to find an outlet. Thus one may say that the *Soledades* is the expression of the essential solitude and sense of deprivation of the Spanish seventeenth-century mind under the hard crust of social armour that had grown over it, and of the half-aesthetic, half-mystical consolation it could, in this case at least, discover in the uncertain, coming and going beauty of Nature. This poem is one more interpretation of that never ending quest—*la recherche du temps perdu.*

Let me then try to sum up once more the career of this most elusive of poets. As a young man, gay, brilliant, frivolous, witty as Pope and equally dangerous when attacked, but at bottom sensitive and uncertain of himself, he underwent towards the age of fifty a sort of conversion—not to the religious life but to that of pure poetry. Shutting himself up with his memories of childhood and of travel, he embarked on the most self-conscious and experimental poem attempted since classical times. Even in our day it seems as adventurous as Mallarmé's poems or Joyce's *Finnegans Wake.* It was, like all poems in search of aesthetic purity, an uncompromising attempt to express those feelings which he regarded as being nearest to the core of poetry, and to leave out whatever did not consort with this. But his poem was never finished. Dismayed by the uproar it excited, perhaps bored by the labour of composition and lured away by the temptations of court, he settled in Madrid. Here he resumed, with less verve than before, his mocking, burlesque poetry.[1] But what he had written was sufficient to seal his already great reputation. Seen through the perspective of the centuries, he must be called, if not the greatest Spanish poet—the term is ambiguous—at least the greatest and most enchanting artist in the language.

The readers for whom Góngora wrote were the new nobility and *hidalgos* who had been educated in the Jesuit colleges. Well versed in Latin literature and mythology and highly competitive, they prided themselves on the subtlety of their intelligence. For them an understanding of the *Soledades* was a test of *agudeza* and sensibility. Through these young men—born after 1590— it swept the country and helped to form the idiom of every poet and dramatist of the succeeding age. By the time of his death Góngora was already a classic, discussed and annotated in the same manner as Homer and Vergil. The Jesuits, with their zest for whatever was new, made the study of his works a part of the curriculum in their colleges.

This did not happen, however, without a great deal of opposition, especially from the elder writers, and a furious and highly abusive war of sonnets and lampoons broke out in the Spanish Parnassus. The leader of the hostile party was Quevedo. He represented the school of literature that came to be known as *conceptismo*, whereas the followers of Góngora stood for *culteranismo*. The adherents of *conceptismo* insisted on a correct and idiomatic Spanish and disapproved of obscurity, but they favoured—hence their name—the use of vivid and far-fetched conceits: what *culteranismo* stood for we already know. It is the opposition between Donne on the one hand and Milton on the other: between poetry for the eye and poetry for the ear: between poetry that takes in the contemporary scene and poetry that uses the poetic material of the past as a sounding-board to give a greater richness of meaning: between *Prufrock* and *Finnegans Wake*. This will be clearer when we discuss Quevedo in the next chapter. Here we need only observe that no one who cared for the vigour and integrity of the language could

---

[1] Góngora wrote towards the end of his life a few lyrical *romances* in the manner of *La Colmenera* which rank with his best. And his Nativity song, *Quién oyó*, is one of the most lovely songs in Spanish. But the long burlesque *romance* on the fable of Pyramus and Thisbe, to which he devoted so much time and effort, must be pronounced a failure.

pprove of the principles on which Góngora wrote, however much
hey might admire the results. Contemporary criticism in litera-
ure is necessarily ideological and takes more account of the direction
nd tendency than of the merit of the existing work, and while
Góngora was giving to Spanish poetry a power of expression never
dreamed of before, he was leading it away from its fertilizing
ources in life.

But we must not suppose that Góngora was the only poet of this
ge. The first half of the seventeenth century saw a prodigious
efflorescence of poetry in Spain, and more especially in Andalusia.
The elder generation of these poets derived from the coloured and
rhetorical school of Herrera. At Seville Juan de Jáuregui (1583-
1641) translated Lucan's *Pharsalia* into admirable Spanish verses
and wrote a finely phrased poem in the *culto* style on Orpheus.
Francisco de Rioja (1583-1659), less influenced by Baroque motives,
wrote sonnets and *silvas* full of delicate melancholy on landscapes
and flowers. Rodrigo Caro, an archaeologist, wrote a famous
poem on the ruins of Italica. These Sevillian poets were all great
Latinists and took their tone from Seneca. At Granada, on the
other hand, the tendency was towards a more decorative verse.
Pedro Espinosa (1578-1650), who came from Antequera, a small
town near Granada where poetry was much cultivated, not only
wrote some beautiful sonnets and *canciones*, but brought out in 1605
the famous anthology—*Flores de Poetas ilustres*—which marks the
beginning of the new poetic era. His life is curious. Disappointed
in love at the age of twenty-eight, he retired to a cave in the
mountains and here and in another cave above Archidona, the
hermitage of the Virgen de Gracia, spent some twelve years.
In this he was following the example of Amadis of Gaul, who had
become a hermit on the Peña Pobre after an estrangement with
his lady, the Princess Oriana. We realize that the love-lorn *solitario*
whom we meet with in *Don Quixote* was not a figure of Cervantes'
imagination, but a regular feature of the landscape.

Espinosa is probably the best of the minor poets of this century.
His verse, coloured, ornate and sensuous, revelling in elaborate
descriptions of natural scenery viewed under their more Arcadian
aspects, is highly characteristic of the Baroque age. One may

admire it for its rich arabesque surface or dislike it for its lack of thought and controlling purpose. His longer poem, the *Fábula de Genil*, 1604, and the two *Soledades*, 1613 and 1623, show a parallel development of approach and subject matter to Góngora's *Polifemo y Galatea* and *Soledades*, though they lack of course all trace of that poet's deeper intention. There is even the same sharp eye for natural detail, exemplified, in the *Soledad* he wrote at Archidona, by a profusion of botanical information. But there is no *culto* influence in the diction. We cannot help being grateful for this, yet when we read Jáuregui's *Orfeo*, written some dozen years later, we can see that the *culto* style, with its taut latinized syntax, is the natural form for this kind of poetry, because it provides the best means of giving in verse that appearance of frozen, arrested movement and glowing colour which is the aim of Baroque decorative art.

The last phase of this poetry is seen in *Paraíso cerrado para muchos, jardines abiertos para pocos*, written by Pedro Soto de Rojas and first published in 1652. It is a long poem on the garden of his *carmen*, or villa, in the Albaicín of Granada, written in the stiff and obscure *culto* manner, with many mythological allusions and descriptions of detail, and, as its title declares, open to few.

One should note the pre-eminence of Andalusia, which provided almost all the painters and wood sculptors and poets of this time, as well as the great minister and Maecenas of the age, the Conde Duque de Olivares. But the poetry, Góngora apart, must be said to be disappointing and to grow more disappointing still as the century wears on. Inevitably one is reminded of the Spanish Arab poets of the early Middle Ages. These sonnets and *silvas* and *canciones* contain many beautiful passages, but they lack depth and character. Too much is sacrificed to style and surface decoration, and there is a complete neglect of popular lyric verse.

At the opposite pole to this somewhat anaemic poetry is Quevedo —we shall speak of him in the next chapter. But the Conde de Villamediana also requires a word. This fantastic nobleman, who was murdered, it is said, to avenge the king's honour for having dared to pay court to Queen Isabella, was the friend and disciple of Góngora and a remarkable poet. Besides some brilliant epigrams, he wrote a number of sonnets in the *culto* style of uncommon beauty and a long poem in the Baroque idiom, *La Fábula de Faetón*. His death in 1622 at the age of forty was a loss to Spanish literature.

Meanwhile what was happening to popular poetry? The old forms, *romances* and *villancicos*, were rapidly dying out. New songs, to suit the new dances of the time—*zarabandas, chaconas, fandangos* and the like—were springing up, but not so much in the country districts as among the populace of the large towns. Few of these have any literary merit. Here, however, is the beginning of a *chacona*, dated 1616, which gives an idea of what they were like:

> *Así vida, vida bona,*
> *Vida vamos a chacona.*
> Acuérdome un tiempo cuando,
> dulce y amada Señora,
> la noche me halló en tus brazos,
> y en ellos el alba hermosa.
> Y en medio destos contentos,
> aunque mejor diría glorias,
> con la grana de tus labios
> mesclan mis dos amapolas.
> Y aunque acertaron a hallarse
> dos lenguas en cada boca,
> en un profundo silencio
> pasamos la noche toda.
> ¡Ay, cuánto un amor se aumenta,
> y una afición se acrisola
> entre sábanas suaves,
> y entre las oscuras sombras!

I remember a time, sweet and most dear lady, when the night found me in your arms and after it the dawn. And in the midst of these pleasures, or I had better say glories, your lips' crimson was mingled with my poppies. And though two tongues found themselves in each mouth, we passed the whole night in a profound silence. Ah, how love mounts up and passion refines itself when it lies between smooth sheets and among deep shadows!

The rest of this ditty is somewhat obscene. In the same class were the *jácaras*, roistering ballads derived from ballads in thieves' slang, that acquired an enormous popularity towards the middle of the century and were sung on the stage between the acts of plays.

One new form of genuinely popular verse did, however, appear at this time and spread all over Spain. This was the *seguidilla*, the ancestor of the modern *copla*. I have quoted one in speaking of Lope de Vega, but will postpone further discussion of this fascinating poetry till we come to the nineteenth century. But I must mention the popular religious verse. Here the *villancico*, that most ancient of all lyrical forms, acquired a new lease of life as a Christmas carol. This, it will be remembered, was the use to which it had been put in the thirteenth century by Jacopone da Todi and Alfonso el Sabio. A delicious poet, Josef de Valdivielso, chaplain of the Mozarabic chapel in Toledo Cathedral (his dates are 1560-1638), appeared as the exponent of this type of verse. He wrote *romances* and *villancicos* round snatches of popular love songs on such subjects as the Nativity, the Childhood of Jesus, the Holy Sacrament, the Passion and so forth. Some of these lyrics are charming: they show that tender and naïve imagination in matters of religion which is only found in Mediterranean countries. In one carol, as the bells ring for Christmas matins, the Virgin comes into the church among white swans, whilst the Child Jesus laughs joyfully among the choir boys, cherubs sing treble to the accompaniment of the minstrels, the *seises* dance by the altar and shepherds sing the Gloria. A *romance* on the Immaculate Conception shows a bull-fight in which the Virgin, crossing the plaza, is saved by a gallant from the bull. Another pastiches *a lo divino* a famous early ballad, the *Serranilla de la Zarzuela*, which describes how a traveller was seduced by a shepherdess on a lonely heath. Another shows Christ on the Cross as the King of the May. But the most original of all, perhaps, is the *Ensaladilla del Retablo*, a long poem full of snatches of popular songs, in which we are shown the drama of the Nativity taking place on a stage whilst the audience comments and applauds and, in the interval, eats its supper. The Virgin, *una niña de cristal*, arrives seated on a mule behind Joseph, whilst a snowstorm of jasmine and orange petals falls on them, and, when the innkeeper refuses to take them in, the audience gets angry. The shepherds arrive, there are songs and dances, and squadrons of cherubs throw toy darts into the air.

In these poems and in Valdivielso's *Autos Sacramentales* we are carried straight into the heart of the religious imagination of ordinary people living in an age of faith. The poet is so much a part of this life that his mind offers no personal barriers: what he writes is almost folk poetry. But it is the folk poetry of the baroque age, influenced by the new pictures and statues and retables that were beginning to crowd out the older medieval decorations in the churches. If we want to catch an earlier note, the same which lingers on in the *seguidillas*, we must go to some of his *estribillos*, which he had taken down from the songs he heard in the street.

> Vientecico murmurador,
> Que lo miras y andas todo,
> Haz el son con las hojas del olmo,
> Mientras duerme mi lindo amor.

Little murmuring wind, you who look and go everywhere, make a sound among the elm leaves while my sweet love lies sleeping.

CHAPTER XI

QUEVEDO AND GRACIÁN

THE poets and dramatists we have been considering in the last two
chapters may be said to have owed their greatness to impulses that
came down to them from the political and religious triumphs of the
previous century. Although they lived in a period of increasing
decline, they either, like Góngora, deliberately turned their eyes
away from it or, like Lope and his fellow dramatists, were too sunk
in the enjoyment of their private lives to be aware of what was
going on around them. The general temper of the country was one
of intoxication with the thought of its national greatness, and few
were capable of seeing that this was rapidly vanishing. The outstanding exception to this was Quevedo. Alone among the writers
of his age he chose the painful course of living in the present and
of warning his fellow countrymen by a steady stream of satires
and denunciations of the ruin that was awaiting them. Even apart
from his merits as a writer, this gives him a special claim to our
attention, because our poets and novelists today have to face a
similar predicament.

Francisco de Quevedo y Villegas was born in Madrid in 1580.
His family came, like that of Lope de Vega, from La Montaña, the
mountainous district to the north of Burgos which had been the
cradle of the Castilian race and language. His worldly position
was fortunate, for his father was the queen's secretary and his
mother her lady-in-waiting. Yet his childhood was very unhappy.
His father died soon after his birth and he was left to the care of
governesses and tutors in the dreary atmosphere of Philip II's court.
He had, besides, two physical disadvantages: he was lame, and so
shortsighted that in order to see at all he was compelled to wear
spectacles.

After some years in the Jesuit college of Madrid he went to the
University of Alcalá, where he remained till he was twenty. Here

he must have crammed mercilessly. When he left, he could read not only Latin and Greek but also Hebrew, and had passed out with honours in theology and philosophy. (Later on he learned Italian and French as well as some Arabic.) But his prodigious energy, which his physical defects seem to have exacerbated, did not allow him to be merely a bookworm: he took a full part in the sports of the students, frequented brothels, kept a mistress and fought a duel in which he almost killed his opponent. All through his life he was to be a very pugnacious man, who knew how to defend himself with a sword very nearly as well as with a pen.

On leaving the University the young prodigy went to live at Valladolid, where the court was then established. He had private means and sought no appointment. Scarcely had he arrived when he began to pour out that stream of satirical verses and pamphlets and *jeux d'esprit* that was only to end with his death. With his genius for making enemies he picked a quarrel with Góngora, the most formidable wit of the time, and in another mood began a learned correspondence with Lipsius, the great Flemish humanist, editor of Tacitus and hero of Catholic Europe against the Protestant Scaliger. One of his letters to him, dated 1604, shows how quickly he had taken in the moral condition of his country. 'As for my Spain,' he wrote, 'I cannot speak of it without grief. If you are a prey to war, we are a prey to idleness and ignorance. In your country we consume our soldiers and our gold: here we consume ourselves. There is no one to speak out, but numbers to tell lies.' This was to be the theme of all his writings and we see from it that he had already chosen his vocation. He was to be the man who spoke out. One is struck by the precocity of his attitude, and in fact by the time that he was twenty-eight he had already written a large part of what, in the way of literature, he had to give us. His pessimism too is remarkable in a man so young: his picaresque novel, *La Vida del Buscón*, was apparently begun in 1603 and the lugubrious and fantastic visions of the Last Judgement and Hell, which form the first numbers of his *Sueños*, were written a few years after. In the whole of literature there can be few books showing such a horror and disgust for life written by a man of that age.

17-2

Quevedo followed the court to Madrid when it moved there in 1606, but in 1612, after a brief visit to Italy, he went through a revulsion against court life and its dull debaucheries (in which he had joined as fully as anyone) and withdrew to his mother's estate in the village of Torre de Juan Abad. This is a small place on the plain of La Mancha, not far from the Sierra Morena. Here, in a low, white-washed house that still stands today, he sank himself in his favourite studies of theology and Stoic philosophy. But he was not to remain in his seclusion for long. In 1613 he received an invitation from the Viceroy of Sicily, the Duque de Osuna, to fill an important and confidential post as his political agent. He accepted.

The Duque de Osuna was one of those brilliant, ambitious, self-centred noblemen, fond of art and letters and women, of whom Europe in that age produced so many examples. Like all the Spanish viceroys in Italy, he was out to make a fortune and also, it was whispered, to build up an independent kingdom for himself. Quevedo served him for seven years, during which he came to know European politics from the inside. To judge by the remarks of later viceroys, he does not seem, for all his Stoic principles, to have been more scrupulous in his conduct than were other Spanish officials, though there is no evidence of his having amassed money. But his dismissal was not due to his private actions, but to the failure of a plot to overthrow the independence of the Venetian Republic in which Osuna overplayed his hand. Quevedo was the chief conspirator, manipulating the strings in Venice, and only escaped with his life because, having learned to speak Italian like a native, he was able to leave the city in the disguise of a *lazzarone*. After a disagreement with Osuna, who was himself on the verge of being disgraced, he returned to Spain and was ordered to confine himself to his house at Torre de Juan Abad pending an investigation into his conduct.

Whilst his fate hung in the balance, the king died and his son Philip IV came to the throne (1621). With him came the new broom, the great, all-powerful minister, Olivares. The Duque de Osuna was thrown into prison and Quevedo's position became very critical, for the court was full of his enemies. In this predicament he took the step of dedicating his long moral-political work, *La Política de Dios*, to the minister. He accompanied this with a letter to Olivares' uncle, full of nicely chosen flatteries and ending with an encomium of his own services. His advances were accepted and, though all Osuna's other ministers were punished, he, after some delay, was released from his detention and taken into favour. But before we condemn Quevedo for his servility, we should remember that Olivares' programme of reforms and the energy with which he set to work carrying them out must have been entirely to the satirist's heart. In all good faith he became for a time the most enthusiastic of his supporters.

The next ten years were the happiest and most peaceful of Quevedo's life. He refused all employment, wrapping himself in his stoic's cloak and declaring that Zeno and Epicurus forbade the sage to take office. Books, pamphlets and verses flowed unceasingly from his pen. He defended St James' right to be sole patron of Spain against the claims put forward on behalf of Santa Teresa, attacked the *gongoristas* and published Fray Luis de León's poems to show what good poetry ought to be like. He also published his own prose works and carried on a lawsuit against his vassals of Torre de Juan Abad who owed him money. He was a man who could not live without some quarrels and altercations. Then, at the age of fifty-two, following on a period of discouragement, he was persuaded to marry. The lady chosen for him by his friend the Duque de Medinaceli was a widow of noble family with two children. But it was not to be expected that the writer of so many satires on women would be able to settle down to married life. After a few months the couple separated.

As the state of Spain grew more and more wretched, the opposition to Olivares' dictatorship—as we should call it today—grew. Quevedo joined the army of the discontented. He was living at Torre de Juan Abad and every few weeks some new composition in verse or prose would reach Madrid, to be copied and recopied by his friends and passed around. But though his attacks on the morals of his countrymen were unceasing, it does not appear, in spite of what has been said, that he began to attack the Government before 1636 or 1637. Then one day in December 1639, whilst

Quevedo was on a visit to Madrid, he was arrested and carried off to prison in a monastery in Leon.

The story told to account for this is that, a few days before, the king, as he was sitting down to table, found in his napkin a sheet of verses setting out in plain terms the condition to which Olivares had reduced the country. These verses were believed to be by Quevedo. But a good deal of doubt has now been cast on this. His offence, it is said, must have been greater, since the king himself hesitated to forgive him, and it is suggested that he was repeating his Venetian intrigue and was in touch with French agents. But whatever his fault was, he remained in close confinement in a damp, unhealthy room till July 1643, six months after the fall of Olivares. When he came out, it was to die, a broken man, before two years had passed.

Quevedo has left his mark both as a poet and as a prose writer. But though some of his verse is good, it is in his prose that we get the full impression of his originality and power. Let us look at this. His first work of any length was the picaresque novel, *La Vida del Buscón*, or 'The Life of a Sharper', begun apparently when he was only twenty-three. Its hero is a boy called Pablos, who was the son of a notorious witch and of a thieving barber, and whose uncle was the hangman of Segovia. At the age of about twelve he becomes the servant of a young gentleman of his own age, follows him to his school and thence to the University of Alcalá. After some time there, he inherits a sum of money from his father, who has just been executed, and with this in his pocket goes to court to make his fortune. His first plan is to pass himself off as a gentleman of means and so make a rich marriage. But his attempts to do this break down and, having run through his money, he becomes a card-sharper. Forced to leave Madrid, he makes his way to Seville and, getting into trouble there, sails for America.

We can best describe this novel by saying that it is a *tour de force*, written with wit and brilliance, but with little of the sympathy or power of conveying the feeling of life that are expected of the novel. It owes a great deal to *Lazarillo de Tormes*, and its most brilliant chapter, that describing the miserly schoolmaster Cabra who starved the boys, is an expansion of the episode of the miserly priest in that book. Here is a sample of it:

His eyes, stuck close together in his head, seemed to be peering out through wicker baskets, and were so sunk and shady that they would have been a good place for a market stall. His nose, having been eaten by some rheumy pimples, was between snub and Roman, but not poxy, because that costs money. His beard was pale from terror of his mouth which, out of pure hunger, seemed to be threatening to devour it. Many of his teeth were lacking, I suppose because he had banished them as idlers and vagabonds. As for his neck, it was as long as an ostrich's, with an Adam's apple that stuck out so far that it seemed to be looking for something to eat. His arms were withered: his hands like a bundle of dry vine-shoots. Seen from below, he looked with his long spindly legs like a fork or a pair of compasses, and he walked very slowly, because if he tried to go faster his bones rattled like a pair of clappers.

This is the style of a caricaturist and, though it could not, I think, have reached such a pitch of concentration if there had not been behind it a powerful recollection of childish misery, it fails to move us as does the sober narration of *Lazarillo*. The chapters on university life were obviously written from personal experience. They describe the pranks of the students and their servants and the very disgusting and scatological initiation ceremonies which new boys had to put up with. One realises the terrible effects upon a sensitive youth of the dirt, violence and gnawing hunger that in those times were the ordinary accompaniments of a good education. We are now taken to Madrid and the tone of the book changes. This part was probably written much later: at all events we get a very amusing and well observed picture of the half-starved *hidalgos* and fortune hunters who hung around the court.

The greatest of Quevedo's writings are by universal agreement the *Sueños*, or 'Visions'. In these we see his style and manner at its best and most characteristic. Their models are Dante and Lucian. They are visions of the Day of Judgement, Hell and the Kingdom of Death which, starting off from some point of profound melancholy, break down into satire, macabre buffoonery and a sort of fantasmagoric nonsense. The characters who appear in them are very various. Most noticeable are those professions which Quevedo hated: the doctors, barbers, tailors, judges and Genoese bankers. There are then the various kinds of bores, the poets and dramatists, and of course every sort and age and variety of women. But there are also proverbs, familiar sayings and figures of popular parlance such as (to give an English equivalent) Tom Tiddler or Hobson of Hobson's Choice, so that we seem at times to be reading a seventeenth-century version of *Alice in Wonderland*. These characters come on like puppets, got up in grotesque accoutrement and hung about with puns and hyperbolical metaphors, and, moving with a sort of jerky motion which Menéndez y Pelayo compared to a dance of death, are pulled this way and that by their sardonic manipulator.

But what makes this book of visions one of the masterpieces of prose literature is its style. It moves easily between a tone of great elevation and one of pungent or farcical description. One is aware of an immense force and ease behind every sentence and, though we may sometimes find what is expressed to be feeble or crude, there is rarely any weakening in the pulse of the language. Take this passage from the *Visita de los Chistes*:

Con esto, bajamos a un grandísimo llano, donde parecía estaba depositada la oscuridad para las noches. Díjome la Muerte:
'Aquí has de parar, que hemos llegado a mi tribunal y audiencia.'
Aquí estaban las paredes colgadas de pésames. A un lado estaban las malas nuevas, ciertas y creídas y no esperadas; el llanto, en las mujeres engañoso, engañado en los amantes, perdido de los necios y desacreditado en los pobres. El dolor se había desconsolado y creido, y solos los cuidados estaban solícitos y vigilantes, hechos carcomas de reyes y príncipes, alimentándose de los soberbios y ambiciosos. Estaba la envidia con hábito de viuda, tan parecida a dueña, que la quise llamar Alvarez o González. En ayunas de todas las cosas, cebada en sí misma, magra y exprimida. Los dientes, con andar siempre mordiendo de lo mejor y de lo bueno, los tenía amarillos y gastados.

On this we went down to a very great plain, where all the obscurity for the nights seemed to have been deposited. Death said to me:
'Stop, for we are come to my tribunal and judgement seat.'
Here the walls were hung with condolences. On one side was ill news, certain and credited rather than expected: [on the other] wailings,

deceitful in women, deceived in lovers, wasted in the foolish and discredited in the poor. Grief had become without remedy or consolation, and only the cares were active and vigilant, gnawing like worms at kings and princes and feeding themselves on the proud and the ambitious. Envy was in her widow's weeds, so like a duenna that I had a mind to call her Alvarez or Gonzalez. Fasting from everything, fed on herself, thin and desiccated. Her teeth, from their continually biting at the better and the good, were yellow and worn to the roots.

The book is full of fantastic, Bosch-like scenes. A coachman takes on a bet with a devil that he can use the whip to more effect than he can. A foreign business man expresses the wish to take over the instruments of torture and rent them out. The devils sow a crop of judges (*jueces*), because from each judge they sow they can reap every day six attorneys, two legal councillors, four notaries, five lawyers and five thousand business men. The poets are tortured by hearing the works of their rivals praised and the women by having their exact age in years, months, days, minutes and seconds calculated by an astronomer. But the greatest scene—too long to quote—comes at the beginning of the *Visita de los Chistes*. Quevedo wrote this in 1621, some dozen years later than the other visions, after an illness in which he had been tormented by one of those terrible apothecary-surgeons of the day, of whom Cervantes' father had been one of the more obscure examples. A procession of physicians appears before us, riding on mules draped in black housings that make them look like coffins with ears. They are followed by a huge mob of apothecaries, laden with mortars and pestles, clyster pipes and syringes, and dressed in recipes. After them come the surgeons, carrying their pincers and catheters, their knives and saws and lances, and crying out in a terrible voice, 'Cut, tear, saw, open, flay, prick, slice, scald, burn'. And since, as Quevedo observed on another occasion, one ought not to say that anyone died of such and such a disease, but rather that he died of Doctor So-and-so, this fearful procession makes a fit prelude to the discovery of Death, seated on his throne, and surrounded by all the particular deaths—of love, cold, hunger, fear and laughter—hung with their various insignia.

The *Sueños* then, as Dr Karl Vossler has well said, are a 'grotesque and exorbitant, feverish and arbitrary caricature, behind which Reality disappears'. I would emphasize the word arbitrary. Quevedo's satires are not well directed. Although his sense of the brevity and suffering of life and of the increasing ruin of his country are present all the time in his mind, he has no rational understanding of what should be attacked and no real discrimination. At least half his abuse falls on women (whom most people would regard as the real backbone of Spain) and on tradesmen. For him the world is an absurd and paradoxical place of suffering, a confused nightmare in which everything is either vain and useless or else totally repellent. It is in fact Hell, and that is the reason why, in describing what he calls Hell, he gives us not a place of rationally apportioned punishment, but a bewildering and grotesque region that is really his notion of the earth. The greatness of the book thus comes not from any ordered view it displays, but from its power of revealing this frantic vision in language unequalled for its force and vividness, for its sardonic wit and for the novelty of its images. One could call it the equivalent in prose of Goya's *Caprichos* and *Disparates:* or rather, since Goya was greatly influenced by Quevedo, these may be said to be the painter's commentaries on it.

Some of Quevedo's other prose writings are of interest. There is *El Entremetido y la Dueña y el Soplón*, written in 1627-8, and *La hora de todos y la Fortuna con seso*, written in 1635-6. These are both visions. The former contains, among other things, a short account of human life from its conception in the womb to middle age, which I think must be the most concentrated exposition of pessimism ever written. More entertaining is the *Premáticas y Aranceles Generales*, a *jeu d'esprit* of his youth, with its curious list of common oddities of behaviour, such as putting the feet on the joints of paving stones when walking, touching the walls with one's fingers, spitting from heights, asking how far it is to one's destination although one knows already how far it is in the hopes of making the distance shorter, seeing lions and whales in the clouds like Polonius, examining one's handkerchief after one has blown one's nose 'to see if any pearls have come out'. There are also lists of indulgences, tables of human desires, pages from an astrologer's almanac and other examples of the *sottisier* that recall Swift's writings in a similar style, for the good reason that Swift was imitating them. There is then the famous skit on the Gongorist poets in *La Culta Latiniparla*. This is not the only occasion on which he has a knock at them. In one of the *Sueños*, when a poet reads his work, the air becomes so dark that bats and owls come out and the audience has to light lanterns. In another there are so many *nieves* and *hielos* (snow and ice) in a poet's description of a woman that she becomes a mountain pass that one can only cross in a sledge with overcoats and top-boots, whilst a snow storm rages all round. In a third passage it is suggested that the gold and silver in contemporary poetry should be melted down to pay off the national debt.

Quevedo, however, was not always witty or fantastic. The books to which he devoted the greater part of his life were long moral-political and didactic works that, because their subject matter has dated, are little read today. The two most important of these are *La Política de Dios* (1617-26) and *La Vida de Marco Bruto* (1632-44). Like everything else by him they are admirably written, the latter with a clarity and elevation of language that make it one of the unread masterpieces of Spanish literature. His political-religious works contain passages that, for their combination of power and fancy, remind one of the great English sermon writers of the day.

Finally we must speak of Quevedo's poetry. There is an enormous bulk of this—five hundred pages in double columns in the great Rivadeneyra edition. The greater part of it consists of sonnets, *letrillas* and *romances*. Some of the sonnets are very fine, especially those that express disillusion and the poet's sense of the brevity of life. They compare—high praise—with those of Lope and Góngora. The *romances*, on the other hand, have as a rule little merit as poetry. He used this form to express his satirical feelings and, though often extremely witty, they justify Góngora's comment that their verse is slovenly and their diction flat and depressing. They suffer from the common Spanish vice of facility.

Of the longer poems in hendecasyllables some, rather surprisingly, are good. Quevedo lacked altogether that sense of the enchantment of life, those moments of plenitude of being, out of which most poetry is made, but he had a prodigious gift for language and a versatile temperament and was thus able to imitate in a convincing way the verse of other poets, including that of the hated Góngora. It is only in some satirical and moral poems that one feels an authentic note. His *letrillas* are examples of the first: his stoic epistle to Olivares in *terza rima* is a magnificent example of the second. In the famous lines:

> ¿No ha de haber un espíritu valiente?
> ¿Siempre se ha de sentir lo que se dice?
> ¿Nunca se ha de decir lo que se siente?

Should there be no valiant spirit? Must we always feel what we say? Are we never to say what we feel?

he put his finger on one of the chief vices of the age and reiterated that determination which he had expressed so long before to Lipsius—to be the man who spoke out.

Quevedo was a man who saw life in very black colours. The unhappiness of his childhood, his hatred of women and his one cynical reference to his parents make us suspect that, like Schopenhauer, his feelings had been perverted by his antagonism to his mother. His mind, over-stimulated at the University, then closed in early. He became a lonely egoist with few friends and innumerable enemies. A man who did not know the meaning of love, a poet with no feeling for beauty, with obsessions that drove him hard and paranoiac tendencies, quarrelsome and inclined to meanness, he makes an unsympathetic impression till we remember his great qualities of honesty and moral courage and the public spirit which caused him to feel so intensely the evils of his century. To an Englishman he recalls both Donne and Swift. The former through his obsession with death, his power over language, the chaotic sweep of his imagination, nourished on medieval lore and theology and expressing itself in an idiom of violent conceits and hyperboles; the latter through his disgust with life and sex, his sardonic humour and his passion for politics. But he had some features which they did not share. Chief among these I would mention an extraordinary instability of temperament. He could not hold a mood for long: in his *Sueños* the note of despair and melancholy, which is always the starting point of the explosion, rapidly dissolves into the play of fantasy. He escapes from his painful feelings by the sheer

exuberance, and one might say gaiety, of his invention. In his
political and didactic works, where he is obliged to maintain a
serious tone, he reveals the same shortness of wind by a lack of
design and coherence. His conversation, an astonishing medley
of reason and fantasy, ingenuity and coarseness, seriousness and
buffoonishness, had apparently the same character.

He was, too, one of those people whose temperament is so
overpowering that they are always, as it were, the prisoners of
themselves. Love had never come, as it had to Donne, to modify
this. One suspects that not only had he never known what it was,
but that he regarded it as just one more of those conventional
hypocrisies with which men gild over their lusts. This inability to
escape from himself is the cause of that extraordinary tarantellic
dance that he called a Vision. It deprived him of the ability to
create calmly in a chosen medium as Cervantes and Góngora both
did, for such creation involves immersion in something outside
oneself. Quevedo, when he wrote, was never calm, but always
inspired and almost always by his own suffering. An Existentialist
before Sartre, a person sick with the stale fumes of himself and
knowing nothing outside his ego to love and value—nothing, that
is, but a few moral and political abstractions—he took refuge, as
such people do, in his own pride and courage and, armed with the
books of the Stoics, daily faced the scene and place of execution.
But such writers never move us very deeply. Their performance
thrills us like a dance on the tight-rope, we imbibe for a moment
their dizziness and terror—then we cry out that life is more than
this and turn to those really humane writers for whom love and
beauty and pity are the major constituents of existence.

Such was Quevedo as a man. But let us glance at his political
ideas and try to place him better in his age. If there was one thing
he saw steadily and clearly it was the decline of his country. Yet he
never understood it. The causes of this decline were the decay of
trade and industry, the inflation brought about by the imports of
silver from America, the military commitments in Europe and the
strangling of the intellectual life of the country by the Inquisition.
Quevedo took the wrong side on every one of these questions. He
detested industry and commerce, spoke of the export of silver and

gold to finance the wars in Europe as robbery and at the same time applauded the crowning folly of Olivares—the renewal of the war with the Netherlands. He was an ardent supporter of the Inquisition and, though he sympathized with the cause of the American Indians —for they were subjects of Castile—he hated, with the irrational hatred of the professed patriot, not only the Jews and the Moors but all foreigners. Then, though a learned man, he was superstitious: for example he believed in the authenticity of a letter said to have been written by the Virgin Mary to the people of Messina, and which he himself had seen.

Such views show, I think, the great weakening in the sense of reality that had taken place since the beginning of the century. Spaniards were living among wraiths and shadows. Quevedo's *Visions* with their phantasmagoric imagery and their startling conceits reflect the confusion and suffering of the time. 'There are many things here', he wrote a few months before his death, 'that seem to exist and have their being, yet they are nothing more than a name and an appearance.' Quevedo knew that, yet could not free himself. For he too clung to the dream that, by some sort of miracle, the glories of the days of Charles V could be restored. This would happen, he thought, if men were more moral. But morality can only flourish if men are adjusted to reality, and such an adjustment required sacrifices to pride that neither he nor anyone else would hear of. Thus if Quevedo, with his deep concern for the condition of the country and his violent, critical attitude towards abuses, can be said to announce the appearance of the opposition journalist and revolutionary, the course he advocated was the opposite of that suited to the needs of his times. The great satirist belonged to that body of political idealists, so characteristic of Spain, whose utopia lies not in the future, but in the past. He believed that it was possible to return to it.

A book that shows the strong influence of Quevedo's *Sueños* is *El Diablo Cojuelo*, which came out in 1641, by the Andalusian dramatist, Luis Vélez de Guevara. It owes its fame chiefly to Le Sage's *Diable Boiteux*, which derives from it. The plot is slight. A student releases a lame devil from an astrologer's phial (a Spanish transmogrification of the genie in the *Arabian Nights*) and is taken by him to a number of places in Madrid and then to various cities in Andalusia. It is a satirical-fantastical work, written in a breathless style of elaborate conceits and endless clauses in apposition which makes it tedious to read. We realise from it how both the *culto* style of the poets and the *conceptista* manner of the prose writers and novelists led away from reality and towards an excessive development of verbal decoration.

Spanish literature down to the twentieth century has been sparing of those discursive books that deal in a general way with human life and thought, such as for example Montaigne's or Bacon's *Essays* or La Bruyère's *Caractères*. The principal exception to this are the works of Baltasar Gracián. Gracián (1601-58) was an Aragonese who was born in a village in a dry, wind-swept plain near Calatayud. Educated at Huesca, he joined the Company of Jesus at the age of eighteen and made his profession in 1635. For the next twenty years his life was the uneventful one of schoolmaster in various Jesuit colleges in Aragon. But a man of outstanding intelligence found it difficult to live at peace in an order which demanded absolute obedience—'that of a corpse', as St Ignatius put it—from its members. Forbidden to publish his books, he tried to leave the Company, but instead was put on a diet of bread and water and imprisoned. Under this treatment he died.

Gracián's principal works comprise several short treatises: *The Hero*, 1637; *The Politician*, 1640; *The Man of Discretion*, 1646; *The Manual Oracle and Art of Prudence*, 1647; *Agudeza y arte de ingenio*, 1640 (a book of literary criticism); and a long allegorical novel, *El Criticón*, 1651-7. The titles of the first three books explain themselves: they are treatises on the ideal qualities that should be possessed by heroes, politicians and courtiers. They aim at doing for that age what Baldassare Castiglione's great book *The Courtier* had done for the Italian Renaissance. As one would expect, they are deeply tinged with the Jesuit ideology. The great quality of the hero is prudence, by which is meant knowing how to adapt means to ends. He must be aware of his own limitations and be free from illusions. Moreover, he must be a man of general culture, refined in his manners, keen in his perceptions, a perfect master of himself and well able to conceal his thoughts and feelings. He must love subtlety and ingenuity and prefer new styles to old. This last is a point to be noticed. The sixteenth century, though it had shown more originality and creative power than the seventeenth, had suffered from a great dread of novelty. The word 'new' had come to have for most Spaniards the meaning of 'bad'. The fact that no sooner was Philip II dead than this fear of the new gave way to a deliberate search for it was due partly to the general law of reaction, partly to the fact that the court was now the centre of fashion, but still more perhaps to the influence of the Jesuits, who were trying to impose on the medieval Catholic world a more polished and up-to-date conception of society and of religion.

Gracián was a strong opponent of Machiavelli. Refuting the ethics of *The Prince* had become one of the duties of every writer on politics, yet one cannot help noticing that a good deal of diluted Machiavellianism creeps into his precepts. This is understandable when one remembers that the success of the Jesuits was due more than anything else to their assimilation of the political theories of the Italian Renaissance and its preoccupation with the idea of power. Hence the *Spiritual Exercises,* their great system of education, their new casuistry, their monopoly of the office of confessor to kings and ministers. But, being realists, they were necessarily also men of common sense and so Gracián's criticisms of the cult of illusions and unrealizable ends are very much more to the point than Quevedo's. What one misses, in comparing his views to those of Castiglione, is the note of simplicity and generosity. The Baroque age, one cannot say it too often, was a tight, contracted age, turned in on itself and lacking self-confidence and faith in the future.

Gracián is a notable stylist. He writes in a dry, clipped, epigrammatic idiom in which every phrase has been carefully polished and refined. He expresses himself in understatements which keep back a certain part of his meaning: his conceits are few, but well chosen: every word is premeditated. Nothing more unlike the grand diction of Quevedo or the copious arabesque of Vélez de Guevara can be imagined, yet he is a more affected writer than they are, for his language smells of the study and is little touched by the rhythms of ordinary speech. Now a stilted or distorted idiom is justified when it produces effects of vividness or emotion that cannot be obtained in any other way: when, that is, it takes a step nearer to poetry. But Gracián's tone is never raised above that of ordinary conversation: the effect he aims at is *agudeza* or subtlety. I confess therefore that I would regard it as a bad style, especially as I find it tedious to read, if it were not that so many good judges admire it extremely.

Gracián's principal work, composed towards the end of his life, is *El Criticón*. This is a long, closely written allegorical novel in which he sets out his philosophy of life. It begins with the shipwreck of Critilo, who stands for rational and civilized man, and his meeting on an otherwise uninhabited island with a savage called Andrenio, who represents the man of untamed passions and instincts. They become friends and, by reasoning upon the order and beauty of Nature, convince themselves of the existence of God. It is curious that Gracián should thus be repeating the theme of the famous philosophic romance by Ibn Tufail, a Spanish Muslim philosopher who was born at Guadix early in the twelfth century. But it was a coincidence, for Ibn Tufail's work was not then known in the West.

The part of the book describing the life of the two men on the desert island occupies only four chapters. The rest is a description of their adventures when they leave the island and visit the world. The picture we get is a very pessimistic one. 'O life, you should never have begun, but once begun you ought never to end', exclaims Critilo as he battles with the waves, and these words may be said to form the text on which the book is written. Critilo and Andremio suffer innumerable deceptions and misfortunes, yet the pessimism is not complete, for we see them rise out of their difficulties and by a continual struggle for self-perfection acquire a share in the only kind of immortality that human society offers— that of the great heroes, poets and artists.

The book is packed with acute observations on human nature, with anecdotes, epigrams and critical judgments. It is clearly the work of a man of unusual culture, intelligence and originality and it offers us a sympathetic and civilized approach to life, similar to

that which we may suppose to have been held by Góngora.
Dragged out of the limbo of forgotten tomes by Schopenhauer's
extravagant praise and, it must be said, partly misunderstood by
him, it is today one of the best known (though perhaps least read)
of Spanish classics.

CHAPTER XII

CALDERON AND THE LATE DRAMA

WHEN Lope de Vega died in 1635, Calderon stepped into his place as the first of Spanish dramatists. Each of these men represented to a remarkable degree his own age. Whereas Lope had been a romantic and naturalistic writer and the pioneer of a vast, unexplored territory, Calderon was a formal and baroque writer, whose career shows a steady retreat and contraction from the human scene to that of mythology and religious allegory. Lope too had been a popular figure, writing for the Madrid theatres and idolized by the people, whereas Calderon wrote almost entirely for the court, except when he was turning out religious dramas for various municipalities. In other words Lope was the culminating figure of a great and glorious era, the *Siglo de Oro*, and Calderon the poet of a catastrophic decline and decadence. When he died in 1681, there was nothing left.

Let us look first at the bare collection of facts that are all that we know of his life. Pedro Calderón de la Barca was born at Madrid in 1600, one year after Velazquez. His family, like those of Lope de Vega and Quevedo, came from La Montaña in the north of Castile and his father had a good though modest position as secretary to the Council of the Treasury. The boy was sent to the Jesuit college at Madrid and then to Salamanca, but before his education was completed both his parents had died, and he and his two brothers were involved in a lawsuit with their stepmother over their father's property.

Pedro had been intended for the Church, but chose instead the stage. He made his début at the literary fêtes held in 1622 in honour of the canonization of San Isidro. But in the following year he seems to have changed his mind. At all events he was away from Madrid for two years and, if his first biographer is to be trusted, he spent this time as a soldier in Milan and Flanders, Back in 1625, with a post in the household of the Duque de Frías, he again took up play-writing and during the next twelve years wrote nearly all the *comedias* for which he is famous.

When we think of Calderon it is generally of a grave, reserved, dignified man with a high lined forehead, white dangling locks and an intense preoccupation with theology. So he was in his later years. But for his youth we must imagine an altogether different person. Two episodes throw a light upon him. In 1621 the three Calderon brothers were prosecuted for killing a certain Nicolás de Velasco, son of a servant of the Duque de Frías, and had to pay 600 ducats as compensation. Then in 1629 an actor stabbed Calderon's half-brother, the son of his father's mistress, and took refuge in a convent. Calderon, accompanied by his friends and also by the *justicia*, or baliffs, broke into the convent, mishandled the nuns and tore off their veils. When the court preacher, Fray Hortensio Paravicino, reprimanded them for this in a sermon, Calderon repaid him with some sarcastic lines in his next play, *El Príncipe Constante*. Nor were these the only incidents of the kind, for we are told that the dramatist had a scar on his forehead as the result of a knife wound that had been given him in a quarrel over a woman.

These things tell their own story: we see from them that Calderon, when a young man, led the roistering, duelling life of the *galán* of the period. This view is amply confirmed when we turn to the plays. Making every allowance for a dramatist's power of projecting himself into other lives, we find there a man of the most passionate nature. Not a connoisseur of women like Lope, with far more depth of character and far more pride, he still had nothing to learn about love or the arts of courtship. His lovers' speeches are the most convincing in the Spanish drama and, as we shall see when we come to discuss his plays, there was no subject on which he had meditated more deeply than jealousy. But he was also a man who could not be content with what life had to offer. Like Segismundo in *La Vida es Sueño* and Semíramis in *La Hija del Aire*, the strength of his desires working on his imagination made the world seem small:

> La causa es, que de mi pecho
> tan grande es el corazón,
> que teme, no sin razón,
> que el mundo le viene estrecho.

The reason is that my heart is so large in my breast that it fears, not without reason, that it will find the world too narrow for it.

And so even in his early plays we get the familiar note of disillusion—of life being unequal to the demands of man, of being therefore no more than a dream. This feeling was to grow on him till, with the decline of his strength and the deaths of those he loved, he went over to it altogether. Like St Augustine, he was drawn to religion by his insatiability.

The years 1635-7 saw the culmination of Calderon's worldly success and fame. The new palace of the Buen Retiro had just been completed and he was chosen to give the principal dramatic representation for its opening. This was a musical play on the theme of Ulysses and Circe, which was later printed as *El Mayor Encanto Amor*. No play had ever been given under such splendid circumstances. A floating stage was built on the large *estanque* or oblong pond and lit with 3000 lanterns. Cosme Lotti, an Italian stage machinist, designed the décor, which included a shipwreck, a triumphal water-car pulled by dolphins, and the destruction of Circe's palace to the accompaniment of artillery and fireworks. The king and his suite watched from gondolas. Such was the success of the performance that Calderon was made a Knight of the Order of Santiago—an honour only given to Velazquez twenty years later.

But in 1640 the disastrous revolt of Catalonia and Portugal from the Spanish crown put an end to all dramatic entertainments. Calderon enrolled in a troop of cuirassiers and spent some eighteen months at the front. Disillusioned by the conduct of the militia, as his play the *Alcalde de Zalamea* shows, he retired on grounds of ill-health, and since both the court theatre and the public theatres were closed, entered the household of the Duke of Alba. But personal disasters now followed the national one. In 1645 his brother José was killed in action: two years later he lost his other brother. Then sometime between 1648 and 1650 his mistress died, probably in giving birth to a son whom he adopted. This decided him. He resigned from the king's service and became a priest.

Thirty years of life were left to him. They were years of steady output. Every summer he produced two *autos* for the municipality of Madrid and wrote plays on mythological subjects for performance at one of the court theatres. Except for the time given to rehearsals, he seems to have lived in great retirement. For some years he was at Toledo, occupying a room at the Hermandad del Refugio, to which he was chaplain. Then he lived in Madrid in apartments which he filled with pictures, reliquaries, ivory crucifixes, gilt vases, polychrome statues—a whole museum of religious *objets d'art* which the painter Claudio Coello was given the task of valuing after his death. Here he spent much of his time in reading. But it is a mistake to think of him as a scholarly man: the scope of Calderon's interests was very limited and his notions on history and geography wildly inaccurate.[1] The subjects he studied in his retirement were those he needed for his plays—pagan mythology and theology.

The most convenient way to approach the study of Calderon's drama is to make a division between the realistic plays and the poetical plays which he wrote before he was forty, and then to go on to a study of his later work. The great majority of his realistic plays are *comedias de capa y espada*, comedies of cloak and sword, which deal in a light way with contemporary life. Their subject is always the love intrigue of two pairs of lovers, and the business of the playwright is to introduce such a succession of obstacles and misunderstandings that the situation appears quite irretrievable—until, at the very last, it is retrieved. The concept of honour provides an added complication, because at any moment swords may be drawn and the lovers be faced with the alternative of killing the

---

[1] Calderon's indifference to fact was very great. He thought, for example, that Fez, which is only a hundred miles from Spain, was a seaport. Even after he had become a priest, he confused Syria with Assyria and when writing a play on the war in the Alpujarras, close to Granada, he invented the name of the town where the action took place, although two well-known accounts of the campaign had been published. Lope de Vega, on the other hand, had been very accurate.

fathers or brothers of their lady-loves and so ruining their prospects, or else of being killed by them.

Calderon did not of course invent this genre: he took it from Lope de Vega, from whom he often borrowed his plots as well. But he perfected it. What strikes one chiefly about the best of these plays is the admirable management of the plot. In his *Casa con dos Puertas Mala es de Guardar*, which he wrote when he was twenty-nine, we see a very complicated dual intrigue worked out with the precision of a mathematical problem. *La Dama Duende*, given in the same year, and in every respect a most perfect and delicious play, is another example. Or one may cite *Mañanas de Abril y Mayo*, given in 1632, which shows the May Day courtship of the young people of Madrid and puts on in Don Hipolito an amusing example of the fashionable lady-killer of the time, who talks, of course, in a *culterano* idiom.

The *discreteo*, or lovers' repartee and argument, in these plays is generally excellent, the versification is easy and all the parts well proportioned. But the form is of course highly artificial. Here we see the characteristically Calderonian contribution. The merit of Lope lies in his spontaneity and fertility of invention: that of Calderon in his talent for systemization and putting everything rather tightly in its place. We see this particularly in his treatment of the *gracioso*. As his style developed, Calderon took to relegating all the humour of his plays into a single person, usually a servant and always of lower-class origin, who fulfils much the same function that the fool does in Shakespeare. This was necessary because the increasing decorum of the age—let us remember that Philip IV never permitted himself to smile in public—was making it difficult to allow men of the upper classes to show any sense of humour, much less to appear ridiculous. The *gracioso* was therefore needed to provide comic relief, and he tended to become more and more a stereotyped figure, rather like the music-hall comedian of the present day. Many, though by no means all, of Calderon's *graciosos* are extremely funny. He had a fine vein of wit which he kept to the end of his life. We need to bear this in mind because nearly everything else that we know about him inclines us to think of him as a man of weight and gravity.

More interesting than the plays of cloak and sword, though naturally less delightful, are the tragedies on jealousy and honour. The two chief examples of these—and they rank among the greatest of Calderon's productions—are *El Médico de su Honra* and *A Secreto Agravio Secreta Venganza*, both written in the same year, 1635. But before considering them, let me say something about Spanish ideas on honour at this time.

The concept of honour, as the code of a gentleman's life, distinguishing him from the merchants and peasants, began to take on exaggerated forms in various European countries towards the beginning of the seventeenth century. In Spain it was carried further than anywhere else. A number of factors contributed to this: the intense competition, both economic and amatory, set up by court life: the need of the nobles, who no longer volunteered for foreign wars, to find a convention that would canalize their aggressive instincts: the general idleness, and most of all perhaps the uncompromising temper of mind and what I should like to call the idealistic egoism, that from this time on stand out as one of the most characteristic features of *homo hispanicus*.

'*Valgo yo más que yo mismo*', declares a character in one of Calderon's plays, when he forgives an enemy, 'I can rise higher than myself.' Here we see the almost religious estimation in which honour was held. It was the private banner or escutcheon that a man hung up in the temple of his ego, the symbol of his pride and self-respect, by means of which he could rise superior to his own nature. It was the source from which, if it was kept inviolate, courage, loyalty and generosity flowed. But it was not easy to keep it inviolate. As Calderon's characters frequently complain, the slightest breath of gossip or suspicion could sully it. It depended, that is to say, less upon a man's own actions than upon the public report of them. This is where the Spanish conception of honour differed from that of other nations: it was not so much a department of the individual conscience as a sort of tyranny, not unlike that of the Inquisition, which society exercised with the aim of procuring greater uniformity and cohesion. We owe to it the sudden silence that, in the matter of gossip, private correspondence and biographical material generally, descends upon Spanish life in the first quarter of the seventeenth century. But for the drama and the reports of foreign ambassadors, this age, so full and luminous in other countries, would be almost as dark to us as is Russia today.

In the plays, taken as a whole, we get a fair picture of how the code of honour worked out. The ordinary *caballero* lived easily enough, provided that both he and his family showed reserve and circumspection. But in certain circumstances the strain of keeping one's honour pure and above reproach could be very severe. It could call for a constant vigilance. For honour was a defensive conception. As Kathleen Gouldson says, 'Whilst the honourable man would not brook the slightest offence against himself, he never hesitated to satisfy his own passions. Dishonour consisted not in committing, but in receiving an injury. Thus a code which owed its origin to high motives... ended in the perversion of all ethical sense whatever.'[1] And then, as if the ordinary rules were not enough, there were the purists who made their honour hang upon the finest points of conduct or etiquette—the so-called *pundonor* or *puntillo*. For many people the whole affair became an obsession.

The test of a man of honour was his readiness to risk his life at any moment in defence of his good name. Out of this grew the universal custom of duelling. But in Spain the duel gave rise to something much worse—the blood feud. When a man killed another in fair fight, the matter was not necessarily over, for the relatives of the dead man might feel obliged to seek out and kill the slayer. In practice this was not always done, for friends would step in and arrange the matter, but when strong passions were aroused such arrangements were not easy. It was, however, in their sexual applications that the laws of honour showed their most sinister side. They canonized jealousy. To preserve his honour, a man might feel authorized to kill both his wife and the person he suspected of being her lover, whether he had proofs of her infidelity or not. It was enough if she had given cause for gossip. Moreover, the lover must be killed secretly, by a stab in the back, to avoid giving scandal. In the large towns such assassinations were frequent. In the same way a father or brother could kill, not only

[1] 'Three Studies in Golden Age Drama', by Kathleen Gouldson, from *Spanish Golden Age Poetry and Drama* (1946). An excellent essay.

a man who had compromised his daughter or sister, but, in the heat of his rage, the girl as well. This added a spice to courtship. Young people in Spain have always insisted on marrying for love, but although, like the Moslem poets, they developed the faculty for falling in love at first sight, they naturally desired to confirm their sentiments by meeting and talking. If the girl's male relatives were touchy about their honour, they did so at the risk of their lives.

This extreme sensitiveness about the good name of women corresponded to a wave of suspiciousness that passed across Spain in this century. Although to their face they were treated like goddesses, an apparently quite unjust belief in their frailty was general among men. To have a beautiful wife or daughter or sister was a responsibility that many men dreaded. And, if we put ourselves in their place, we shall understand this. The streets of Madrid and Seville were full of young and reckless gallants whose chief occupation in life was the spying out of beautiful girls and, if possible, conducting secret intrigues with them. Love was the great business of the day: a host of servants, pimps, porters and the like were its agents and the man whose position required him to defend the prizes had often an anxious time. One of the commonest images for the lover in Spanish poetry is that of a hawk chasing a heron, and the smallest imprudence on the part of a girl of good family might lead to her ruin and to that of her male relatives. Although we must remember that these matters were more often solved in a common-sense way than the plays of the time suggest, it is significant that the Jesuit casuists were compelled by the strength of public opinion to find excuses not only for duelling, but even for secret assassinations, whenever questions of honour were involved. For

> El honor es reservado
> lugar, donde el alma asiste.

Honour is a reserved place, where the soul is engaged.

Let us now turn to Calderon's tragedies. It was Lope de Vega who had first seen the dramatic possibilities that lay in the idea of a conflict between love and honour, but Calderon in these two plays concentrated the whole of his genius and of his power of plot organization upon this theme. *El Médico de su Honra* is the story of a man who comes to suspect that his wife is having an affair with the king's brother, the Infante Don Enrique. He resolves to say nothing, but to wait and see if he can obtain further evidence of her guilt or innocence. Although she is innocent in act though not in feeling—for before her marriage she had been in love with the Infante—the evidence against her accumulates and becomes irresistible. Her husband cannot avenge himself on his rival because his position is too high, but honour, reinforcing jealousy, requires that he kill his wife. He does so in a manner which is at once secret and dramatic. Sending all the servants out of the house, he warns her of her approaching death so that she may make her peace with God. Then he fetches a *sangrador*, or blood-letter, brings him blindfolded from his house to the room where Doña Mencia is lying drugged on the bed and orders him to open a vein. When the king knocks at his house at dawn, having discovered by a chance meeting with the *sangrador* what has happened, the bed is soaked in blood and Don Gutierre explains the terrible 'accident'.

The central part, or pivot, of the play lies in the conflict that goes on in the mind of Don Gutierre between his love for his wife and his jealousy of her. With each new piece of evidence that turns up, he balances the pros and cons of her guilt or innocence and, till he finds her actually writing to the Infante, puts off a decision. The uncertainty causes an agony of mind that breaks out on one occasion in uncontrollable ravings that remind us of similar outbursts in Webster or Ford, and in the last scene, when the king knocks at the door of his empty mansion, we see Don Gutierre, his hands red with blood, in the state of crazy exaltation of a man who has forced himself to perform terrible things.

The play has been compared to *Othello*. In the movement of its plot, in the economy of its material, in the adjustment of the different characters to their functions in the whole, it is decidedly superior. The fact that everything that happens after the beginning of the second act leads us straight to the conflict between love and jealousy in Don Gutierre's mind gives it a concentration and unity, which are increased by our knowledge that he had broken off a previous engagement to a lady upon very slight grounds. Calderon, at his best, is a master of plot construction. The versification too is as pure, as stripped and, when the situation requires, as passionate as the thin *romance* measure of Spanish plays will allow. A Spaniard might well argue that the torrents of great poetry that Shakespeare pours into his tragedies are mostly wasted when they have to be spoken by actors. But the play has, it seems to me, two serious defects. Don Gutierre, though not a broad or rich character, is perfectly alive—but he is unsympathetic. It is not that we are shocked by his murder of his wife, for that is dramatically excused by his sufferings: what we cannot stomach is his prudence, his secretiveness and his mastery of himself. Calderon has drawn him in the mould of Gracián's *Discreto*, the man whose passions are entirely subordinate to his will. His value as a tragic hero is weakened when we see him, in spite of his very real love for his wife, planning to kill her with such secrecy that his act will not be discovered and that he will be able to resume his normal life and even, as happens at the end of the play, to marry again. The real character of the laws of honour stands out in all its freezing egoism. How different from Othello, who, when he killed Desdemona, did not stop to count the consequences to himself!

The second objection I find to this play is Calderon's clearly shown approval of Don Gutierre's action. This secret, premeditated murder of an innocent wife is held up to us as a course to be followed. It is for this reason that the murderer is not tried for his crime, but on the contrary secures the king's approbation. Now this means that the play is not a tragedy at all, so far at least as the chief character is concerned, but on the contrary a drama offering a moral example. As such we cannot take it. The sinister smugness of the final scene, where we have to listen to Don Gutierre's self-congratulatory boasts on the skill and discretion with which he has avenged his honour, produces a revolt and we are left with a feeling of the gulf that separates the moral standards of this neurotic and convention-ridden country and age from those of the rest of Christendom.

The other play that Calderon wrote in the same year, *A Secreto Agravio Secreta Venganza*, is closely modelled on *El Médico de su Honra*. Here again we have a husband, Don Lope, deeply in love with his wife, who before her marriage had been in love with someone else. The lover, whom she had thought was dead, returns, and Don Lope becomes suspicious. But his suspicions do not lead to conviction. He murders her lover treacherously, when he is his guest on a boat, kills his wife and, to cover up his deed, sets fire to her bedroom—not because he believes her to be guilty, but because he has been asked by the king to accompany him to the Moorish wars and fears what will happen in his absence. The king, on learning what he has done, expresses his approval.

The chief interest of this play, which is not so good as *El Médico de su Honra*, lies in the long soliloquies of the husband, Don Lope. He expresses the view that a suspicion that one's wife may betray one is a sufficient reason for killing her, and that honour is better served by acting at once than by waiting till the evil has taken place. His friend, Don Juan de Silva, who is presented to us as a man of the most honourable views, agrees with him. But Don Lope also complains of the tyranny of the 'mad laws of the world' which place a man, without any fault of his own, in such a hateful situation. (Needless to say, he does not for a moment consider the injustice to his wife.) One may thus, I think, call this drama not so much a bungled tragedy on the theme of jealousy as a problem play. Calderon poses the question—can a view of honour that permits a man to kill his wife on the grounds that she is likely to be unfaithful to him be a reasonable one? And though he answers this question in the affirmative, the fact that he has asked it shows that it has disturbed him.

Two years later Calderon wrote a powerful but imperfect play on the subject of jealousy from which the trappings of honour have been left out. This is *El Mayor Monstruo los Zelos*, 'Jealousy the greatest monster'. The Tetrarch of Judaea is in love with his wife Mariene, but on being imprisoned by his enemy Octavius, orders his servant to stab her to prevent her falling into his hands. She discovers this, saves her husband's life by appealing to Octavius' chivalry and then punishes him by refusing to cohabit with him. But the tetrarch's jealousy is a disease he cannot control, and in the end he kills her. As the title shows, we have here a very different approach to the whole question. Jealousy is seen as a monstrous and irresistible passion and the play is therefore a genuine tragedy.

Calderon never again confuses jealousy and honour. By the time he is sixty he is putting forward quite different opinions. In his musical *comedia*, *Eco y Narciso*, for example, a shepherd called Febo declares that, because his jealousy is noble, he can forgive his rival. His companion replies:

> En amor, Febo, no hay
> sofisterías; y advierte
> que en zelos nunca hay nobleza;
> Lo que se siente se siente.
> Y así tengo de matarle.

There is no sophistry in love, Phoebus, and no nobility in jealousy. What one feels one feels, that's all. And so I shall kill him.

Here, I think, we have the mature Calderon: honour is on the side of generosity and is opposed to the violent passions. Yet, the world being what it is, jealousy keeps its rights. If he had felt differently in the two plays we have discussed, that is, I think, because at the time he wrote them he was going through a personal crisis.

We now come to that little group of Calderon's plays, written before he was forty, which for want of a better term I will call poetical. The first of these is *El Príncipe Constante*, given to the stage when he was only twenty-eight. It tells the story of a Portuguese prince who, when captured by the Moors of Africa, preferred a cruel exile to accepting the ransom asked—the fortress of Ceuta. Side by side with this tale of loyalty and heroism we are given a picture of the hopeless love of the Moorish general, Muley, for Fénix, the daughter of the King of Fez, who has been betrothed against her will to the King of Morocco, and of the chivalrous relations that bind the prince and Muley. The play breathes out the noble and generous instincts of the young dramatist, but it strikes also that lyrical philosophical note of the illusoriness of life and the evanescence of beauty that is the thing we most prize in Calderon.

Very characteristic is that scene in the second act where the prince, now a slave employed on manual labour, is seen picking flowers for Fénix. He offers them 'as hieroglyphs of his fate, since they were born with the sunrise and died with the day'. She recoils with horror from the spectacle of his wretchedness, which seems to presage her own, and refuses to take them. 'What fault have the flowers committed?' he asks. 'That they resemble the stars', she answers. In this contrast between flowers, as the Christian's symbol of the brevity and illusion of life, and stars, as the Moslem's symbol for fate (or perhaps more generally for the unchanging order of Heaven), and in the two human figures, the conscious martyr and the girl frozen in hopeless grief, we get one of the first and most typical examples of Calderonian allegory. Altogether this play, in spite of a certain weakness in the plot, is one of the most beautiful he ever wrote and its language has a freshness rarely shown by his usually rather heavy and emphatic muse.

El Príncipe Constante was written in 1628 and is one of a small group of plays that deal with the theme of loyalty in religion and in friendship. It was followed by a four years' spell during which Calderon perfected his talent for plot construction, but wrote only light comedies. Then, from 1633 to 1635, comes a period of intense creative energy, devoted chiefly to those plays of a tragic sort on vengeance which we have already spoken of. *La Cena de Baltasar*, an *auto* containing Calderon's most tremendous burst of poetry, the stanzas spoken by Death, is also from this time and at the end of it comes *La Vida es Sueño*. After this, till the outbreak of civil war in 1640, there is a falling off in intensity.

The play I wish to speak of first, *La Devoción de la Cruz*, dates from round about 1633. This is a religious melodrama of the most romantic and extravagant kind, showing attempted incest, violation of a convent, murders committed by an escaped nun, and all taking place in an exalted atmosphere of mingled faith and passion among surprising events and miracles of every sort. In the last scene, for example, we see the brigand hero raised from the dead in order that he may make his confession to a bishop turned anchorite, whose life he had once saved and who miraculously happened to be passing the spot at the moment: after absolution has been given, he sinks back into the grave again. Calderon derived the general idea of this play from the recently acted *El Condenado por Desconfiado*, a drama attributed to Tirso de Molina but almost certainly not by him.[1] But he disregards entirely its doctrinal intention, piling up the melodramatic effects, accentuating the morbidity and perverted sensuality and throwing to the winds all care for probability. One can best compare *La Devoción de la Cruz* to the paintings and polychrome statues of ecstatic saints and martyrs that were so popular at this period. In them death and physical suffering have acquired almost sexual attributes: they constitute a kind of pornography dedicated to religious ends, the aim being, by squeezing out the last drop of emotion from sin and suffering and salvation, to produce a sort of gloating ravishment.

The play in which Calderon most movingly expresses his feelings upon the human situation is *La Vida es Sueño*, 'Life is a Dream', which he wrote in 1635. It is a play so well known in England that I will spare the reader a description of its plot. It is, or has always been regarded as, a philosophical play, expressing general truths about the world by means of allegory. When, however, we try to interpret that allegory, we do not find it easy. The unreality of life is, obviously, one of the things it aims at expressing, but who is Segismundo? In the first act we naturally take him to represent Man, condemned to unhappiness through no fault of his own: we wonder whether the king, his father, is not God and the astrologer's prediction the curse of original sin. The third act undeceives us. Segismundo's pride, we learn here, is the result of a bad education, the king has been much to blame and the astrologer's prediction is falsified: we return with a jar to the plane of actuality. Moreover the reason that Segismundo gives for dominating his evil impulses does not make sense, for if life is really a dream, then surely it is

---

[1] *El Condenado por Desconfiado* deserves a mention. Its theme is the contrast between a brigand who, after committing every imaginable crime, is saved by a confession on the scaffold and an anchorite who, in spite of all his austerities, suffers from a conviction that he cannot be saved, and is therefore damned. Behind the play lies a theological controversy between a Dominican, Báñez, who inclined to predestinarianism, and a Jesuit, Molina, who held that anything could be achieved by an act of the free will, assisted by grace. But the play shows how far in fact the religious temper in Spain had swung over from the balanced medieval position on these matters to something like Luther's doctrine of grace. Works no longer count if salvation can be assured by a death-bed repentance: a single act of faith is a sufficient justification. By giving way to this unrestrained antinomianism, Spain was showing how, when the social fabric of a country decays, it is the religious attitudes of the East that spring up and flourish. On the other hand she escaped the smugness so prevalent in the more moral atmosphere of Protestant countries.

outside the dreamer's control and the acts he performs in it have no moral consequences. We have to resign ourselves to getting no philosophical interpretations out of this play beyond the rather vague one expressed in the title. As an allegorical drama, it is a muddle.

Yet one cannot read it or see it acted without being deeply moved. The scenes in which we see Segismundo first in the dungeon, then in a palace, then in the dungeon again are not only intensely dramatic, but they carry up our thoughts to philosophic regions. They make us feel the situation of Man in a broad and poetical way and leave us free to draw any conclusions that may occur to us. We thus become alive to the mystery of human life and destiny without having to submit to the tedium of having it explained to us. Allegory is a form that is hardly ever successful because, whilst we get an exhilaration from our awareness that what we read has 'higher' meanings among which our thoughts wander, we resent the tight organization by which the allegorist seeks to rob us of our liberty and tie us down again to some conceptual framework. We feel like Segismundo returning to his dungeon a second time: our freedom in the upper regions has been taken from us and we are in a worse prison than before. Now in this play that does not happen. Calderon, through his own haste and vagueness, has failed to impose any irksome discipline upon us, and though we might wish the plot had been better thought out and a little more direction given to our philosophizing, we do feel that we are breathing a higher and purer air as we read it.

The only other play of this sort that I will mention here is *El Mágico Prodigioso*, which Calderon wrote for the Corpus Christi festival in the little town of Yepes in 1637, but revised later. It is a play on the theme of the Faust legend and takes place during the first centuries of the Christian era. A young pagan called Cipriano, deeply taken up with speculations about the nature of God, falls in love with Justina, who is a Christian. The Devil offers his services in procuring her, on condition that Cipriano makes over to him his soul. The young man accepts and retires with him to a cave in the mountains to learn the arts of magic. But even diabolic magic has no power over the free will of a human being who invokes the aid of God. The incantations fail, Cipriano embraces Christianity and dies with Justina on the scaffold. The Devil appears to seize Cipriano's soul, but is defeated and put to flight.

It is a beautiful play, rich in poetry. A note of exhilaration runs through it, reaching a climax in the scenes of love and death in the last act. Historically too it is one of the best of Calderon's dramas. His indifference to politics and the business of the world gives a thinness and inadequacy to most of his representations of courts and kings, but he had a special feeling for the period when Christianity was emerging from paganism, which enabled him to write about it with understanding and conviction. We are taken straight back to Prudentius, who, it will be remembered, was the first European to write an allegorical poem. These two great poets both lived in ages of decay verging on calamity and, if we allow for the fact that the one breathed in the sense of reality and political responsibility of the Roman Empire and the other the very different atmosphere of the Spanish baroque age, we shall find that they have many features in common.

Calderon's great period of production ended in 1637. The *comedias* he wrote during the next three years are of little interest: then came the long interval of the Catalan War and the closing of the theatres, and when he began to write again in 1648, he had lost much of his skill and zest. One feels that he was repeating himself. One remarkable play does, however, date from this period: this is the *Alcalde de Zalamea*, which he is thought to have written round about 1642, after his experiences in the Catalan campaign. It stands in a different category from anything else he ever wrote. Founded on a play of the same name by Lope de Vega, it treats of the honour, not of a gentleman or *caballero*, but of a *villano*—a rich peasant whose daughter has been violated by a captain of the militia who was billeted in the village. This alone makes it unique. Lope, the son of a poor man, had written many plays on such themes, but one may search the rest of Calderon for any mention of a *villano* who was not a simpleton or a buffoon. The play too is charged with social criticism. We are shown Don Mendo, the starving village *hidalgo*, who declared he would have refused to be born from anyone not of *hidalgo* blood: the vulgar captain of militia, drunk with his new power, like some of the militia officers in the recent civil war, and the tough but honourable commander, Don Lope de Figueroa, who had spent his life in Flanders and suffered from gout. Best of all is the peasant, Pedro Crespo, who during the course of the play is elected Alcalde. Calderon, whose weakest point is his inability to create character, here shows us a magnificent type of prosperous peasant, honourable, decent, very obstinate and yet with a curiously comical, almost buffoonish streak in his nature that makes him one of the most solid and convincing figures of the seventeenth-century stage. His altercations with Don Lope, who is also a 'character', are high comedy.

Calderon was, of course, the most intellectual of the Spanish dramatists and so it is natural that, once embarked on social criticism, he should have found some telling things to say. 'Can a villein have opinions?' asks the captain of militia. 'As well as you', replies the Alcalde's son. 'There would be no captains if there were no labourers.' In another place, when the soldiers are about to set fire to the village, one of them cries out 'Kill those villeins!' '*Que mueran?*' replies the Alcalde. '*Pues qué, no hay más?*' 'They're to die, are they? Well, aren't there plenty more?' These retorts have an almost revolutionary ring about them. And there are those famous lines upon honour, spoken by Crespo:

> Al Rey la hacienda y la vida
> se ha de dar; pero el honor
> es patrimonio del alma,
> y el alma sólo es de Dios.

To the King we owe life and goods, but honour is the patrimony of the soul, and the soul belongs to God alone.

One cannot help regretting, when one reads this magnificent play, that Calderon spent so much of his early life at court, among people for whom love affairs and points of honour were the only topics of interest, and that in later life theology, which he got from books, weakened his interest in conduct, which must be studied from human beings. This regret will be strengthened by reading the fine *auto*, *El Gran Teatro del Mundo*, also written at this time, in which he shows in a moving way the Catholic attitude of the day to social inequality.

As we have said, Calderon's drama seemed to have reached a dead end by the time he was forty-five or fifty. His wonderful powers of plot invention had depended upon his adhering to the strict convention of the realistic *comedia*. Whenever he had followed more romantic or poetical themes, he had had difficulty in keeping his play together, more especially when he began to increase the number of the characters and to throw in allegorical meanings. A good illustration of such a failure is *La Hija del Aire*, a very ambitious play in two parts, which was given before the king in 1653. It is a return to the theme of *La Vida es Sueño*, in which the part of Segismundo is taken by a woman, Semiramis, who becomes Queen of Syria. Another play of the same sort is *En esta Vida todo es Verdad, y todo Mentira*, written a few years later. Like so many of Calderon's plays of a melodramatic-allegorical kind, they both contain a few good scenes, lost in a mass of absurdities.

Perhaps we may see how this happened if we turn to a passage in one of his earliest *comedias* (*Saber del Mal y del Bien*, 1628) in which he gives what one might call his formula for life:

> El mundo todo es presagios,
> El cielo todo es avisos,
> El tiempo todo mudanzas
> Y la fortuna prodigios.

> The world is all presages,
> Heaven all warnings,
> Time all changes
> and fortune all prodigies.

Now such a statement, if taken literally, implies a denial of the order of Nature and of the laws of causality. The Moslems, since the time of their great schoolman Ash'ari, had formally accepted this and their prose literature had led to the *Arabian Nights*. Although Calderon as a theologian could not hold such a view, as a playwright he was strongly inclined to it. Released from obedience to the laws of probability, he found his material in a mixture of presages, warnings, omens, heaven-made coincidences and miraculous events—the world of the baroque imagination. The justification for works of art composed of such material is that, if well selected, they give an increased importance to inner elements at the expense of outer ones. Just as some modern writers and painters endeavour to create a world in which the unconscious suffuses every detail and gives it significance, so Calderon aimed at writing plays in which sin, grace and divine interposition operated continually and dramatically at every point. Nothing, of course, can be said against such a method (accusations of superstition are quite beside the point), but in practice the wide choice of resources offered to the dramatist and the release from the discipline of having to adhere to probability made the construction of coherent plays much more difficult.[1] Nor had Calderon any longer got to direct him that powerful eruption of feeling that had given their freshness and vigour to *La Vida es Sueño* and *El Mágico Prodigioso*. A certain drawing-in and reorganization therefore became necessary.

Towards 1657, therefore, we see Calderon's dramatic work crystallizing into two different types of production—the *zarzuelas* or musical comedies, and the *autos sacramentales* or allegorical religious plays. The change was gradual, for there were no complete breaks in his literary life: he had tried his hand at both of these types before and he continued to write other kinds of plays to the end. As a court dramatist he worked to order. What we can say, however, is that from this time he set himself to evolve the best possible organization for these two different types and to give his most careful attention to them. Let us take the *zarzuelas* first.

The original form of these plays goes back to *El Mayor Encanto Amor*, the musico-dramatic piece which was given to celebrate the opening of the Buen Retiro Palace in 1635. Calderon continued to write other mythological dramas of this sort for open-air festivals at the same place. Towards 1656, however, plays began to be given at La Zarzuela, a hunting box close to the palace of the Pardo that belonged to the king's brother. They were plays of a light kind, rather short, to suit an audience that had spent the day in the open

---

[1] An extreme example of this sort of composition is provided by the Chinese story *Monkey*, translated by Arthur Waley. One can call it Buddhist Baroque.

air: for subject they had some legend from pagan mythology and many of the dialogues and choruses were sung to a musical accompaniment. They were a sort of *divertissement*, half-way between a play and an opera.

The first of these *zarzuelas*, as they came to be called, was *El Golfo de las Sirenas*, described as a 'piscatorial eclogue' and of one act only. It was performed in 1657. After this came *El Laurel de Apolo* and in 1660, to celebrate the peace with France and the marriage of the Infanta Maria Teresa to Louis XIV, *La Púrpura de la Rosa*, on the fable of Venus and Adonis. In the *loa*, or prelude, to this play, Calderon alludes to himself as a swan of the Manzanares, *cantando en su edad postrera*, and announces that the play is to be in a new style, *toda música*, so that other nations (i.e. the Italians) may see their best works equalled. It was in fact an opera, in which the *recitativo secco* mode of singing was introduced for the first time from Italy, though the music was Spanish. But the recitative did not catch on, so that Calderon reverted to his earlier custom of having songs, choruses and selected dialogues sung to music, but leaving the rest of the play to be spoken. In this form he wrote two *zarzuelas* of remarkable beauty, *El Hijo del Sol*, *Faetón* and *Eco y Narciso*, both given at the open air theatre of the Buen Retiro in 1661. To the end of his life he continued to turn out plays of this sort, the most notable of his later years being *El Monstruo de los Jardines* in 1667 and *La Estatua de Prometeo* in 1669.

These plays belong to a genre of Calderon's work that has not been sufficiently appreciated. Operas or half operas, they realize a form of collaboration between music and poetry in which each art has been given its fair share. Their technique is highly stylized. To quote A. A. Parker, writing of a similar but less elaborate technique in the *autos* of this period, 'whole scenes are constructed in a fixed metrical pattern, often built up round a *leitmotif* which is developed and repeated at regular intervals. The pattern is invariably symmetrical, the different parts balancing and contrasting with each other. . . . Just as Calderon made scenery, costumes and the movement of the characters serve his dramatic end, so too does he adapt his style to the requirements of choral music, thereby giving his dialogue a remarkable and, usually, very effective symmetry and balance.' As an example of this kind of writing, which should be of interest to poet-dramatists and librettists today, I would recommend the curious choral passages in *El Golfo de las Sirenas* and also the beginning of *El Hijo del Sol, Faetón*. In this we see Calderon taking one of the most joyful and melodious of Góngora's *romances*, breaking it up into short fragments and distributing them among three choruses. The characters develop each piece as it is sung and the combined choruses repeat the first verse at the end. One can call this an adaptation of the *villancico*, or of Góngora's own technique, to the uses of the stage. But it is also a form highly suited to opera, while at the same time it produces a musical effect on the person who reads it.

The treatment of the mythological subjects of the *zarzuelas* also deserves to be mentioned. Calderon took a great interest in Greek mythology and saw the rich field it offered to symbolical treatment. It seems that, influenced by two books that had come out on the philosophical interpretation of classical mythology, he regarded the pagan myths as foreshadowing in some way the coming of Christianity. That is to say, he believed that God had revealed himself to the pagans as well as to the Jews, though in a less distinct and authoritative manner.[1] Thus in *La Púrpura de la Rosa*, we find that Adonis prefigures Christ:

> El que en pena tan enorme
> con su sangre les infunde
> nuevo espíritu a las flores.

He who in such enormous pain infuses with his blood a new spirit into the flowers.

This is a more intelligent attitude than that of Milton, who, writing the first book of *Paradise Lost* in the same year but taking the Old Testament point of view, has no excuse to offer for turning this same myth of Adonis into enchanting poetry.

Another sort of interpretation is offered in that loveliest of *zarzuelas*, *Eco y Narciso*. Narcissus is represented as having been

---

[1] *La gentilidad—teniendo de las verdades—lejanas noticias.* See the long speech by the Prince of Darkness in the *auto*, *El Divino Orfeo*.

brought up alone in a cave by his mother Liriope, to avert some evil omen. That is to say, he is a variation of the solitary man, sequestered from childhood in a cave or dungeon and so deprived of all experience of society, of whom Calderon's plays offer so many examples.[1] But he had doted on his mother, and it is on this account that he turns away from the nymph Echo and falls in love with his own image. Here we have what looks like a case-history from a book of modern psychology. But Calderon was looking beyond this: his Narcissus is simply another example of his view that the fundamental thing in Man, the thing he carries out of his mother's womb, is his self-love and egoism.

The other type of drama that Calderon set himself to perfect was the *auto sacramental*. These *autos* were one-act plays, performed on Corpus Christi, in which the mystery of the Eucharist was represented symbolically. In the Middle Ages they had been known as *farsas* and acted in churches. After that they were given in *carros* or movable cars and formed part of the slowly moving procession with its fantastic Carnival figures, the *tarascas* and *gigantones*. But by Calderon's time the arrangements had become more elaborate: a fixed stage, surrounded by movable cars, was set up in the street and on these the *autos* were acted with a great display of scenery, costumes and fireworks, to the accompaniment of instrumental music and dancing. The needs of Catholic propaganda brought about a movement towards the fusion of the arts which, under the influence of Latin literature, had become separated during the Middle Ages.

Like most of the other playwrights Calderon had written *autos* during the first period of his life—indeed two of his most moving

---

[1] Perhaps we may some day have a study of this theme, which so fascinated the seventeenth century, of the child brought up in isolation from the world. We find it touched on in *The Tempest*, novelized by Gracián, made the basis of Descartes' philosophy, developed by Defoe. It marks the new interest in man as an individual—what is he, what can he be or do when taken out of society? Sometimes this theme is connected with theories of the noble savage and the visionary life of childhood. But in Calderon it is always associated with pride and self-love. Man is born an egoist, life is the testing ground and the aim to be achieved is self-mastery. Segismundo is the classic example of the aggressive egoist who conquers his egoism, and incidentally one of the two great representations of the Spanish character. It is a pity that the play that Calderon wrote on Don Quixote, that more subtle portrait of *homo hispanicus*, has been lost. (Sr A. Pastor's *A Spanish Robinson* (1930) confines itself to the study of the Spanish Arabic romance on this subject by Ibn Tufail.)

and poetic date from then—but it was not till he was ordained priest that he wrote them regularly: after that, from 1652 till his death in 1681, he produced two every year. As with the *zarzuelas*, he began towards 1660 to elaborate their form and the last he wrote are, in the opinion of some judges, his best.

The distinction between the *auto* and the *zarzuela*, subject apart, is that the former is an allegorical play with its symbols and correspondences fully worked out, and the latter a play with at most a vague allegorical tendency. The *auto* has therefore a much stricter and more intellectual form and contains as a rule more argument and less 'poetry'. It is also more didactic in tone than are most works of imagination, for the object of the *auto* was to instruct the common people in the dogmas of the Church and to show them their application to their own lives, and only incidentally to entertain them. This, I think, is sometimes an obstacle to their enjoyment by modern readers, whether they are Catholics or not. We miss too, as Calderon himself pointed out in his preface to the 1677 edition, the pomp and magnificence of the setting, the music and the singing, whilst the unreality attaching to abstract characters such as Thought, Sin, Sight, Memory and so forth requires to be counteracted by their being impersonated by real actors. Yet in spite of all these disadvantages the best of the *autos* are remarkable dramatic poems which will repay the attention of the reader who is prepared to go a certain way to meet them. Calderon's skill in devising plots and situations to illustrate Catholic dogmas is quite amazing and the form of allegory itself, usually so tedious in its precision and tightness, sometimes takes on a real beauty in his hands. Besides, the subjects chosen—the misery of man, free will, sin and redemption, the same as those taken by Milton for his two great epics—are in the highest degree significant and dramatic, even for those who do not accept the Catholic solutions.

The most impressive of the *autos* are undoubtedly *El Gran Teatro del Mundo* and *La Cena de Baltasar*, both of them early. After that one may read *El Divino Orfeo*, a mythological *auto* of great charm, and *Tu Prójimo como a Ti*, with its strange and beautiful allegory. The reader will then be ready to take up the more dogmatic *autos*, such as *La Nave del Mercader* and *El Nuevo Hospicio de Pobres*, which

Calderon wrote towards the end of his life. A recent study of these plays, *The Allegorical Drama of Calderon* by A. A. Parker, provides an excellent introduction.

Calderon might be called the perfect example of a Baroque writer. All the different elements included in that much abused word are represented in his plays. The love of extremes, the delight in marvellous and phantasmagoric effects, the tendency away from realism towards allegory and melodrama, the feeling for pagan mythology, the impulse to fuse poetry with music and dancing and so create an art in which all the senses are affected at once, the love of pattern and repetition, the strong contrasts, the ponderous style, the lack (so unusual in Spain) of any influence of popular verse. Most of these elements have their corresponding feature in the painting, sculpture or architecture of the century. But Calderon is also a very personal writer, whose voice can be heard in almost every scene that he wrote. It is an attractive voice, noble, passionate, a little melancholy, but above all decided and affirmative.

Calderon's strong affirmation comes of course from his faith. He is the poet of certitude. The world is a dream, a place of vague confusion and suffering, but Reality lies beyond and the road there is open to anyone who will exert his free will to follow it. Yet though this world is unreal, it is not simply a base and ugly place, but is full of reflections and adumbrations of what comes after. One of these is physical love. Calderon writes of love in a thrilling, passionate, manly tone that is very different from the excited rapture of those addicts; Lope de Vega and Shelley, and from the obsessionary concentration of Donne, who found a kind of spirit in the flesh. Love, even when misplaced and sinful, is for Calderon a property or similitude of the soul.

> Aunque es verdad, que en la calma
> del morir se ve perdida
> la acción de aquello que es vida,
> no el ser de aquello que es alma.
> Alma en mí ha sido mi amor.[1]

Although it is true that in the calm of death the action called life is lost, the being called soul is not lost. My love in me has been soul.

[1] *La Hija del Aire II*, act 2.

On the question of beauty Calderon is even more definite. He adopts the attitude which St Augustine derived from Plato. The beauty of the world is a reflection of heavenly beauty—illusory if taken as subsisting in itself, but real in so far as it is derived from eternity. The situation is well conveyed in a passage from the *auto*, *El Gran Teatro del Mundo*, in which a voice sings and Hermosura, Beauty, answers, defending herself:

> *Voz.* (*canta*) Toda la hermosura humana
> es una temprana flor.
> Marchítese, pues la noche
> ya de su aurora llegó.

> *Hermosura.*   Que fallezca la hermosura,
> dice una triste canción.
> No fallezca, no fallezca,
> vuelva a su primer albor.
> Mas ¡ay de mí! que no hay rosa
> de blanco o rojo color
> que a las lisonjas del día,
> que a los halagos del sol
> saque a deshojar sus hojas,
> que no caduque; pues no
> vuelve ninguna a cubrirse
> dentro del verde botón.
> Mas ¿qué importa que las flores,
> del alba breve candor,
> marchiten del sol dorado,
> halagos de su arrebol?
> ¿Acaso tiene conmigo
> alguna comparación
> flor en que ser y no ser
> términos continuos son?
> No, que yo soy flor hermosa
> de grande duración,
> que si vió el sol mi principio,
> no verá mi fin el sol.
> Si eterna soy, ¿cómo puedo
> fallecer? ¿Qué dices, Voz?

Voz. (canta) Que en el alma eres eterna,
y en el cuerpo mortal flor.

Voice (singing). All human beauty is a morning flower. Let it fade
then, since night has succeeded dawn.

Beauty. A sad song says, beauty must die. No, it must not die, not
die, it must return to its first prime. But, alas, there is no rose white or
red that opens its petals to the caresses of the sun and the flattery of the
day, which does not wither; none returns to hide in its green bud again.
Yet what matter if the flowers, those brief glints of the dawn, fade in
the golden sun, victims of its rays? Can a blossom in which being and
not being follow one another bear any comparison with me? No, for I
am a flower of lasting life and the sun that saw my beginning will not
see my end. If I am eternal, how can I die? What say you, Voice?

Voice (singing). That in the soul you are an eternal, but in the body a
mortal flower.

The contrast expressed in these verses between the pathos of the
human situation and final affirmation is typical. They help one to
see why Shelley felt such enthusiasm for Calderon: the Romantic
poet who was a Platonist and the Baroque poet who read St
Augustine had much in common. But Calderon had stronger and
more robust instincts than the youth who died at thirty, whilst the
ready-made structure of Catholic dogma, with its complex view
of human nature, provided a better framework for poetry than the
arid rationalism from which Shelley never entirely disengaged
himself. If the characteristic notes of Calderon are exhilaration,
pathos and a dream-like sense of the unreality of life, there lies
behind them a proper amount of human experience.

Calderon's moral attitude is also clearly defined. For him the
principal vice, governing all others, was egoism, which showed
itself chiefly in pride, arrogance and rebelliousness. A theme repeated again and again in his plays is that of the man (or woman)
who has some great inheritance in store for him but who, as a
result of a fear as to how he will use it, generally expressed in the
form of an astrologer's prediction, has been brought up in ignorance
of this and in great seclusion. Here, being thrown back upon
himself, he develops an inordinate pride which leads him, when

the truth about his prospects is discovered, to break out into acts of violence and *hubris*. Sometimes, as in the case of Segismundo, the reverses he suffers teach him to reform himself; but more often, as with Semiramis, Narcissus and Phaethon, he is irreclaimable. One remembers Milton's Satan. Pride was the great vice of the seventeenth century, the age of the break-up of the social structure of the Middle Ages and of the emergence of the solitary individual, and it should be noted that, contrary to what one might expect, it was even more strongly marked in Catholic countries than in Protestant ones. We may suppose too that for Calderon, as for Milton, this was a personal problem. All that we know of Calderon's youth suggests that he was a man of violent, headstrong character. Then, in the second half of his life, we see him given up to the task of reform and self-discipline. But the only letter we possess of his—addressed to the Patriarch of the Indies in 1652—shows him as a man to whom, even then, humility and obedience did not come easily.

There remains to be discussed the question of Calderon's poetic diction. Of his ordinary dramatic versification in octosyllabic metre there is little to be said. Often very diffuse and long-winded, and made more tedious still by its fondness for arid scholastic distinctions and sophistries, it can also be admirably terse and direct, lending itself to epigrammatic statement. But such unadorned writing must be distinguished from the 'poetry' which is generally, though by no means always, in longer metres. Here the use made of Nature is important. Unlike Góngora (but much like Shelley) Calderon reduces Nature to a number of fixed, discrete and often contrasted properties: flowers and stars, sea and air, fishes and birds, water and earth, day and night, and so forth. These are brought in, either as components of a landscape or, in metaphorical formations, to enrich a narrative passage, and when they appear we get the impression that they constitute for the poet the separate items of which the harmony of the world is composed. The metaphors tend to be simple contrasts or parallels of two of these stock items, so that, for example, when he speaks of a garden with its flowers and birds, he usually takes the opportunity to compare it to the sea with its tossing waves and fishes. Objects in one element are compared to those in another. Such comparisons are not intended to throw light on the thing described, but are introduced, one might almost say mechanically, both to give a broader view and for the sake of symmetry. They suggest the style of Baroque ornament in retablos and façades rather than that of Baroque painting, which seeks to blend objects with one another. However, Calderon also paints more complex landscapes. These consist for the most part of a series of highly melodramatic stock pieces, suggesting the movable back-cloth in a theatre and generally representing some great cataclysm or monstrous condition of Nature. For example, there is the tempest at sea with its shipwreck and the sailors clambering on shore, the uninhabited island with its crags and grottoes, the volcano belching out lava, the storm with lightning and thunder, the whirlwind and earthquake; when needed, these pieces are brought out in their appropriate metre, touched up a little to prevent monotony and taken away again. Once more we see in this Nature poetry a certain resemblance to Shelley. Bertrand Russell once said that Shelley's poetry was the kind of poetry most suited to the mathematical mind, because it presents Nature in such a discrete and universalized manner. This might be said with even more truth of Calderon's. Like Shelley, he had a philosopher's intellect and a melodramatic imagination. He broke up and articulated his world, partly because he had an analytical and classifying mind and partly because he wished to produce out of its separate elements a series of symmetrical and contrasting patterns.[1]

---

[1] Professor E. M. Wilson has written an interesting study of Calderon's imagery in the *Modern Language Review*, vol. 31 (1936), which I did not read in time to make use of in this chapter. Here very briefly are its conclusions. Calderon imagined the world as divided into the four elements, fire, air, earth, and water. To each of these elements he assigned both an animate and an inanimate creature which typified it, and to these, as well as to the element itself, he gave a fixed number of attributes or characteristics. Thus to air correspond bird and cloud, and their attributes are feather, wings, and exhalations. To water, fish and ship, with foam, scales, sail, and rigging. To fire, sun, comet, star, salamander, phoenix, Phaethon, with for attributes light, smoke, ray, lightning, and so forth. With these tables to draw on, he could then establish correspondences between the different elements, comparing flowers to stars, ships to birds, waves to feathers and constructing epithets which illustrated the correspondence, such as, to designate a ship, sea-horse, foam-bird, wind-dolphin, sailing-rock, canvas hurricane, and grove of rigging. These comparisons reach a sort of climax in those set passages, so plentifully provided in his plays, in which he describes the violent disturbances of Nature—storms, shipwrecks, earthquakes, volcanic eruptions—for here the various elements really do interfere with and compenetrate one another. Nature is, as it were, doing the poet's work of fusing metaphors.

There can be no doubt, I think, that Professor Wilson has correctly explained the very

Calderon is usually spoken of as one of the most poetic of dramatists. This is so and yet his poetry is of a peculiar kind. Sometimes, especially in his early plays, it wells up in a spontaneous way in short melodic passages, but in general it was written, not for the inner ear like Shakespeare's, but to be declaimed on the stage. That is to say, it is rhetorical poetry. In this it is, of course, the precise opposite to Góngora's, to which it is often compared. Calderon, as his plays show, knew Góngora by heart, but what he took from him he adapted to his own very different purposes. One will see this if one takes a few lines from the elder poet and notes how finely they are phrased and how they linger and reverberate in the memory. Then one may turn to Calderon and observe that most of his poetical set pieces are written in very strong rhythms and with little or no melody. Their grain is coarse and it is not easy to find single lines that stand out on their own merits. In the few passages, epigrams apart, where his poetry can be detached from his plays, it lives by the force of its long, sweeping rhetorical periods.

What Calderon chiefly learned from Góngora was his use of pattern and his *culto* idiom. His poetical passages are made up of symmetrical patterns and stylized tropes and epithets that recur again and again. This gives to many of these passages a barbaric quality of richness and monotony that is unlike anything else in European poetry. One of the favourite devices of his first period

artificial sytem by which Calderon did his image-making and which in a vague way strikes every reader of his plays. His explanation shows us why it is that so much of his poetry is that of the hurdy-gurdy. Calderon set out to invent a mechanical way of writing his decorative passages and stuck to it. In a poet such a method must, I imagine, be regarded as reprehensible, but Calderon was a playwright and in that capacity his system served him well. His formal image patterns suited his notions of what an allegorical play required, and it is quite likely that they also corresponded to some philosophical theory of the value of metaphor as a way of interpreting the world, and even of the general illuminative function of poetry. Besides he relied on method and systemization to solve his personal problem. Calderon's excessive love of order and symmetry is a reaction to his chaotic, spasmodic imaginative faculty. Nature had made him a loose and slovenly writer with occasional bursts of 'inspiration', when his one strong feeling about the evanescence of beauty and the unreality of the world rose and flooded his mind. As the schoolmaster or sergeant-major in him took charge to combat this, the unruliness of his class or squad forced him to become more and more a disciplinarian; he drilled his words and images and scenes mercilessly. But if much verse that is merely decorative and empty is produced in this way, we also owe to the drill book some of Calderon's best poetry. And it is by his poetry that he lives: scattered about among those seventy-odd plays, there is a note which, once heard, can never be forgotten.

is to enumerate a number of features, giving to each two or three lines of description and then summing them up rapidly at the end. The most elaborate example of this is Cipriano's description of Justina in the second act of *El Mágico Prodigioso*. Here, in the description of a garden from *La Cisma de Inglaterra*, is another. I select it, in spite of its being a rather poor illustration, because it is taken from one of the most beautiful passages of Calderon's poetry—Don Carlos's account of his falling in love with Anne Boleyn.

> Allí el silencio de la noche fría,
> El jazmín que en las redes se enlazaba,
> El cristal de la fuente que corría,
> El arroyo que a solas murmuraba,
> El viento que en las hojas se movía,
> El aura que en las flores respiraba,
> Todo era amor. ¿Qué mucho, si en tal calma
> Aves, fuentes y flores tienen alma?

> And there the silence of the chilly night,
> The jasmine that on the lattice was entwining,
> The crystal of the fountain, ever running,
> The stream that to itself was murmuring,
> The wind that in the leaves was moving,
> The airs that on the flowers were breathing,
> All, all was love. What wonder if in such calm
> Birds, fountains and flowers a soul take on?

In itself there is nothing remarkable about a rhetorical figure such as this: Italian poetry from Tasso on contains many examples of it. What is remarkable is the continual use that Calderon makes of it. In his poetical plays he appears to seize on any stylistic device, any opportunity for formal pattern that comes his way, and is never afraid of repeating it. This has led to his being accused of monotony by people who have not understood the ritual element in Baroque art. But in Calderon's plays symmetry, stylization, repetition all have their function. The whole tendency of his drama is towards a ritual performance in which every act shall be symbolical and every gesture balanced by another gesture. If we call that performance opera or ballet (and the ritual of the Mass is both), then we may say that the poetical pieces correspond to arias or set dances and the passages in plain octosyllabic measure to recitative or miming. The poetical pieces have therefore to be as formal in their language as possible, whilst in the others formality is provided by the arrangement of the plot and the grouping of the characters.

Although Calderon's most thrilling poetry was written in the first half of his life, when he was still open to new impressions, his most deliberate and artistic verse dates from his sixties. The best of this is found in the *zarzuelas*. I have already said something about the complicated writing of their choral passages; however, it is the dialogues or set pieces in a florid or rhetorical style that make most impression as poetry. An early example of these is the description of the magic storm in the second act of *El Mágico Prodigioso*. Another is the scene of the landing on Circe's island in *El Mayor Encanto Amor*. But later on, when he was working on his *zarzuelas*, he began to experiment in new verse arrangements that should give a better musico-dramatic effect. In one of these—the beginning of the third act of *El Monstruo de los Jardines*—he imitates the very beautiful opening of Lope de Vega's play *El Remedio en la Desdicha*, referred to in chapter IX, in which two lovers come on to the stage without seeing one another and declaim in alternate strophes on the subject of their love. In another passage—it is the opening scene of *Eco y Narciso*—he uses the same device, except that the speakers are not lovers but rivals. Here are the first stanzas of it. Though meant to be spoken and not sung, both the measure and the arrangement suggest music. It may be noted too how much better the florid Baroque diction is suited to declamation than Lope's delicate lyric style, delightful though this is when read to oneself.

> *Silvio.* Alto monte de Arcadia, que eminente
> Al cielo empinas la elevada frente,
> Cuya grande eminencia tanto sube
> Que empieza monte y se remata nube,
> Siendo de tu copete y de tus huellas
> La alfombra rosas y el dosel estrellas. . . .

Febo. Bella selva de Arcadia, que florida
Siempre estás de matices guarnecida,
Sin que a tu pompa, a todas horas verde,
El Diciembre, ni el Julio se le acuerde,
Siendo el Mayo corona de tu esfera
Y tu edad todo el año primavera. . . .

Silvio. Pájaros, que en el aire fugitivos
Sois matizados ramilletes vivos,
Y, añadiendo colores a colores,
En los árboles sois parleras flores. . . .

Febo. Ganados, que en el monte divididos
Música sois de esquilas y balidos,
Y en la margen de aquese arroyo breve
Cándidos trozos de cuajada nieve. . . .

Silvio. High mountains of Arcadia that eminent
Against the sky upraise your lofty front,
Whose mighty eminence so proudly rises
That what begins as mount as cloud surprises,
Having to clothe your feet and shade your head
A baldequin of stars, a rose-strewn bed. . . .

Febo. Lovely Arcadian woods that, full of flowers,
Are always decked with variegated colours,
Such that no July drought nor cold December
Your ever verdant pomps can e'er remember,
Perpetual May the regent of your sphere,
Your only age the springtime of the year. . . .

Silvio. Small birds that flying fugitive in the air
Are little coloured branches living there,
And, adding on to colours other colours,
Among the trees appear as chattering flowers. . . .

Febo. White flocks that, scattered through the mountain,
Music of sheep bells are and distant lowing,
And on the edges of that trickling river
Are slabs of beaten snow [or gleaming silver]. . . .

But it is difficult to sample Calderon in small fragments. Here, to conclude this subject, are the famous octaves spoken by Death in the *auto*, *La Cena de Baltasar*, 'The Feast of Belshazzar', given in 1634. They are in *rimas agudas*, with the accent falling on the last syllable of the line—a kind of rhyme which Spanish critics dislike, but which is here appropriate both to the speaker and to the occasion. Although the versification is crude by comparison to that of Garcilaso or Góngora, they have an organ-like power and resonance that make them, in my opinion, one of the outstanding passages of Spanish poetry.

> *Daniel.* ¿Quién eres?
> *Muerte.* Yo, divino profeta Danïel
> De todo lo nacido soy el fin;
> Del pecado y de la envidia hijo cruel,
> Abortado por áspid de un jardín.
> La puerta para el mundo me dió Abel,
> Mas quien me abrió la puerta fué Caín,
> Donde mi horror introducido ya,
> Ministro es de las iras de Jehová.
>
> Del pecado y la envidia, pues, nací,
> Porque dos furias en mi pecho estén:
> Por la envidia caduca muerte di
> A cuantos de la vida la luz ven;
> Por el pecado muerte eterna fuí
> Del alma, pues que muere ella también;
> Si de la vida es muerte el espirar,
> La muerte así del alma es el pecar.
>
> Si *Juicio*, pues, *de Dios*, tu nombre fué,
> Y del juicio de Dios rayo fatal
> Soy yo, que a mi furor postrar se ve
> Vegetable, sensible y racional,
> ¿Por qué te asombras tú de mí? ¿Por qué
> La porción se estremece en ti mortal?
> Cóbrate, pues, y hagamos hoy los dos,
> De Dios tú el juicio, y yo el poder de Dios.

Aunque no es mucho que te asombres, no,
Aun cuando fueras Dios, de verme a mí;
Pues cuando El de la flor de Jericó
Clavel naciera en campos de alhelí,
Al mismo Dios le estremeciera yo
La parte humana, y al rendirse a mí
Turbaran las estrellas su arrebol,
Su faz la luna y su semblante el sol.

Titubeara esa fábrica infeliz,
Y temblara esa forma inferior;
La tierra desmayara su cerviz,
Luchando piedra a piedra y flor a flor;
A media tarde, joven e infeliz
Espirara del día el resplandor.
Y la noche su lóbrego capuz
Vistiera por la muerte de la luz. . . .

Yo abrasaré los campos de Nembrot,
Yo alteraré las gentes de Babel,
Yo infundiré los sueños de Behemot,
Yo verteré las plagas de Israel,
Yo teñiré la viña de Nabot,
Y humillaré la frente a Jezabel,
Yo mancharé las mesas de Absalón
Con la caliente púrpura de Amón.

Yo postraré la majestad de Acab,
Arrastrado en su carro de rubí;
Yo con las torpes hijas de Moab
Profanaré las tiendas de Zambrí;
Yo tiraré los chuzos de Joab;
Y si mayor aplauso fías de mí,
Yo inundaré los campos de Senar
Con la sangre infeliz de Baltasar.

Daniel. Who are you?
Death. O holy and prophetic Daniel,
Of all things that are born I am the end,
The son of sin and of envy cruel,

Aborted by a serpent in a garden.
The door into the world gave me Abél,
But he who opened it for me was Cain,
By which my horror having entered once
Became the instrument of Jahveh's wrath.

Of envy was I born then and of sin,
And so there are two furies in my breast.
Because of envy I gave wretched death
To all who saw the light: because of sin
I am the death eternal of the soul,
Since you must know that that may die as well.
For if of life death is the parting breath,
Sin to the soul is death its very self.

If *Judgement of God* is then your name
And of God's Judgement the fatal ray
Am I, at whose furie you see laid low
Things vegetable, sensible and rational,
Why do you stand amazéd thus, and why
Does your O mortal part tremble at me?
Collect yourself and let us act the two,
I the power of God, his judgement you.

Yet it would not be strange that you should fear,
Even though you were God, to look on me;
Since when He, from the flower of Jericho,
Carnation is born in fields of *alhelí*,[1]
I shall make tremble even of God himself
The human part, and when He yields to me,
The stars will falter and their colour change,
Its face the moon and the sun its semblance.

Then that unhappy fabric will be rocked,
And shaken too that form inferior;
The fainting earth will low bow down its neck,
Contesting stone by stone and flower by flower.

[1] The *alhelí* is the Elizabethan gillyflower, comprising both the modern stock and wall-flower. Observe the beauty given by the Spanish verb tense, which, though known to grammarians as the imperfect subjunctive, conveys, as the subjunctive mood tends to do in Spanish, a sense of the future and of expectancy.

In the mid afternoon, unhappy and brief,
The splendour of the daytime will expire,
And its lugubrious hooded cloak the night
Put on in mourning for the death of light. . . .

I shall dry up the pastures of Nembroth,
I shall confound the people of Babél,
I shall unloose the dreams of Behemoth,
I shall pour out the plagues of Israel,
I shall infect the vineyards of Naboth,
I shall bring low the forehead of Jezebel,
I shall defile the tables of Absalóm
With the incestuous purple of Amnon.

I shall bring low the majesty of Ahab,
Hurling him from his chariot of ruby;
And with the shameless daughters of Moab
I shall profane and soil the tents of Zimri;
I shall thrust home the javelins of Joab,
And, if a greater fame you demand of me,
I shall bedrench the lowlands of Shinar
With the unhappy blood of Belshazzar.

Calderon was not the only dramatist of his generation. A number of playwrights, working both for the Madrid theatres and for the court, were turning out their three or four plays a year. Two of them—Rojas and Moreto—require to be mentioned.

Francisco de Rojas Zorrilla was born in Toledo in 1607 and died in or soon after 1648. He lived chiefly in Madrid, where he made a place for himself at court, wrote plays for the royal theatre and, like Calderon, was awarded a knighthood of the Order of Santiago. That is all we know about him. But it is a real pleasure to read the best of his plays. When, after a session with Calderon, we open a Rojas comedy, we find ourselves in a world that is much more varied and entertaining. Reading Calderon might be compared to attending a function in a seventeenth-century palace or cathedral: there is an elaborate ceremonial, an opulent decoration, a droning voice that sends us to sleep and then moments when the ear is charmed and the mind uplifted and immense vistas are opened.

But there is generally very little that can be called life, and it is precisely life—seen through the eyes of a man who had a fine sense for it and enjoyed it—that Rojas gives us.

Let us take his best known play—*Del Rey abajo, Ninguno*, usually called, after its principal character, *García del Castañar*. It is a play about honour: a rich *labrador*, or farmer, García, who later turns out to be a nobleman in disguise, has reason to think that the king is trying to make love to his wife. Although he adores her, the laws of honour leave him no option but to kill her. In a confused way he attempts to do this, but cannot bring himself to the point: then, while his intentions are still in suspense, he discovers that the would-be lover is really a courtier. He kills him and the king forgives him.

The play, in spite of its conventional theme, is remarkable in several ways. In the first place there is the wonderful ease and naturalness with which the plot moves. If we allow for a certain artificiality in the premises, there is perhaps no Spanish or English play of that century in which one gets quite such a feeling of events casually succeeding one another yet always tending towards a certain end. Nor do we feel ourselves shut in within the narrow limits of dramatic conventions, as we do in Lope's *comedias*. From all sides, in small details and suggestions, there seeps in a sense of actuality and of the way in which things are in practice managed in the world. But what especially charms us is the picture of the prosperous and happy life of the *labrador* and his beautiful wife Blanca. Whether we listen to García discoursing on the pleasures of partridge shooting, or watch Blanca cooking the dinner or playing at riddles with her women whilst she awaits his return, or see the two of them making love to one another, we find a whole-hearted enjoyment of the simple things of life for which the great writers of this century have not prepared us. And this is expressed in a poetry in which exactness of delineation is combined with a fine ear and a delicate but restrained lyrical feeling. It is true that Rojas, unlike Lope de Vega, looks at the country with the eyes of a man of property: he paints an idyllic picture for the same reason that Tolstoy painted idyllic pictures in *War and Peace*—because he saw it from a privileged position. Yet that picture is more detailed than Lope's: the touches more finely observed and casually presented, and the savour of country things equally strong. On reading this play we get the feeling—fallacious, as it turns out—that the novel of country life is not far away.

García del Castañar is one of the most enjoyable of Spanish plays and Rojas Zorrilla wrote nothing else that can be compared to it. Most of his other work is disappointing. He followed Calderon in trying his hand at every sort of production, from comedies of cloak and sword and plays on revenge to grand rhetorical pieces on mythological and classical subjects. If these are sometimes good of their kind, they run too closely to type to allow Rojas to show his special qualities. Where he broke new ground was in three of his lighter comedies—*Abre el Ojo*, *Lo que son Mujeres* and *Entre Bobos anda el Juego*. These are delightfully humorous plays, offering a rich variety of bores and pompous personages and thus throwing over the convention by which humour had to be confined to the *gracioso*. Like all comedies of cloak and sword, their plots consist in a juggling feat with endless embarrassing situations and misunderstandings, but the intrigue is not too closely woven (the fault of most of these Spanish comedies is the over-ingenuity of the plot) and allows scope for comic passages of great brilliance. As an example, read the opening of *Abre el Ojo*, in which a young man is shown complaining of the jealous scenes which his mistress, a widow who piques herself on her respectability, is always making to him. It is a passage that even the greatest comic writers would have been glad to have written.

What, however, is especially notable in Rojas Zorrilla is the way in which he enlarges the focus of literary consciousness by incorporating material that had never been used previously. In *Abre el Ojo*, for example, the furniture of one of the ladies' apartments plays a considerable part in the action. We get two scenes of her moving house—these three plays abound in those trifles of daily life which the Spaniards call *costumbrismo*—and then we have a duel that has the same relation to the innumerable duel scenes in Lope de Vega and Calderon that Stendhal's description of the battle of Waterloo in *La Chartreuse de Parme* has to the battle scenes in history books or paintings. Rojas is inclined too to treat the sacred theme of honour in the same spirit, showing the compromises to which it was subject in practice and so allowing its rules to be contrasted with those of common sense. Thus one might say that if Lope de Vega and Calderon are the great poets of Spanish auto-intoxication, Rojas Zorrilla is a de-intoxicator, not so much through overt satire, as by the ironic pleasure he takes in showing the casual way in which things usually regarded as important actually take place. Yet we must be careful not to exaggerate the scope of his innovations. Rojas was a man of instinct rather than a self-conscious artist, and he failed to press on in the direction in which his intuitions were leading him. And since the generation that followed him produced no writers of talent and was completely under the spell of Calderon's allegorical plays, the hints he had offered of a new and less formal dramatic art were not taken up.

Agustín Moreto was a man of less originality and creative power than Rojas, but he was a finished artist who knew exactly what he wanted to do. He was born in 1618 at Madrid, spent most of his life at court and died in 1669. The plays for which he is read are comedies dealing with love, restrained in tone and keeping within the limits of a narrow field. But they are extremely well written and adapted to the stage, their dialogue is excellent and the characters they present of courtiers and young ladies, usually so conventional in Spanish plays, contain nuances that show a delicate power of observation. The best known of his plays is *El Desdén con el Desdén*. This has for its leading figure a princess, Diana, who, though courted by several lovers, refuses to marry any of them because she is incapable of feeling love. One of these lovers has the ingenious idea of pretending that he too is incapable of seriously loving any woman. This piques her vanity and she resolves to make him fall in love with her and then to turn him down. A courtship follows in which each plays a part he does not feel until, out of sheer mortification, the princess finds that she is hopelessly in love. The young man then reveals his true feelings. It is a play that calls out the best in good actors and Moreto does his part by providing an admirable plot and a dialogue of considerable subtlety. The duel-like form of the courtship, which would have pleased Stendhal, was an especially clever idea because it did away with the need for an artificial intrigue by providing internal obstacles to be overcome.

Another play, *El lindo Don Diego*, centres on a comic character, a very preposterous fop, whilst *La Confusión de un Jardín*, with one of those Chinese-box plots of misunderstandings, has an overtone of deep night and tree-shaded gardens, expressed in subdued imagery that, as Sr Valbuena remarks, suggests the paintings of Watteau. Moreto, one may say, is the perfect playwright of a refined and self-contained court, cut off from the general life of the country and given up, on the surface at least, to a life of love affairs and pleasure. One feels too in the fine grain of his versification and in the delicate touches of his dialogue and characterization the beginnings of French influence, though the dates would suggest that these were an indigenous development.[1]

The last readable playwright of this century is Bances Candamo (1662–1704). He was a disciple of Calderon. In him the great torrent of Spanish drama comes to an end in a pool of minor poetry, fantasy and shallow symbolism. The art for art's sake ideal concealed in the heart of baroque literature killed it, because it prevented it from taking in new draughts from the outer world. If the seventeenth century in Spain must be called an age of faith in religion, it was even more an age of lack of faith in life. In the previous century these two faiths had not been mutually exclusive.

---

[1] Another dramatist of note at this time was Antonio de Solís (1610–82). He may be described as a court playwright of a similar kind to Moreto, but with a more satirical tendency. He also wrote a *History of the Conquest of Mexico* in a pure Spanish, free from all Baroque affectations. It is one of the best prose works of the century.

CHAPTER XIII

THE EIGHTEENTH CENTURY

SPANISH literature entered on a long decline with the death of Calderon. For nearly two hundred years no writer of major importance, unless we include Moratín, made his appearance, and for sixty or seventy years scarcely a single book came out that can be read today except for its historical interest.

The first part of this period—from 1681 to 1760—was taken up with a struggle between the Spanish forms and ideas of the seventeenth century and the new ideas that came from France. The old forms had taken too strong a hold of the country to die easily, but they no longer had the vitality to inspire fresh works of interest. The new ideas of reason, simplicity and common sense that filtered across the Pyrenees were equally incapable of stirring the creative imagination. They took therefore a doctrinaire and propagandist tone and were put forward not so much by young poets and dramatists as by a tribe of critics, pamphleteers and men of erudition, who laid down rules and attacked abuses, but were themselves unable to give birth to a new literature.

The most important of these figures was Padre Benito Jerónimo Feijóo. He was a Benedictine monk from Galicia, born in 1676 and dying at an advanced age in 1764. He was a man of unusual intelligence and breadth of mind, who read several languages and was well versed in the scientific, philosophical and theological speculation of the day. In a series of papers, later published in book form as *Teatro Crítico* and *Cartas Eruditas*, he set out to attack the superstitions and absurd beliefs that had grown up in the course of the previous century and to bring a little light into the abysmal ignorance to which his countrymen had sunk. But he was not guided solely by French ideas: he drew his principal inspiration from Luis Vives, the Catalan humanist who had been the greatest of Erasmus' disciples. One may say that his aim was to lead Spain back to the state of intellectual activity and participation in the life of Europe that she had possessed before the Inquisition and the struggle with the Protestants had isolated her.

Feijóo has been called the Spanish Voltaire, but his counterpart is really Pierre Bayle, the author of the famous *Dictionnaire historique et critique*, which came out in 1695-7. Although he was a persistent critic both of the superstitions of his day and of its barbarous and inhuman practices, he lacks the fierce party spirit of the men of the *Encyclopédie:* his tone, though occasionally tinged with irony, is persuasive and reasonable. For this reason he does not write so well. A Spanish critic of the last century, who thought his style too colourless, declared that a statue ought to be put up to him and his works burned under it. But that is carrying the cult of elegance too far. Feijóo is always clear and easy to read, and he is never pompous or pedantic. We feel ourselves in the company of a modern man when we open his pages, and his essays on the science, learning and philosophy of his time and on its superstitions and false miracles can still be dipped into with pleasure. To give an example: if we read his essay on the intelligence of animals, we shall discover what the Greek, Roman and medieval philosophers thought on this subject, be treated to a number of absurd and entertaining anecdotes and at the same time take part in a serious and reasonable discussion.

But what draws us most of all to this man is the openness of his mind and the warmth of his sympathies. Thus we see him arguing against the use of torture and showing, as Montaigne had done, how useless it is for obtaining true confessions: defending women against the unjust opinions of men and standing up for the freedom of the arts and sciences. In a country where heretics were hated, he ventured to admire the English, whom he regarded as more judicious and serious than other races, though the Elizabethan drama showed, he thought, that they had a strain of the bloodthirsty and neurotic. And he preferred Bacon to Descartes, whose narrowly intellectual approach to life he distrusted.

Feijóo is a strange phenomenon in the ignorant and anarchic society of his time. He did not begin to write till he was almost fifty. Then, from his cell at Oviedo, where he lectured on philosophy, or from the still remoter convent in Galicia to which he retired in 1739, he poured out till his death a stream of articles and essays upon every subject imaginable—articles that were always well informed, up to date and intelligent. If the purpose of literature is to change and educate, then this Benedictine monk must be classed among the greatest of Spanish writers. But since no one has ever regarded him as such, we must suppose that it is something different.

The literary counterpart of Padre Feijóo was Ignacio de Luzán (1702-54). He was an Aragonese who had been brought up at Naples, where he is said to have been a pupil of Vico. A man of finer and more polished intelligence than Feijóo, he had also considerable erudition, for he knew the Greek and Latin poets well, was familiar with Italian and French literature and had enough English to translate a part of Milton. His great work was his *Poética*, published in 1737, which became the bible of all the new Spanish writers of the century.

The Baroque movement in literature had come in insensibly, like feudalism or capitalism, without rules or programmes to guide it. It was the result of a tendency, so little aware of itself that it did not even acquire a name, that appeared spontaneously in every West European country at somewhat different dates. When, for example, it broke out in Spain and Italy, it was dying in England. But neo-classicism entered, like Socialism, with books and doctrines. Essentially the reaction of French common sense and realism to the anarchy of the imagination, it spread rapidly through Europe with the prestige of the Court of Versailles and because it was the counterpart in aesthetics of a more lucid and objective view of conduct and society.

The first exponent of the new ideas in literature was of course Boileau. His *Art Poétique*, published in 1674, has the narrow emphasis and doctrinaire tone of a militant pamphlet. Luzán's *Poética* is by contrast a much broader, more serene and more thoughtful work. He wrote at a later date, his knowledge of literature was wider and he had the advantage of drawing on the finest critics and scholars of the day, who were all Italians. His book is written, not in verse like Boileau's, but in a pure and elegant prose: and although it breaks no new ground, its clarity in exposition and the breadth and aptness of its critical judgments make it one of the classics of literary criticism. Its weakness lies in the fact that it was a product of the academies and not of an active, creative movement.

Luzán's approach to Spanish literature must be briefly stated. He greatly admired Lope de Vega for the energy and variety of his genius and he felt the charm of Calderon: he also praised Góngora's *romances* and his great natural talent. But the only authors he entirely approved of belonged to the previous age. Something had gone wrong, he thought, about the turn of the century, when the language had contracted the diseases of obscurity and turgidity and there had been a general lapse from good sense and truth to nature. Moreover in the drama he supported the French view that plays should satisfy the three unities of action, place and time. This was a severe view to take, because plays made to these specifications must generally require more time and labour to write than others. This could not be done without a complete transformation of the conditions governing theatrical life, because the Spanish theatre was a popular affair, existing to provide excitement and melodrama, and suffering from an insatiable appetite for new works, since (except during a rainy spell in winter) no play, however successful, could hope to hold the stage for more than a week. To satisfy this monster, dramatists had to write quickly and to rely on improvisation.

Luzán's general view of literature was that it exists partly for entertainment or the giving of delight and partly for didactic reasons, in which case it should express moral and political truths and natural philosophy in the form best suited to make an impression. Although, he held, lyric poetry may aim at delight only, in all works of any length the two purposes ought to be blended. But Luzán had been educated in Italy, where pleasure has always been cultivated as an end in itself, whereas to the Spanish mind it is more likely to need excusing. It thus came about that the enlightened circles in Spain who supported the new ideas stressed the didactic motive, because they believed that everything, including art, should justify itself by its utility. That is to say, they tended to regard literary creation as a form of propaganda. It was a situation that has some resemblance to that which we see in Russia at the present time. Spain under its Bourbon kings was in process of becoming an enlightened autocracy, and the intellectuals, who were in sympathy with all projects of reform, conceived their function to be the imposition from above of a ready-made culture upon a people whom, not without reason, they regarded as ignorant and barbarous. The intention was no doubt laudable, but it was carried out with too much dogmatism and with too little regard for the special qualities of the Spanish temperament. The consequence was that it set up a gulf between life on the one hand and ideology and literature on the other, which was an obstacle to the revival of a genuinely national literature.

Two prose works, however, stand out in this barren age. One is the autobiography of Diego de Torres Villarroel (1693-1770). He was the son of a bookseller at Salamanca who, after a rowdy career as an undergraduate, ran away from home and saw life as a bullfighter in village *corridas*, a seller of patent medicines, a dancing master and the begging partner of a hermit. Then one day he came across a book on solid geometry, and felt the charm of mathematics. At that time mathematics was regarded in Spain as an adjunct of witchcraft and pacts with the Devil. The chair assigned to it at Salamanca had long been vacant and, if we are to believe our author, the subject had not been taught there for 150 years. Torres Villarroel, however, restored its popularity by the astrological calendars which he had begun to bring out under the name of Piscator. In one of these he happened to foretell correctly the death of the king, Luis I, and it was as a result of this prediction that in 1726 the authorities at Salamanca decided to appoint a new lecturer to this valuable science. After a public contest with two other competitors upon the geometry of Ptolemy's *Almagest* (arithmetic was not yet known in Spain) and among scenes of terrific enthusiasm, he was appointed to it.

Torres Villarroel's autobiography is a very readable book, full of curious details about Spanish life in this rather blank century. We are told how he learned medicine in thirty days, investigated a poltergeist who afflicted the Countess of Arcos and had an adventure in the Sierra de Guadarrama, in which his horse was caught in a wolf trap not far from the spot where the Archpriest of Hita had an encounter with the ugliest of the cowgirls. His character too is interesting, with its mixture of extravagance and turbulence. A pleasant trait was his habit of treating his servants as social equals. Like Jean-Jacques Rousseau, whom he resembled in some ways, he combined a strain of egalitarian idealism with a very un-Spanish snobbishness. Both were signs of his feeling of social insecurity, for, like a bull-fighter of today, he had risen suddenly from very humble circumstances to familiarity with the great. The whole book is so much an explosion of his craving to exhibit himself that we look in vain for portraits of other people, but he did not lack a certain malicious acuteness, as when, in a prologue breathing distrust and defiance, he dedicates his work to the hypocritical reader.

As to style, this book is written in the rather taut manner of the picaresque novels of the seventeenth century. The model was evidently Quevedo, whose hatred of doctors he shared. But there is nothing old-fashioned in the contents; Torres Villarroel was in every way a man of his age. Especially one notices his zest for life, which never deserts him except once, when he is in trouble with the Inquisition. His abject submission to it reminds us of Communist Russia. In all other respects his book offers a striking contrast to the carking tone and denigration of life affected by the novel writers of the previous century. The cloud of original sin has lifted and men have a future on earth once more.

The other prose work which deserves to be remembered is the *Historia del famoso predicador Fray Gerundio de Campazas* by Padre José Francisco de Isla. Padre Isla was a Jesuit, born at Leon in 1703, who, like all intelligent men of his day, belonged to the reforming school of Feijóo. From boyhood he had been a voracious reader of French literature and it is significant that his favourite author was Molière. His duties as a Jesuit led him to preach and his preaching to taking some notice of other sermons. At this time the art of sermon writing had fallen into a remarkable decline under the influence of baroque literature. Preachers filled their harangues with allusions to pagan mythology, allegorical interpretations were carried to fantastic lengths and a Gongoresque idiom took the place of ordinary language. Sermons were in fact pieces of fine oratory, which the congregation applauded or hissed, as they felt inclined, and in which moral exhortation was almost entirely neglected. *Fray Gerundio* was an attempt to kill this state of things by ridicule, as Cervantes was thought to have killed the novels of Chivalry. The first part was published under an assumed name in 1758.

The book begins like a picaresque novel. We read of the young Gerundio's early life and upbringing in one of those dull, benighted, treeless villages of the Leonese Tierra de Campos. We are given portraits of the various schoolmasters to whom his education was entrusted and of the absurd methods of teaching that they practised. Then we see him choose the monastic career because, as a lay brother tells him, 'there is no better life than that of a friar, since the most stupid can be sure of getting his rations. . . while those who preach often make a great deal of money and when they retire live at their ease like bishops.'

After this we are introduced to the various inmates of the monastery. We meet the lector, Fray Toribio, with his powerful lungs and his 'clear, thick corpulent voice, a man who is perpetually arguing and a furious Aristotelian because he has never read any other philosophy and cannot endure to hear one mentioned'. Then we see Fray Blas, the preacher, well built but inclined to paunchiness, natty to the point of coquettishness in his dress, with a slight lisp in his sonorous voice, very fluent at finding the right word, a famous *raconteur*, with the free and easy manner of a man who knows his own popularity. With him we enter on the business of sermons: Fray Blas has taken a liking to Gerundio, so, inviting him into his cell, he treats him to a rehearsal of the sermon he is to preach on the following day for the feast of St Benedict. The title of this sermon is 'The Science of Ignorance in the Wise Ignorance of Science', and we are given the full text. Its leading idea is what Fray Blas calls 'the vernal parallel'. The meaning of this is that, since the feast of the Saint falls in spring, a parallel can be drawn between him and the pagan deity, Faunus, whose festival, with its licentious rites, fell at the same time. 'But how are you going to find anything in common between St Benedict and the God of Rejoicing?' asks Gerundio. 'In the easiest way in the world', replies Fray Blas. And he goes on to explain that, since St Benedict spent three years in a cave in the wilderness, castigating his body with penances, and Faunus passed his time in gardens in pleasant repose, the parallel is clear.

This young man in the fields, the other in the desert: this one stretched on the ground, the other in a cave: this one naked, the other in rags: this one crowned with flowers, the other pricked with thorns. . . . What better parallel could one find? For as to the rest, that Faunus was the god of riot and dancing and St Benedict an image of tears and penitence, why, that does not matter one jot. Surely it could not be expected that parallels, even when they are vernal parallels, should apply at every point!

This is not the only sermon we are given. Two by Fray Gerundio himself, composed in a jargon of Gongoresque phrases and images and stuffed with Latin quotations that do not fit the context, are provided for our entertainment. But the nonsense of past ages is less amusing as well as less credible than the nonsense of present times, and so the book begins to pall. Even *Bouvard et Pécuchet*, that most stupendous of *sottisiers*, is not as readable as it used to be. Yet the early chapters, with their pictures of village and school and convent, have a permanent fascination. We see in them what one is sometimes tempted to call the real Spain, the Spain of vast plateaux and earth-coloured villages and bad communications, and the almost inconceivably monotonous life that goes on there. The convent is just such another pool of tedium, lacking the consolations of manual work and family affection, and finding its only alleviation in browsing on intellectual material which, from sheer dullness and stupidity, it cannot digest. These poor devils, Fray Toribio and Fray Blas, who today would be tolerable motor engineers or commercial travellers, have nothing else to do but to grind their way through the arguments of St Thomas's *Summa* or concoct preposterous sermons out of dictionaries of classical mythology and Gongoresque imagery. At all events we see that Padre Isla has hit on the right approach. It was not vice that was destroying this society, as the men of the previous century believed. It was ignorance, boredom and stupidity. The nation had settled down, cut itself off from all possibility of outside stimulus and was sunk in the deep sleep of provincialism. We are once again reminded of Russia—this time the Russia of Gogol's *Dead Souls*.

But Padre Isla, like all the other writers of his age, was a teacher and a reformer as well as a creative writer. Thus while we get in the first chapters of this book a wonderful picture of Gerundio's family life, in which by means of an ironic description of their furniture we enter into the whole circle of their activities, we also encounter that inevitable bore, the model friar, and have to read, or skip, many pages of his wise counsels. This is, of course, an aesthetic blemish, because it crams down our throats something that we can infer for ourselves if the satirist has done his work properly. Not everything that an author wishes to convey needs to be said. But the didactic impulse in this century was too strong to be resisted. Later on we shall see that the *hombre de bien*, the ideal man of good sense and feeling, becomes an almost indispensable figure in drama and poetry.

Fray Gerundio is the only readable Spanish novel between 1640 and 1849 and it would never have been written if a Jesuit father had not been interested in reforming sermons. This dearth of novels is surprising when one remembers the point of development reached by the Spanish drama in the seventeenth century and the way in which the English novel grew out of Restoration plays and Spanish picaresque writings. It must be attributed to the general decay of the creative faculty in literature from the reign of Philip IV onwards. But one would be unjust to this century if one did not make it clear that a very large number of books on historical, critical, scientific and technical subjects were published in the course of it. The impulse began with the foundation, under royal auspices, of the *Biblioteca Nacional* in 1712, the *Real Academia* in 1713 and the *Academia de la Historia* in 1735. Between 1726 and 1739 the *Real Academia* brought out the six massive volumes of the *Diccionario de Autoridades*, which was the most comprehensive dictionary of its time in any language. But the work of the academies is best seen in the encouragement they gave to scholars to produce books on learned subjects. In this the Jesuits especially distinguished themselves, Masdeu writing a critical history of Spain, Hervás an important work on philology and Arteaga a treatise on aesthetics. After the expulsion of their order from Spain, they continued their studies in Italy, where Padre Isla, who was also one of the exiles, employed his leisure in translating *Gil Blas*.

A characteristic feature of some of these works is their enormous length. Padre Flórez's *España Sagrada*, a compilation of documents bearing on the history of the Spanish Church, reached twenty-nine folio volumes: Larruga's work on Spanish economics reached forty-five, whilst—to quote the inevitable absurd example—the history of Spanish literature by the brothers Mohedano reached ten volumes and took twenty-five years to write, though it did not get beyond Seneca. The style of all these books, from Feijóo on, is flat and pedestrian; both the florid writing and the clipped sentences of Baroque prose have gone and there is no trace of the pompous period that appeared in England and reached such amplitude in Gibbon. The only aim one can detect is clarity and the usual fault verboseness—Luzán, who wrote well, being an exception. It is not till the end of the century that one finds, in Jovellanos, Cadalso and Moratín, prose writers who can express themselves with distinction. But they, and especially the two latter, belong to the age of sensibility.

We must now consider the drama. All through the eighteenth century the theatres continued to put on plays that followed, with little innovation and scarcely any merit, the tradition of Calderon and Moreto. After 1750 a few tragedies in the manner of Racine, composed in alexandrines instead of in octosyllabic measure and observing the unities, began to be written, but rarely found their way on to the stage. The extraordinary manner in which plays were given, with both an *entremés*, or short dramatic interlude, and a *tonadilla*, or miniature operetta, sandwiched between each act, encouraged bad play-writing because it prevented the audience giving their attention to the principal piece. Then, in the last years of the century, a genius in the art of writing comedies, who, if his character had been equal to his talent, might have risen to the greatest heights, made his appearance.

Leandro Fernández de Moratín was born in Madrid in 1760. His father Nicolás was a well-known man of letters who had written comedies in the French manner and a poem on bull-fighting that, chiefly for lack of better examples, occupies a place in every anthology. Brought up at home, in an atmosphere of doting parents and grandparents and conversations on literature, he was apprenticed at the age of twenty to a goldsmith. But his talents were too great to allow him to spend his life at a bench, so on his mother's death in 1785—his father had died a few years previously —he left it and settled in his uncle's house to write a play. Then, the play finished and his money at an end, he obtained from Jovellanos, who was a friend of the family, the appointment of secretary to the Embassy at Paris. Here he spent two years, visiting the salons and the theatres and meeting Goldoni, who was then an old man of eighty.

Back in Madrid in 1788 without any means of support, he had the luck to be taken up by Godoy, who, whatever his other faults, was an intelligent and generous patron of the arts. He received a pension and was able to see his first play, *El Viejo y la Niña*, performed. But he was not a courtier. Retiring to the country to his grandmother's town of Pastrana, he settled down to work on two plays, *La Mogigata* and *La Comedia Nueva*. The second was given in 1792 and, as it was a satire on contemporary dramatists, created a great sensation. Immediately after it Moratín applied to Godoy for a further sum of money to enable him to travel abroad.

Moratín's character was very different from what one expects of a great comic genius. He was a man of extraordinary timidity and shyness. In the company of intimate friends he could be gay and witty: he had a strong sense of ridicule and was a brilliant mimic. But a stranger had only to enter the room for his self-confidence to fail and silence to fall on him. 'Then', as he put it himself, 'my assurance vanished and a fear of being mistaken in what I was saying came over me.' In his relations with women he was equally timid. He was attracted to them, but his attraction led nowhere. A long sentimental love affair ended in his sheering away from marriage. The consequence of this was that, in spite of his passion for the stage, he began to shrink more and more from the society of actors and from the discussions of the coffee houses, and to shut himself up with books and learned subjects. A second way of escape was travel. To a man who in his home country must either defend himself by ridicule or barricade himself behind books, the stage coach and the foreign city gave the elation of active flight and of anonymity. It was not surprising therefore that, once launched on his travels, he did not return to Spain for five years.

Travel developed another side of his character. In London, where he spent a year, he read at the British Museum, translated *Hamlet* and admired Greenwich Hospital and St Paul's. In Italy he read history and looked at works of art. His memoirs, published posthumously, show an indefatigable sightseer and a man of taste and sensibility. His letters, which are probably the best ever written by a Spaniard (excepting only those of Santa Teresa) confirm the same impression. But what was happening to his talent? Back in Spain, in the new house he had built at Pastrana, he rewrote *El Barón*, a comedy originally composed in 1787, and in 1805 finished what was to be his last play, *El Sí de las Niñas*. A reflection of his sentimental courtship of Paquita Muñoz, it is still the most popular of Spanish plays.

The rest of Moratín's life was a long and singularly inappropriate tragedy. Caught in Madrid by the events of 1808, shocked by the violence of the national rising and convinced of the impossibility of defeating the French, who in any case represented for him civilization, he ended by accepting a post—that of Director of the Royal Library—from King Joseph. This was no more than what most other Spaniards in Madrid, including his friend Goya, had done. But when the French armies withdrew to Valencia in 1812, his fear of the reprisals that might be taken against him by the Nationals led him to make the mistake of going with them and finally of letting himself be shut up in the rock fortress of Peñíscola. Here he had to endure a year of siege, with all its horrible accompaniments of famine and bombardment. Escaping from this, and after other painful and humiliating adventures, this timid, bookish man of fifty-five, who happened to be the greatest European dramatist of his day, found himself free at last, with his confiscated property restored to him. But the Inquisition had been re-established in Spain. No longer a tribunal for defending orthodoxy, but a secret terrorist body at the service of the blind hatred of the clericals, it showed signs of moving against him. Warned in time, he fled to Montpellier and thence to Bordeaux, where he spent most of the remaining years of his life. He died in 1828—a few months after Goya.

Moratín's later history illustrates the horror of that double catastrophe—the invasion of the French and the rise of the clericals —that put an end to literary production in Spain for a quarter of a century. But let us look at his plays. At one glance we can see that they are as different as possible from the old drama. The plots are simple, the unities are observed and the dialogue is condensed and brilliant. The characters too are realized with extraordinary vigour: they live with every word they utter and the best of them have that terrifying exuberance that is known as comic force. The influence, we do not need to be told, is Molière, but it is Molière adapted to the feeling of the age, the last decades of the eighteenth century, when the modern sensibility is beginning to show through the older forms.

Let us take the plays one by one. *El Viejo y la Niña*, written when Moratín was only twenty-six, has as its theme an old man, fussy and parsimonious, who has married a young girl against her will. Shortly after the wedding her former love turns up and the husband, who is called Don Roque, becomes suspicious and spies on them. In a fit of jealousy he compels his wife to quarrel with her lover, whilst he listens to their conversation from the next room, at the very moment when the young man, in despair at the situation, has come to say goodbye to her before embarking for America. The boat sails and the girl, outraged by her husband's conduct, enters a convent.

The end is too sad and too full of dejection to please a theatre audience and the play has therefore never been popular. Yet it is a remarkably fine one. The presentation of the old man's character is a marvel of comic genius. Moratín has had the original idea of revealing to us Don Roque's inner life through his relations with his servant Muñoz, one of those rude, crusty retainers who have grown sulky and domineering through a lifetime of service in the family and who delight in showing their independence by retailing home truths to their master. Don Roque and Muñoz are the real married couple of the house and in their conversation the dull, pedestrian life of the elderly is brought out with wonderful vividness and comic force. The servant is the stronger character because he is a realist who has reconciled himself to the limits imposed by old age, whereas Don Roque is at one moment querulous and full of self-pity and at the next given to sudden illusions and *coups de tête*. The comedy of their relations springs from the fact that, though Don Roque is dependent on Muñoz for advice and sympathy, he can also, since he is master, compel him to act as he pleases. Each, that is, takes turns in bullying the other.

The result of all these scenes between master and man is that we realise that the shocking mistake of this marriage bears as heavily on Don Roque as on his bride, for, while she is destroyed by it, he must wear out what remains of his life in a twitter of suspicion and jealousy; and so, though the two young people touch us by their pathos—and their discourse is made all the more moving by being couched in a restrained yet vibrating poetry, in which one feels the beginning of a new power of expressing feeling—it is to the tormented old man, who has been driven by his jealousy to act in a very odious manner, that our final sympathies go. For if they are young, he is complicated and has more of the stuff of human life in him. We get, when our delight at the comic situations has vanished, a prodigious lesson in human sympathy and understanding.

Moratín's next play is *El Barón*. An impostor, who pretends to be a grandee in temporary disfavour at court, takes rooms in a small town near Toledo and completely turns the head of an elderly widow, *la tia* Mónica, who hopes to marry him to her daughter. When the situation becomes too hot, he escapes out of the window, carrying the woman's savings with him. The principal character in the play is the widow, pigheaded, conceited, ignorant and infinitely gullible, because there are no limits either to her greed or to her desire to revenge herself on the wives of the local gentry, who have the right to put *Doña* in front of their names. She too has a servant, a woman this time, who, by playing on her curiosity to know what the neighbours are saying, is able to insult her with impunity. But there is no intimacy between them, because the *tia* Mónica cannot love anyone who is not lit up by the beam of her reigning ambition. The play is really a study after the manner of Molière of an obsession, and the character of the widow —hard, egoistic and entirely focused on her dream of aristocratic grandeur—lacks the redeeming features that could allow us to sympathise with her.

It is the object of her infatuation, the baron, who supplies the charm. As a man we learn nothing about him: all we see is a part. But what a part! Only an impostor of imagination could have conceived the vision of a great nobleman that he presents to us. Airy, superior, yet exquisitely kind and condescending, a thousand miles removed from all possibility of mundane circumstances or worldly calculations, he seems to have floated down to earth from a cloud castle where kings and counts and archbishops of Trebizond and knights of the Holy Roman Empire meet and bow and go through their lordly ceremonies. Nothing can ruffle him, nothing mar his air of being pure and *sans reproche*—except—except the threat of physical violence, which causes him to hurry out of the room with the remark that he has certain letters of importance to write. But he remains an artist to the end. Even when he has decided to abscond during the night, he devotes half an hour to working up the *tia* Mónica's infatuation to fever heat by the promise of marrying her to his uncle, the Prince of Syracuse. What a performance! We are tempted to see in this crook of genius some mute inglorious Cervantes who, after soaking himself in all the bad plays of the day (which themselves were the lineal descendants of the novels of Chivalry) has produced in his own person a joyful, satirical masterpiece. It was of course because the *tia* Mónica had also seen itinerant players that she believed in him so implicitly.

The next play of Moratín's was *La Comedia Nueva*, which is also known as *El Café*. It is a satire, written this time in prose, on the bad playwrights of the time. The action takes place in a coffee house, where we see the dramatist with his wife and sister putting the final touches to a comedy that is to be acted that night. With them is Don Hermógenes, one of those Catos of the coffee house whose habits Moratín has described in a verse epistle addressed to

Godoy—an insufferable pedant, swollen with conceit and envy, who has taken a hand in the composition of the play because, if it is successful, he will marry the author's sister and receive a dowry from the proceeds that will pay off his debts. But the play is not successful: it is such a failure that the audience leave their seats in the middle of the second act and the little group returns in dismay to the coffee house, where Don Hermógenes, cad that he is, rats on them and goes off.

As a satire on bad plays *La Comedia Nueva* is amusing, but there is a human side too. The little group are all at their wits' end for money: most of their conversation runs on this and we get a moving insight into the hardships and exigencies of an author's life. Since the dramatist is just a poor devil trying to support himself, the play must be given a happy, if ironic, ending. For this purpose Moratín calls in a certain Don Pedro, a bear who since the first act has been growling in a corner at the degeneracy of the stage, but who, like all bears, turns out to have a heart of gold. He offers the despairing author a job as steward on one of his estates, and the curtain falls with the whole family wiping the tears of gratitude from their eyes and abjuring their dramatic errors. But the end does not ring true. Don Pedro is a cardboard figure, the ideal *homme de bonne volonté* of the day, who, while refusing all truck with vice or folly, uses his wealth to redress the misfortunes of their victims. At this time a hero of the reforming party, we shall meet with him again in conservative dress right down to the end of the nineteenth century.

La Mogigata is a play about hypocrisy. A certain *dévot* brings up his daughter to be a nun, because he hopes to inherit the money that has been left to her. The daughter, who wants to keep her money and marry, plays the part assigned to her, but uses her feigned religiosity as a mask for husband hunting. The schemes of both are thwarted and the money goes elsewhere. I do not think this play is successful, because it falls between two stools. On the one hand it lacks the concentrated drive of Molière's *Tartuffe* and on the other it presents a view of hypocrisy that is too crude to interest us. We live after all in days when thoroughgoing bigotry is out of fashion.

The last play that Moratín wrote was *El Sí de las Niñas*. The subject is the rivalry of an uncle and a nephew for the hand of a young girl and the action takes place in an inn at Alcalá during a hot summer night. There is the usual overpowering mother, ambitious, silly, egoistic and an inexhaustible talker who beats everyone else down; and there is the uncle who, though he suffers from the impetuosity of the elderly, is at bottom a decent man and gives way to his nephew when he discovers that the girl is in love with him. The play has always been by far the most popular of Moratín's: the end is happy, the pleasant characters, as well as the unpleasant, are carefully drawn and more scope than usual is allowed to the comedy of situation, for which Spaniards have a special predilection. It is, one may safely say, his most mature piece: the easy way in which new situations are created and the suspense maintained make it a model of the dramatic art, whilst a certain ironic humour, falling impartially on all the characters, compensates for the weakening of the *vis comica* and produces an effect of detachment and mellowness.

The most interesting feature is the way in which the young lovers are treated. Moratín had a theme, present in almost all his plays, about the relations of youth to age. He believed that the severe method in which the children of his day were brought up led them to suppress their real thoughts and feelings in the presence of their elders and to become incapable of speaking the truth to them. In *El Sí de las Niñas* he puts this view over deliberately and earnestly: it is, just as much as Ibsen's *Doll's House*, a play with a message. But the effect of this message, or rather of the perception that preceded it, is to make us see the young in a new light. They no longer live in a world apart, as all previous writers have depicted them, but are brought into focus with the rest of the characters. The effect of this is surprising. We see the two lovers—charming, touching, high-spirited, as such people both in and out of plays are apt to be—but we also see their moral weakness and lack of stamina. They cannot stand up to their elders, and even when it is to their obvious interest to tell them the truth, they continue to practise evasions and to tell lies. And this is not simply the effect of bad education. The chronic vice of the young is a feeling of their own unreality: invaded by a succession of voices, attitudes, ideas, influences, they do not yet know what they are and therefore cannot resist those definite, pachydermatous monsters, whom time and experience have fixed and hardened. Nor do the old on their side know how to deal with them. We see how dangerous the two ages can be to one another and how difficult they find it to communicate. However, this is a comedy: everything is going to end happily, so we merely smile at the precipitous flight of the young officer when he learns that his uncle is his rival and at the senseless prevarications of the girl from which the piece takes its name. The author's general attitude is one of indulgent irony.

Moratín's special contribution to literature is thus an exploration of the relations of youth and age. There are no characters between twenty-five and fifty-five in his plays. We see the weakness and insubstantiality of youth—a notion somewhat shocking to our romantic convictions—and also the monstrousness of age, with its obsessions, its hardening of the arteries and its bolting of the doors on reality. In his first play he shows an astonishing power of presenting old men in their most unattractive guise and yet of making us sympathize with them and understand their predicament. This fierce comic penetration he learned of course from Molière: *El Viejo y la Niña* is a study of character in the French manner. But it was not sufficiently in keeping with the spirit of an age whose mode of feeling had been formed by Jean-Jacques Rousseau. So at the end of his literary life we see him moving towards a more balanced and harmonious, but gentler and less searching, presentation of the same theme. *El Sí de las Niñas* is a modern comedy: we see the advance, yet cannot help feeling a certain disappointment. For, compared to his earlier pieces, the play is tepid.

Moratín's style requires a few words. His first two plays are in verse: it is an excellent verse, pure and simple, and so plastic that it seems to take on the tone and accent of the characters. In every line one sees a gesture. It is thus a perfect instrument for comedy. When he turns to prose he is, I think, less successful. It is not that his prose is bad: on the contrary it is very good. But, as we know from reading Congreve, good prose is more suited to express wit than character. Verse is a less cumbrous medium: the effects it gives are more immediate, more suggestive of miming, and some day, no doubt, when the present vogue for surface realism has passed, we shall see writers of comedy return to it.

We have seen the classical drama triumphing in Leandro de Moratín and leading to works that, though strongly influenced by French comedy, are entirely Spanish in feeling. We must now look at the very different products of the popular drama. The pressure of French ideas led, in the second half of the eighteenth century, to a vigorous national reaction against them. This is the age of the growth of the bull-fight, of the flowering of the minor arts and handicrafts and above all of popular music and dance. The Spanish people fell in love with themselves and their national customs, and turned their backs on the enlightened Government and its small group of intellectuals, who were trying to instruct them in the ways of reason. The very success of the agricultural and commercial reforms of that Government assisted the growth of this popular movement by producing prosperity. The severity of the laws of honour were relaxed, *autos de fe* fell into disuse and customs generally became milder. The dominant note of Spanish city life between 1760 and 1808 is gaiety and love of enjoyment.

The writer who best expresses this resurgence of popular life is Ramón de la Cruz. Born at Madrid in 1731, he spent his life as a humble Government official and died in 1794. As a young man he had tried his hand at plays of the conventional kind: then in 1764 he took up the *zarzuela*, abolished its mythological characters and put in their place figures taken from popular life.[1] At the same time he began to turn out *sainetes*. The *sainete* was a derivative from the *pasos* and *entremeses* that had first been written in the sixteenth century by Lope de Rueda and then developed by Cervantes and others: it was performed between the second and third acts of a play, lasted about twenty minutes and contained from a dozen to twenty characters. Its object was to put on for the entertainment of the audience a slice of typical Madrid life.

[1] The *zarzuela*, after being revived by Ramón de la Cruz, gave way towards 1776 to the *tonadilla*, which was a miniature operetta, lasting some fifteen minutes and containing only two or three characters. The music was a medley of Spanish popular airs, such as *seguidillas, tonos de folía* and *jácaras*. In the nineteenth century the *zarzuela* was again revived as a sort of musical comedy, but its history now belongs to that of light opera rather than of literature.

Ramón de la Cruz's *sainetes* are very pleasant reading: they show us the social life of the capital from the lowest circles to the highest. We visit the yearly fair of San Isidro, the *saraos* and *bailes de candil*, the cafés and *tertulias*, the picnics, the formal visits of the middle classes and the street scenes. We meet the *majos* and the *majas*, the *petimetres*, or dandies, and the ordinary people, from gentry to beggars—all the types and scenes so vividly depicted by Goya. The dramatist shows great skill in portraying life going on in its casual, customary way: he has a satirical eye and a nice touch of malice, and there is just enough plot to keep the conversation going. But the *sainete* is essentially a minor art, of less scope than the *pasos* of the sixteenth century with their three or four characters and their primitive but vigorous comic force.

I have left the poetry to the last because there is so little of it. The dearth begins some thirty years after Góngora's death—that is, towards 1660. One remarkable poetess, Sor Juana Inés de la Cruz (1651-95), appeared a little later, but she was born and spent her life in Mexico and her work therefore lies outside the scope of this book.

The eighteenth century came in with bad omens: the native tradition was exhausted and the only foreign influence was that of France. The verse of this period consists, therefore, of dull regurgitations of earlier poets such as Lope de Vega and of frigid, academic imitations from the French classics. It was not till the last decades that a new wind began to blow, the wind of sensibility and love of nature, and made it possible for poetry to be written again.

Juan Meléndez Valdés, who was the representative poet of this age, was born near Badajoz in 1754. Sent to the University of Salamanca to study law, he made friends there with two young men, Jovellanos and Cadalso, both several years older than himself and already on their way to being well-known writers. From them he got encouragement and advice in his reading—which included Greek poetry, Jean-Jacques Rousseau and Edward Young —and later on protection in his legal and professorial career. Till 1808 his life passed uneventfully. Then the calamity which destroyed all the writers of his generation fell on him. Uncertain which side to take, he wrote first a *romance* urging resistance to the French and then an ode to King Joseph. The latter almost cost him his life. Caught by the enraged Nationals in Asturias, he was tied to a tree and on the point of being shot when someone rescued him. This experience threw him back into the arms of the French, so that when they withdrew, it was all up with him. He saw his library burned, his manuscripts destroyed, and he escaped on foot to France, where he died at Montpellier a few years later.

In character, Meléndez Valdés was a weak, gentle, irresolute man, given to solitary walks in the country and to quiet reading in his study, and completely dominated by his jealous and aggressive but very loyal wife. His poetry reflects his disposition. It is a watery verse, diffuse, pellucid, monotonous but never careless, treating of the country with its trees and flowers and streams in a manner that, after his favourite poet, he called anacreontic. The measure he most commonly employs is the lyrical quatrain of seven syllables, which since Lope de Vega's time had fallen into disuse: he shows something of the great poet's lightness and delicacy in his management of it. Some of his *romances* too evoke Lope by their charm and limpidity: to write freshly in this metre since Góngora had laid his stamp upon it had become as difficult as for an English poet to write heroic couplets that did not recall Pope. But the comparison to the poets of the Golden Age cannot be pushed far. In Spain, as in England, the language of poetry in these prosaic decades seems tired, as if it still remembered the uses it had been put to in earlier times, but could not rise to them. And Meléndez Valdés did not have, like Gray and Collins, the device of the nicely chosen epithet to tighten up his verse: in this respect he is nearer to Wordsworth. Impossible though it is to give a just impression of such a diffuse poet by quotation, here are a few quatrains from one of his odes, to serve as an example.

> ¡Con cuán plácidas ondas
> Te deslizas tranquilo,
> Oh gracioso arroyuelo,
> Por el valle florido!
>
> ¡Cómo tus claras linfas,
> Libres ya de los grillos

Que les puso el enero,
Me adulan el oído!

¡Cuál serpean y ríen,
Y en su alegre bullicio
La fresca yerbezuela
Salpican de rocío!

Sus hojas delicadas
En tapete mullido
Ya se enlazan, y adornan
Tu agradable recinto. . . .

Ya entre juncos te escondes,
Ya con paso torcido,
Si una peña te estorba,
Salvas cauto el peligro:

Ya manso te adormeces,
Y los sauces vecinos
Retratas en las ondas
Con primor exquisito.

With what placid waves
You tranquilly meander,
O charming rivulet,
Through the flowering valley!

How your clear waters,
Freed now of the chains
With which winter bound them,
Delight my ear!

How they twist and laugh
And in their happy babbling
Sprinkle with dew
The fresh turf and grasses!

Their delicate leaves
In a yielding carpet,
Close enlaced, adorn
Your cheerful shores. . . .

Now you hide in the reeds,
And now with twisting course,
If a rock confronts you,
Safely avoid the danger.

Now, tame, you fall asleep
And the bordering willows
Mirror in your flood
With exquisite perfection.

Meléndez Valdés also wrote a good deal of poetry on moral and philosophical themes. But this vein of his is much less attractive and foreshadows the frigid academic verse of his successor, Quintana. His gift was his sensibility: tepid though it is and tinged with the rosy sentimentality of the times, whenever he yields to its influence he is a genuine poet. To break a long age of sterility, to raise a new poetic idiom out of a slough of dead clichés and rhythms, is no small feat, and Meléndez Valdes must stand, I think, as the most considerable poet between Calderon and the lyric poets who usher in the twentieth century.

CHAPTER XIV

NINETEENTH-CENTURY POETRY AND POETIC DRAMA

LITERATURE suffered a long eclipse in Spain during the Napoleonic War and the clerical reaction that followed it. Not till Ferdinand VII died in 1833 could the writers, who were all Liberals, return from exile and renew their activity. We feel the agitation of these years in their works. *Exaltados* in politics, they were feverish, rhetorical and shallow in their poetry and drama. And of course romantics, because romanticism, as they saw it, was the expression of the Liberal ideal in literature.[1]

The first of these to appear was Angel de Saavedra (1791-1865), a nobleman from Cordova who later became the Duque de Rivas. A Radical abroad, his experience of Liberal politics at home quickly converted him to Conservatism. His poetry expresses a romantic glorification of the past, more particularly of the Middle Ages and of the period of the Catholic Kings. This was of course a common attitude of Romantic writers everywhere, but it was also in keeping with the ideology of the Spanish Liberals, who aimed at restoring the greatness of Spain to what it had been before (as they thought) the tyranny of Philip II and the religious bigotry of the clergy had ruined it. Rivas' best known poems are his *Romances* on historical subjects: unevenly written, often diffuse, but abounding in highly coloured descriptive passages, they can be compared not too unfairly to Scott's *Lay of the Last Minstrel*. His *Leyendas*, 'Legends' —narrative poems composed in a variety of metres—owe something to Lamartine and Victor Hugo. If the general quality of his verse is not high, he writes with energy and *brio*. We remember as we read him that he was a man of action who had fought with

---

[1] Manuel José Quintana (1772-1857) is an exception to this, because he belonged to an older generation. An Encyclopaedist and Liberal down to 1835 and then a Conservative, he continued in his verse the eighteenth-century tradition of classicism. Once regarded as a great poet, he is today seen to be empty, turgid and rhetorical, without any of the stuff of poetry in him.

courage in the Napoleonic War and been left for dead on the battlefield.

José de Espronceda is better. Born in 1808 near Badajoz, spoiled by his parents, he grew up to be the typical Spanish revolutionary. While still a boy he became involved in one of the many secret societies of the capital: obliged on this account to fly to England, he picked up on his way a woman called Teresa, the daughter of an exiled Spanish colonel, who became his mistress and the great love of his life. In 1833 he returned to Spain with the other exiles and here he continued his career of romantic poet and now rather lukewarm revolutionary until his death in 1842. Teresa had already preceded him: she died of tuberculosis brought on by drink in 1839. They were living apart at the time and his famous poem to her was written after looking in through the bars of a window and seeing her dead body lying on its bier.

Espronceda liked to be known as the Spanish Byron. As a man he was very unlike Byron, because his amatory career was modest and he remained all his life an adolescent, but as a poet there are some resemblances. He is the great romantic egoist, the poet organist who makes the air throb with the sound of his laments and exaltations. The instrument is superb. The lines roll out one after the other in perfect sonority, impelled by the surge of his inspiration. He possesses to a magnificent degree one of the necessary faculties of a great poet—the power of amplifying feelings. But unfortunately most of the other requirements are lacking. Espronceda is the prisoner of his own cyclical processes. Gigantic desires and aspirations break down as he writes into unutterable despair, which is followed by a childish cynicism. As we read, we cannot resist being caught up in the enveloping atmosphere of his moods, yet we feel that the wheels run so smoothly just because they are never engaged in external reality. Still one cannot refuse admiration to his poem *A Jarifa en una orgía*, that splendid expression of the inner life of drunkenness, or to his *Canto a Teresa*, a poem in octaves which rivals at moments the great streams of nostalgic melody poured out by Camoens in the *Lusiads*.

22-2

Es el amor que al mismo amor adora,
El que creó las Sílfides y Ondinas,
La sacra ninfa que bordando mora
Debajo de las aguas cristalinas;
Es el amor que recordando llora
Las arboledas del Edén divinas;
Amor de allí arrancado, allí nacido,
Que busca en vano aquí su bien perdido.

It is Love who Love herself adores,
Love who the sylphs and river undines made,
The sacred nymph who, as she broiders cloths,
Beneath the crystal water ever stays:
It is Love who in remembrance pours
Tears for the groves of Eden and their shade:
Love snatched away from thence and yet there born,
Seeking in vain on earth her lost good fortune.

The Spanish Byron, we may say, was the perfect example of an exuberantly adolescent age, too drunk with its new-found liberty to be able to take in anything from the outer world. A situation portrayed with prophetic insight by Calderon in *La Vida es Sueño*, and of frequent occurrence in Spanish political life. But if he does not approach his English model in intellectual force or in understanding of the world or in psychological complexity or even in myth-making power, he does reach levels of poetic expression that (*Don Juan* apart) are considerably higher. This is because he knew how to abandon himself to his lyrical impulse.

The third of the famous exponents of romanticism in this century was José Zorrilla (1817-93). Born nine years later than Espronceda, he missed the grim years of the repression and the exciting ones of the Revolution. He lacked therefore both the oratorical gifts and the utopian faith and chaotic feelings of his predecessors. His poetry is the poetry of romantic disguises. Gifted like Swinburne with a good ear and an endless capacity for spinning verses out of the thinnest material, he deluged his age with torrents of fluent, graceful, sometimes charming but always commonplace poetry. He is at his best in his lyrical-narrative *leyendas* and in his long unfinished poem *Granada*, but the modern reader is discouraged by the quantity of merely tinkling verses he is obliged to read before lighting on a passage that contains a few lines of authentic magic. He was, however, the poet who most impressed himself on the nineteenth century. One might say that he consolidated the romantic attitude in Spain as General Narváez consolidated Liberalism, by making it harmless and respectable. The purveyor of romantic colour and sentiment to a feebly convalescent age, he caught the ear of the public and till his death was the most read poet in the Peninsula.

As a man Zorrilla was of a piece with his work. A romantic flight from a severe father, a period of bohemian poverty and concealment, a second flight from a wife who was sixteen years older than himself, frequent wanderings across the more picturesque regions of Europe and America, a sense of guilt that made him shy and evasive, an inability to hold on to his money—these are the features that stand out in the brief accounts that have been published of him. Like his poetry, his life was a continual escape from actuality into make-believe. In an autobiographical poem on his flight from home he gives an apt illustration of this. Leaving the *tranquilo hogar paterno* (in fact he jumped out of a coach in which he was being forcibly conducted to it), he mounted a mare that he had seen grazing by the roadside and reached the oak forest. Here, fearful of being followed, he looked about him:

> Cada rama que del viento
> Una ráfaga movía,
> Colosal me parecía
> Brazo alzado contra mí;
> Y el perfil de cada tronco
> Sobre el cielo destacado,
> Ser fantástico apostado
> A atajar mi paso allí.

Every branch that was moved by a gust of wind seemed to be a colossal arm raised against me; and the outline of every tree-trunk upon the sky a fantastic being waiting there to ambush me.

As an account of a boy's feelings in such an emergency these verses are appropriate as well as beautiful: what is more serious is that they are typical of the adult Zorrilla's whole attitude to life. His poetry is simply a romantic dramatization, a dressing up in picturesque colours of what without this would be completely trite and commonplace. The monotony of the process and the terrible mediocrity of the poet's mind and sensibility end by making his fancy-dress charades tedious.

The drama of this period is romantic in feeling and was written, not by dramatists in close contact with the stage, but by poets. It opens with a tragedy in mixed verse and prose by the Duque de Rivas. This was *Don Álvaro o la Fuerza del Sino*, which was first performed in 1835 with the same sort of demonstrations as five years before had accompanied the performance in Paris of Victor Hugo's *Hernani*. In Spain as in France the Romantic Movement fought its battles on the boards of the theatre rather than in books of poetry.

Don Álvaro is a play on the theme of honour. Written in sonorous language, coloured, vigorous, but inflated in feeling and poorly constructed, it is the typical romantic play of the age. The defects of this kind of drama are obvious: its sources lie in a superficial reading of earlier dramatists, including Shakespeare, and in a grandiose frame of mind for which there was no justification in the sordid realities of contemporary life. Rivas wrote another play, *El Desengaño en un Sueño*, much influenced by *La Vida es Sueño* and *The Tempest:* it is less bombastic, for it was founded on his recollections of two years of exile spent at Malta, but still it is not easy to read today.

Few other romantic plays of this period need be mentioned. One is *Los Amantes de Teruel*, first given in 1837, by Juan Eugenio Hartzenbusch, a minor poet and student of Spanish classical literature. It is a relatively sober work, strongly influenced by Montalbán and Tirso de Molina and owing little to foreign literature. Zorrilla too was a playwright and a prolific one: his best known piece, *Don Juan Tenorio*, which was first performed in 1844, gives a softened and romanticzied version of the famous hero that has been much admired by successive generations of Spaniards. It is still put on in Madrid every autumn. One thing we may note about these verse plays is that, though written by poets who had little experience of the stage, they are all actable. In this they contrast with the verse dramas written by English poets during the same century. Spaniards, even in a bad period, seem born with stage sense.

I must now speak of the poets of the second half of the nineteenth century. If we consult the histories of the time, we find two patriarchal figures, both famous and respected, spreading their branches over these pleasant but nerveless years—I mean Ramón de Campoamor (1817-1901) and Gaspar Núñez de Arce (1834-1903). Campoamor is the poet of the upper middle classes at their most philistine moment: dropping all romantic disguises, he gives us little sketches, flat, tepid and prosaic, about family and provincial life. His tone is gently ironic and disillusioned: that of the elderly bachelor uncle who, having passed his life as an *homme à bonnes fortunes* in the salons, smiles indulgently at his young nephews and nieces who still find some thrill in it. Once placed on a level with Shakespeare, Goethe and Calderon, he is today unread. I should like, however, to put in a good word for his *Humoradas*, if only as a social document. These are little epigrams in the manner of Martial, only much, much more genteel: their form approximates to that of the popular *coplas* of the day. They are just readable in idle moments, and a few have *chiste*. Here are two examples:

> Van y vienen, por sitios alfombrados
> con hojas de los árboles caídas,
> la grey de engañadores engañados,
> unas cuantas esposas aburridas
> y otros tantos maridos fastidiados.

> They come and go by places carpeted
> with the fallen leaves of trees
> the flock of the cuckolded cuckolds—
> bored wives
> and husbands who are bored also.

> Cuando te cases, Lola,
> te encontrarás con él dos veces sola.

> When you marry, Lola,
> you will find yourself with him alone twice over.

One feels the pulse of the age, or rather of Madrid society in the reign of Isabella, in such verses.

Núñez de Arce, on the other hand, is a Romantic whose romantic faith, like his Liberal faith, has been put in cold storage. A politician and orator from the plush seats of the Senate, the principal themes of his poetry are regret at the decline of a religion in which he does not believe and fear of those modern ideas which officially he welcomes, but privately considers are bound to have unfortunate consequences. But if his matter is half-hearted, his tone is loud and self-confident. A virtuoso in rhymes and metres, with all the sonority of language of the disciples of Victor Hugo, he suffers from the disadvantage of having nothing to say.

The poets of this age who move us today are two obscure figures whose lives were passed in poverty and wretchedness and who till after their deaths were unknown outside a small circle of friends. The first of these to be considered is Bécquer. Gustavo Adolfo Bécquer was born in Seville in 1836, the son of an unsuccessful painter. An orphan at ten, he was brought up by his godmother, who gave him a good education in the expectation that he would adopt a regular profession. But the young man had had his head turned by poetry. When barely eighteen he took the train for Madrid with only a few pesetas in his pocket in the belief that, like Zorrilla, he could achieve fame by his literary talents. The usual fate of indigent poets awaited him. For sixteen years he managed to support himself by translations from the French and articles in the daily papers, then (in 1870) he died of consumption brought on by malnutrition and accentuated by a catastrophic marriage and an unhappy love affair.

Bécquer's poems are not easy to appraise. They consist of short lyrics, arranged in a series to show the progress of a love affair from its hopeful beginnings to its end in separation and death. This idea of a string of poems forming an artistic whole he took from Heine's *Lyrisches Intermezzo*, which he had read in full in Gérard de Nerval's French version and incompletely in the admirable Spanish translation of Eulogio Sanz. But the result is very different. Bécquer lacked almost completely the poetic afflatus which is the birthright of every romantic poet and without some trace of which it is difficult to write poetry at all. His language is plain to the point of bareness: only rarely does he allow himself any word or image that is not trite and obvious, and he returns to the old Spanish habit of using assonances instead of rhymes. Even his rhythms, on which his power to put his lines over depends, are often weak and faltering, so that on a casual reading one might say that his verses scarcely deserve the name of poetry. But this is not so. Bécquer is a poet, only he gains his effects by keeping as close as possible to his original feeling rather than by allowing it to expand, and for this reason he is obliged to abstain from most of the expedients employed in poetic elaboration.

To read Bécquer's *Rimas* from beginning to end, as they should be read, is a strange experience. I do not know any other poetry which conveys an impression of such hopeless, irremediable sadness. It exhales suffering. In most melancholy poetry the delight of composition gives to some of the lines at least a winged quality, which lifts us up above the painful circumstances. Not so in Bécquer. His lines never rise, but take us down, deeper and deeper, into the heart of his discouragement: the feeling seems always to be in excess of the means of expression. It might be held that there is something to be said for this on the score of honesty. There is an inflationary quality in even the saddest poetry, an involuntary but welcome optimism, that carries us away in a flight of released feeling from the immediate experience. The abuse to which this escape is put by some romantic poets makes us at times rebel against it, yet the function of melancholy poetry is surely to show us a way of transcending painful feelings and not to leave them lying on our minds. But Bécquer does not recognize this: he is intent only on conveying to us, as well as he is able, precisely what he feels.

In his earlier poems, written before his love affair began, we see him struggling to fix and put down certain delicate and fugitive experiences, chiefly on the subject of aridity and inspiration—those inevitable obsessions of the self-cloistered poet. It is to these poems that the words airy, diaphanous, tenuous, so often applied to Bécquer's work, chiefly apply. Here, as an example, are four stanzas from a longer poem, which give some idea of the impalpable quality of his work in this phase. The Spirit of Poetry is imagined as speaking:

> Yo río en los alcores,
> Susurro en la alta yerba,
> Suspiro en la onda pura
> Y lloro en la hoja seca.
>
> Yo ondulo con los átomos
> Del humo que se eleva
> Y al cielo lento sube
> En espiral inmensa.
>
> Yo, en los dorados hilos
> Que los insectos cuelgan,
> Me mezo entre los árboles
> En la ardorosa siesta. . . .
>
> Yo soy el invisible
> Anillo que sujeta
> El mundo de la forma
> Al mundo de la idea.
>
> I laugh on the hill tops,
> rustle in the long grasses,
> sigh in the clear stream,
> and weep among the dry leaves.
>
> I curl with the atoms
> of the smoke that rises
> and slowly mounts upward
> in an immense spiral.
>
> I rock between the trees
> on hot afternoons
> by the gilded threads
> which the spiders hang. . . .
>
> I am the invisible
> ring that fastens
> the world of form
> to the world of ideas.

Then, a little later, the subject of love begins and soon Bécquer's verses become a succession of *cris de coeur*, weak though penetrating cries of a man who is crushed and frozen by his misery and whose gift of poetry is of a kind that cannot give him relief.

> Antes que tú me moriré: escondido
> En las entrañas ya
> El hierro llevo con que abrió tu mano
> La ancha herida mortal.
>
> Antes que tú me moriré: y mi espíritu,
> En su empeño tenaz,
> Sentándose a las puertas de la muerte,
> Allí te esperará.
>
> Con las horas los días, con los días
> Los años volarán,
> Y a aquella puerta llamarás al cabo. . . .
> ¿Quién deja de llamar?
>
> Entonces que tu culpa y tus despojos
> La tierra guardará,
> Lavándote en las ondas de la muerte
> Como en otro Jordán;
>
> Allí donde el murmullo de la vida
> Temblando a morir va,
> Como la ola que a la playa viene
> Silenciosa a expirar;
>
> Allí donde el sepulcro que se cierra
> Abre una eternidad. . . .
> ¡Todo cuanto los dos hemos callado
> Lo tenemos que hablar!

> I shall be the first to die: already
> in my vitals hidden
> I bear the steel which, wielded by your hand,
> opened the fatal wound.
>
> I shall be the first: and my spirit,
> in its fixed resolve,
> seating itself at the gates of death,
> will await you there.

With the hours the days, with the days
   the years will unroll,
till at length you will call at that door. . . .
   Who does not call?

For then the earth will have in keeping
   your guilt and your mortal remains,
washing you in the river of death
   as in another Jordan.

There, where the noise and fret of life
   tremble away to die,
like a wave coming up the beach
   to expire silently:

There where the sepulchre that closes
   opens an eternity. . . .
All that we two concealed in life
   we shall have to say!

It will be seen at once how very different this poem is from any that had appeared before it in Spanish literature. The diction is flat and prosaic, the words lack all resonance, but the concepts and images spring from a single deep core of feeling and are expressed with economy. The poem is held together by a poignant, vibrating rhythm, which, if at first sight it seems a little crude and insistent, one will find on a second reading to contain passages of great delicacy. (In his habit of grafting delicate and subtle variations on crude rhythms Bécquer resembles Poe.) Other outstanding poems are *Volverán las oscuras golondrinas* and *Cerraron sus ojos* with its dirge-like monotone, or his half-dozen lines to his wife Casta with their famous last couplet:

Tú creces de mi vida en el desierto
Como crece en un páramo la flor.

You grow out of the desert of my life
as a flower grows in a waste.

But Bécquer is a poet who only comes through fully when one has read and re-read his work. His poems lean on one another and their muted language requires an apprenticeship before it can be heard by the inner ear. However, this initial difficulty did not prevent him from becoming after his death the most felt poet of the age—most felt, I mean, among that small body of people, chiefly the young, to whom poetry makes a real appeal. He was the first Spaniard to write intimately about love and he came at a time when poets had lost sight of the connection between language and experience. If it is true that the innovators in art are often people who lack the current artistic gifts of their age and so are driven to discover new methods, then one may say that Bécquer re-oriented Spanish poetry precisely because he lacked what had till then been considered the principal faculty of poets—the power of ordering words so as to make the most of their aural properties. His tentative search for the unrhetorical yet telling phrase, his determination above everything else to keep true to his feeling are really very different from Heine's masterly simplicity, and the poems in which the German comes nearest to him—the terrible and poignant *Aus der Matratzengruft* series—he had not read. There is, however, another and perhaps more significant influence—that of Andalusian folk-poetry. In 1859, just as Bécquer was beginning his career, Fernán Caballero published her volume of popular *coplas*, which she had collected in his native city of Seville. We shall speak of this poetry later. All I need to say now is that the plaintive tone and stark concentrated expression of a single feeling or situation, which is characteristic of many of these little ditties, is in complete accord with the poetic principles on which Bécquer was working. Indeed his verses are sometimes so close to the *coplas* (for example XIX and XXXVIII) that it is impossible not to suppose that he had them in his mind.

Bécquer also wrote a considerable quantity of prose. His *Leyendas* are stories in the romantic manner of the day, influenced by Poe, Hoffmann and Charles Nodier. They are written in a rich cadenced style, with chiselled periods and great wealth of description, that recalls Chateaubriand. That is to say, he put into his prose all the fantasy and luxuriance of language that he refused to his verse: an unusual reversal of the roles of prose and poetry.

The other poet of this period whose reputation has risen steadily since her death is Rosalía Castro. She too had a life of poverty, bitterness and disillusion. But her verse has an extraordinary lyrical and musical appeal and, had she written in Castilian rather than in her native Galician dialect, she would, I feel sure, be recognized as the greatest woman poet of modern times.[1]

Rosalía was born in 1837 in Santiago de Compostella under mysterious circumstances. Her mother was a young woman of good family, whose ancestral mansion dominates the neighbouring town of Padrón, but she was not married and her child was therefore brought into the world in secrecy and given to a peasant woman to bring up. Then at the age of nine she was adopted by her mother, taken into her grandparents' house and given as good an education as provincial girls at that time could obtain. Both physically and mentally she was precocious: by the time she was eleven she was writing verses, whilst at sixteen she could play the guitar and the piano, draw well and read French. Of equal importance in her development was a family servant, known as La Choina, who told her stories and sang folk-songs. Rosalía herself had a fine contralto voice and, it is said, as much musical as poetic talent. These quiet years spent round the family *llar*, or hearth, at Padrón or in brief visits to Santiago were perhaps the only really happy years of her life.

Then in 1856, a tall buxom girl with a large mouth, thick chestnut hair and dark luminous eyes, she set off, on the pretext of family business, for Madrid. From this moment the period of her sufferings began. In a strange city, far from the soft landscapes and watery light of the Galician *rías*, she was overcome by that *soidade*, or home-sickness, to which her countrymen are so prone. She saw no beauty in 'the desert of Castile', as she called it, and she hated the harsh, dry temperament of the Castilians and the unkindness with which they treated their Galician labourers. However, she made friends among the young poets and writers of Madrid and married one of them, a youth from Santiago called Manuel Murguía, who was writing a history of their native province. It was an unfortunate choice, for though Murguía was a Galician, he

---

[1] Galician, or *Galego*, is to all intents and purposes the same language as medieval Portuguese, with a certain number of Castilian words added. Anyone who knows Spanish and devotes an hour or two to a Portuguese grammar can read it with fair proficiency, though naturally a Galician-Spanish dictionary is necessary for complete understanding.

was also a dwarf, who, out of envy of her talent, or for other reasons, maltreated her. With marriage too came poverty, sickness and five children. Her health—for home-sickness can be a real illness—made it necessary for her to return for long periods to Galicia and here in 1885 she died in her house at Padrón—the little decaying town at the head of the estuary about which most of her poetry is written and for which she had such a passionate attachment.

Rosalía Castro's first book of verse, the *Cantares Gallegos*, came out in 1863. All the poems contained in it are in Galician. Since the *jograles* of the thirteenth century had made their songs, no poet of consequence had written in this language, and their verses were unknown to her because the *Cancioneros* that contained them were still sleeping on the shelves of Italian libraries.[1] Rosalía's poetry was therefore founded upon her native folk-songs in which, as we have seen, she had had such exceptional opportunities for saturating herself. When, however, we turn to these folk-songs, we are likely, so far as the words go, to feel some disappointment. Lyrics of more than four lines in length had almost ceased to exist and, as elsewhere in Spain, the folk-poem, sung in the fields and streets and as an accompaniment to dancing, had shrunk to the dimensions of a single verse. Of these there were three main kinds: the three-lined *tercetos*, known as *cantares de pandeiro*, because they were sung to the accompaniment of the *pandeiro*, or timbrel: the four-lined octosyllabic *coplas* of Andalusian origin: and the *muiñeiras*, which were also four-lined poems, but having eleven syllables broken by a caesura in each line and rhyming *a a b b*. These *muiñeiras* were the direct descendants of the old *cantigas de amigo*, only differing from them in that, under the influence of the invading *copla*, they had generally been reduced to one verse. However, the tone of these songs was the important thing; as Rosalía said, 'Galician poetry is all music and vagueness, all complaints and sighs and gentle smiles'.

[1] Some of the poets of the fifteenth-century *Cancionero de Baena* had written verses in Galician, but these verses are poor and have no specially Galician characteristics. Among them were two famous figures, Macías el Namorado and Juan Rodríguez de la Cámara, who were not only Galicians but natives, like Rosalía, of Padrón. Macías, is, however, known for the legend of his unhappy love rather than for his poetry, and Juan Rodríguez, though he is the author of the first romantic novel in Spanish, a book very Galician in feeling, wrote only in Castilian.

For this reason these little verses had sometimes retained traces of that peculiar movement, the bringing forward to the beginning of a new verse of an echo of the last, which, under the name of *leixa-pren*, had been the special feature of the *cantigas de amigo*. It is a mark of Rosalía Castro's amazing sensitiveness to the spirit of her native muse that she was able, from such slight indications as were provided by a few *coplas* and *muiñeiras*, to reproduce this pattern in her poetry.

Here is an example: it is one of a series of six interconnecting poems written on the theme of a *cantar de pandeiro*:

> *Campanas de Bastabales*
> *Cando vos oyo tocar,*
> *Mórrome de soidades.*

Bells of Bastabales, when I hear you ring I die of longings.

One will observe how the form of the little popular ditty has been expanded to make a poem in *tercetos* of a kind entirely new to Spanish poetry.

> Cada estrela, o seu diamante;
> Cada nube, branca pruma,
> Trist'a lua marcha diante.
>
> Diante marcha crarexando
> Veigas, prados, montes, ríos,
> Dond'o día vai faltando.
>
> Falta o día, a noite escura
> Baixa, baixa, pouco á pouco,
> Por montañas de verdura.
>
> De verdura e de follaxe,
> Salpicada de fontiñas
> Baixo a sombra d'o ramaxe.
>
> D'o ramaxe, donde cantan
> Paxariños piadores,
> Que c'á aurora se levantan.
>
> Que c'á noite s'adormecen
> Para que canten os grilos
> Que co'as sombras aparecen.

Every star its diamond, every cloud its white plume, sadly the moon marches on.

Onward marches while it lights up fields, hills, meadows, rivers, where the day is failing.

Fails the day, the dark night falls, falls, little by little, over the green mountains.

Green and leafy, sprinkled with rivulets, beneath the shade of the branches.

Branches where sing the twittering birds that rise with the first light.

Which all night sleep that the crickets may come out and trill among the shadows.

Rosalía de Castro's more usual procedure, however, is to start with a popular *copla* and then to develop it in a lyrical *romance*, somewhat as the Castilian poets of the Middle Ages had done with the *estribillo* of a *villancico*, only in a looser and less formal manner. The most wonderful example of this is the poem *Airiños, airiños, aires*, which she wrote when she was only twenty. It is a poem of nostalgia for her native country put into the mouth of an emigrant, a lyrical musical complaint evoking the life of the Galician country-side with its trees and waters and gentle rain, its country dances and its shady cemeteries, and moving with a hurry and passion that calls to mind the torrent of notes poured out by a missel-thrush when it is singing on a tree top during a storm. It is, I think, one of the most entrancing lyrics ever written by a Spaniard and, just as Galician poetry had provided an essential element in the formation of the Castilian lyric of the fifteenth and sixteenth centuries, so this poem was to have an influence in the great revival of Spanish poetry that began thirty years after her death. In particular, the *Romancero Gitano* of García Lorca, with its richly musical idiom, its continual repetitions and allusions to folk-poetry and to popular themes, owes much to it. Unfortunately it is too long for me to quote here.

There are half a dozen other poems in this book of almost equal merit: *Nasín cand' as prantas nascen* with its echoes of the fifteenth-century lyrical *romances*; *Adiós, ríos; adiós, fontes* with its farewell-to-my-town theme so common in popular *coplas*; *Cantan os galos pr'o día*, an *aubade*; *Cómo chove miudiño* with its recollections of

Rosalía's childhood; and *Campanas de Bastabales,* which I have already quoted from. All these poems spring out of folk-poetry, starting off with a popular *copla* and developing and paraphrasing it in the authentic Spanish manner. Nor should we, with our English contempt for peasant arts, imagine that there is anything precious or anachronistic in the fact of a nineteenth-century poet adopting such a procedure. Spain is a country where popular poetry is still very much alive and its most modern poets have shown that they can draw strength and sustenance by building on it. Thus Rosalía Castro found no difficulty in being at the same time a mature and civilized poet, living in her own age, and an interpreter, in their own forms and idiom, of the feelings of the Galician peasantry. So close is she to the popular sensibility that, as her fellow countrywoman, Emilia Pardo Bazán, has said, within twenty years of the appearance of her book, verses written by her were believed to have a popular origin, whilst others, which were genuinely popular, were attributed to the poetess. When we compare her work to that of Thomas Hardy and William Barnes, who were attempting the same sort of thing at approximately the same time, we can see how much of the clumsiness of these poets was due to their having no genuinely popular forms or poetic traditions to write in. The English agricultural labourers and industrial workers have long been inarticulate.

Rosalía Castro's next book of poetry, *Follas Novas,* was not published till 1884, though most of the verses in it had been written a dozen years earlier. It belongs, as she said in her preface, to a different inspiration from that of the *Cantares.* That is to say, most of the poems in it are subjective and personal. The first part consists of a series of short pieces written in a variety of metres, all expressing deep despair and melancholy. In a poem to the moon, for example, she begs to be carried body and soul to a place, neither in this world nor in 'the heights', where she may remember nothing. Many of these pieces show a strong influence of Bécquer, whose collected verse had been published in 1871, but she was not by nature a concentrated poet and her subjective poems lack as a rule those poignant rhythms which inject the little versicles of her contemporary under the skin of the reader. Other longer poems follow on a variety of subjects, but all in the same melancholy strain, the most notable being two on the cathedral of Santiago, *N-a Catredal* and *Amigos Vellos*, one beginning *Aquel romor de cántigas e risas* and one entitled *Adiós*. In these pieces Rosalía shows her powers as a sophisticated poet, surprising one by the beauty of her descriptions, by her continual and often daring experiments in form and metre and by the floods of feeling that from time to time seem to carry her verse away. All the same I think that Emilia Pardo Bazán is right in saying that it is in the poems in which she developed folk-song themes that she shows her lyrical gifts at their best. Most of these are to be found in the *Cantares Gallegos* volume. Here, however, as an example of her later style and of the nostalgia for the past that had now become habitual to her, is a short lyric which is one of a series of three farewell poems to Padrón.

Aquelas risas sin fin,
Aquel brincar sin delor,
Aquela louca alegría,
⸮Por qué acabou?
Aqueles doces cantares,
Aquelas falas d'amor,
Aquelas noites serenas,
⸮Por qué no son?

Aquel vibrar sonoroso
D'as cordas d'a arpa y os sons
D'a guitarra malencónica,
⸮Quén os levou?
Todo é silencio mudo,
Soidá, pavor,
Ond'outro tempo a dicha
Sola reinou. . . .

¡Padrón!. . . ¡Padrón!. . .
Santa María. . . Lestrobe. . .
¡Adiós! ¡Adiós!

That ceaseless laughter
Those light-hearted leaps,
That crazy gaiety,
Why did it end?

> Those songs sung so sweetly,
> That talking of love,
> Those nights so serene,
>   Why are they gone?
>
> That sonorous trembling
> Of harp strings and the sound
> Of the guitar's melancholy,
>   Who took them away?
> All is mute silence,
> Vain regret, dread,
> Where in other days happiness
>   Reigned alone.

Rosalía Castro's last book of poems, *En las orillas del Sar*, came out just before her death. It was written in Spanish. Like *Follas Novas*, its inspiration was personal and subjective and, as she was suffering from the slow but painful cancer that carried her off, in great straits for money and anxious about the future of her children, it is, if possible, even more pessimistic and despairing than her previous volume. The principal theme is the longing for a life beyond death. Although it contains several notable poems, one feels that the dry, clear language of Castile did not suit her so well as the soft, caressing idiom which she had learned as a child. In Galician she is usually warm and tender: in Castilian her coldness and aloofness chill one.

Rosalía Castro is above all the poet of nostalgia: most of her best poems were written when she was away from her country, in the stone and brick wilderness of Madrid or on the treeless plains around Simancas: her longing for her native land, which she shared with so many Galician emigrants, provided her with a rich and varied subject. But under her home-sickness—*soidade, morriña*—there lay a deep, indescribable dread and horror that became more pressing as she advanced in years: as her husband observed, she seemed to have sucked in from her mother all the secret terrors she had felt when she held her in her womb. These fears, being less related to the outer world, offered a poorer material for poetry.

Her life, too, after the first few years of her marriage and the death of her mother, contracted. She became absorbed in the daily tasks of maintaining a family on an insufficient income and educating her children. She had always shunned publicity—her first volume of poems had been published by her husband without her consent—and now she began to avoid all society. The shame of her birth dogged her and the cold shoulder which the *familias acomodadas* of Santiago turned on her, at a time when all the young people of Galicia were reading her verses, threw her back still more into herself. During the last twelve years of her life, the ravages which her disease caused in her appearance made her unwilling to see anyone.

There is one other feature of Rosalía's poetry to which I must draw attention, and that is her preoccupation with the condition of the poor. In her prologue to *Follas Novas* she tells us that these poems had been written to express the endless sufferings of the Galician peasants and sailors, *soya e verdadeira xente d'o traballo n-o noso país*, which we may translate as 'the only people in our country who do any real work'. She constantly puts her poems of *soidade* into the mouths of Galician emigrants and day-labourers—Galicia, like Ireland, is a country where the land cannot support the population—and shows a special sympathy for the women, on whom, in the absence of their men-folk, the brunt of poverty chiefly falls. It is true that this feeling was at first associated with her passionate love of her own countrymen and her almost equally passionate hatred of their oppressors, the people of Castile. When, for example, in one of her poems she asks how God could have made anything so ugly as the plain of Simancas, the reply comes pat—that he made it for the Castilians. But in her later years she was equally outspoken in her scorn for the hypocrisy of the middle-class Gallegos, who spent so much of their time praying yet remained callous and hard-hearted, and in her *romances* she treats the theme of poverty realistically, but with an almost excessive warmth and bitterness.

Now this, it must be observed, is a note that had not been heard in Spanish poetry since the time of the Archpriest of Hita. Before Rosalía, poetry in Spain lacked the sentiment of pity—or rather banished it to religious topics such as the Crucifixion—because it avoided subjects that had a social content. But she lived in a circle of people who held extreme federal and left wing sympathies. One of her best friends, Eduardo Chao, was Minister of Supply in the Federal Republic of 1873-4 and her husband was given a post as archivist by that Government and deprived of it during the Conservative reaction that followed. Although there are no allusions to politics in her work, for Spanish women at that time took no part in public affairs, there can be little doubt as to where her sympathies lay. And by associating her own troubles with those of the poor—'those accustomed to unhappiness', she wrote, 'come to feel the afflictions of others as their own'—she greatly strengthened the appeal of her work.

If the object of lyric poetry is to enchant, to enrapture, to lift the reader out of his surroundings, then Rosalía Castro is a fine lyric poet. By their repetitions, their *Ai Ai*'s, their caressing diminutives, by the way in which the lines follow one another in a cataract of emotion, her poems carry one away in a sort of musical flight. Her best lyrics produce on the mind the effect of an impassioned aria sung by Galli-Curci: the impression is more immediately overpowering than is the case with most poetry. But there are some things that these poems—written as they apparently were without effort—do not give. When in Burns—who is not, I think, so fine a lyric poet, though he was a richer human being—we come on the line 'The dance ga'ed thro' the lighted ha' ' we are arrested by its beauty as we are never arrested by any fragment of Rosalía's. Her poetry, pure and idiomatic though its language is, and smelling, as Emilia Pardo Bazán said, of the village (it has no trace of the sultry overtones and plush surface of Christina Rossetti), never condenses into a single epithet or phrase, but flows on from line to line in a musical sequence. Nor does it show any sense of that special and peculiar relation of word to word that came in at the Renaissance from Latin poetry. Under the wind of lyric feeling that blows through them, all the words in her poems lean in one direction. There is no pause, no measure, no restraint in this exuberantly passionate verse and there is sometimes, it must be said, a displeasing note of hysteria.

Rosalía Castro was not the only poet of her day to write in the Galician dialect. Her appearance coincides with a revival of Galician literature, which was all the more remarkable because the language spoken by the middle classes in their everyday life was not *Galego* but Spanish. The only one of these poets to achieve real distinction was Eduardo Pondal (1835-1917), who after a brief revolutionary exploit which led to his being exiled for two years to the Mariana Islands, spent the rest of his long life in a village near Corunna. His first poem, *A Campana d'Allons,* written when he was only seventeen, made him famous: composed on the same popular *copla* of the *Campanas de Bastabales* that was to inspire Rosalía Castro a few years later, it is a poem of *soidade* in the manner of Camoens' famous verses on the waters of Babylon. His two books of lyrics, *Rumores de los Pinos* and *Queixumes d'os Pinos,* were published in 1879 and 1886 and are now hard to obtain. An epic on the discovery of America, which I have not seen, came out after his death.

Pondal is a very different sort of poet from Rosalía Castro: aloof, melancholy, sceptical, more Portuguese than Spanish and entirely pagan in his pantheistic feelings for Nature and in his tragic attitude to human life and destiny. His poetry is steeped in melancholy allusions to the remote past—to the days when the Galicians were, as he supposed, Celtic tribes, with the same sort of gods and heroes and bards as are described in Macpherson's *Ossian.* It is the Galician nostalgia focused on pre-history and it is curious to see that he professed a similar belief to that which runs through Yeats' poems in the *Wind among the Reeds,* that the spirits of the past have left behind them a legacy of unsatisfied desires to torment the hearts of men who, in an outworn time, have grown tired and old. Here is a poem from *Queixumes d'os Pinos* which gives a good idea of the sort of vague and lofty, yet deeply felt, *soidade* which is his most characteristic note.

> Salvage val de Brantóa,
> En terra de Bergantinos;
> Ou val, amado dos celtas,
> E dos fungadores pinos:
> Cando Gundar prob' e 'scuro,
> Sea d'este mundo ido;
> No teu seo silencioso,
> Concédelle, val amigo,

Sepulcro á modo dos celtas,
Tan só de ti conocido.

Qu' hai tempo que n'este mundo,
Anda o bardo peregrino,
Deseando chegar ó cabo,
D'un traballo escurecido;
E somente repousar,
Deséa do seu camiño.

N'hé a vellez a que causa
O fondo dolor que sinto;
Pois que son do tempo voso,
Carballos de Carballido:
Suidades de non sei qué,
Recordos quezáis do espirito,
D'algunha perdida patria,
Ou d'antigo ben perdido,
N'esta peregrinación
Miña, van sempre comigo;
E son os meus compañeiros,
No travalloso camiño,
Suspiros por non sei quén,
E por non sei qué suspiros.

Wild valley of Brantóa
in land of Bergantinos,
valley beloved of the Celts
and of umbrella pines;
when Gundar unhonoured and in darkness
has departed from this world,
grant him burial in your silent nave,
friendly valley,
after the manner of the Celts,
known only to you.

For a long time now the poet has wandered,
seeking to reach the end
of an obscure labour
and desires only to rest on his road.

Not old age is it that causes my deep sorrows,
for they, oaks of the oak forest, are as ancient as you;
longings for I know not what,
memories perhaps of some lost country
or of some lost good
go with me always on this pilgrimage
and are my companions on the rough road—
Sighs for I know not whom
and, for what I know not, sighs.

It will be seen that though Pondal adopts the notion put forward
with all sorts of romantic implications in Matthew Arnold's *Celtic
Studies*, that the Celts are a defeated people who masochistically
draw their spiritual strength from their defeat, the tone of his verse
is different from that of the poets of the Celtic twilight. There is no
languidness, no over-sweetness: the style is bare and almost without
adjectives. There is a pseudo-classical restraint and the bardic mantle
is worn like a toga. But he is not really a poet of false attitudes:
loneliness, disdain and longing for a nobility that has vanished
from the world make up the natural temper of his mind. Through
the mists of his native moorlands he catches glimpses of gigantic
and simplified shapes that shrink and become commonplace when
the sky lifts. That is to say, under his Galician romanticism there
is a Spanish stoic.

Another Galician poet, very well known in his day, was Manuel
Curros Enríquez (1851-1908). Turned out of his home by his
father for his irreligious views, he became a successful journalist
and a furious anti-clerical. As a poet he is a disciple of Rosalía Castro.
His *romances* on village life in Galicia have a certain sentimental
charm and no one else has described so feelingly the miseries of the
peasantry. His denunciations of the Church, which led to a prose-
cution for blasphemy, are the most bitter and outspoken in Spanish
literature.

It was not only in Galicia that regional poetry was written.
From the 'seventies on, this sort of poetry, based on the life of the
villages, became the fashion, and almost every corner of the
Peninsula came to have its local poet. The best of these poets,
outside Catalonia, was José Maria Gabriel y Galán (1870-1905).

He was a schoolmaster from Frades de la Sierra, a country of rolling hills and ilex woods situated at the foot of the Sierra de Gredos to the south of Salamanca, who married at the age of twenty-six, took over his father-in-law's farm near Plasencia and died prematurely. He wrote poems in the local patois and also in Spanish.

Gabriel y Galán suggests to the English reader an unintellectual Wordsworth. He is in love with his native country, with its huge empty landscapes, its grey stone villages, its lonely farms and its old-fashioned, god-fearing ways of life. His poems consist in rather monotonous incantations in its praise, written in a flat prosaic idiom in which the descriptions of landscapes—and these are the best parts—pile up into catalogues that remind one a little of Walt Whitman. Rather tedious to read at length, because they always strike the same note, they contain passages that move one by their delicacy and limpidity. It is the kind of poetry in which, in the next century, one of the greatest of Spanish poets, Antonio Machado, was to excel, but unlike him Gabriel y Galán is a versifier who has only one string to his bow and, besides this, a man with a limited range of feeling and thinking. He sees his country world entirely *couleur de rose* and his dogmatic optimism ends by producing a reaction. Here is a passage from a poem on the death of his wife which gives some idea of what he can do:

> Todo lo pudo la mujer cristiana,
> logrólo todo la mujer discreta.
>
> La vida en la alquería
> giraba en torno de ella
> pacífica y amable,
> monótono y serena. . . .
>
> ¡Y cómo la alegría y el trabajo,
> donde está la virtud se compenetran!
>
> Lavando en el regato cristalino
> cantaban las mozuelas,
> y cantaba en los valles el vaquero,
> y cantaban los mozos en las tierras,
> y el aguador camino de la fuente,

y el cabrerillo en la pelada cuesta. . . .
¡Y yo también cantaba,
que ella y el campo hiciéronme poeta!

Cantaba el equilibrio
de aquel alma serena
como los anchos cielos,
como los campos de mi amada tierra;
y cantaba también aquellos campos,
los de las pardas, onduladas cuestas,
los de los mares de enceradas mieses,
los de las mudas perspectivas serias
los de las castas soledades hondas,
los de las grises lontananzas muertas.

She could do everything, this Christian woman
with her woman's discretion.

The life of the farm turned upon her,
peaceful and kind, equable and serene. . . .
For oh how joy and work
mingle together where there is virtue!

The girls sang as they washed clothes in the water channel.
the cowherd sang in the valleys
and the farm lads sang in the fields.
The waterman too sang on his way to the spring
and the goatherd on the bald hill slopes.
And I sang as well,
for she and the countryside made me a poet.

I sang the fixed balance
of that soul serene as the broad skies
and as the fields of my dear country.
And I sang of the fields—
those with the brown, undulating slopes,
those with the seas of shut-in corn,
those of the dumb, grave perspectives,
those of the deep, chaste solitudes,
those with the dead, grey distances.

Here we see the three things that make up the ideal world of this Salamancan poet—work on the land, love in the home and trust in God. He preaches them day in day out with all the self-satisfaction and persistence of the man who believes that he alone has the secret of happiness. But there is a lyrical passion in his love of the great rolling plains with their clumps of ilex trees and glassy streams and clear mountain air, a monotonous, reiterating ecstasy that reminds us that this is also the country of *cantos y santos*, of Santa Teresa, San Juan de la Cruz and San Pedro de Alcántara.

We may call him a primitive. He had read scarcely anything and the romantic poets he admired, Espronceda and Zorrilla, had no influence on his poetry. He invariably wrote out of doors, lying prone under an ilex tree and looking out over the immense landscape, whilst his ploughboys and herdsmen carried on with their work under their master's eye. Decidedly he is a poet to dip into, all the more because he is one of the few writers in this nation of peasants to have any real feeling for country life.

The most important example of a revival of regional poetry took place, however, not in Castile nor in Galicia, but in Catalonia. The *Renaixença*, as it is called, is really the rebirth of a literature. It is generally regarded as starting with the publication in 1833 of a patriotic ode by Aribau. During the generation that followed, a great scholar, Milà i Fontanals, helped to fix and establish the literary language out of the various local dialects into which medieval Catalan had broken up, and three considerable poets, Jacint Verdaguer (1845-1902), Joan Maragall (1860-1911) and Josep Carner (b. 1884) came forward and wrote in it. Their work has been amplified and continued by a number of other writers. But the scope of this book does not allow me to embark on an account of such a considerable movement in a language which is nearer to Italian than to Spanish and whose productions, unlike those of Galicia, have had little influence on the literature of the rest of the Peninsula. For the sake of completeness, I included in a previous chapter a brief study of the short-lived literature of Catalonia and Valencia during the Middle Ages, but I cannot resume that study now. Modern Catalan literature requires a separate volume.

POPULAR POETRY

We have had occasion, in discussing Bécquer and Rosalía Castro, to speak of the influence on them of the popular poetry of the day —the *coplas*. We must now say something about these little poems. *Coplas*—to give them their usual name, though in books they are sometimes spoken of as *cantos* or *cantares*—are verses of, as a rule, three or four lines only, and are intended for singing. Until the early part of the last century or later they were sung as an accompaniment to dancing at weddings, *verbenas*, *fiestas*, etc., the voice of the singer breaking out while the lute and guitar stopped playing and the dancers continued to revolve. They were also used in that invariable feature of courtship—the serenade, particularly on Midsummer Night and May Day. That is to say, they were a part of the ritual of peasant and working-class life and their words had the character that marks folk-poetry in every age and country, except where, in the large towns, they had become corrupted by the poetic idiom of the eighteenth century. But the convenient form of these little verses—easy to remember and improvise—led to their having an extraordinary and quite unritual popularity. Sung on the roads by muleteers, on their way to work by labourers and peasants, at their household tasks by women, they became incorporated in the life of the people in a way that had never been possible with the older folk-poetry of *romances* and *villancicos*. Even very simple and untaught people could invent new ones and so it happened that, in the early years of the nineteenth century, they began both to extend the range of their subject-matter and, in many cases, to take on a more particular and individual accent, which allowed them to express a greater variety of feelings and situations. This change was undoubtedly a reflection of the Liberal revolution in Spain, which, at the same time that it destroyed the old social conditions in the countryside, stressed the value of the individual and encouraged him to express his own feelings in his own language. Indeed one might almost say that the real lessons of the new age in the art of poetry were drawn by the peasants of Andalusia and Castile before the literary poet had managed to

365

divest themselves of their bardic mantles and come to grips with them.

Before considering the subjects of the *coplas*, let us look at the verse forms in which they are written. There are two main kinds, common to both Castile and Andalusia—the *seguidilla* and the *cuarteta*. The *seguidilla* is a four-lined verse in which the second and fourth lines are shorter than the other lines: this gives it a characteristic rhythm, which makes it suitable for singing to the gay air and dance of the *sevillana*. In the chapter on Lope de Vega I gave an example of one of these: here are two more modern examples:

> La iglesia se ilumina
> cuando tú entras,
> y se llena de flores
> donde te sientas.

The church lights up when you come in and is filled with flowers where you take your seat.

> Tus ojos y los míos
> se han enredado,
> como las zarzamoras
> por los vallados.

Your eyes and mine have become tangled together, like the black-berry bushes in the hedges.

Sometimes the *seguidilla* is lengthened by the addition of three lines—a lovely form apparently invented in Seville.

> Desde que te ausentastes,
> sol de los soles,
> ni los pájaros cantan,
> ni el río corre.
> ¡Ay, amor mío!
> ni los pájaros cantan,
> ni corre el río.

> Since you went away,
> sun of suns,
> the birds do not sing,
> nor the river runs.
> Oh, my love!
> The birds do not sing,
> nor the river flows.

Some of the most beautiful *seguidillas* have been discovered in Asturias, which, being a very isolated region, has preserved in its folk-song some of the delicate and nostalgic fragrance of the seventeenth century:

> Al cantar de las aves
> mi amor durmió.
> ¡Ay, mi Dios, quién supiera
> lo que soñó!

At the singing of the birds my love fell asleep. Ah, God, that one could say what her dreams were!

> A Castilla vanse, vanse
> ya los pastores;
> y la nieve cuaja en el puerto;
> ya non hay flores.

The shepherds are now leaving for Castile. The snow piles up in the pass. There are no more flowers.

The *cuarteta* is simply a verse of octosyllabic ballad measure:

> Yo me asomé a la muralla
> a ver las olas pasar;
> y se volvieron arenas
> las aguaïtas del mar.

I went up on the sea-wall to watch the waves come in, and the waters of the sea turned themselves to sand.

Or this, to a girl dancing:

> Jaléate, cuerpo bueno,
> que te vas aniquilando
> con los fríos del invierno
> y el calor del verano.

Dance, my beauty, you are wearing yourself away in the frosts of winter and the heat of summer.

As will be seen, the *cuarteta* is more condensed and realistic than the *seguidilla*, whereas the latter is more lyrical. It was through the *cuarteta* that the *copla* achieved its great range and popularity and developed its most characteristic and modern features; at least three out of every four *coplas* are of this kind.

Besides these two main verse forms, there is a third form, the *soleá*, confined to Andalusia, which has only three lines. (The *cantar de pandeiro* of Galicia, which we have already spoken of, is a parallel development.) The word *soleá* is a dialect form of *soledad* and so *soleares* are songs expressing grief and loneliness, like the American Blues, which are also in stanzas of three lines. They differ from most other *coplas* in that, though they have a special air of their own, they cannot be danced to. These *soleares* are for the most part the poetry of the very poor and often compress into their tiny space an astonishing beauty and poignancy.

> Clareando viene el día.
> Ya lo avisa la corniz.
> Adiós, prenda de mi vida.

See the day is breaking. Now the quail announces it. Farewell, joy of my life.

> Madre mía del Socorro,
> de la noche a la mañana
> me perdí sin saber como.

Lady of Succours, between the night and the morning I lost myself without knowing how.

> Ya yo me voy a morir.
> Gitanitos de la Cava,
> Venid y llorad por mí.

Now I am going to die. Gipsies of La Cava, come and weep for me.

> ¡Virgen del Mayor Dolor!
> Como la negrita mora
> tengo yo mi corazón.

Virgin of the greatest sorrow, like the black mulberry is my heart.

> Arrímate a mi querer
> como las salamanquesas
> se arriman a la pared.

Draw close to my love, as the little lizards draw close to the wall.

Besides these there is the *alegría*, also confined to Andalusia, which is merely a two-lined *piropo*, or compliment, and the *playera* or *siguiriya gitana*, which is the word form of an ancient gipsy air and dance. Here is one in which the mint plant is used as a symbol for a girl:

> Apenas nacía
> la yerbita buena
> como se iban—alimentadito
> las raíces de ella.

Scarcely was the mint flower born than its roots began gathering food.

As will be seen, the verse form of the *playera* is not very successful: it is a sign of its primitiveness that it requires music.

The subjects of these little ditties are almost as extensive as those of popular life itself. There are religious songs, among which one must single out the *coplas de navidad*, or carols, and the *saetas*, sung in Holy Week to the images that pass in procession. There are cradle songs, prison songs, tavern songs, wedding songs, songs for sailors, soldiers, miners, smugglers, bandits. There are songs addressed to towns and villages, which are often surprisingly beautiful, because Spaniards have an intense love of their native place.

> Sanlúcar de Barrameda
> ¡Quién te pudiera traer
> metido en la faltriquera
> como un pliego de papel!

Sanlucar de Barrameda, would that I could carry you folded up in my pocket like a piece of paper!

> ¡Qué gusto es en Zaragoza
> oir un niño cantar,
> con la bandurria tocando
> si serena noche está!

Oh how pleasant it is in Saragossa to hear a boy singing to the bandore's music when the night is clear!

There are also satirical songs, songs expressing proverbial philosophy, songs of farewell on being called up to the army, songs on political subjects. But by far the most extensive and also the most successful category is that of the love songs. To read them through in Rodríguez Marín's great collection is a curious experience. The *copla* is by its terseness designed to express one feeling, one sentiment and no more, and many of the best *coplas* are those where that feeling rushes up like a *cri de coeur* that cannot be kept under. Others are more indirect and subtle. But, whatever their manner, there are thousands of these minute poems, each expressing one moment and one situation out of all the possible moments and situations of a love affair. Taken together they form a sort of amatory dictionary such as would have delighted Stendhal. Yet none of these poems is personal in the sense given to that word in cultured poetry. That is to say, they express the idiosyncrasy of a situation rather than of a character.

The *coplas* show various styles and types of imagery, corresponding to the different cultures from which they have come. Very common is the old symbolic imagery of folk-lore, which one finds in the *villancicos* of the sixteenth century and in some ballads:

> Cuando una mata se muere,
> al tronco llega el dolor.
> Las raíces lloran sangre,
> de luto se viste la flor.

When a plant dies, the pain reaches the stem. Its roots weep blood, its flower puts on mourning.

> Pajarito de la nieve,
> dime ¿dónde tienes el nido?
> Lo tengo en un pino verde,
> en una rama escondido.

Little bird of the snow, tell me where you have your nest?—In a green tree I build it, hidden in a branch.

There is also the style of the *coplas de requiebro* and serenades, with their *piropos*, or compliments:

> Yo creí que era la luna
> la que estaba en el balcón.
> Yo creí que era la luna
> y era la luna y el sol.

I thought it was the moon there on the balcony. I thought it was the moon, but it was the moon and the sun.

> Asómate a esa ventana,
> a la que da sobre el río,
> manojo de clavellinas
> cogidas con el rocío.

Come to the window that looks on the river, bunch of carnations gathered with dew.

> ¡Ole con ole, graciosa!
> Parece tu cuerpecito
> una botella de gaseosa.

Ole, my lovely. Your body dances like a bottle of soda-water.

But the most interesting, though not necessarily the most beautiful category is that of the indirect or allusive statement:

El candil se está apagando.
La alcuza no tiene aceite.
No te digo que te vayas.
No te digo que te quedes.

The lamp is going out. The oil jar has no more oil. I do not tell you to go. I do not tell you to stay.

A mí se me da muy poco
que un pájaro en la alaméa
se pasée de un árbol a otro.

It makes little difference to me if a bird in the poplar grove flits from one branch to another.

Ahí, no hay naïta que ver,
porque un barquillo que había
tendió la vela y se fué.

Now there is nothing to be seen, since a little ship that was there has spread its sails and gone.

These last are all in the modern, individualistic style of the nineteenth century, though, as we have seen in treating of the *villancicos*, allusion and suggestion have long been a typical procedure in Spanish folk-poetry, as they also are in the everyday speech of the people. Here, to conclude, is one more *copla* to illustrate the almost metaphysical subtlety of some of these little love poems.

Por donde quiera que voy,
parece que te voy viendo;
es la sombra del querer,
que me viene persiguiendo.

Wherever I go I seem to see you; it is the shadow of love that is pursuing me.

The beauty and interest of the *coplas* first struck the cultured world of Madrid when the well-known woman novelist, Fernán Caballero, published her Andalusian collection in 1859. Until then some interest had been taken in popular melodies and dances, but it had been supposed that the words that were set to them were insignificant. Other collections followed, culminating in the great anthology of more than eight thousand *coplas* by Rodríguez Marín in 1882. Since then a great deal of work has been done, especially by Sr Torner, in almost every province of Spain in the transcription of folk-songs and music. But what, one may ask, is the origin of this brief and condensed kind of poetry, which is so different from anything to be found in the north of Europe? If we consult Spanish sources only, there is very little information. The *seguidilla* first appeared in Andalusia towards 1600 with the dance and air of that name, though isolated examples are found as early as 1520; it would seem to have been just a special form of the *estribillo* or theme-stanza of the *villancico*, which, under the influence of new kinds of music, had dropped its development. There must, however, have been some feeling that it was too short, because the *seguidillas* of this time are often found in couples or in longer series, as they still are in Asturias today and as Sr Torner has usually arranged them in his *Cancionero Musical*. Perhaps the vogue of the single stanza, which spread rapidly, was connected with the diffusion of the ornate Andalusian style of singing with its elaborate *appoggiature*, known as *cante jondo*, or 'deep song', which, as those who have heard it will realize, is only suited to the enunciation of a few lines at a stretch. The *cuarteta* came in later, after the custom of singing single *seguidillas* had been well established and, as we have seen, gave the *copla* new opportunities for development. Nothing is known of the origin or age of the *soleá*.

It is only when we turn to other countries that we are able to see the *copla* poetry of Spain in its true perspective. We then discover that it is almost as general and widespread a form as that of the ballad or epic and that it provides the ordinary vehicle for popular love poetry over a large part of the Mediterranean region and of the Far East. Take first of all the case of Italy. Here, to speak very briefly, there are the six- or eight-lined songs written in hendecasyllables and known in Tuscany as *rispetti* or *canzoni*, and the three-lined songs, known as *stornelli* or *strambotti*. Both of these go back to at least the thirteenth century and are the sources from which the two classical measures of Italian poetry are sprung. There is also a more modern version of the *stornello* which is known as *fiore* because it begins with the name of a plant or flower and, less common, certain four-lined songs in octosyllabic metre known as *maggi*, or May songs. The style of the *rispetti* is, as their measure requires, more diffuse and musical than that of the Spanish *coplas* and their diction and that of the *stornelli* have been greatly affected by the cultured poetry of the Middle Ages and Renaissance, which, from Dante to Tasso, was widely sung by the artisans and peasants. There is, therefore, no very close parallel. One has to go to the *ciuri* (i.e. *fiori*) of Sicily and Calabria to find ditties that are at all close in feeling to anything Spanish: many of these recall the Andalusian *soleares*.

In Greece, however, the situation is almost precisely the same as it is in Spain, except that the three-lined form is lacking. The Greek distich is a sixteen-syllabled rhyming couplet with a caesura after the eighth syllable (the early Spanish *seguidillas* were also written in two lines) and its style and content are very much the same as those of the octosyllabic *coplas*. It is sung too in much the same way, to the accompaniment of a small stringed instrument called the *lura*, and in recent times it has separated itself from the older body of folk-poetry, acquired a general popularity and extended its subject matter. New distiches are often printed in the newspapers. In Turkey too there is the *mani*, a seven-syllabled rhyming quatrain, which in style and imagery is very similar to the Spanish love *coplas*, whilst in Syria and Palestine there are Arab ditties of the same type. Then, if we go to the Far East (for Persian folk-poetry contains only accidental examples) we find that the *copla*—that is to say, the poem of from four to six short lines—is the characteristic type of popular love poetry over a very wide area. In China, it is true, there are none today. But from the first to the sixth century octosyllabic four-lined poems, very similar in style to the Spanish *coplas*, were sung there as courting songs, chiefly by women. In Japan folk-ditties of a similar type were taken up by the cultured poets and became the classic form of Japanese poetry. Dr Arthur Waley has compared the indirect, allusive style of many of these *hokku*, with their three to five short lines, to that of some of the Spanish *coplas*. It is, however, in the mountain regions bordering on China and in Annam and the Malay States that we can best see this kind of poetry in its primitive setting. Here it is the ritual courting poetry of the young men and girls, sung to a certain extent all through the year but with especial appropriateness at the celebration of the spring rites, when, as in the European May festival, the spirits of vegetation and of love are propitiated in the same ceremonies. As in Spain, contests in poetic improvisation are held, there are dances, and betrothals are made. According to Marcel Granet, this was once the case in China also.

It is the Greek distiches, however, that have most relevance to the matter we are considering. In form, style and content they are, as we have said, almost precisely similar to the Spanish *coplas*, and, as it happens, we can trace their descent back a long way. Émile Legrand in his *Chansons populaires grecques* has published distiches from a fifteenth-century manuscript, preserved in Vienna, some of which he considers on linguistic grounds as having been composed in the thirteenth century. Moreover, the tenth-century epic, *Digénis Akritas*, contains a pair of rhymed distiches which are sung by a girl to her lover in the typical spring setting of a May poem. There is, besides, another very significant feature. The Vienna MS. contains a poem made up of a series of distiches, each one of which expresses the praise of some feature of a girl's face or body. The poem, as it stands, is rather corrupt and has been mixed up with material drawn apparently from the Song of Songs, but its general character can be confirmed by similar poems current in Greece today. Now these poems exist in Spain (as well as in Italy) and were till quite recently sung by young men to their girls on May Day. They are generally known as *trovos de ronda*, and in Estremadura as *Loh Mayo*. They are not alphabetical, but consist of a string of *coplas*, each *copla* describing with exaggerated imagery some feature of the girl, beginning at the head and working down to the feet. Moreover many of the ordinary courting *coplas* sung today can be shown to have been taken from these series, and this is the case in Greece and in Italy also. The implication is obvious—that the Spanish love *copla* in *cuarteta* form derives from the medieval *trovos* sung on May Day in a more or less ritual manner.

What then do we get from this (very abbreviated) excursion into comparative folk-lore? This, I think—that the courting *coplas* are fragments of the long-sought-for May poem of the early

Middle Ages, of which the descriptions of spring and of birds singing that have come down to us in sophisticated versions are the mere introit or introduction. Their regional extension has been decided by the habits of courtship. The *copla* is the love poem of those countries where the sexes are severely segregated, for naturally, when they are not segregated, when they can walk out together as in England, no ritual of love poetry is necessary. Essentially the *copla* is a functional poem, composed and sung as a means to attaining a definite object; and it is also a ritual poem, because it is connected with rites carried out at the spring festivals. All the evidence points to its being of pagan origin, brought in from the East with the introduction of agriculture and of agricultural ritual. And if one wishes for further evidence of antiquity, there is the Song of Songs, in which, as Rodríguez Marín long ago observed, the strings of compliments ('thy hair is as a flock of goats. . .thy teeth are like. . .thy lips. . .thy temples. . .thy neck. . .thy breasts. . . thy navel. . .thy thighs. . .') so amazingly resemble those in the *trovos de ronda* and where also there is to be found the earliest known example of a 'spring passage'. Now not only is the Song of Songs a collection of Jewish bridal songs of the third century B.C. which has come down to us in a confused form, but the Syrian bridal songs of today contain very similar passages of compliments which are in the form of octosyllabic rhyming quatrains. In this part of the world, I should add, the bridal ceremonies, which are usually performed in the spring, have taken over the ritual of the old Spring rites, which also celebrated a marriage—that of the May King and Queen, in other words, of the Vegetation Deities. The conclusion seems unescapable—that the *copla* is a poetic form of the greatest antiquity, coeval with those agricultural rites and superstitions described by Frazer in *The Golden Bough*. What is even more surprising is that in Spain and in Greece it should recently have emerged from its ritual, folk-lore background and, without ceasing to be popular, taken on a new lease of life.[1]

---

[1] See Song of Songs iv, 1-5: v, 10-16: vi, 4-7: vii, 1-7 and for the Spring passage ii, 11-13. Also J. G. Wetzstein, *Die Syrische Dreschtafel* (1873) and Hilma Grandquist, *Marriage Conditions in a Palestinian Village* (Helsingfors, 1935).

CHAPTER XV

NINETEENTH-CENTURY PROSE

WE HAVE seen that the principal kinds of literature that sprang up in the 1830's, after the long period of savage wars and reaction had come to an end, were romantic poetry and poetic drama, and that these were really the propaganda weapon of the new Liberal ideology. It was natural that the prose of the day should reflect the political ideas also—in modern parlance, 'be engaged'. We need not be surprised therefore that the greatest writer of this time, the only one whom we can still take up with much pleasure, was a journalist.

Mariano José de Larra—for that was his name—was born in 1809. His father, a man of parts, was an army doctor who, having served under Joseph Bonaparte, was obliged to leave the country in 1814. His son went with him. When in 1817 the child was sent back to live with his mother's relatives in Castile, he spoke only French. Put to school with the Escolapians in Madrid, he grew up to manhood under the *ominosa década*, or terror. His first post was in a Government office. Then, as the censorship weakened, he left it to become a journalist, and within a year or two was the greatest journalist that this people so given to reading newspapers has ever had.

The rest of Larra's brief life can be quickly told. His success as a journalist gave him fame and an entry into the best society. He visited Paris and London and married. But he remained an unhappy man. A novel on the Middle Ages and a romantic verse play which he had written were both failures. His marriage turned out a failure too and he formed a liaison with another woman. When she, for reasons of conscience, decided to break with him, he shot himself. He was just twenty-eight.

The articles that Larra scribbled in haste at night for his paper are what we read of his today. It was the age of great journalists.

Paul Louis Courier had only a few years before been making a name for himself in Paris. There was Leigh Hunt in England and Heine in Germany. Larra's articles deal with literature and the drama, with contemporary types and customs, with Madrid society, but above all with Spain, her character, her place in the world, her predicament—the Spain that 'like a new Penelope, spends her time in alternately weaving and unweaving her dress'. Larra was one of those unhappy people who would like to believe, but cannot. A romantic by inner conviction and a Liberal because he hated tyranny, he saw no grounds for romanticism or for optimism in the world about him. Unlike his poet contemporaries, who suffered from all the false hopes and easy expectations of men who have been exiles, he had spent the dark days of the reaction in Spain. There the iron had entered into his soul: he knew what conditions were, he realized how desperate was the state and how unalterable the character of his countrymen, and he felt a deep pessimism. The failure of his play and of his marriage increased this. Where divorce is impossible, love affairs outside the framework of marriage are necessarily unstable and full of torment. What we find therefore in his articles is the reporting of a very intelligent and observant man who has lost all his illusions. He writes in a style that is admirably direct and spontaneous; since Quevedo, no one had written prose with such force and economy and, though he lacks the great satirist's command of the full resources of language as well as his powerful and tormented imagination, his dry tone of understatement makes an admirable background for his flashes of sardonic wit and irony. Larra is not so witty as Heine, but he is nearly so: he is more astringent and tonic and therefore more in keeping with modern taste. Although his themes are too local and Spanish to make a very general appeal (here painters such as Goya have an advantage), there is no one, I think, except the great German, who can approach him as a journalist. His early death was a tragedy for Spanish literature.

The characteristic prose form of the nineteenth century is the novel. This, however, developed much later in Spain than in England or France. More than any other kind of literary production, the realistic novel requires for its appearance a prosperous middle class and settled conditions, and these did not exist in Spain before 1850. What took its place were those short prose sketches of types and customs known as *costumbrismo*.

This kind of thing was not new. As we have seen, during the last decades of the previous century Ramón de la Cruz had been delighting theatre-goers by his short, casual presentations of Madrid life. When it became possible to write again, journalists and men of letters began to offer the same fare to their readers. Larra wrote *costumbrista* articles: Mesonero Romanos described characteristic scenes and types in Madrid, and Estébanez Calderón, writing in a tediously affected style, did the same for Andalusia. His *Escenas Andaluzas*, first published in 1832, mark the end of a six-centuries-long silence about the life of this province and the first step in its popularization as the picturesque region of Spain. During the following decade it was to be discovered and written up by the foreigners—Borrow, Ford, Gautier, Mérimée and the Russian composer Glinka.

The importance of the *costumbristas* is that they decided the main lines that the novel was to follow during the rest of the century. The novelists, with a few exceptions, sat down to write with the aim of describing the life and customs of the city or province in which they lived and only secondarily of telling a story of general human interest. Sometimes they wrote in praise of their *patria chica*, more often they drew a dark picture of it, but they always took care to describe its general pattern, even when this meant making considerable interruptions in the plot. If this approach had obvious disadvantages, it at least made certain that the Spanish novel should draw its strength from the observed social life of a community rather than from the personal experience of the novelist. Such a rule, in Spain at least, was salutary.

The first of these novels—for I omit those historical romances inspired by a misunderstanding of Scott—was *La Gaviota*, which came out in 1849. Its author was a woman, Cecilia Böhl de Faber (1796-1877), who wrote under the name of Fernán Caballero. Her father was the German consul at Cadiz, who, by his translation of a work by August Wilhelm von Schlegel and by the collections he brought out of Spanish poetry and drama, had been one of the forerunners of the Romantic Movement. Her mother was half Spanish and half Irish. She herself had been born in Switzerland and educated in a French pension at Hamburg, but from the age of seventeen had lived in Andalusia and so regarded herself as a Spaniard. Three times married and widowed, she made her home in Seville, where she moved in aristocratic society.

Fernán Caballero is a woman who deserves well of her adopted country. She was the first person to interest herself in the artistic talents of the peasants and working classes, collecting and publishing the stories they told and the *coplas* they sang. Since Lope de Vega no Spanish writer had thought any of these worth listening to. She also, as we have said, wrote the first novel of contemporary life. It is true that *La Gaviota*, which is the best of her works of fiction, is not, artistically speaking, a good book. The characters, though plausible, are types rather than living people and do not change or grow as the plot develops. There is also too much emphasis on *costumbrismo* and too much Germanic zest for instructing us. But she has a wide range of observation and sympathy: her crude, egoistic heroine and her bull-fighter are convincing in their static way and, even when we feel the weakness of the novelising, we go on reading. As an intelligent and widely travelled woman explaining to us the social pattern of Andalusian life, she contrives, I think, to hold the attention.

The first Spanish novelist of real talent—first, that is, in point of age—was Juan Valera (1824-1905). He was an Andalusian from Cabra in the province of Cordova, who had had the luck to be born into one of the great Liberal families that, as a political and social force, were supplanting the old aristocracy. Educated at Malaga and Granada, he chose as his career the diplomatic service and spent the best part of an agreeable youth in various foreign capitals—Naples, Lisbon, Rio de Janeiro and later Washington, Paris, Vienna, St Petersburg. Then in 1858 he retired and settled in Madrid, becoming the director of a number of periodicals, a deputy to Congress and finally its secretary. But these activities represented only one side of his life: the other half was devoted to literature, and thus it was that the serene and Olympian figure who moved so easily through aristocratic salons and congressional corridors came also to be regarded as the *doyen* of Spanish letters.

Valera was a man who by temperament belonged more to the late Italian Renaissance than to his own age. A hedonist rather than a stoic, a pagan rather than a Christian, a classicist and not at all a Romantic, he took as his aim in life that simultaneous development of the intellectual and aesthetic faculties and social graces which had been prescribed by Castiglione in his famous book, *The Courtier*. Badly educated in the wretched Spanish universities of the day, he acquired by study and travel a very wide culture. His clear, well-ordered mind and fine sensibility enabled him to absorb what was best in the literature and philosophy of half a dozen countries and to give out his reflections on these in a long series of essays and articles. His complete works number forty-six volumes. After Menéndez Pelayo he is the best Spanish critic of the century, standing above the literary fashions of his age and examining the books he discusses in the light of first principles and of a general aesthetic theory. His clear, flowing style, almost French in its smoothness and limpidity, makes the reading of his work pleasantly effortless.

Valera had tried out his talents in poetry, criticism and philosophy before he came to novel writing. His first novel, *Pepita Jiménez*, did not appear till 1874, when he was fifty. He came to write it, he tells us, after a study of the theological and mystical works of the sixteenth century, into which he had been drawn by a controversy that had broken out between the intellectuals of his day, with their German-inspired pantheism, and the clericals. But he was a believer in art for art's sake; didacticism in literary works seemed as improper to him as it did to Turgeniev or Flaubert and he therefore made use of the insight he had acquired into the theological mind to create the character and mode of thinking of an ardent and pious divinity student.

The plot could not be simpler. A young man, who is about to be ordained priest, goes to spend a few months with his father, who is the *cacique*, or boss, of a small town in Andalusia. Here he meets a lovely and sedate young widow called Pepita. He falls in love with her, and the rest of the book is a description of the conflict that goes on in his mind between his love and what he believes to be his religious vocation. In the end Pepita, who is equally in love with him, contrives that, on his visiting her to say goodbye, he shall seduce her in her bedroom, and the young man, overcome by his act, realizes that what he had taken to be a call to a religious and ascetic life had really been no more than youthful pride, ambition and self-deception.

Pepita Jiménez has the fame of being Valera's best novel. Certainly the realization of the characters and the management of the plot are admirable. The gradual awakening of the young man's love, the sophistries he uses for concealing it from himself and the opposition it finally encounters in his religious scruples are conveyed with a fine truth and subtlety. Then, in the second half of the book, we are taken into Pepita's feelings and character and are shown to what lengths a virtuous but passionate woman will go to secure her ends. But it is not enough for novels to tell stories and portray character; they have to entertain. It is here that, from the twentieth-century point of view, *Pepita Jiménez* falls down rather badly. We resent the intractable dullness of much of the material—in particular the seminarist's lengthy excuses and theological disquisitions. And we feel too, I think, a certain *malaise* at the ambiguous tone in which these subjects are treated, which comes from Valera's being one of those sceptics who reject with their intellect the dogmas of the Church, but are drawn back to religious matters by a sort of prurient curiosity.

Doña Luz, which appeared five years later, is a less perfect but more varied novel on a similar theme. Here the issue is even more piquant: a monk who has reached an advanced stage of holiness falls in love with a young woman, but suppresses his feelings. The heroine, however, does not return his love, so that the situation fails to come to a head and other events supervene. Although we are not spared a lengthy theological disquisition, this is partly redundant to the plot and can be skipped.

Las ilusiones del Doctor Faustino (1875) can be called an interesting failure. Valera sets out, like Turgeniev in *Rudin*, to depict the typical young man of the day, with his boundless hopes and illusions, his talent which leads only to writing bad verses and his pride which causes him to neglect the practical management of his small estate and so ruin himself. It is a sort of *Éducation Sentimentale* in the setting of the Andalusian countryside, with the old feudal landowners sinking into poverty and the money-lenders and successful farmers rising and enriching themselves. But the novelist makes his hero reflect and philosophize too much—this is his common failing—and the second half of the book breaks down completely.

Doctor Faustino was followed by *El Comendador Mendoza*, which in my opinion is Valera's masterpiece. Like most of his novels it introduces us to a small circle of people of the landowning class living in a country town in Andalusia. These people are carefully chosen: there is something distinct and attractive about each of them. Their houses are clean, cool and airy, with dark polished furniture and patios full of well-cultivated flowers. There is a background of farming with its various seasons of harvest, vintage and olive gathering, but the painful and abject side of country life —the poverty and hunger of so many of the agricultural labourers —is scarcely touched on, though Valera shows that he is aware of it. And naturally there is the subject of love, with, as usual, a trace of violent sexual passion or crude sensuality breaking through the polite and urbane narrative.

Love is the subject that interested Valera most. An *homme à bonnes fortunes* who married late in life—married, too, a girl in her early twenties—he studied it in all its aspects and has much to say about it. His women in love are nearly always excellent. He has much to say also about the conflict between love and pride, and love and self-interest. His curiosity over religion is chiefly derived from the same thing, because religious fervour is so often a diversion of sexual love to an unchanging object. In his portraits of religious people he is careful to show the foundation of pride, guilt and frustration that underlies their devoutness. Only his elderly priests and monks and his young girls are allowed to be naturally pious.

In the *Comendador Mendoza* the great passion lies in the past; it is its consequences—a child born in adultery—that provides the theme of the book. There is, however, a second theme: the marriage of a girl who is under twenty to a man who is over fifty. Valera, who was himself fifty-two at the time, shows a sort of obsession for the possibilities of such matches, which in Spain have generally had public opinion against them. What causes more astonishment to the English reader is that the happy couple are uncle and niece and that this seems to have been regarded as a perfectly normal situation.

Two novels written towards the end of Valera's life deserve a mention—*Juanita la Larga* (1895) and *Genio y Figura* (1897). The former is an excellent novel about life in an Andalusian town; it has a sinuous plot that provides new situations with every chapter and the picture it gives of the social gradations among the middle classes is drawn with great skill and malice. Only the *dénouement* is poor. *Genio y Figura* is an altogether different sort of work. It describes the life of a Spanish courtesan who marries a rich and elderly Brazilian. The scene is laid in Rio de Janeiro and then, twenty years later, in Paris. Although, as in all Valera's novels, the tone is discreet and on occasion sugary, it is really a meditation on sex, and especially on the sexual life of the middle-aged and elderly. One feels an old man dreaming and sentimentalizing about past delights and triumphs and, because he is a pyschologist and philosopher, reasoning and novelizing about them. Although one can hardly call the novel good, for it reeks too much of the stale perfumes of *La Dame aux Camélias*, it has interesting passages, among which I would include an extraordinary anecdote about an old man's impotence.

Valera is a novelist who attached great importance to form. His best novels are built round a single situation and take place in one locality within a comparatively short space of time. Nothing is allowed to occur that does not contribute to the elucidation of the central problem or theme. In an age when other writers were either romantics or realists he—by his tone, his treatment of character, and his plot—is aloof and classical. We feel a mind at work that likes to survey the field of human action from a certain distance and not to be emotionally mixed up in it. But if he is Olympian like Goethe, he can also be sentimental and unctuous. He flatters his characters in the soft Andalusian way, though often under his flattery there lies a good deal of malice. His caressing, feline approach suggests at times the manner of Renan, whilst on other occasions the acuity of his observation reminds one of Stendhal.

He is inclined to spoil his novels by his desire to make them end as happily as possible and to show even his most venomous characters lying down like lambs.

The great gift, however, of this writer is his flair for the dramatic tensions that exist in quite ordinary situations. In his novels we are kept constantly aware of the contrast and opposition between different minds, aims and points of view. This is often done with a fine irony. Take, for example, the scene in *Doña Luz* where Don Acisclo, a rough, uncultivated but otherwise excellent man, who has acquired a large estate by lending money, is so impressed by the sanctity of his missionary nephew that he decides to reform his life. While his friends are expecting him to announce that he will enter a convent, he amazes them by declaring that he has decided to take up politics, set himself up as a local boss, or *cacique*, and send a suitable person to Parliament to represent his interests. For what has impressed him about his nephew has been his success: if, he argues, the success of a religious man lies in acquiring holiness, then that of a practical man must consist in acquiring wealth and power. Since he already has wealth, it only remains for him to add to it power and prestige. In other words, his nephew's reputation as a saint has stimulated his ambition, and the fact that the politics of the day were based on corruption, bribery and the crude pressure of the money-lender and had no ideal content whatever was from his point of view irrelevant. In this way, quietly and without comment, Valera lifts the veil of conventional appearance and language that holds people in a false conformity to one another and shows us what the thoughts of a successful man, even on such a time-honoured subject as religion, really are.

We may say then that Valera, though limited in scope, is a psychological novelist of considerable penetration and subtlety. He is also a man of mature mind and wide knowledge of the world. His sense of order, his clear narrative style and his fine irony are further attractions. Yet there is something lacking. This something is the heart. Under all his curiosity about human beings we discern a cold, egocentric nature, with more than the usual quantity of sensuality but little capacity for genuine love or passion. The qualities one most dislikes in him—his desire to please and flatter,

his occasional sentimentality, his smugness and facile optimism—
are attempts to cover up this lack of feeling. His lack of force and
pungency have the same origin. He is an uneven writer, who only
novelizes well when he relies on his intelligence. But then he is
admirable.

Hitherto, in the course of the past three chapters, we have been
dealing with prose writers and poets who, for all their unique and
remarkable qualities, must be regarded as figures of secondary
importance. We now come to someone who is very much greater
—to Pérez Galdós. He is a writer of the first order, comparable to
Balzac, Dickens and Tolstoy, and it is only the strange neglect in
which nineteenth-century Spanish literature has been held by the
rest of Europe, and, one must add, the narrowly aesthetic views of
some Spanish critics and intellectuals, that have failed to give him
the place that is due to him as one of the great European novelists.
None of his mature works have been translated into English and
only one into French.

Benito Pérez Galdós was born at Las Palmas in the Canary
Islands in 1843, the youngest son of a large and fairly wealthy
middle-class family. We know little of his youth except that he
was timid, silent and studious. Sent to an English school in the
city, he learned to speak English fluently, to read French and to
draw and paint. But his principal love was for literature, and he
read everything he could lay hands on.

Such talents could not be wasted and when he was nineteen he
was sent to Madrid University to study law. Madrid was at this
time in the full glamour of the late Isabelline period, pleasure-
loving, animated, idle and enormously given to conversation upon
every conceivable subject. From midday to midnight the streets
and cafés were crowded with people; plots and revolutions were
in the air, and yet such was the mildness of the age that little was
left of that fear and hatred which had been so noticeable thirty
years earlier. In spite of the Carlist War brewing in the north and
the risings of peasantry in Andalusia, clericals and anti-clericals sat
at adjacent tables without scowling at one another. The young
Galdós threw himself into this pleasant life with zest. The theatres,
the cafés, the *Ateneo*—Madrid's club for writers and politicians—

and no doubt too the usual love affairs drank up the time he should have given to his law books. But he had private means, and when no one else who could avoid it worked, why should he? One of his favourite amusements was to take long, solitary rambles round the city and its suburbs, loitering to watch any particular scene that struck his fancy and making conversation with other onlookers. Perhaps it was his island background or even his English education —but he had fallen in love with Madrid with all the passion and curiosity of a foreigner.

Galdós was not long in discovering his literary vocation, but the first step he took in this direction was a false one. An enthusiast for the theatre, he imagined that his talent lay in writing plays. It was a visit to Paris and the reading of Balzac that put him on the right track. He began to write his first novel, *La Fontana de Oro*, in 1867, immediately after his return—that is to say, just seven years before Valera published *Pepita Jiménez*. It was an historical novel, set in the revolutionary era of Liberal rule in 1820-3. He had been led to the subject by his desire to account for the deplorable condition of his country—its backwardness, its chaotic political regime, its poverty and idleness. The roots of these things lay, so it seemed to him, a generation or more back in the struggle between the Liberals and the Clericals. He felt the same need to discover and explain the causes of this situation as has been felt by almost every Spanish intellectual since his time, and the revolt of the Artillery Sergeants of a Madrid barracks in 1866 and their brutal execution afterwards had made this task seem more pressing. But *La Fontana de Oro* did not satisfy him. The matter needed to be treated at greater length. In 1873, therefore, after a period of active journalism which gave him a close-up view of the dramatic events that followed the dethronement of Queen Isabella, he embarked on that long series of historical novels, commencing in 1805, which are known as the *Episodios Nacionales*.

From now on, for the next forty years, Pérez Galdós became a man of regular habits and of steady, almost unbelievable industry. Not even Scott or Balzac left so many books behind them. The *Episodios Nacionales* alone number forty-six volumes. There are then the thirty or so novels of contemporary life, one of them almost

25-2

as long as *War and Peace*. Although perhaps a third of these books are of little merit, half a dozen are among the best novels ever written. In addition to this there are more than twenty plays, which in their time had considerable success.

To achieve this vast output Galdós had to make a complete change in his habits. Cafés, *tertulias* and even visits to the theatre were given up or reserved for special occasions. In summer he rose at five, in winter at seven, and from then till nine at night, with a short break for lunch and two longer breaks for exercise, he worked steadily at his writing table. His two unmarried sisters kept house for him and protected his hours of work from interruption. Then from time to time he took holidays. Packing a gladstone bag, he would set off to explore some foreign country or province of Spain that he did not know. He was an enthusiastic tourist, wandering guide-book in hand round the principal towns and cities of Western Europe. His favourite city was London, which he visited several times, exploring all the places mentioned in the novels of his *maestro más amado*, Dickens. He also travelled a good deal in Spain, going third class with his servant among the peasants and their baskets of vegetables and poultry, and staying in the most out-of-the-way places. His other hobbies, which he took up chiefly in later life, when he owned a summer villa at Santander, were painting, gardening and playing the harmonium. In Madrid he never missed a concert.

Such was the mode of living of this tremendous worker: a succession of strictly regulated habits that tell us merely that his real life lay in his books. To them alone he gave himself completely. It is for this reason that we find so little—almost nothing—to say about his personality and character. He was for one thing very reserved about himself. Genial with people of a lower social position, at ease with children, he was silent and a little constrained in company and did not expand much even with his friends. Everyone who knew him speaks of his simplicity, modesty and quiet unassumingness, and his novels show that, while others talked, his small, deeply set eyes, which in old age were to fail him completely, were taking in more of the people round him than any writer except Tolstoy had taken in before. He was, or seemed to be, the complete extrovert who, unhampered by any veil of egoism, gave his eyes, his ears and above all his sympathies to the persons with whom he came into contact.

Let us now consider his work. He began to write the *Episodios Nacionales* in 1873 and had completed the first two series, of ten volumes each, by 1879. They then covered the period from the battle of Trafalgar in 1805 to the cholera epidemic and sack of the convents in 1834. At the same time that he worked on these episodes, he wrote four novels about contemporary life: *Doña Perfecta* (1876), *Gloria*, *Marianela* and *La familia de León Roch* (1878). These are the works in which he was discovering his talent. Then in 1880 he sat down to that great series of contemporary novels, beginning with *La desheredada*, reaching its climax in *Fortunata y Jacinta* (1887) and ending with *Misericordia* in 1897. After this he returned to the *Episodios Nacionales*, writing twenty-five volumes between 1897 and 1912: the last episode, *Cánovas*, takes the series down to the 'eighties. This concludes Galdós' career as a novelist. In 1912 his eyesight, which had for some years been weak, failed and he went blind. The only works that he produced after this were four plays.

The *Episodios Nacionales* are short volumes in which history and fiction are mixed in various proportions. In some of them the chief events and characters of the day are seen directly, whereas in others they are only alluded to. Galdós's aim was to give the feeling and tone of Spanish society in each epoch rather than to describe the strict succession of historical events. To provide continuity, there are certain fixed characters who appear and reappear through a number of volumes, so that we may consider each of the series of ten episodes as a single novel. The treatment is objective and realistic, without any trace of political prejudice or romanticism. His approach to the subject had been influenced by Erckmann-Chatrian's *Histoire d'un conscrit de* 1813 and *Waterloo*, which had come out a few years earlier, so that, when he describes historical events, he tries to show them just as they would have appeared through the eyes of a person who took part in them. But he is much more lively and inventive than the Alsatian novelists. The *Episodios* contain many vivid and brilliant scenes and characters. He has a particular talent for putting over the confusion of street fighting and rioting—compare his account of the rising against the French in *El Dos de Mayo* with Dickens' description of the Lord George Gordon riots in *Barnaby Rudge*—whilst in other passages the comedy of civil war, bad government and revolution is shown as well as the tragedy. For this reason and because they provide Spaniards with a living history of their country, the *Episodios* are probably better known in Spain than any of Galdós' other books. But foreigners must necessarily have a different attitude. These volumes, entertaining though they are, require from the reader some preliminary curiosity as to their subject matter. And, unfortunately, the history of Spain during this period is not of such a kind as to make it likely that many people, other than Spaniards, will wish to delve deeply into it.

As we have seen, Galdós wrote between 1876 and 1878 four novels about contemporary life. The first and best known of these is *Doña Perfecta*. It is a book about clerical obscurantism in the provinces. A young engineer of Liberal ideas arrives at the small Castilian town of Orbajosa with the object of marrying his cousin, who is the daughter of the principal landowner of the place, Doña Perfecta. From the moment of his arrival he finds himself enveloped in a dense Tibetan atmosphere of intolerance and fanaticism: thwarted in his hopes of marrying the girl he loves because he is regarded as a heretic, he attempts to elope with her and is killed by a Carlist partisan. The girl, who has from the beginning shown signs of hysteria, is removed to a lunatic asylum.

In its general plan, in the terrible and on the whole convincing picture it paints of a small cathedral town in Old Castile, the book is an imposing one. We see the Spain against which the Liberals were contending, the stagnant, stupid, fanatical Spain of the country districts. Once and for all Galdós has portrayed it for us in fierce black and white. Some of the characters are well drawn, notably the priest, Don Inocencio. His ironic humility—'How are we ignorant people to contend with you who know all the marvels of science?'—and the aggressive way in which he presses it on the young man till he has succeeded in infuriating him are especially telling. The notables of Orbajosa have the angry sulkiness of people who have once been powerful, but are now defeated. Yet the novel is not up to the level of the mature works of Galdós. Many of the scenes are weak, and the indignant mood in which it has been written—for the book is a satire—has prevented him from displaying that fine understanding of character and motive which he was later to excel in. Doña Perfecta herself is one of the few failures among his female characters.

The next novel, *Gloria*, is also on a religious theme: it treats of the love of an intelligent Spanish girl for a Jew of noble character. It too has a strong polemical bent, but, though less boldly constructed than *Doña Perfecta*, it marks an advance in subtlety of characterization. *Marianela*, which follows, is a book about a mining village; conceived in a romantic vein, it is one of the worst of Galdós' novels and also one of the most popular. *La familia de León Roch*, the last of this series, marks the transition to his mature period of novel writing.

The twenty-one novels that follow and that contain the best of this writer's work are all sited in Madrid. Galdós is the novelist of the Spanish capital. In the course of these books he treats of every aspect of life in the rapidly growing city, every social class and almost every profession. There is a change of accent from the earlier works. In them the principal characters personified ideas: now he draws individuals, seeking in the conjunction of all these individuals to give a balanced account of the national temperament. He draws his characters life-size, neither exaggerating them nor diminishing them, and, since the whole of Madrid is his subject and streets and shops have their human facets too, he is careful to give them also a prominent place in his picture. But he is far from aiming, as the *costumbristas* had done, at a mere description. Galdós, more than any other of the great novelists except Proust, is a moralist. We see this, not in his comments—for he rarely makes any—but in his choice of themes. He had a very clear picture in his mind of the social and political vices of Spanish society and every one of his novels is devoted to the analysis and portrayal of one or more of them. The Spanish character, the Spanish predicament are his eternal subject, and since Spain with its *grandeurs* and its *misères*, its political cataclysms and its economic misery can be called the microcosm, or even at some moments the caricature, of Europe, we other Europeans should have no difficulty in finding ourselves at home among the scenes that he represents.

Let us take a few of his best novels and see what they are like. The first, *La desheredada*, owes its theme to a meditation on *Don Quixote*. It depicts the conflict, so deeply rooted in the Spanish character, between imagination and reality. Isidora Rufete is a girl of the lower middle classes who has been brought up by her uncle—a fantastic person who very appropriately lives at el Toboso, the village of Dulcinea—to believe that she is the daughter of a marquesa. She has what she supposes to be documentary proof of this and the novel takes her from her arrival in Madrid, to press her claim, through a long series of events that end in the failure of her lawsuit and in her sinking to the level of a prostitute. Isidora is a girl who, if she had not been brought up under false expectations, would have had a better fate. She has beauty: she is decent and honest and in many ways a likeable person, but she has one great vice that springs from her mistaken view of her origin—an unshakable conviction of her own transcendant value. '*Eso merezco yo*', she says when she sees an expensive dress in a shop window, 'I deserve to have that.' Or, of a not sufficiently presentable suitor, '*Yo valgo infinitamente más que él*,' 'I am worth infinitely more than him'. This conviction gives her a loathing for everything that is vulgar, cheap and commonplace and makes her feel with every cell of her body that she was born for a life of ease and elegance. Thus, in spite of the efforts of her friends and relatives to help her, she passes on from lover to lover and, when at last she loses faith in her claim, finds it impossible to adjust herself to the narrow but respectable position that is offered her. She is a Manon Lescaut who is ruined by pride even more than by love of luxury.

La desheredada is the freshest, the most lyrical of Galdós' novels. The early chapters offer a picture, not usual in this author, of young life beginning, of adventures unrolling, of unshaped opportunities and possibilities. This is partly due to the presence of Augusto Miquís, a young doctor who is one of the few really witty characters in fiction. His flirtation with Isidora, their walk round Madrid together, their visit to the Zoo have a spring-like charm and gaiety. Then we are given a view of lower middle-class and working-class life. The girl's aunt keeps a shop in a very poor quarter, and her brother is a hooligan. These descents into squalor, where the atmosphere grows thick and dense as in a Dickens novel, and is shot by oblique lights, occur in most of Galdós' works. But meanwhile Isidora's character is developing. We see her unable to resist the temptations of the shop windows, unable to refuse the pleasures of new clothes and hot baths, unable to say no to any form of ostentation or luxury. With every fresh extravagance or folly her difficulties increase and she takes another step down. Galdós draws the struggle that goes on in her mind with wonderful tact and sensitivity. We are never allowed to forget her pride and egoism, her false refinement with its morbid dread of vulgarity or her essential hardness: they are not pleasant characteristics, but they are redeemed for us by her sense of her destiny that drives her forward and by her reckless generosity. She pays in full the price of her faults and does it without remorse or self-pity. Ordinary though Isidora is, her story has all the cleanness and inevitability of classic tragedy.

Galdós' next book is *El amigo Manso*. It is a novel of a more conventional sort and lacks any dominating theme. The story is made by the rivalry of various men of the upper classes for a girl who, because she has no private means, becomes a governess. Young women in dependent positions often play the part of heroine in Galdós' novels, as they do in English ones, the chief difference being that in Spain they ran a great risk of being seduced and ruined. In this case the merit of the novel consists less in the story, which ends happily, than in the amusing scenes and characters that are thrown up by the way. There is, for example, the wealthy Indiano, Don José Maria Manso, with his Cuban family, who, in order to cut a figure in society, decides to use his money to found a new political party; the eminent nobodies who collect round him, their conversations and programmes and social functions, provide a rich comedy. Best of all is that mosquito-like horror, Doña Candida, a once wealthy widow who has squandered all her money and now supports herself by ingenious forms of pestering her old friends. With her lies and her snobbishness and her chatter, and her crude, virulent egoism, she is one of the high watermarks of Galdosian comedy.

El Doctor Centeno, an interesting but uneven book, followed, and then, in 1884, two short novels that should be read in conjunction—*Tormento* and *La de Bringas*. *Tormento* is another novel on the subject of the impoverished young lady. Amparo Sánchez Emperador, who is also known as Tormento, is a poor relation who sews and does the shopping for a family of eminently respectable civil servants, the Bringas. A cousin of the Bringas', a millionaire who has made his money in the wilds of Mexico, falls in love with her and wishes to marry her. But Amparo has a secret past: as a young orphan in dire poverty, she had let herself be seduced by a dissolute priest. If she had confessed this to her fiancé, he would have forgiven her, but she cannot quite bring herself to do so. She is one of those humble, self-effacing, warm-hearted women who seem to owe their good qualities to the fact that they have no character and no moral courage. So the slow torture of the book begins. First the priest, who is still madly in love with her, blackmails her: then his sister, a sinister mahogany-faced *beata*, who spends her life in churches, throws out hints. But still she cannot confess. At last it comes out: the match is broken off and it is only on the final page that a bearable ending is provided by her fiancé carrying her off to Bordeaux as his mistress. Once again we get a picture of a young woman struggling with her character—this time, her weakness of will—and suffering cruelly over it. And in the background there is the magnificent comic spectacle of the Bringas family—Don Francisco, the perfect man of order and method, and Doña Rosalía with her envious, *agridulce* temperament.

La de Bringas, the novel that follows and continues *Tormento*, is Galdós' comic masterpiece. The centre of the picture is taken up by the Bringas couple and their young children. They are now living in the Royal Palace, a vast building which houses a heterogeneous population of court employees, ranging from ladies of the bed-chamber and royal pensioners to charwomen. They have apartments there because Rosalía is an attendant of some unspecified sort on the queen, while her husband works in the Royal Commissariat for Holy Places. The book opens deliciously with a description of a fantastic work of art which Bringas has undertaken in his evenings —a picture of a classic mausoleum with angels, weeping willows, urns and garlands disposed around it, all made of human hair. It is to be a present to the wife of a high official, Don Manuel Pez, as a memorial of her dead son. It is a work requiring immense patience and a watchmaker's skill, but Bringas is an adept at every sort of domestic handicraft, from mending furniture to carving toys and polishing silver, so that making a picture of four different colours of hair, all taken from the heads of various members of the Pez family, is just the sort of task he likes. But while he works at his picture, his partner Rosalía enters on a new course of life. Hitherto she has always been a model wife and mother, prudent, economical and submissive to her husband and to his meticulous routine. But the presents given her (in *Tormento*) by her millionaire cousin and the envy aroused by Amparo's engagement to him have turned her head. She now longs to shine, to make the most of what is left of her youth and beauty, to dress well, and her spendthrift friend, the Marquesa de Tellería, urges her on. She is soon in debt and turning feverishly from one recourse to another.

The plot of the book consists in an alternation between her orgies of extravagant spending on clothes and a search for the means of preventing the debts thus incurred from becoming known to her husband. Never, I think, has a novelist introduced us so deeply or minutely to the secret of this feminine passion as Galdós here does. Rosalía cannot resist the lure of clothes, and the tale of her desperate borrowings and of those of her even more extravagant and bankrupt friend takes us from one crisis to another. As in *La desheredada* and *Tormento*, the main part of the novel consists of a description of the *passio* or suffering of the heroine, which she brings on herself by her inability to resist her leading vice. The alternations of hope and despair are skilfully arranged. For example, just as the whole thing seems about to come out, Bringas' eyesight, strained by the labours of his hair picture, gives way and he goes blind. Rosalía seizes on this to pawn the silver candlesticks and to abstract part of his private hoard, but, when his sight returns suddenly, there is a further crisis. The highest comic moment in the book occurs when, in spite of her strict principles, she decides to give herself to Don Manuel Pez in return for a 'loan', which will allow her to replace what she has taken from the family savings. The Pez family—the word means 'Fish'—are the type of the higher bureaucrats who appear in a number of Galdós' books. Don Manuel, elegant, poised, superior, is of a rank only just below that of minister. He has been courting her in a discreet way for some time and she has been flattered by his attentions. Oh that she had for a husband a really distinguished man such as he, who could afford to dress her as she deserves to be dressed! So she gives herself to him—clumsily choosing the wrong moment—but, when she asks for a loan, Pez has to confess that he is as much in debt as everyone else and at the moment cannot afford a penny. In the end Rosalía saves herself in the most humiliating way by borrowing from the sister of the despised Amparo, who is a dress-maker turned courtesan.

The story has taken place during the sweltering summer of 1868. Looking out from the windows of the Palace, the country lies white and inert in the heat. Now in September the curtain falls. The army, the navy, the middle classes and the workmen rise with one accord, and Queen Isabella takes the train to France. Rosalía and her husband lose their jobs and vacate their rooms in the Palace. And so this phantasmagoric society, so brilliant when seen from outside but built on poverty and debt and emptiness, melts and disappears. The cold breath of reality puts an end to the brittle dream. We may say that *La de Bringas* is the application to Spanish society of the leading idea of *Don Quixote* and *La Vida es Sueño*.

In 1886-7 appeared Galdós' greatest novel, *Fortunata y Jacinta*. This enormously long book can be called the epic of Madrid: as we read its seventeen hundred or more dense pages, we become so caught up in the life of this self-absorbed city that we forget that there is anything outside it. Yet *Fortunata y Jacinta* is, like *War and Peace*, a universal book, giving, in Menéndez Pelayo's words, 'the illusion of life itself, so completely have the characters and ambience been worked out'. Unlike most of Galdós' previous novels, it has no simple or definite theme. Such guiding ideas as it can show are quite vague—a contrast between two women, the upper-class wife and the mistress who comes from the people, and behind these perhaps between civilized society and Nature. The plot, which in its main outline is simple, is complicated by an immense ramification of subsidiary events and characters.

Let us look at this main subject or plot. A young man, Juanito Santa Cruz, who belongs to a wealthy middle-class family, marries a girl called Jacinta from the same class as himself and has also a working-class girl called Fortunata for his mistress. The principal part of the novel consists of the description of his varying relations with both of them and in the feelings that the two women who are both in love with Juanito, have for one another. But not more than half the book is taken up in this way. Behind these three persons are grouped their numerous friends and relatives—rich on the one side and poor on the other—as well as the family of Fortunata's husband Maxi, who belongs to the respectable lower middle classes; and the history and adventures of all these people are worked into the general picture.

Let us consider the three major characters first. Jacinta is a sweet, refined, warm-hearted, generous girl—'an angel', as her friends put it—who has been brought up by adoring parents to a sheltered life. Fortunata, on the other hand, is a typical woman of the people—a term that means so much more in Spanish than it does in English. Although she is generous and warm-hearted too, she is much more full-blooded than Jacinta: her passions are stronger and she thinks and feels from instinct. Thus she believes that she is more truly married to Juanito than Jacinta is, because she has had a son by him, whereas Jacinta's great tragedy is that she is childless. This sterility of the wife—let us say in passing—has a symbolic value. Galdós had always castigated the frivolity of the upper classes, and here— with many reservations, no doubt—he is putting forward an idea that was widely held in Spain at the time—that the vital force of the country lay in 'the people' and that the upper classes were feeble and decadent. As Cánovas, the restorer of the monarchy, expressed it, 'the surface of our country constantly decays, but never the depths'.

But if Galdós ever really held this rather simple view, he does not allow it to influence his sympathies as a novelist. His two women—Jacinta especially—are drawn with marvellous skill and delicacy. No writer, except perhaps Tolstoy, has shown such a deep and intimate understanding of women's characters and feelings. As we read, we forget the printed page and feel the living presence of this wife and mistress, and the tremors of love, jealousy, doubt and reassurance that pass through them. Juanito, on the other hand, is a poor creature. Handsome, agreeable, selfish, not exactly unkind but always putting his own pleasure first, the spoiled child of rich parents who takes the love of his wife and mistress for granted, he sums up for Galdós the whole class of *jeunesse dorée*.

One of the most delightful chapters in the novel is that which gives an account of the young couple's honeymoon. First Jacinta's feelings as she sits in the cab beside her new husband are described with a delicacy of intuition that Henry James would have envied. Then, a little later, we see her tantalized by the suspicion that she has not been the first woman in her husband's life and, half jealous and half merely curious, setting herself to wheedle out of him the story of his encounter a short time before with Fortunata. Serenely happy though these weeks are, all the seeds of the young couple's future discords come out and show themselves. And, as we read, we cannot help being amazed by the knowledge which this confirmed bachelor had of the intimate life of married people. Their conversations when undressing, their baby language, their half-affectionate discords and jealousies and reconciliations are revealed by him with the most complete naturalness. These are matters which other novelists, dazed perhaps by their own marriages, have rarely been able to present in their proper focus. He is fond too of showing us children. Most of his novels contain some, and these children have their own thoughts and characters and take their place in family life just like anyone else. Altogether I would say that there is no writer who gives us such vivid and detailed pictures —sometimes comic but in this novel straightforward—of the interior of middle class ménages. He is a master of the ordinary, the average, the commonplace, of life as it is lived by the majority of people, but—this is the peculiar triumph—under his touch it ceases to be commonplace and becomes alive and tremulous with human feelings and desires. To Galdós no human being, no moment of existence is unimportant.

However, the world contains exceptional people too, and Galdós, sometimes successfully, at other times less so, sets out to give them to us. *Fortunata y Jacinta* contains one character, Doña Guillermina Pacheco, who is very unusual indeed. She is a saint—a woman of the upper classes who devotes her life to works of charity. Galdós drew her from an actual person, well known in Madrid at the time, a sort of Catholic Florence Nightingale, and the portrait he gives of her, which has a superficial resemblance to Santa Teresa, is alive and convincing. I must single out too among the many vivid characters in this book that brilliant comic figure, Doña Lupe, '*la de los pavos*'. She is Maxi's aunt, with whom he boards, and into her buxom, determined, matronly person are packed all the humours of Spanish lower middle-class women.

But there was something in Galdós that drew him away from the sphere that he knew best towards extreme types and situations. Already in *La desheredada* he had begun to show the fascination that slum life had for him. This melodramatic craving for scenes of poverty and degradation, inspired no doubt by Dickens, began to increase from now onwards till, at the end of his career of contemporary novelist, under the further impulse of a growing social conscience, he was to devote whole books to it.

At the same time he began to show a great interest in abnormal psychic states and in madness. The young heroine in *Doña Perfecta* was a hysteric: the father of Isidora in *La desheredada* was mad and its first chapter opens in a lunatic asylum: she herself had abnormal symptoms and her brother became an idiot. Many of the characters in his later novels are neurotics and we are often told their dreams. Dreams, indeed, occupy a large part in the technique of Galdós' character drawing. Now, in *Fortunata y Jacinta*, we get a full-length history of a schizophrenic. Maxi Rubén is a man who, under a crushing sense of his own insignificance, has shut himself off from the world and taken refuge in day-dreams. He falls idealistically in love with Fortunata and persuades her to enter a convent for the redemption of Magdalenes. To get out of it she marries him. But marriage meant nothing to her and when Maxi realizes this he shuts himself up in his room to concentrate on the interior life. Here—he is to all intents and purposes mad—he invents a religious philosophy in which death is proclaimed as the only liberty and suicide the only duty. A new Messiah will come to announce this. But—here we have a remarkable anticipation of Freud—as soon as he realizes that this philosophy and the hallucinations that have accompanied it are due simply to his subconscious jealousy of his wife's lover—'jealousy fermented and putrefying', as he puts it—he becomes well again. Other border-line cases in the same book are José Ido, who has appeared in previous novels, and that strange Dostoevskian being, Mauricia la Dura. In his later novels we shall see much more of these types.

Miau, which came out in 1888, is on the classic subject of the *cesante*. *Cesantes* are Government officials who have lost their jobs because a new party has come into office. Owing to the clan-like way in which social and political life in Spain is organized, every change of Government is followed by a sort of musical chairs among the personnel of the bureaucracy. *Miau* is consequently a story of middle-class distress and ruin, brought about by no fault of the persons concerned. In this way it marks a change in the theme of Galdós' novels from the personal fault or vice to the social one. As a novel, it is one of the most condensed and painful that he wrote. From the way in which everything seems to combine to crush the unfortunate man who has lost his job, it reminds one of Balzac's *Le Cousin Pons*. The characters are all well drawn, one of the more original being an epileptic child who in his fits sees and talks with God. These conversations, reported in Galdós' dry manner, are extremely amusing, for the God whom Luisito talks with is the God of a small boy's imagination, something between a schoolmaster and a grandfather, and they are also interesting because they take us into the boy's mind and reveal to us what later physchologists have termed the super-ego. Where can Galdós have obtained his amazing knowledge of the workings of the abnormal mentality? We are also given a very entertaining picture of the interior of a Spanish Government office (compare it with the descriptions of the Royal Palace in *La de Bringas*) and of the system of nepotism by which promotions and jobs were obtained. But the book is a little too long. Galdós, like his contemporary Dostoevsky, could not always control his characters' loquacity.

La Incógnita and its continuation, *Realidad*, are psychological explorations into a crime story. They reflect Galdós' interest in a sensational murder case that had just taken place, and their theme is that the psychological motives in crimes are always different from what they appear to be. Their chief defect lies in their form; the first is told in letters and the second in dialogue. Galdós' increasing interest in the drama was leading him to write novels in dialogue form, which he regarded as 'purer' than narrative. But it did not suit him.

Angel Guerra, the second longest of Galdós' works, came out in 1890-1. It is a book on the theme of religious conversion, treated from a psychological angle and with sympathy. The plot is briefly as follows. Angel Guerra is a rich young widower who quarrels with his mother, plunges into a life of dissipation and takes part in a Republican rising. On the death of his mother he falls violently in love with Leré, who is governess to his child, and asks her to marry him. But Leré refuses, because she wishes to give herself to religion. She enters a convent at Toledo and Angel follows her there. The scene now shifts from Madrid to the religious capital of Spain. As a result of his constant conversations with Leré, Angel is converted from the agnostic philosophy he had previously professed to Catholicism. With the same impetuosity and wholeheartedness with which he had previously taken to revolutionary activities, he throws himself into his new faith and decides to devote his entire wealth to founding a Brotherhood of Mercy, of which Leré shall be the head of the female branch and he of the men's. But before this plan can be put into effect he is murdered by relatives of his former mistress.

As an account of a religious conversion this book is admirable. The gradual sublimation of Angel's love for Leré and the sudden, violent plunge into the new faith are convincingly drawn. Galdós would have nothing to learn from William James's *Varieties of Religious Experience*, which came out ten years later. Angel's abnormal character is presented in great detail and we are given not only his dreams, but also certain vivid experiences of his youth which had made a deep impression on him. Leré too, another pathological case, is excellent: she was not beautiful and her eyes were affected by a continual oscillation 'which gave her the look of one of those mechanical dolls whose eyes move from right to left on a swivel'; yet we believe in her fascination. But the book, powerful and arresting though it is, fails, I think, to please. Unlike most of Galdós' novels, it contains little irony or humour. And among the subsidiary characters there are far too many criminal and neurotic types, some of them very repulsive. The physiognomies of these abnormals are presented to us with a sharpness and detail that is almost clinical. How different from the manner of Dostoevsky, who, though he fills his books with border-line cases, uses them to real imaginative effect. The neurotic storms that whirl and tear through his pages raise the action to a higher level of significance. Galdós, on the other hand, is confined to the limits of the realistic novel, and the comparison that occurs to our mind on reading *Angel Guerra* is rather to some of the veristic painting and wood sculpture done by Spanish artists in the seventeenth century. We feel a stress laid on morbid states of mind and on suffering that, artistically speaking, defeats its own purpose because it fails to liberate us.

Angel Guerra is the last of Galdós' contemporary novels that we can read with much pleasure. He was fifty and had written forty books in twenty-three years. Some spiritual crisis, similar to that which overtook Tolstoy as he was finishing *Anna Karenina*, had come over him. He continued writing, however, and in 1895 produced *Nazarín*. In this book he portrays a Christ-like figure who lives as a priest among the lowest and most abject types in Madrid, practising literally the teachings of the Sermon on the Mount. *Halma* continues the same theme, but the priest is a mere copy-book saint and neither book, in spite of some good scenes of low life, is likely to find many readers today. Then in 1897 he published his last novel of contemporary life, *Misericordia*. It is a book about the poorest class in Madrid, the down-and-outs and beggars, and before writing it he spent several months in investigating their mode of life. The heroine is an old beggar woman who, without being consciously religious, has carried out to the full

Jesus' teachings about love and charity. Although it shows in many passages the wonderful power of the novelist's imagination in entering into situations with which he was unfamiliar, I feel that it has been over-praised.

The spiritual crisis that produced the last three novels requires a few words. We can feel it coming on gradually from the time of *Fortunata y Jacinta*. Galdós had become convinced that there was something radically wrong with European bourgeois society and that the cure must take place on a deeper level than politics. A religious renovation was needed, but a renovation that did not run contrary to the findings of reason and that would take a wider and deeper channel than the narrow and hide-bound Spanish Church would allow. He had read Hegel and then, with greater sympathy, Schopenhauer. The Sermon on the Mount seemed to him to express the latter's philosophy of the need for escaping from the blind biological urge, the Will to Power. Men were saved by love, but love could only operate freely when the Will was destroyed. Poverty, therefore, was not merely the deadly cancer that sapped the nature and corrupted the heart of the community, it was also the sole condition under which the good life could be practised. The road to freedom lay, as the Church had once taught, through renunciation.

A complete acceptance of this view required, as Tolstoy saw, a radical change in the habits and mode of living of the person who professed it. Galdós did not attempt any such change, but he found that his power of writing was affected. He fell into a great discouragement about his work and for a time believed that he had wasted his life. It was his will power that saved him. Under his outwardly calm and controlled character there were, we cannot doubt, all sorts of neurotic and psychopathic tendencies, but he had kept his sanity, as writers do, by projecting them into his characters. Now in 1898 he overcame his sense of being at the end of his tether by forcing himself to take up again in a perfectly objective spirit the *Episodios Nacionales*, which he had abandoned twenty years earlier. His crisis passed. Before long we find him, pessimistic but determined, returning to his earlier view that the solution lay through politics. In his plays

26-2

he entered the field once more as an anti-clerical and a socialist.

If the reader who does not know Spanish wishes to get a rough idea of what a novel by Galdós is like, let him take one of the better works of Balzac, add the warmth and colour and melodramatic sense of Dickens and the grave ironic tone of Cervantes, and he will have something that approximates to the picture. Galdós had in fact been deeply influenced by these three writers. Further, as I think I have already made clear, he is one of the great psychological novelists, endlessly curious about the varieties of human conduct and character. He keeps, however, within the range of what his very objective eye had seen: most of his characters are mediocrities, some are almost pitiful in their lack of personality and none are above life-size. We look in vain in his portrait gallery for outstanding figures, such as Prince Myshkin or Pierre Bezukhov or M. de Charlus. One reason for this is that he never treats his characters in isolation, but always as members of a class or group or family. He is a social historian who aimed at giving the pattern of a society (and what is more, of a society which he regarded as corrupt and frivolous) rather than an individualist seeking to show to what magnificence of branch and leaf and root the human tree could grow.

He is especially good in his pictures of family circles. More than any other writer, he succeeds in conveying that peculiar, dense atmosphere that middle-class families, each in their own way, give off. He is able to do this because of his extraordinary eye for the significant detail of everyday life. In reading his books we are never far away from the sewing, the ironing, the children, the housekeeping and general economy of the ménage, and it is through these things that the feelings and idiosyncrasies of the various characters are made known to us. Then every member of one of his family groups is shown in relation to the other members; they are all the time acting on one another and being acted upon. No one is isolated. And since we have also had time to take a good look at the furniture of the house and to cast our eye over the dossiers of the relatives and friends, we end by having a sense of the corporate existence of the family such as no other novelist gives us. The same thing is true of his Government offices, his café *tertulias* and so forth.

We have said that Galdós' outlook on the world was above everything that of a moralist. No weakness escapes his eye: he is the incorruptible reporter who cannot be flattered into putting a good face on bad things. But, unlike the French novelists, he is very tolerant. If, as Blake said, the artist is the eternal forgiver of sins, then Galdós is one in a large way. He forgives because he understands all the particulars of the case and because, when one understands that, one must either forgive everyone or no one. The only people excluded from his compassion are those who have no heart, and who lack therefore the organs to which such a sentiment can be applied. And then if, as he believes, it is society that shapes men, how can one expect them in bad societies to behave well? Under Galdós' skin there was both a Christian who gave absolution and a Marxist who attributed the sins of the children to the fathers.

In a formal sense too Galdós is an artist. His plots are usually admirable. His skill in devising a natural enchainment of events and in producing and maintaining tension are equal to those of any other novelist. But his style? This has been criticized. Here, however, we have to make a distinction. His dialogue is usually alive and racy, his descriptions are vivid, and full—as Dickens' are—of striking and effective images, and his narrative manner is excellent whenever it is in his characteristic tone of Cervantine irony. He attached great importance to this quality of *socarronería*, as he called it, regarding it as the Spanish equivalent of English humour and the sauce with which the solid fare of the realistic novel required to be seasoned. But this sly or ironic tone is the only personal element to be found in his work. When it is absent, his writing is apt to become diffuse and colourless and, worse than that, long-winded.[1]

But the critics of Galdós' style are really, I think, upset by something else. The basis of a personal style is temperament, and

---

[1] In his introduction to Leopoldo Alas' novel *La Regenta*, Galdós gives us his view of the history of the novel. First appearing, he says, in Spain, it passed to England, where its dry Spanish realism and *socarronería* were converted into English humour in the hands of Fielding, Thackeray and Dickens. Then it passed to France. What it lost there in *gracia* and *donosura* it gained in analytic force and extension, being applied to psychological states that do not easily fit into the picaresque form. Thence it returned to Spain as *naturalismo*—by which Galdós means the manner of Balzac and of the early family novels of Zola. 'Let us accept', he continues, 'this reform that the French have made in our own invention, restoring to it the humour

this Galdós did not have. His greatness as a novelist consists in his having given himself completely and impersonally to his characters. To this end he had been ready, in Auden's phrase, to 'become the whole of boredom', but he had only been able to do so because he had no ivory tower of his own. His personal attitude to the world is always connected with his feelings for human beings. For this reason his books lack that extra dimension, so richly provided by Tolstoy and Turgeniev and Flaubert, which comes from the writer's having a secret fund of poetry and contemplation which he can draw on and dissolve through his work. They exhale the suffocating atmosphere of human contacts, and it is typical that one of his most noble characters, Villaamil, notices for the first time the beauty of the Madrid parks when he is on the point of killing himself. One can understand therefore why the aesthetic 'nineties felt a certain flatness and lack of savour in these immense canvases and regarded them as being out of date almost as soon as they had been written.

There is one last question about Galdós that seems to require an answer, and that is—how could a man who led such a secluded life acquire the necessary experience to write the books that he did? We must first remember that he did not start working seriously at novel writing till he was thirty. For more than ten years he had been idling, theatre-going and doing parliamentary reporting for the press. Madrid at this time was just the right size—a little larger than Dublin is today—and during these years it went through a great political and social convulsion. The institution of the *tertulia* too gave to a moderately sociable person a large and varied range of acquaintances. But Galdós possessed another key to Madrid life that is less generally known. Although he never married, he had, like so many other men of his time, mistresses. One of these gave him children and there are people alive today who remember seeing him—an erect military figure, wearing dark glasses and

that they have taken from it and applying this in the narrative and descriptive parts in accordance with the tradition of Cervantes. . . . . For we must recognize that our native art of realism, with its happy concert of the serious and the comic, answers better to human truth than does the French sort; that the crudest descriptions lose their repugnant quality when expressed through the burlesque mask employed by Quevedo, and that profound psychological studies only reach their perfection when treated, in the manner of D. Juan Valera, with grains of Spanish salt.'

dressed as usual in shabby clothes—calling on one or other of them. Readers of his novels will appreciate how much these relations with women of a different social class, each no doubt with her particular bevy of relations and friends, must have given him. They also allow one to understand the warmth and sympathy with which he wrote about family life.

Although Pérez Galdós is by far the greatest of Spanish novelists, there are others of this century who deserve some mention. First of all let me speak of two who were his contemporaries.

José María de Pereda (1833-1906) was a regionalist novelist from the district called La Montaña, near Santander. He was a man of means who after a few years in the artillery retired to his native *solar*, or country house, and never left it. Here he led the life of a country gentleman, fond of the open air, of books and of the society of his neighbours. In appearance he was one of those *hidalgos* whom El Greco had painted, and his opinions matched his looks, for he hated large towns, foreign customs and everything modern. In politics he was a Carlist.

Pereda's first novel, *Escenas Montañesas* came out in 1864, before either Galdós or Valera had written anything, and attracted a good deal of notice by its realistic drawing of country scenes. Every few years after that he produced a new book, the best being *Sotileza* (1884), on the fishermen and sailors of Santander, and *Peñas Arriba* (1894), on the life of a small mountain village. These novels are really sketches of characters, customs and scenery held together by a slight plot. He shows a real, though not very lively, art in depicting country society. His priests and patriarchal farmer-squires are solidly drawn and his sailors and fishwives belong to the sea. He also writes well, in one of those heavy styles that reflect sensibility and a love of letters. But his books have great drawbacks. In some of them the reader has to wade through long disquisitions on the moral superiority of country people to townspeople and on the disruptive nature of modern ideas. In others he has to face lengthy descriptions of mountain scenery. Pereda had the same sort of mystical feelings about Nature that Wordsworth had, but what is suited to poetry is apt to become tedious in prose. Perhaps one has to have visited La Montaña to get much pleasure from these novels: like most works of *costumbrismo*, they are vignettes to a guide-book.

Another writer of this generation was Pedro Antonio de Alarcón (1833-91). He was a journalist from Guadix in the province of Granada who wrote novels, books of travel and short stories, and made a second living out of politics. The type of the unrooted man of his age, without fixed beliefs or principles, he moved within a short space of time from the extreme Left to the extreme Right. His novels, romantic and insincere, have little to be said for them, but some of his short stories are excellent. The best of these is *El Sombrero de Tres Picos*, a brilliant tale set in the last years of the eighteenth century, coloured, realistic and steeped in a pleasantly archaic *españolismo*. It provided the subject for Manuel de Falla's famous ballet as well as for an opera by Hugo Wolf.

In the next generation we have Emilia Pardo Bazán (1851-1921), Countess in her own right of Pardo Bazán, the novelist of Galician life and a writer of considerable distinction. She was a woman of great wit and vitality, but of remarkable ugliness. After a youth spent in her family manor near Corunna, she married and went to Paris and Madrid. Leaving her husband a few years later, she settled in the Spanish capital, where she held a literary salon, kept up with the developments of French literature and wrote regular critical articles for the press. She had an excellent mind, firm, clear and well-informed, without any trace of the *saudade*, or melancholy, so characteristic of her fellow countrymen. On the contrary, the tone of her writings is so vigorous and outspoken that we often find it difficult to believe that they were written by a woman.

Doña Emilia wrote a number of novels, but only those on Galician life are worth reading. Of these *Los Pazos de Ulloa* is recognized as being much the best. Its plot centres on one of the ancient *pazos*—that is, *palacios* or mansions—of that country, which since the breaking up of the *mayorazgos*, or entails, and the consequent impoverishment of their owners, had fallen into decay. There is a Brontëish atmosphere of *Sturm und Drang* in the description of the melancholy house and its sinister occupants, involved in a mesh of greed, lust and violence, but this is modified by the hard and realistic presentation of events and characters. Here we feel the influence of Zola. The authoress is particularly successful in her group pictures—confabulations of priests, sportsmen and local politicians—and in her account of the rivalries of the two leading *caciques*, or bosses, and of the fraudulent election in which they fought one another. Writing of a country proverbial for its wistfulness and charm, she never allows herself to idealize anything except the scenery. The full squalor, violence and anarchy of the Galician countryside is brought home to us without bias or *parti pris*, and we realise why Galicia is called 'the Ireland of Spain'.

Deliberateness is the word to use about *la* Pardo Bazán. She has decided to write a novel about Galicia and so she has written one. We feel the conscious intention of the feat: there is no sense of compulsion in her art, no suspicion that she has hidden stores of feeling to express. She is completely outside what she is writing about. The same applies to her technique: romanticism, realism, naturalism—she has chosen the proportion of each which she thought best suited to her purpose and applied them as a doctor prescribes medicines. This is both the strength of her book and its weakness. *Los Pazos de Ulloa* is a very fine novel, but it does not, I think, quite get hold of us as the works of less competent novelists (Charlotte Brontë, for example) sometimes do. We feel a lack—extraordinary in a Galician—of temperament.

Cuentos de la Tierra is also worth looking at. It is a collection of short stories or sketches, some romantic, others Zolaësque, about the peasantry. Again we feel that the authoress uses too eclectic a palette.

Leopoldo Alas (1852-1901) was an Asturian who under the penname of Clarín was one of the leading literary critics of his age. In 1884 he brought out a very long and ambitious novel called *La Regenta*. It is a study of life in a cathedral city which he called Vetusta, but which is really Oviedo, and when one has read it there is little about the upper middle classes and cathedral clergy of the Asturian capital that one does not know. The picture we get is of a dull, stagnant provincial town where it is always raining and where there are only three occupations—gambling, gossip and thinking about sex. *La Regenta* has many of the marks of a good novel: the characters are finely analysed, the plot is adequate and the comment intelligent and spiced with irony. Yet the book is dead. The author lacks the secret of making his scenes come alive and is besides extraordinarily long-winded. He is a critic of Spanish life rather than a novelist with the power of recreating it.

A very different sort of novelist who also came from Asturias was Armando Palacio Valdés (1853-1938). He is a light, gay, spontaneous writer with no settled attitude to life, but plenty of talent. His characteristic vein is comedy of manners, set in a small circle of rich, upper middle-class people who have no serious problems to contend with. He specializes in light drawing-room conversations and courtships, related in a half-frivolous tone. For this reason, perhaps, even his early novels make such a modern impression that one has difficulty in believing that they did not come out in the 1920's. However, most of his books are too casually written and too unorientated to be classed as literature: all one can say is that they make pleasant books for a railway journey, easy to read, with some clever scenes and descriptions.

There are, however, two exceptions to this. One is *La aldea perdida*, a *novela de costumbres* on an Asturian village. Though unevenly written, it has at least its roots in something. Without *costumbrismo* to fall back on, the Spanish novel of this century loses its hold on reality. The other is *La Hermana San Sulpicio* (1889), a book which I find entirely delightful. It is a novel told in the first person by a young Galician poet. On a visit to an Andalusian watering place he comes across a party of three Sevillian nuns and falls in love with one of them. Sister San Sulpicio has only taken temporary vows, so that the fact of her being a nun is no obstacle to his marrying her: it merely adds spice to the situation and difficulties to the courtship, which is of course what the novel requires.

The young man now follows his nun to Seville and the emphasis of the book changes. In his efforts to rescue her from her convent, he has made a number of new acquaintances and been introduced into aristocratic circles. Gradually we realize that the love affair is mainly an excuse for showing us some of the different sides of Sevillian life. Palacio Valdés has a lively and amused eye for people and types and his descriptions of *tertulias*, picnics, drinking parties and *pensions* (though we get a little tired of them towards the end, for the novel is too long) are for the most part very entertaining. We take it in all the more vividly because the hero is a northerner and almost as much at sea in this society of easy-going chatterboxes as we should be ourselves.

La Hermana San Sulpicio is a novel that recalls *La Chartreuse de Parme*: lighter, gayer, with more superficial charm and of course far less penetration, it is all the same in the Stendhalian vein of romance, curiosity about manners and psychology of love. And it is the best guide the tourist can have to Seville. Yet, it must be added, the picture is just a little false. Written at the time of the craze for Flamenco dancing and singing, when the modern legend of the Andalusian capital was taking shape, it gives us what other Spaniards think Seville to be when they go there for their honeymoons and what some Sevillians try to pretend it is themselves. But there is a great deal in Seville besides its *andalucismo*.

The last novelist we have to consider here is Vicente Blasco Ibáñez (1867-1928). He came from Valencia, a region of Spain that has produced little literature since the Middle Ages. He was a man of great brute force and vitality who did many other things in his life besides writing books. At sixteen he ran away from his parents, with whose narrow religious views he was out of sympathy, and worked as amanuensis to a seedy and decrepit thriller writer in Madrid. When the old man fell asleep, he would continue the story. Then he became implicated in a Republican plot and fled to Paris. On his return, more of a radical than ever, he founded a federalist newspaper and printing press at Valencia, but, becoming again involved with the authorities, was sentenced to a year's imprisonment with ordinary criminals. His offence was that he had opposed the jingoistic feeling of the country over the war with Cuba.

Released in 1899, he became the *caudillo* of a political party, the *Blasquistas*, that engaged in street battles with its opponents; at the same time he fought duels, had notorious love affairs and was elected deputy. Then in 1909, finding Spain too narrow a field for his energy, he sailed for the Argentine and founded there a colony in the icy regions of Tierra del Fuego and a few years later another colony in the tropical forests of Paraguay. On the outbreak of the First World War, he returned to Europe and became one of the most active propagandists of the cause of the Allies. His last years were spent in the expensive villa he had bought at Mentone on the proceeds of his film rights, from which he kept up a furious campaign of pamphlets and articles against King Alfonso.

Blasco Ibáñez's period of real creativeness as a novelist dates from 1894 to 1902. During these eight years, which were also his years of greatest political activity, he published the five novels and one book of short stories, all on his native province, upon which his literary fame rests. The sociological novels on other regions of Spain which he wrote after 1902 have much less merit, and the same can be said of his famous book on bull fighting, *Sangre y Arena*. The best sellers he wrote at the end of his life are without interest.

In temperament Blasco Ibáñez may be said to resemble Maupassant. He had the same animal vitality, the same earthiness and incapacity for sublimation. He possessed an extraordinary power of entering into the feelings of simple people such as peasants and fishermen—this was increased by his political activities, which taught him how they were exploited—and the sort of almost physical passion for nature that one sometimes finds in keen sportsmen. But he had a fire and a passion which Maupassant had not, and his artistic sensibility had a coarser grain, possibly because he did little to cultivate it.

As a novelist his masters were Zola and Flaubert. From Zola—the minor influence—he took the idea of portraying the life of primitive communities: from Flaubert, his general method of telling a story and also whatever a man who works at white heat can use of such an elaborately distilled style. His heavy, coloured writing —which, though often careless and journalistic in its phrasing, rises at times to passages of great beauty—perfectly suits the subjects he used it for. His method of composition was to meditate on his subject for a long time—no doubt it is for this reason that the form of his novels is so excellent—and then to write the book in furious haste in a few weeks. Although he documented himself carefully beforehand, it is only when he is writing of his native country, of which he had an intimate knowledge since childhood, that he writes well.

His first book, *Arroz y Tartana*, came out in 1894. It is a *costumbrista* novel about the shopkeeping classes of Valencia, among whom he had been brought up. As a picture of the life of the city it is interesting, but the middle classes were not his subject and one feels something lacking. In the following year appeared *Flor de Mayo*, a novel about the fishermen of el Cabañal. Here we have the real Blasco Ibáñez, sure of his subject and his style. It is a novel of fishing, smuggling and jealousy and, as one reads it, the smell and glitter of the southern sea seem to rise out of its pages and to throw a cloak of poetry over the bare-footed fishermen who wring a precarious living out of it. He wrote it at a great speed to the deafening rattle of the printing press, between midnight when his editorial work ended and the first streaks of the day, and some of this hurry and excitement is passed on to the reader. The wonderful account of a smuggling voyage to Algiers in an unseaworthy boat is the reliving of a similar voyage he had just made himself, with the object of learning what a smuggler's life was like. Since the *Odyssey* and the *Aeneid*, I do not think that the life of the seafaring people of the Mediterranean has ever been presented so vividly.

In 1898 appeared *La Barraca*, a novel about the peasantry of the Vega, or cultivated plain of Valencia. Its subject is a vendetta between the landlords and the peasants, and the ruin which the latter brought on a family of *churros*, or Aragonese labourers, who persisted in occupying a farm which they, to pay out an oppressive landowner, had decided must remain vacant.

In every respect it is a masterpiece. Its plot has the firmness and cleanness of the plot of a Maupassant story and yet it has been able to take up and digest all the innumerable details required to convey the life of a peasant community. From the very beautiful opening, with its description of day breaking over the Vega and the work of the farms beginning, to the terrific scene of the burning homestead and the stampede of the scorched animals that closes the book, it moves with an art that is sure and faultless. And as a picture of peasant life it is unequalled, I think, in any language.

Blasco Ibáñez's next book was *Entre Naranjos*, a lyrical work reflecting a love affair he had had in a village near Valencia with a Russian prima donna. Then in *Cañas y Barro* (1902) he produced another masterpiece. It is a novel about the fishermen and rice growers of the Albufera, the large fresh-water lagoon that lies between the plain of Valencia and the sea. A week's shooting expedition gave him the immediate impression he needed and the result is a novel in which the people really seem to be a spontaneous growth of the water and soil. Of all the 'pattern of culture' novels that seek to show how the life of a primitive community has been determined by its geographic environment, this seems to me by far the best. There is a unity of tone and colour in the book that make it, with *La Barraca*, one of the most aesthetically satisfying novels of the century.

Blasco Ibáñez is a writer who has too often been judged by his worst novels: these made him famous abroad and damaged his reputation in Spain. But even his best books have, I think, something that makes them antipathetic to the Castilian mind. There is a certain gulf of incomprehension between the peoples of the Mediterranean seaboard and those of the table-land, and in his coloured style, his lack of ironic comment, his pagan feeling for nature, Blasco Ibáñez is a pure Levantino. There was also a crudeness and vulgarity in his nature that, when he lost touch with his native soil, allowed him to sink to the lowest depths of popular writing. Perhaps one can best sum him up in the language of painting as a *fauve* and point to Paul Gauguin as the artist who most nearly resembles him.

As we have seen during the preceding pages, the Spanish novel of the nineteenth century drew its strength from its attempt to depict the life not so much of individuals as of societies. One consequence of this was that even its poorer examples—and there are many *costumbrista* novels of provincial life which I have not mentioned—have a certain interest, if only as documents. In the drama, however, one does not find anything of this sort. In the main (apart from the plays of the romantic poets which I have already spoken of) it continued along the lines set by such seventeenth-century playwrights as Alarcón, with of course appropriate modifications to suit the times. Bretón de los Herreros, an admirer of

Moratín, wrote pleasant but artificial comedies in the 'thirties and 'forties. In the middle of the century Adelardo López de Ayala and Manuel Tamayo y Baus wrote plays in a freer and more realistic manner, which act and read well. Then in the 'seventies and 'eighties appeared the fantastic figure of José Echegaray, with his preposterous revival of romantic melodrama. Galdós, without success, attempted to introduce the new technique of Ibsen and it was not till the last years of the century that a drama of real importance made its appearance. But Benavente and the brothers Quintero belong properly to the next chapter.

Of other forms of literary enterprise there is little to be said. The age that produced Macaulay and Michelet saw no Spanish historians who can be read with pleasure: the new zest for historical studies that began towards 1870 led to works such as Altamira's great *History of Spain*, which makes no claim to literary merit. Of the few memoirs and biographies that came out in this century, none can be said to have much interest as literature. If Quintana's *Vidas de españoles célebres* is solidly written, its material has been superseded. One prose writer, however, deserves to be mentioned—the Catalan, Jaime Balmes (1810-48): a Catholic polemist and philosopher, he not only writes but argues well. His work is altogether superior to that of his better known contemporary, Juan Donoso Cortés, whose defence of the neo-Catholic position is empty and rhetorical. The very different oratorical mode of writing that was fostered by the great parliamentary jousts of the last two decades of the century is best represented by Emilio Castelar (1832-99), who combined a passion for Christian democracy with a wide culture, a Hegelian philosophy and a fine feeling for literature. But his works have dated.

In turning over books on Spanish literature the name that comes up most often is that of Marcelino Menéndez Pelayo (1856-1912). This great scholar and critic occupies a unique position. Following on an earlier generation of scholars who had made it their business to rescue Spanish classical literature from its long neglect by re-printing texts (the chief names here are Agustín Durán [1793-1862], the Austrian, Fernando Wolf [1796-1868], and the Catalan, Manuel Milá y Fontanals [1818-84]), he gave to Spanish literature the kind of critical, biographical and historical organization which in other countries has required the labour of half a dozen scholars.

He was a Castilian from La Montaña, that small region near Santander which has produced so many poets and writers, and he was a devout Catholic. His earlier work, such as the *Historia de los heterodoxos españoles*, is strongly polemical and suffers further from insufficient documentation. But he became more Liberal as he grew older and in any case he never allowed his religious views to influence his literary judgments. His aesthetic formation was humanistic—Horace, Vergil, Shakespeare, Cervantes—and this prevented him from appreciating Góngora's *Soledades* and even from doing full justice to Calderon. But outside the Baroque period his understanding and judgment are sure and infallible, and illuminated by a wide knowledge of European literature and thought. His best works are his *Antología de los poetas líricos castellanos*, which he did not live to carry beyond Boscán, his *Orígenes de la novela* and his seven volumes of studies of Spanish history and literature. His *Historia de las ideas estéticas en España*, though too ambitious in scope, is also of interest. He is one of the best prose writers of the century, with a heavy yet not pompous style that takes one back to Jovellanos and Quintana.

CHAPTER XVI

THE TWENTIETH CENTURY

As one approaches modern times, every art tends to become more interesting. That is why I have written on the literature of the nineteenth century at greater length than its merit, in comparison to that of earlier periods, deserves. If I were to continue in the same way, the past forty years would require at least as much space —all the more since it has been an exceptionally brilliant period. However, as the reader will probably agree, this book is already long enough. Besides, recent literature properly requires a volume to itself, because, being so close to us, it must be viewed with a different focus. Some sort of compromise seems necessary. I propose, therefore, to continue this book on a diminishing scale, discussing only the most important authors and breaking off when I come to the generation that started writing in the 1920's.

Two different and quite unrelated tendencies moved and directed the writers of the twentieth century. One was the patriotic urge to discover the soul of Spain, to analyse the symptoms of her long decline and sickness and to prescribe a cure for it, and the other was the influence of the symbolist, *fin de siècle*—call it what one will—literature of France, which, reaching Spain at this time, opened up new and exciting possibilities. Let us begin by speaking of the first of these two tendencies.

We have seen that the Spanish predicament, as I have called it, had imposed itself on some of the greatest writers of the nineteenth century—in particular on Larra, Galdós and Leopoldo Alas— with almost the force of an obsession. To a small group of people in the 'seventies, the principal cause of the weakness of their country seemed to be the lack of an élite of able, patriotic men who would fill the most important posts in science, politics and civil administration, and contribute to art and literature. To produce them a reform was needed in the system of higher education. Some such reform had in fact been initiated during the Revolutionary Government of 1868, but when, to please the clerical faction, the Restoration Government of 1876 began to interfere in the affairs of the universities and to dismiss the best professors, a few of these decided to open a free school for higher studies on their own account. Thus the famous *Institución Libre de Enseñanza* was born. Its leading spirit was Francisco Giner de los Ríos, a pedagogic genius whom one may call the Ignatius Loyola of the liberal-minded, and its aim was to turn out men with a sense of vocation in life, who would feel a real responsibility for the state of their country. Then in 1898 came the war with the United States and loss of the last vestiges of the Spanish colonial empire. The corruption and inertia of the politicians and behind them of the whole governing class stood out more nakedly than ever. A movement grew up, led by a small group of intellectuals, the so-called generation of '98, almost all of whom were connected with the *Institución*, which set itself the task of analysing the symptoms of disease in the institutions and social framework of the nation and of prescribing remedies.

A strong influence in this movement were the writings of a young Andalusian diplomat, Angel Ganivet (1862-98), who had committed suicide at Riga as the result of an unhappy love affair. Ganivet, like so many other educated Spaniards of his time, was a man of strong religious and even mystical inclinations, whose reason did not allow him to accept the dogmas of the Catholic Church. As a consequence he was profoundly unhappy and sought consolation in a stoic attitude. In Seneca he found the perennial philosopher of the Spanish race. The book of his, however, that most influenced his successors was not on philosophy but on politics. This was a collection of notes and aphorisms which came out in 1897 under the title of *Idearium español*. It represented an attempt to define the racial character of Spaniards, the place in the world that naturally belonged to them and the steps that they ought to take to occupy it. One might call it a work of national stocktaking. If by Anglo-Saxon Liberal standards it may appear to be a somewhat reactionary and authoritarian book, coloured by a pessimistic view of the capacity of men for governing themselves, it was optimistic in that it showed how Spain could be reorientated in the modern world so as to regain, not her former power—for that had passed for ever—but her dignity, her self-esteem, her soul.

Ganivet's book helped to canalize a great deal of scattered thinking and criticism. A new, intenser stage began of that long interior dialogue and self-examination that had occupied the best Spanish brains since the eighteenth century. Spain became more than ever the patient on the psycho-analyst's couch. Among the older generation of writers who led this movement were Joaquín Costa (1846-1911), with his formula of 'school and larder', Manuel B. Cossío (1858-1935), the educationalist, art critic and rediscoverer of El Greco, and Miguel de Unamuno (1864-1937). Among the younger generation were two writers on political and philosophical subjects, José Ortega y Gasset and Ramiro de Maeztu; the essayist on the Spanish countryside, 'Azorín'; the novelists Pío Baroja and Ramón Pérez de Ayala; and the poets Antonio Machado and Juan Ramón Jiménez. To these should be added other names from the field of science, especially the great biologist Ramón y Cajal. Most of these men were closely connected with the *Institución* and its offspring, the *Residencia de Estudiantes*, or Residential College for Students, which was founded by Alberto Jiménez in 1910. Here, over a long course of years, Unamuno, Cossío and Ortega taught, walking about the garden or sitting in the shade of the trees in the manner of the ancient philosophers: here Juan Ramón Jiménez wrote and recited his poems, and here too a later generation of poets, among them García Lorca and Alberti, learned their trade, coming under the influence of the school of music and folk-song which Eduardo Martínez Torner organised. Never, I think, since the early Middle Ages has any educational establishment produced such astonishing results on the life of a nation, for it was largely by means of the *Institución* and the *Residencia* that Spanish culture was raised suddenly to a level it had not known for three hundred years.

The leading intellectuals of this critical and reforming movement were José Ortega y Gasset and Miguel de Unamuno. Ortega—born in 1883 and therefore a few years younger than the generation of '98—received his intellectual formation in Germany, where for some years he read Kantian philosophy. His first work of importance was *España invertebrada* (1921), a masterpiece of social and political analysis which everyone interested in modern Spain should read. It is marred only by his strong prejudice for Germanic as against Latin civilization, which lead him to underestimate the value of Spanish culture and to accept a number of rather wild historical hypotheses. His next book, *El tema de nuestro tiempo*, is one of his best. In it he sets out his philosophical position—a kind of vitalism—and shows how he derives the values from it. His theory of the relativity of truth has become famous. Reality can be seen from many different points of view. Each point of view has its peculiar perspective, which can be described by the observer either correctly or incorrectly. But when the point of view changes, the perspective changes too and there is usually no valid way of relating one point of view to another. After this book came *La deshumanización del arte* (1925). Ortega's view being that art, morality and reason exist to serve life, he sets out to explain how it is that, in an age when the social values are increasingly democratic and egalitarian, art and literature are seeking to get rid of all human content and to imprison themselves in style. Why, for example, has poetry become 'a higher algebra of metaphors'? Although in my opinion he is wrong in his interpretation of modern art, or is describing only a very brief phase in it, his observations are often suggestive and stimulating.

La rebelión de las masas (1930) deals with the position of an élite in a country where the masses (by whom he means chiefly the educated masses of the middle classes) are continually menacing them. Though influenced by Nietzsche, this book can only be understood by reference to the situation in Spain, where a very small body of intelligent and disinterested people was struggling vainly to leaven the horde of the inert and reactionary. But it has a bearing on other countries too: although he is by nature an optimist, Ortega wrote it in the prophetic mood of Spengler, seeing in the rising importance of 'the man in the street' and of the specialist and technician the doom of Europe.

Ortega is at bottom not an original philosopher but a superior sort of journalist—a journalist who deals in ideas. He makes great efforts to live always in the present—to give the attitude and ideas that the moment requires. His views have changed and developed to suit the changing social and political situation and it is this that makes him a stimulating writer rather than a profound one. His articles appearing in the daily press and in the *Revista de Occidente* —most of his books have first come out in this form—have had an important influence on the young and on those—they are many in Spain—who draw their intellectual fodder from the newspapers. His style, which at its best is elegant and enlivened by vivid phrases and images—strange that so French a writer should be so passionate a Germanophile!—is often made diffuse and prolix by his love of parentheses and divagations. This is a pity, because he has an alert and well-stocked mind, a subtle approach to every question and a fear, which sometimes amounts almost to priggishness, of the obvious. He is also one of the very few Spanish writers to write with a full awareness of what is happening in the world; the majority, even when they learn foreign languages or travel, feel little solidarity with the countries beyond the Pyrenees.

If Ortega y Gasset is a writer who mirrors his age, Unamuno is one of those granite figures who seem to live in their own right, very much in space but out of time. He was a Basque, that is to say an unfinished, unpolished Castilian, a Castilian in his raw highland state, and his name with its suggestion of uncouthness perfectly expresses his primitive, bearlike nature. He had a very strong, rather childishly aggressive personality and a great heart. Those who have seen him talking, arguing, gesticulating, yet also in his own way humble and receptive, an egoist who accepted other people's egoism and without a trace of vanity or arrogance, will never forget the experience. His style expresses this perfectly. It is a simple style, without qualifications or refinements, going straight to the point and addressed *ad hominem*. The style of a great talker rather than of a writer, but of a talker who talks to convince, to persuade, to overwhelm: a talker for whom talking is a violent exercise because he talks and thinks with his whole body and mind. But no trace of rhetoric or irony: his sincerity and urgency exclude such artifices, and he is always urgent because for him the issues are always great.

One might be tempted to call Unamuno a naïve or simple writer because there are so many considerations that he brushes aside on his path. But his simplicity is a little deceptive. It comes from his determination to reduce everything to its elementary human terms. 'What does this proposition by this man Kant really mean?' he asks. And digging under what he regards as the professional jargon of the metaphysicians, he tries to show us what it meant in terms of Kant's personal desires and feelings. In interpreting these feelings, he is guided by certain notions which his own inner nature told him were fundamental—for example, the longing for an existence after death. If this incapacity of his for seeing people except in terms of his own personal experience sometimes makes his judgments appear rash and arbitrary, it is also the mark of his being a true philosopher—that is to say, a man whose obsession with the great problems of human life enables him to integrate them in a system.

The most obvious feature in Unamuno's make-up was his passion for having things as he wanted them. When he was in one of his fighting moods, he overrode inconvenient facts and blustered his way through difficulties. In this and in a certain attractive childishness he reminds one of Winston Churchill. But, like Churchill, he could listen to the voice of his enemy Reason when he wanted to. For example, in his search for truth he had read a great deal. Professor of Greek at Salamanca, he also read French, English, Italian, German and Latin with fluency. He had more than a smattering of the sciences and had picked his way through the philosophers and theologians. But he was never a learned man, because he lacked the historical sense and took from books only what he personally needed. He put the same questions to every writer and noted their answers.

Unamuno's work comprises plays, novels, poems, essays and books of a philosophic sort, but a man who is more interested in what people have in common than in what divides them can scarcely be a good novelist or dramatist. His poems, too, are not in my opinion very good as poetry: they are rough and amateurish and show an unusual insensitivity to the auditory values of words, although it is true that they sometimes make an impression through their sheer force and sincerity. We are left therefore with the essays and philosophic books. Perhaps the chief interest of the essays, published by the press of the *Residencia* in seven volumes, is that they show how his mind worked on the questions of the day. What we usually discover is a struggle going on between two opposite principles, which one may call Faith and Reason, or Past and Future, and though the battle sways furiously this way and that, it was an essential part of Unamuno's nature that neither side could ever win a victory. Take for example his attitude as a reformer. His whole life was devoted to the work of educating his countrymen, which, as he always said, meant Europeanizing them. Yet in 1898, in the very year from which the reforming generation took its name, he was violently attacking this policy and declaring that the unlettered peasant of Toboso was happier, nobler and saner than the highly paid workman of New York. And how much better in this world of philistine values Spain was for its ignorance and backwardness! *Es una ciencia divina la ciencia de la ignorancia; es más que ciencia, es sabiduría.*

To understand, however, what Unamuno made out of this irresolvable conflict within himself we must read his great philosophical work, *Del sentimiento trágico de la vida*. It came out in 1913 and is without doubt the greatest book of its kind to have been written in Spanish. It is one of the most representative too, for the conflict that tormented its author is also the conflict of the Spanish people, who are sceptical by nature but, because they find their scepticism hard to bear, are easily driven to the most absolute and dogmatic faith. To this people who see only in black and white, who demand of God some personal satisfaction and are usually incapable of detachment, the kind of penumbra between doubt and faith in which most Europeans pass their lives is as intolerable as their grey climate. It must be all or nothing, *Todo* or *Nada*.

Unamuno begins his book by saying that his subject is man, not abstract Man, but the concrete man of flesh and blood who is born, suffers from love and toothache and in the end dies. In the end dies. The sovereign instinct of all living things is their desire to live for ever, and yet, in spite of that, death comes to them. That is unjust and intolerable. The foreknowledge of his death, which Man alone has, makes his life too painful, too senseless to be endured, unless he can believe that he will live again after it.[1] But no vague after-existence, no myth of being gathered into the spirit of Nature can satisfy him. He must live again a real life with his bodily senses and his memory (here we recall Prudentius' passionate declaration) or his life on earth will have been a mockery. The only problem that philosophy is asked to solve, the only problem that matters, is the problem of our destiny.

But philosophy cannot solve this. Its instrument, the Reason, tells us that there are no grounds for supposing that we can live again. Nor does a belief in God necessarily help. The only purpose of God—let the theologians say what they will—is to guarantee to man immortal life. Without that we should take very little interest in Him. But a God who gives immortal life is precisely the kind of God whom our Reason tells us we have no right to believe in. What are we to do then? Either we must find a way of living among subterfuges and illusions, or we must abandon ourselves to utter despair.

There is, however, another alternative. We may turn our Reason back upon itself. Since we must suppose that our faculties have been given us for the purpose of life, would it not be extraordinary if our strongest faculty, our passion to go on living, should turn out to be the very thing that deceives us? Can a strong desire exist without the state or object it desires existing too? In other words, is truth to be found in thought—or in life? If we say in thought, then we must remember that our faith in Reason, which is the law of thought, is exposed to the same rational doubt as is any other faith. By pushing our scepticism far enough, we will arrive at a position where despair will no longer be the appropriate attitude.

However, these considerations cannot give us any certainty: they can merely offer us a hope. And it is in his method of exploiting this doubt and this hope that Unamuno's originality as a philosopher lies. We must not resign ourselves. We must go out, as Don Quixote went out, to battle for our faith. We must be prepared to

---

[1] Not altogether senseless. For, says Unamuno, a life with no death in it, with no katabolism in its incessant anabolism, would be without value. Real life is maintained by death just as real faith is fed on doubts.

spend our lives in uncertainty, in torment, in spiritual agony, but this agony will give us the energy to live and struggle towards our goal. It may be that we shall not after all live again, but, if so, we must see to it that this sentence against us will be an injustice. 'Spend your life so that you deserve to be immortal'.

It will be seen that what we have here is a sort of Existentialism. Unamuno was a great admirer of Kierkegaard and no doubt learned many things from him. But the conception of *Angst* as a source of spiritual energy was something that he did not have to learn from anyone, because it sprang from his own nature. So was the peculiar emphasis that he laid on the isolated, individual man, living his life here and now. His philosophy is, in the most complete way possible, a projection of himself and of the conflict that went on, day in day out, between the two warring people who inhabited him.

Let us, however, note how much it differs from the kind of philosophy that had hitherto been put forward in Castile. One example of this can be seen in that comparison of human life to a river losing itself in the immensity of the sea, which we find in the *coplas* of Jorge Manrique, in Góngora and in Calderon, and later several times in Manuel Machado. It was precisely the prospect of that loss of separate identity that aroused in the Basque sage such anguish and indignation. Still less do we find in his books any trace of the self-forgetfulness of the sixteenth-century mystics: of their love of God for His own sake or of their belief that salvation is to be got by emptying oneself of temporal preoccupations and turning the whole of one's libido upon Him. The sentiment expressed by the famous sonnet:

> No me mueve, mi Dios, para quererte
> el cielo que me tienes prometido . . .

It is not the heaven you have promised me that moves me to love you. . .

belongs to a vein of feeling which is the precise opposite to that conveyed by him. Unamuno could only love God *because* He had promised him a future life. His longing for survival after death was so tremendous that a disinterested attitude on almost any

425

subject seemed to him unintelligible. Thus we do not find in his books any belief that there can be a merit in doing things because they are worth doing, any comprehension of the devotion of the artist or scientist, any faith in absolute values. The whole Oriental element in European culture is absent. For him everything is valued by its duration, and what is forgotten is as though it had never been. We may not unfairly, I think, call this philosophy the crisis philosophy of the ego—as a Spaniard would say, of the *Yo*.

Yet we cannot dismiss it in this way. Unamuno is the great Spanish egoist, hungry for life and determined to win immortality precisely because he attaches such importance to his own personality. His egoism is very great because his personality is very strong (great men have more to lose by death than other people), yet it is after all noble because he respects the egoism of other people and indeed puts himself forward as their champion. Men are for him everything, and so obsessed is he by their overriding importance that even the God he prays to and tries to believe in has to have man-like qualities. Thus whilst he is passionately attached to Christ, who died to give us a second life, and whom he regards more as a struggling hero like Heracles, who had to win his godhead by his sufferings, than as a Prometheus who was divine from the outset, he shows little regard for or faith in God the Father. This is the philosophy of a humanist who has lost his faith in the classic dogma of humanism—that men have the power to create values that transcend them.

Yet, whether one agrees with Unamuno's attitude or not, *Del sentimiento trágico de la vida* is a profoundly moving and stimulating book. The range of reading and quotation brought to bear on the subject is great: the arguments are well set out and the style is clear and forcible. And above all there is a suppressed passion running through the whole work that makes it one of the most searching and heart-felt expositions of the human predicament ever written. And then how Spanish it is, in spite of the fact that it contains no trace of the Spaniard's characteristic virtue of stoic resignation! The obsession with death, the rebellious attitude, the crusading enterprise, the gesture of defiance in defeat, the pride felt in putting the universe in the wrong! And, I would add, the lack of interest in anything outside the human circle. It is a book written in the idiom of heroic Spain, that spoken by Don Quixote and the Conquistadors, but not that in which, in the moment of submission or ecstasy, they addressed their God.

We spoke at the beginning of this chapter of two tendencies running through the literature of this period—one being that of the generation of '98 and the other that of the *fin de siècle* literature of France. We must now say something of this second. It was brought in by the great Nicaraguan poet who went under the assumed name of Rubén Darío.

Rubén, as he was generally called, was born in 1867 and visited Spain for the first time in 1892. He arrived with an official position, that of representative of Nicaragua at the Columbus centenary, and with the prestige of being the rising poet of the New Continent. His first book of verse, *Azul*, published when he was only twenty-one, had taken Latin America by storm and had been praised in Spain by Valera. A tour through Guatemala, Peru and Chile had turned his poetic success into a personal triumph. But he remained in Spain only a few months and met only the older generation of writers. Then he moved on to Paris.

Paris is the natural goal of all Latin Americans who come to Europe and Rubén Darío recognized it at once as his spiritual home. He met the French writers in the cafés of the Rive Gauche and read Verlaine and the new Symbolist poetry: till now he had known only Hugo and the Parnassians. The result was *Prosas Profanas* (1896), the first book of verse to be written in his mature style and which is really a transposition into Spanish of symbolist metres and cadences. It produced a tremendous effect, especially among the young, and when Darío returned to Spain in 1898 he found himself the hero of the new generation of writers—Valle-Inclán, the Machados, Juan Ramón Jiménez and Unamuno. He had opened the door into the garden of modern poetry.

Rubén Darío's verse is the embodiment in Spanish of all that is most magical and rhythmically exciting in French symbolist poetry, with something exotic added. Superficially it often recalls Verlaine, that marvellously unencumbered man who could turn the fleeting moods and sensations of the moment into music, but really it is very different. Darío was not one of those poets who are able to interpret precise experiences, but a *maestro* manipulating an instrument with *brío* and authority. If one wishes to find someone to compare him to, one might choose a composer such as Rimsky-Korsakov. But, though he is unlike Verlaine, his power to thrill his generation came from the skill with which he adopted that poet's metrical innovations and cadences so as to make his dodeca-syllables and alexandrines more supple and insinuating, and his shorter measures lighter and more nuanced. Such an ability to transpose the intimate structure of a poetry into that of another language is very rare and demands high poetic gifts, and Darío's verse moves with an ease and melodiousness that any poet might envy. In the art of writing flowing, musical verse—verse, too, of the greatest rhythmic vitality—he is a master. But the content offers less interest. He took his themes and his rather banal imagery from such second-rate poets as Rostand and Rémy de Gourmont, and his idiom is the conventional 'decadent' one of the time. So though a few of his poems are quite unforgettable—and I would especially single out *Divagación, Mía, A Margarita Debayle, Yo soy aquel que ayer no más decía* and *Canción de otoño en primavera*—the bulk will probably suffer like Zorrilla's from the passage of time.

The shock produced by *Prosas Profanas* has often been compared to that which followed the publication in 1543 of Garcilaso's poems. These new, intoxicating rhythms and cadences burst the narrow banks in which Spanish poetry had long been confined. A larger world was thrown open, which made the poetry of the nineteenth century appear *cursi* and provincial. The tone of these *prosas* too was utterly new. Rubén Darío's verse is hedonistic, pagan and steeped in a violently sensual and erotic atmosphere. Take even one of his most delicate and airy poems:

> Cojamos la flor del instante;
> ¡la melodía
> de la mágica alondra cante
> la miel del día!

Let us pluck the flower of the moment. Let the song of the magic lark sing the day's honey!

This had never been a possible philosophy in Spain, but it was immensely stimulating to the young men who came up to Madrid from the dull, decaying little towns, where life went on as it had gone on for centuries.

Rubén Darío's personality helped to strengthen this impression. His tall figure, usually clad in a frock coat, and strange, white, mask-like face with its fixed concentration of the eyebrows— the face of a man who has more Indian than Spanish blood in his veins —attracted attention. His sayings were repeated like those of Pater or Oscar Wilde in England: 'Poets of our generation should wear gloves and patent-leather shoes, because modern art is aristocratic.' 'The chief enemies of art are the people.' 'The mummification of Spanish rhythms has become an article of faith.' And those who knew him well were astonished at the superstitious ritual of his life, for this man, who usually professed agnosticism, believed in every sort of witch and evil spirit and lived in as great a fear of omens as a gipsy. He was a dipsomaniac, who suffered from terrible attacks of delirium tremens: he had had a fantastic upbringing in a Nicaraguan hamlet: he travelled about openly with his mistresses : he was of a naïveté and gentleness that were more Indian than European. Such a person was too exotic to be digested by the harsh, narrow world of the Iberian Peninsula and it was no doubt largely for this reason that although, like Garcilaso, he started a new movement in poetry, he did not found a school. The principal poets who came after him reacted against him.

The most striking example of this reaction is Antonio Machado. Born in 1875 in Seville, the son of the founder of the Spanish Folklore Society and the great-nephew of Agustín Durán, the collector of *romances*, he was taken to Madrid when he was eight and put to school at the *Institución Libre de Enseñanza*. Here and in its ambience he lived till he was thirty-two, reading philosophy and coming under the influence of Unamuno. Then he took the post of teacher of French at the College of Soria, an ancient, decaying town lying at the height of 3500 feet above the sea among arid steppes and *páramos*, close to the head-waters of the Douro. This was the culminating period of his life. Here he fell in love, married and lost his wife, and when, five years later, in 1912, he was moved to the town of Baeza in Upper Andalusia, he felt all the nostalgia of an exile. Just as his brother Manuel, who was also a poet of talent, became the most typical of Sevillians, so Antonio came to incorporate in his verse, as no poet had ever done before, the ascetic spirit of Castile.

Antonio Machado's first book of verse, written between 1899 and 1907, is called *Soledades*. The title fits the subject. It consists of short poems in many of which a state of mind is associated with a landscape. The general influence of Verlaine's earlier lyrics can be seen, though the tone is completely different. For Machado has not a trace of Verlaine's feminine sensibility, or of the *fin de siècle* malady. His is a grey, melancholy, denuded poetry, written in *la rima pobre*—that is, assonanced instead of rhymed—bare and sober in its diction, with few images and uncompromising in its realistic vision. It is also a poetry that thinks, and by its thought endeavours to reach down to some inner, deeply hidden core. 'I considered', he wrote, 'that the poetic element did not lie in the word with its values of sound and colour, nor yet in the line, nor even in a complex of sensations, but in a deep palpitation of the spirit: what the soul, if it says anything at all, says with its own voice when it is brought into lively contact with the world.' This is the poetic theory of Bécquer, whose work one might say that Antonio Machado continued, though in a more manly tone and without his note of self-pity. But in Machado this language of the soul is expressed through the mediation of natural objects. All through this book we find certain things in nature appearing and reappearing—rocks, poplars, ilex trees, streams, water. Above all, water. Whether in the form of rivers, brooks, springs, tarns or fountains, his verse plays with it and draws from it a symbolical nourishment. Indeed one might find an image for these poems in a pool of water lying under an overcast sky: dark and gloomy from a distance, yet on closer view full of a pellucid inner light.

Machado's next and best volume of verse is *Campos de Castilla*, which he wrote between 1907 and 1917. It reflects the passionate love for Castile which during his five years at Soria had taken possession of his whole being. The first poems in alexandrines— modelled on the *prosas* of the old thirteenth-century poet, Gonzalo de Berceo, but varied by an attention to Verlainean metrics—and also the *silvas* that follow them express this feeling admirably. The emptiness of the great stony plains, the circle of snow-ribbed mountains, the glitter of the river that is curved like a broken scimitar, the rocks and the grey plants that cover them, the innless roads and crumbling towns are described in a strong, resonant, sinewy verse that is as bare and magnificent as the landscapes that it portrays. But Machado was not content with descriptions: the soul of Castile is his subject, and he sees how it has been corrupted by centuries of inanition.

> Castilla miserable, ayer dominadora,
> envuelta en sus andrajos desprecia cuanto ignora.
> ¿Espera, duerme o sueña? ¿La sangre derramada
> recuerda, cuando tuvo la fiebre de la espada?

> Wretched Castile, lording it yesterday,
> wrapped in its rags scorns what it does not know.
> Is it waiting, sleeping or dreaming? Does it remember
> the blood spilt when it had the fever of the sword?

In another poem, *Desde mi rincón*, addressed in reproof to 'Azorín' for his merely antiquarian love of Castile (*Azorín el reaccionario, por asco de la greña jacobina* 'Azorín, the reactionary, through disgust at the Jacobin rabble. . .'), he breaks into a long invocation of the Castile of the *Siglo de Oro*, which is, I think, one of the most splendid passages in Spanish poetry. And he ends it by calling down fire and axe upon 'the Spain that idles and yawns'. This poem is followed by another, *El mañana efímero*, written in the same year, in which he invokes the new fierce and implacable Spain, *España de la rabia y de la idea*, which will take its place. These passionately written poems occupy, however, only a small part of the book. The longest poem, which is no doubt Machado's masterpiece, is the ballad, *La tierra de Alvargonzález*, on the subject of two sons who murder their father in order to possess his land: in it he revives in modern language and in his own great style the epic grandeur of the medieval *romances*. There is also the autobiographical poem *Retrato*, the elegy on Francisco Giner de los Ríos, the lyric entitled *Una noche de verano* on the death of his wife and the beautiful verses to Juan Ramón Jiménez, which I give here:[1]

> Era una noche del mes
> de mayo, azul y serena.
> Sobre el agudo ciprés
> brillaba la luna llena,
>
>   iluminando la fuente
> en donde el agua surtía
> sollozando intermitente.
> Sólo la fuente se oía.
>
>   Después, se escuchó el acento
> de un oculto ruiseñor.
> Quebró una racha de viento
> la curva del surtidor.
>
>   Y una dulce melodía
> vagó por todo el jardín:
> entre los mirtos tañía
> un músico su violín.
>
>   Era un acorde lamento
> de juventud y de amor
> para la luna y el viento,
> el agua y el ruiseñor.
>
>   'El jardín tiene una fuente
> y la fuente una quimera. . . .'
> Cantaba una voz doliente,
> alma de la primavera.
>
>   Calló la voz y el violín
> apagó su melodía.
> Quedó la melancolía
> vagando por el jardín.
> Sólo la fuente se oía.

[1] For some good earlier lyrics, see 'Amada, el aura dice' and 'Fué una clara tarde' in *Soledades*, 'Elegía de un Madrigal' in *Humorismos* and the three lyrics 77, 78 and 79 in *Galerías*. Also his last poem, *Canción*, written at Valencia in 1938.

There was a night, in the month
of May, blue and serene.
Above the sharp point of the cypress
shone the full moon,

Lighting up the fountain
where the water was springing,
intermittently sobbing.
Nothing was heard but the fountain.

Afterwards came the singing
of a hidden nightingale,
and a gust of wind breaking
the curve of the water's plume.

And then a sweet melody
wandered through all the garden;
in the myrtles a musician
was playing his violin.

It was a musical lament
of youth and of love,
played to the moon and the wind,
the water and nightingale.

'There's a fountain in the garden,
a chimera dwells in the fountain. . . .'
A grieving voice was singing—
the soul of the springtime.

At last the voice grew silent
and the violin ceased its playing.
Melancholy alone
still strayed through the garden—
Nothing was heard but the fountain.

When Machado left Baeza in 1919 for Segovia, his best work
had been done. Although his great style never failed him, the
emotion behind his verse became thinner and rarer. We find
gnomic poems, popular *coplas*, epigrams—some of them excellent
of their kind, for Machado was a poet with a point of view on life,

who, like Blake and Yeats, knew how to handle a terse form. But of poetry *de longue haleine* there is little. Old age had come over him prematurely. He seems too to have been discouraged by the fact that a new sort of poetry was beginning to appear in Spain and with it the return to favour of the Baroque poets and in particular of Góngora's *Soledades*. He disapproved of this development and in a prose essay called *El arte poética de Juan de Mairena*, which is included in the 1936 edition of his poetical works, he sets out at length his objections to the Baroque conception of poetry, which in his opinion was shallow and decorative. These pages are worth reading and considering. He died at Collioure in 1939, his spirit broken by the catastrophe of the Civil War.

Rubén Darío has described Machado's appearance in an admirable poem:

> Misterioso y silencioso
> iba una y otra vez.
> Su mirada era tan profunda
> que apenas se podía ver.

> Silently, mysteriously
> he went and came.
> His glance was so profound
> it could scarce be seen.

Shabbily dressed, sunk in his own thoughts, almost always alone, the picture of a provincial schoolmaster run to seed till one looked at him attentively, both timid and proud at the same time—that is how he appeared to Rafael Alberti in the 1920's. His friends, other elderly provincials: his occupations, walking and reading: his severity, that of the inward-looking man who has had to suffer all the boredom of the classroom. But he was the poet of Castile. No one, not even Luis de León, has expressed so intimately or from such a depth the essential spirit of that country. Or shall we say, no one except Santa Teresa? And he is also the poet of the generation of '98.

> Tras el vivir y el soñar,
> está lo que más importa:
> despertar.

Behind living and dreaming
lies what matters most—waking.

This was his message—'Awake!' The eye must be taught to see, not merely to look: the brain to think and the soul to contemplate the eternal, if uncertain, things. Out of the doubt and despondency in which he habitually lived, there came a hope and a call to work and action. As he wrote in his elegy to Francisco Giner:

> Vivid, la vida sigue,
> los muertos mueren y las sombras pasan;
> lleva quien deja y vive el que ha vivido.
> ¡Yunques, sonad; enmudeced, campanas!
>
> Live, for life goes on,
> the dead die and the ghosts pass.
> He holds who leaves and he who has lived lives on.
> Anvils, ring out! church bells, be dumb.

In the genealogical tree of poetry, Antonio Machado occupies a special and solitary place which we can compare to that of W. B. Yeats—the Yeats of the later volumes—in our poetry. He wrote a strong, bare, sonorous verse which has some of the qualities of the best sixteenth-century prose and which is always alive because it is saturated in every part by its rhythm. It has less artifice than that of Yeats and not a trace of mannerism, and when it leaves the ground it takes off with a great spread of wings like, for example, Yeats' two poems on Byzantium. If Machado is not among the very greatest of Spanish poets—Juan Ruiz, Garcilaso, Góngora, García Lorca—he follows close behind them.

The only other poet of this generation of whom I propose to say much is Juan Ramón Jiménez. He was born at Moguer on the tidal estuary of the Rio Tinto in 1881. But although every line he writes proclaims him an Andalusian, he has lived chiefly in or near Madrid, spending some ten years of his life in sanatoriums, then occupying a room at the *Residencia* and, after his marriage in 1916, a house and garden in a quiet surburb. His temperament is that of an aesthete: he loves gardens, music, painting, silence, and protects himself with care against intrusions on his long working hours and his peace of mind. Years of delicate health have given him a languid manner, but his conversation is witty and often agreeably satirical and malicious. Today, like almost every other Spanish writer of repute, he is living in America.

Jiménez's first style in poetry can be seen in the three books of verse that he brought out between 1903 and 1905—*Arias Tristes, Jardines Lejanos* and *Pastorales*. They consist of short poems in octosyllabic metre in which a state of mind is expressed through a landscape. Frequently this landscape is an Andalusian garden and more often than not the moon is shining. There is an air of autumnal vagueness and melancholy: we note the influence of Verlaine's early lyrics and occasionally of Jammes and Laforgue, but these influences have been well asssimilated through the choice of a classical Spanish metre. Jiménez did not borrow rhythms and cadences from the French Symbolist poets as Rubén Darío had done: rather he was writing the same sort of poetry, but with a smaller and more delicate gamut.

> Yo no volveré. Y la noche
> tibia, serena y callada,
> dormirá el mundo, a los rayos
> de su luna solitaria.
>
> Mi cuerpo no estará allí,
> y por la abierta ventana,
> entrará una brisa fresca,
> preguntando por mi alma.
>
> No sé si habrá quien me aguarde
> de mi doble ausencia larga,
> o quien bese mi recuerdo,
> entre caricias y lágrimas. . . .
>
> I shall not return. The night,
> warm, serene and silent,
> will put the world to sleep in the rays
> of the solitary moon.
>
> My body will not be there,
> and through the open window
> a fresh breeze will enter,
> enquiring for my soul.

I do not know if there will be someone to await me
through my long and double absence,
or if anyone will kiss my remembrance
between caresses and tears. . . .

In his next volume but one, *Baladas de Primavera*, his manner is
firmer and there is an invigorating influence that comes from the
popular song-books of the sixteenth century and from children's
ditties.

> Dios está azul. La flauta y el tambor
> anuncian ya la cruz de primavera.
> ¡Vivan las rosas, las rosas del amor,
> entre el verdor con sol de la pradera!
> > *Vámonos al campo por romero,*
> > *vámonos, vámonos*
> > *por romero y por amor.*

> Le pregunté: '¿Me dejas que te quiera?'
> Me respondió, radiante de pasión:
> 'Cuando florezca la cruz de primavera,
> yo te querré con todo el corazón.'
> > *Vámonos al campo por romero,*
> > *vámonos, vámonos*
> > *por romero y por amor. . . .*

> God is now blue. The flute and the drum
> announce the festival of spring.
> Long live the roses, the roses of love!
> Let the green of the meadows enter with sun!
> > *Come to the fields for rosemary,*
> > *come, come,*
> > *for rosemary and for love.*

> I asked her: 'Will you let me love you?'
> Radiant with passion she answered me:
> 'When the cross of the springtime blossoms,
> I shall love you with all my heart.'
> > *Come to the fields for rosemary,*
> > *come come,*
> > *for rosemary and for love. . . .*

Then in his next two books, *Elegías* and *La Soledad sonora* (1908),
Jiménez leaves the short measures for alexandrines. Here one
sometimes feels the touch of Mallarmé.

> Un pájaro, en la lírica calma del mediodía,
> canta bajo los mármoles del palacio sonoro;
> sueña el sol vivos fuegos en la cristalería,
> en la fuente abre el agua su cantinela de oro.
>
> Es una fiesta clara con eco cristalino:
> en el mármol, el pájaro; las rosas, en la fuente;
> ¡garganta fresca y dura; azul, dulce, argentino
> temblar, sobre la flor satinada y reciente!. . . .

> A bird in the lyric calm of afternoon
> sings beneath the marble of the echoing palace:
> the sun dreams vivid fires in the crystal panes,
> the water of the fountain throws up its golden song.
>
> It is a clear celebration with a crystal echo:
> the bird in the marble: in the fountain the roses:
> a throat fresh and hard: a blue, sweet and silvery
> trembling upon the flower, satiny and new. . . .

After this the poetry gets richer, more ornate and coloured: the
metaphors develop, but the influences are classical Spanish rather
than French and there is little trace of Baroque. Among the best of
these poems are the sonnets, which are in the condensed manner of
the sixteenth century. But one begins, among all this poetical
paraphernalia of birds and roses, to feel a certain weariness, in spite
of the continual attention given by the poet to the discovery of
new epithets and images and of the artistic perfection of the verse.

Then in 1916 his style changes. He speaks of this in a poem
numbered 411 in his *Anthology*. His first verses, he says, had all the
charm of innocence. Then he began to dress them, to load them
with jewels as a queen and to find that he secretly detested them.
A moment came when he could bear them no longer, and he
began to undress them. Now they were completely naked.

> ¡Oh pasión de mi vida, poesía
> desnuda, mía para siempre!

What this means is that in 1916 Jiménez abandoned rhyme, assonance and fixed metres and began to write in *vers libre*. The aim he set himself was *depuración*, to take out of his verse everything except its pure poetic essence. This change in his method coincided with a great change in his life. He had fallen in love and his *amada* had sailed for New York; he had followed her, won her and brought her back as his wife. This is the story described in the book of verse that he published at this time, *Diario de un poeta reciencasado*.

Vers libre is a difficult form for a poet who relies upon his fine artistic sense rather than upon the strength of his poetic imagination, because it requires the abandonment of all artificial aids. Jiménez was entirely lacking in Whitman's force and rhythmic power. But he was at this time under the influence of strong feelings, and it is the new tone of seriousness that these feelings gave that raises some of these short poems to a higher level than anything he had written up to now. Particularly fine are the poems on the sea, which he was crossing in the stormy month of January:

> ¡Oh mar sin olas conocidas,
> sin 'estaciones' de parada,
> agua y luna, no más, noches y noches!
> . . . .Me acuerdo de la tierra,
> que, ajena, era de uno,
> al pasarla en la noche de los trenes,
> por los lugares mismos y a las horas
> de otros años. . . .

> O sea without known waves,
> without halts or stopping places,
> water and moon and nothing more,
> night after night!
> . . . .I remember the earth,
> which, though not belonging to us, was yet ours,
> as we passed over it by night in trains,
> through the same places and at the hours
> of other years. . . .

But I will quote a whole poem: here is one, which has for title a question mark:

Vive entre el corazón
y la puesta de sol o las estrellas.
—En el silencio inmenso
que deja el breve canto
de un pájaro; en la inmensa
sombra que deja el oro último
de una hojita encendida
por la yerba.—
   Vive dentro
de un algo grande que está fuera,
y es portador secreto a lo infinito,
de las llorosas pérdidas
que huyen, al sol y por el sueño,
igual que almas en pena,
en una desesperación que no se oye,
de fuera a dentro a fuera.

                          Ella
pregunta, sin saberlo,
con su carne asomada a la ventana
primaveral: ¿Qué era?

   It lives between the heart
and the setting of the sun or the stars.
—In the immense silence
that the brief song of a bird
leaves behind; in the immense shadow
that the last gold of a scarlet leaf
leaves on the grass.—
   It lives within
a something great that is outside us,
and is the secret bearer to the infinite
of the lost sorrows
that flee away, to the sun and by way of sleep,
like souls in purgatory,
in a desperation that is not heard,
from without to within to without.

                            She asks
without knowing that she is asking,
leaning with her body against the window
that opens on the spring: 'What was it?'

What are we to make of this poet who seems so remote from the English scene? His early verse is all spun out of sensibility—a fine eye, a delicate ear and the passive attitude of the aesthete, savouring the poetic moments of life on his palate. Professor Trend has well compared these poems to the piano pieces of Debussy. His poetic philosophy at this time might be described as a sort of adolescent solipsism: the landscapes and gardens he writes about do not exist independently, but are extensions of his mind. Later this attitude is modified and he dreams of a disembodied life, fed by memory:

> ¡Oh qué vivir divino
> de flor sin tallo y sin raíz,
> nutrida, por la luz, con mi memoria,
> sola y fresca en el aire de la vida!

> Oh what a heavenly sort of living,
> like a flower, without stem or root,
> nourished, instead of light, with my memory,
> solitary and fresh in the air of life!

We see Juan Ramón Jiménez as a poet who lives very much on his own resources and, from the convent security of his study or sick-room, keeps at a distance that rude and disturbing thing called Life.

What distinguishes him from other poets of sensibility is the extreme self-consciousness of his artistic sense and the urge he felt not to rest on what he had done, but to advance and explore. He used his fine intelligence to organize and analyse what his sensibility gave him, and his delicate ear to fix it in flawless lines. From his first poems onwards we can watch the increasing subtlety and precision of his metaphors, just as we can with the Spanish Arab poets of the eleventh and twelfth centuries, of whom he often reminds us. In his second period we see his verse reduced largely to a texture of metaphorical expressions and allusive statements, yet, note well, metaphors which are not conceits, but which are intended to convey as simply as possible a recondite perception or experience.

In one of his later poems he asks his muse, whom typically he calls *Inteligencia*, to give him the 'exact names of things':

> Que mi palabra sea
> la cosa misma,
> creada por mi alma nuevamente.

> Let my word be the thing itself,
> newly created by my soul.

Can we say that this request was granted? The power of naming and creating (as a younger poet, Gerardo Diego, was a few years later to assert) has hitherto been effected only through rhythm and melody. Jiménez's early poems are melodious, though their melody is often faint and has to be listened for. But the melody of his *vers libre* poems is, I would say, essentially speech melody. Their total impression, too, is not so much of a thing caught or seen as of a state of mind in which the outside world mingles and takes part. There is a constant interchange of elements between the poet and the object. Nature appears saturated with thought. These poems seem to me therefore to represent not so much an attempt to create *things* as to seize an almost unseizable experience, and we may observe that there is a necessary correspondence between their thin, diaphanous texture—which demands an exceptionally receptive state of mind from the reader—and the abstruse, elusive character of what is conveyed. Jiménez is most decidedly one of those poets who set out to extend the limits of consciousness. In this respect we can compare much of his later work with T. S. Eliot's *Four Quartets*, although both his method and his cast of mind are entirely different. Jiménez looks out at nature to find himself: Eliot looks inward.

The last book of Jiménez's poetry that I have seen is *La Estación Total* (1923-36). In this he takes another step towards 'naked poetry'. In some of these poems he develops the *vers libre* themes of his 1916 volume. A very beautiful (and difficult) example of this is his poem on the Guadarrama, which he calls *Pacto primero*. Others seem to have taken shape round words, rhymes and scraps of old poetry, out of which he builds something new. The forms are more symmetrical and regular and the content very elliptical.

A few of these poems are very lovely: I would single out *Cuatro* and two which copy the forms of the sixteenth-century *villancicos* —*Mi triste ansia* and *Viento de amor*. The latter has the *a-i* rhyming system of the Galician *cossantes*. So we see the most abstruse and recondite of modern Spanish poets returning—but how differently! —to the forms of the medieval dance poetry.

If Jiménez's position as a poet is difficult to assess, there can be no doubt about his great importance as an influence. The whole of contemporary poetry comes out of him. For some of these poets he is the continuer of the introspective and analytical verse of Bécquer: for others an experimenter in form and imagery. Again and again he has provided the themes which more forceful and exuberant poets have developed. Most indebted of all was García Lorca. One cannot read his *Romances Gitanos* without realizing that many things that one regards as characteristic of his style—rhythms, melodies, turns of phrase, uses of refrain—are derived from Jiménez's early poems. But greatly amplified. What in Jiménez is delicate and faint becomes a music of flutes and guitars in Lorca's rich, fully blooded, triumphant poetry.

Another poet of the same generation who requires to be mentioned is José Moreno Villa. He was born in Malaga in 1887 and spent some years at Freiburg-im-Breisgau studying chemistry. On his return he went to live at the *Residencia* in Madrid, where he took up the history of art. At the same time he began to write poetry, publishing his first volume in 1913. His verse, which is mostly written in the form of the sixteenth-century *villancicos*, is not at all what one would expect an Andalusian from Malaga to write. It is extremely dry—like a glass of *manzanilla* before lunch —and is full of a zest for life that is rather unusual in Spanish poetry. This dryness provided a perfect natural defence against Rubén Darío's poetry of moods and colours, and almost without knowing it Moreno Villa became a precursor of the new poetry. Besides being a poet, he is also an interesting painter: his poem *Descubrimiento* describes his excitement at his sudden discovery of the beauty of forms and colours in Nature. Although he has not the scope or depth of a major poet, there is something individual, adventurous, independent in his work that pleases.

The 1920's saw an extraordinary outburst of poetry in Spain. It was as though a poetical Klondike had suddenly been discovered, and from all corners of the Peninsula, but especially from Andalusia and Old Castile, young men flocked to it and began to dig for ore. Among those who found, one can give at least a dozen names: Pedro Salinas, Jorge Guillén, Gerardo Diego, Dámaso Alonso, Federico García Lorca, Emilio Prados, all born in the 'nineties: and Vicente Aleixandre, Rafael Alberti, Luis Cernuda and Manuel Altolaguirre, born between 1900 and 1905. Every one of these poets may be said to derive, in one way or another, from Juan Ramón Jiménez, though José Moreno Villa also had an influence. Among them there were several outstanding figures, notably Alberti, Cernuda, Guillén and Aleixandre, but the greatest of all was García Lorca. His early death at the age of thirty-seven in front of a Falangist firing squad cut short one of the most astonishing poetic careers the world has seen.

Some of the work of Ramón Gómez de la Serna, though written in prose, has a close affinity with the poetry of this period. He is a Madrileño, born in 1891, and one of the few writers of his time to have had no contacts with the *Residencia*. Endowed with a facile, inventive, often rather flippant talent, he has written books on a variety of subjects. The only ones, however, that I wish to speak of here are his *Greguerías*, which he first began to publish in 1910.

Greguerías are—but no exact definition is possible. I will therefore give you a few examples of them:

The umbrellas are widowers who are in mourning for the departed sunshades.

The seagulls were born from the handkerchiefs that wave goodbye in ports.

In the pond in the public gardens where we played as children our nurse is lying drowned with ourselves in her arms.

Stale bread is like a newly born fossil.

They put prisoners in striped pyjamas in the hope that they will not be able to escape if dressed in bars.

On the telegraph wires there hang, when it is raining, the tears that make the telegrams sad.

See in the typewriters the smile of the alphabet's false teeth!
Milk is sleep.

Gómez de la Serna calls his *greguerías* 'attempts to define the indefinable, to capture the fugitive'. Although their success depends upon the instantaneousness of the impression they make, they aim at something more than wit; the best of them reveal the secret correspondences of things, employing for this a peculiar sort of poetic intuition. This kind of writing is of course surrealism, born long before that term was invented and a great deal more entertaining than any so-called surrealist writings that I have seen. It has analogies too with some things in Quevedo and in Spanish Arab poetry. The author generously offers the new form he has invented to anyone who cares to try it out and one can imagine a writer who had access to deeper levels of feeling putting it to even better uses.

We have explored the two principal fields of literary activity during this century—the philosophic writings and the poetry—and we must now turn our attention to the novel. Immediately we notice one great change: the regional novel is dead. The balanced style and manner in which it was written has also broken down and the conception of what a novel ought to be has become looser and vaguer. Every writer has now to invent his own form and method.

The two principal novelists of this period are Ramón del Valle-Inclán (1866-1936) and Pío Baroja (b. 1872), and they are as different from one another as any two writers could possibly be. Let us look at them.

Some time in the middle 'nineties a young Galician called Ramón —his surname I forget—turned up in Madrid and took his seat among the young writers in the cafés. He was very fantastic to look at, with a long, black, goat-like beard and long waving hair —not unlike the portrait of Lytton Strachey in the Tate Gallery— but his conversation was even more fantastic than his appearance. Nothing could be gathered of his antecedents—for his stories about himself were too extravagant to be believed—except that he had spent some time in Mexico. 'I went there', he said, 'because it is the only country in the world that has an X in it.' Prominent in his conversation were descriptions of love affairs of a marvellous kind of which he was the hero. 'A Galician type', everyone said, much as we say, 'A regular Irishman'.

His first book came out in 1895. It consisted of short stories of beautiful, perverse, amorous women, written in poetical prose and in a ninetyish setting. Influences—Barbey d'Aurevilly, Villiers de l'Isle-Adam and D'Annunzio. Then in 1902-5 appeared the four rather long stories that gave him an immediate fame—the *Sonatas*. They bore on their title page the new aristocratic-sounding name, Valle-Inclán, which he had adopted not merely as a *nom de plume*, and purported to be four incidents from the memoirs of the Marqués de Bradomín, a sort of Galician Don Juan who was *feo, católico y sentimental*. Each *Sonata* described a love affair which corresponded to one of the four seasons of the year and took place in an appropriate country, and in each of them a beautiful woman was shown in love with the Marquis, who played a passive role and allowed himself to be adored. As for the rest—no creation of character, no psychological analysis, but plenty of conversation in the style of a bad *feuilleton* and, if portrayal of life is part of the business of a novelist, an extraordinary innocence and ineptitude.

The first impression of a modern reader confronted with this once famous book must be that it is the day-dream of a sex-starved adolescent who has been reading Wilde's *Dorian Gray* and Villiers de l'Isle-Adam's *Axel*. The identification of the hero with the author's picture of himself proclaims itself on every page. But in this *fin de siècle* literature it is the manner that is the important thing, and the musical style of the descriptive passages has been praised. Valle-Inclán certainly wrote these parts with great care, paying special attention to the cadences of the sentences, but their vocabulary and imagery are banal and in any case the effect of a too cadenced prose is to send one to sleep. Also, as it happens, the greater part of the *Sonatas* is written in dialogue. It is here that we come on the original side of Valle-Inclán. Inept though this dialogue is, it has often a harsh, fierce, marionette-like tone that cuts through the pseudo-enchantment. There are abrupt transitions, childish insistences and exaggerations, but in spite of all these crying faults we do feel a force and energy which, however badly employed, shows us that the author is not the sickly purveyor of purple love passages that he often appears to be.

His next book, *Flor de Santidad*—actually it came out before the fourth *Sonata*—is better. It is a story of beggars, pilgrims and peasants in a Galician setting. Its descriptive passages are over-written, but in the conversation of the peasants and beggars one gets a real feeling of the soil and a sense of great though uncontrolled energy. The story is of the sort that George Moore might have selected and there is something too in the richness and spice of the dialogue that reminds one of Synge. But the resemblance is superficial: Valle-Inclán, for all his preoccupation with style, was not a self-conscious artist and his books show a violence of phrase and an unpredictability of action that are entirely *sui generis*.

His next books comprise three novels on the Carlist War of 1870 and some verse plays. The novels show a great increase in the harsh and pungent side of his nature, but they also display to the full the difficulty he had in putting more than a few pages together in a consecutive manner. His mind works in flashes and between these flashes there are the most disconcerting gaps and inconse-quences. The verse plays are better. Valle-Inclán was a delightful poet in the style of Rubén Darío, and *Cuento de Abril* (1910)—to name the best of these plays—is a little *jeu d'esprit* that of its kind is quite perfect. It tells the story of a Provençal troubadour and of a cruel joke which the Princess who employed him, and with whom he was of course in love, played on him. Then an Infante of Castile appears to beg the Princess' hand. The contrast between the civilized and artificial society of Provence and the fierce, predatory, ascetic spirit of Castile is beautifully brought out. Naturally in Valle-Inclán's mind Provence stands for Galicia, but his intuitive feeling for certain societies and situations has enabled him to present a picture that has real historical truth.

From verse plays he went on to prose plays—or rather to novels in dramatic form. These include the trilogy of the *Comedias Bárbaras*, written on the sort of epic subjects that Lope de Vega often chose, and the *Esperpentos* and *Farsas*. The last two categories contain some of his high- water marks. *Los Cuernos de Don Friolera*, for example, is an *esperpento* which can be described as a satire in the

Grand Guignol manner on the Spanish Army officers and their exaggerated code of honour. It is written in a harsh, dry, racy style of extraordinary vigour and cruelty, which recalls at moments Alfred Jarry's *Ubu Roi*. Although tastes will always differ about a writer so arbitrary and fantastic as Valle-Inclán, I personally find this play immensely stimulating. Of his *farsas* the best is *Farsa y licencia de la Reina Castiza*, a grotesque and biting caricature of the life of Isabel II. His aesthetic principle, he said at this time, was to transform the natural appearance of things 'by a mathematics of concave mirrors.' The tragic reality of Spanish life could be conveyed only by a systematic deformation, 'because Spain is a grotesque deformation of European civilization'. That is to say, he belonged in his own way to the generation of '98.

Valle-Inclán's last works consist of three novels—*Tirano Banderas* (1926), which is a satire on a Mexican dictator, *La Corte de los Milagros* and *Viva mi dueño*. The two last, which are both on the court of Isabel II, are generally regarded as his best novels. Written when he was over sixty, they achieve the greatest harmony attainable by him of the various violently contradictory elements in his nature. There is the famous poetical style, made up of short sentences dovetailed together, both sharp and sweet at the same time: the rich vocabulary, drawn principally from the village or street, or else just out of his own head: the abrupt transitions, to which it is now possible to assign some formal purpose: and the dialogue, racy, vivid, satirical—almost whip-like at moments in its cutting power. Few ideas or comments, little interest in character and a sense for form that is aesthetic and stylistic rather than novelesque.

Valle-Inclán is a writer who is utterly unlike anyone else. The roots of his art lie in a fantastic swagger and boastfulness: he scarcely took in the existence of other people except as an audience and much of his best work is of the same order as a display of bargee's language. One must not therefore look for ideas or emotions in his books, but only for verbal assaults and strong sensations. On artistic grounds one can find many things to cavil at, for he had little power of organizing his talents, but in our emasculated times anyone who can use language as richly and arrogantly as he does—and with such flashes of imaginative power—deserves to be highly regarded. When all his faults have been set out, he still remains an exciting and stimulating writer.

The leading Spanish novelist of the century—and after Pérez Galdós the greatest—is Pío Baroja. He was born in 1872 in San Sebastian of Basque parents. His father was a mining engineer. Educated chiefly in Madrid and Valencia, he chose medicine as his career and for two years practised as a doctor in a small town in the Basque Provinces. Disgusted by the intrigues of country life and by the scenes of poverty and suffering he was obliged to witness, he gave up his practice and took over the management of a bakery in Madrid which had belonged to his brother. At this he worked for eight years till the business failed. Then, at the age of thirty, he settled down with one of his sisters and began to write novels.

Since then Baroja's life has been the outwardly monotonous existence of the novelist who turns out two or more books every year. He never married. His only relaxation has been foreign travel. His excessively timid character has obliged him to seek an outlet for his craving for life and adventure in novel writing.

Baroja's books cover many different fields. Some are about the Basque Provinces, others about lower middle-class life in the large cities, others deal with the two Carlist Wars and the struggle against Napoleon: others again take place in Switzerland, Italy, Russia or England and have as their principal characters not Spaniards but foreigners. But they are all alike in one respect— that they are books of adventure. Loosely written, with little that can be called a formal plot, full of characters who appear once and then are never seen again, they aim at giving an objective picture of the passage of events, of that casual opening up and fading out of episodes and situations that we call Life. There is no element of fate; almost anything may happen, but in the place of fate there is a general tendency—a sort of second law of thermodynamics— that operates on human life and reduces every hopeful beginning to frustration, disillusion and absurdity.

The heroes are curious figures. Sometimes, like Julien Sorel in *Le Rouge et le Noir*, they are obsessed by a desire for power, for success, for conquest. Zalacaín, for example, lives to overcome obstacles, even the obstacle of his own desire for life. But these men never succeed in their aim because either their ambition suddenly deserts them or else an accident puts an end to their existence. More often, however, the principal figure is a man without will power or character who feels life passing by without discovering any real desire to seize it. These apathetic and discouraged creatures, whose apathy or *abulia*, we are given to understand, is due to a clearsightedness that enables them to see through the illusions of life, are very frequent in the best of Baroja's novels. They are his real heroes—the men and women who, because they refuse to be deceived, are obliged to live without purpose or faith. But their lives are sad. 'Life is dull and stupid', one of them remarks, 'without real emotions or adventures, and the thoughts become full of terror as a compensation for the emotional sterility of existence.'

It has often been remarked that Baroja's novels are all action. There is a continual movement from one place to another, characters appear and disappear, there are few set scenes, no one is drawn at any length. In the series grouped under the title *Memorias de un hombre de acción*, which deal with the War of Liberation, this action is almost cinematographic in its rapidity. His manner of writing, in short, simple paragraphs without rhetorical building-up or analytical passages, helps to increase this effect. His books read almost like diaries. But Baroja provides another element in his novels besides action: he provides thought and comment. He is after all a man of '98, an intellectual. And these comments and general discussions with which he fills out his books are far from boring; indeed, in my opinion, they are one of the chief delights of his work. As we read him we are carried back to that old picaresque novel, *Guzmán de Alfarache*, where action and moralizing are interwoven in much the same manner.

Guzmán, we may remember, is a book permeated by a sense of the vileness and sordidness of life, which its author appears to ascribe, in the theological language of his day, to the existence of original sin. Baroja feels the same disgust for life, but explains it in a very different manner. In the first place he hates religion, which he regards as a dangerous and disagreeable illusion, introduced into Europe by the Semites. He equally detests conventional morality. In describing a Spanish country town he speaks of it as being in a state of siege, the besieger who pins it down to boredom and immobility being Catholic morality. He hates the State too. 'There should be no laws', he makes one of his characters say. 'Everyone should do as he pleases. The only real crimes are bad faith and hypocrisy.' Nature is to be preferred to the artificial system which men have set up. 'Every subversive instinct—and the natural is always subversive—carries with it its own policeman. There is no pure fountain which men have not trampled with their feet and dirtied.' This of course is anarchism. Baroja was an anarchist of sorts, though in *Aurora Roja*, his novel on the anarchists, he makes a character, who appears to express his own thoughts, declare that nothing can come out of militant anarchism: 'It should only be taken up as a sport.' His anarchism is really that of a morbidly timid man who, because he dare not put into practice his secret desires and aspirations, would like to see everything brought down. Of all the extreme individualists which this century has produced, he is, theoretically at least, the most destructive.

Baroja's views on art are not very favourable either. 'Art, music and books', he says, 'provide a little opium in our lives. At bottom they are of no importance.' (The Basques, one may observe, are noted for their lack of aesthetic feeling.) But Nature is interesting, and still more interesting is science. 'If God is anywhere, he is in the laboratories.' We see that the one value that stands firm in Baroja's system is truth. It is this that leads him to put philosophic speculation above everything. It may not produce the answers that we wish to know, but at least it asks the questions. The philosophers he most admires are Kant, Schopenhauer and Nietzsche and after them Hobbes, Locke and Hume. He has a prejudice against the French philosophers and indeed against everything French.

Baroja's hatred of Catholic morality must not be taken as implying that he is without a moral sense. On the contrary he is obsessed by one. It is precisely his detestation of suffering, cruelty, injustice and hypocrisy that make him judge life so severely. *El Árbol de la Ciencia*, which is both one of his best books and one of his most painful—perhaps because it is founded on the story of his own youth—provides a good example of this exaggerated severity. As one reads it, one finds the words 'stupid', 'absurd', 'disgusting', 'banal', 'silly', on almost every page and sometimes applied to things which the reader is by no means likely to regard in that light. His criticisms of Spain are the most severe ever made by a Spaniard. 'The customs of Alcolea were purely Spanish—that is to say, of a complete absurdity.' When he looked at his own country, he saw no mitigating circumstances. The foreigner was always better.

Yet Baroja's books are not as a rule sad or depressing. One reason for this is, I think, the speed with which events in them move. The air seems to blow in one's face as one reads: one feels the excitement of a journey. There is also a strong lyrical strain which is provided by the descriptions of nature. Though always brief and simply expressed—mere statements about trees and weather—they provide a background of poetry, like glimpses seen between meals and conversation through the window of a railway carriage. In *El mundo es ansí*, for example, where we move through half a dozen countries between Spain and Russia, these grey, subdued, constantly changing vistas give the tone to the novel. Then Baroja's way of feeling life has another peculiarity, which helps to counteract his depressing philosophy. He lives entirely in the present. Unlike Galdós, he has no historical sense: unlike James and Flaubert, no feeling for the past. We live in the moment as we read his books—often plunged in the confusion of rapid events—and never look back. The only pauses for meditation are provided by the glimpses we get of Nature. Thus, though his judgments on life are not very different from those offered by Flaubert in *L'Éducation Sentimentale*, we are much less convinced by them. The total impression we get is indeterminate and complex.

There are two qualities that stand out in the work of this writer: curiosity and sincerity. Every novelist has necessarily a great deal of curiosity, but Baroja's was of a peculiar kind. As he says of the hero of *El Árbol de la Ciencia*, his was *una curiosidad por sorprender la vida*, a curiosity to surprise life. And it is because of this desire to surprise life, to catch it when it was off guard, that he abandons so many of the forms and artifices of the professional novelist and puts down very simply what he has observed and no more. His books are therefore underwritten, full of loose ends, of things suddenly seized and jotted down or that have come into his mind spontaneously. But curiosity needs to be reinforced by sincerity. This is precisely Baroja's strong point: he is the most sincere of writers. Often dull, hurried, sketchy, one will not find anywhere in his books a false touch. Free from the tyranny of the long paragraph, the set passage and the methodical analysis, he never feels the need to put down anything he has not felt. But he is not a mature writer like Galdós: his mind has the penetrating but innocent quality of the child in Hans Andersen's story who cried out that the Emperor was wearing no clothes. At bottom he is always the Basque mountaineer and *aldeano*, living in a city whose customs and ceremonies he does not understand. How could he possibly understand them without some feeling for religion, art and history?

The first decades of this century have seen a revival of the drama. The works of Benavente, of the brothers Álvarez Quintero, of Jacinto Grau and of Martínez Sierra are all of importance. I can, however, do little more than mention them here. Jacinto Benavente, born in 1866 in Madrid, is a dramatist who has written a very large number of plays which give the impression of being slightly constructed when one reads them, but which often made good theatre. The majority of his pieces are comedies of a satirical sort which get their effect through the brilliance of their dialogue and the ironical picture they give of society. He is an isolated figure, too intellectual to belong to the Spanish dramatic tradition and with a very different method of constructing his plots. A play that shows him at his best is *La Comida de las Fieras*, but his work is very uneven and it is not easy to appraise him.

The brothers Álvarez Quintero were born in 1871 and 1873 and died recently. They were Andalusians from Utrera near Seville and the best of their plays, which are all comedies, are upon Andalusian life. They are very delightful playwrights, gay, humorous, full of the *sal* and *gracia* of their native land and a little sentimental. But one must not take their *andalucismo* too seriously, for it is part of that rather self-conscious cult by the Sevillians of their native city which we see in the novel *La Hermana San Sulpicio* and in *flamenco* singing. Their plays must be read or seen for what they are—very good entertainment, with a period flavour of the pleasant, carefree years of the 'nineties. They act splendidly.

Of the other prose writers of this century, interesting though some of them are, only a few words can be said. Ramón Pérez de Ayala, born in 1880 in Asturias, poet, critic and essayist, is also a novelist of distinction who has continued the tradition of Galdós and Clarín from the last century. 'Azorín', whose real name is José Martínez Ruiz, born in 1874 near Alicante, is an essayist whose descriptions of Castilian villages and landscapes should be read by anyone interested in Spanish things. The autobiography of the great bull-fighter, Juan Belmonte, put into good Spanish by a friend, is a book of unusual fascination, which continues directly the picaresque tradition of Torres y Villarroel.

A certain advance has been made in the art of biography, which has long been the most backward of literary forms in Spain, and one may cite as examples of this Dr Gregorio Marañón's life of the Conde Duque de Olivares, with its interesting psychiatric approach, and the Marqués de Villa-Urrutia's books on Ferdinand VII. In scholarship the great figure of Menéndez Pelayo has been succeeded by that of Ramón Menéndez Pidal (b. 1869). With him the focus of interest has moved from the sixteenth century to the Middle Ages, with the result that we now see this as an absolutely capital period in the literature of the Peninsula and one too which throws a considerable light on other European literatures. At the same time Spanish Arabic studies have found a brilliant exponent in Emilio García Gómez (b. 1905), who is one of the very few Arabic scholars to show an intelligent appreciation of the difficult literature of that language. I must emphasize the importance of these two men. One of the great differences between Spanish scholarship and English is that the former, without ceasing to be objective, has worked in close touch with contemporary literature and has therefore had a considerable influence upon it. The work of such collectors of folk-poetry and music as Padre Gabriel Vergara and E. Martínez Torner have also been of value to modern poetry. In Spain the old and the new, the popular and the erudite, touch hands.

CHAPTER XVII

POSTSCRIPT

AT THE end of a long book such as this, covering so many centuries of literature, certain reflections come into the mind and certain authors emerge with especial vividness. It may be useful if I put down a few of the things that occur to me.

In Spanish prose three or four books written before the middle of the nineteenth century stand out above all the others: *La Celestina*, *Don Quixote*, Quevedo's *Sueños* and *Lazarillo de Tormes*. Of these *La Celestina* seems to me the one that is most alive today. Cervantes' novel, great and many-sided though it is, has defects of unevenness, forced gusto and uncertainty of intention that, rightly or wrongly, diminish the pleasure we get from it, but *La Celestina* makes the impression of a clear and untarnished work, fit for the admiration of every age. It is not only the first European novel, but one of the greatest. Quevedo occupies a place by himself: he is an expressionist writer, both bitter and buffoonish, with a vivid imagination and a prodigious power over language. But though he was one of the greatest literary performers of all time, he lacked judgment and spent his talent either on occasional works or on moral and political treatises that have dated. *Lazarillo* could not be more different. Slight and trivial at first sight, because it is deliberately underwritten, it displays to perfection that fine, sad and penetrating observation which is one of the especial things in Spanish literature. For this reason it is among those seminal books that have had a long line of descendants.

In more recent times two novelists stand out as European figures —Pérez Galdós and Pío Baroja. Galdós is one of the major novelists, yet a certain exuberance and wordiness in his manner, despite his fundamental pessimism, have put him under a cloud with contemporary readers. He is, besides, the end and consummation of a great age of novel writing, rather than the beginning of a new one.

We ought to have read and digested him long ago. Baroja, a writer of lower category, is very different. Uneven and slipshod, with little interest either in plot or in character, he contrives by a mixture of rapid narrative and comment to give us in his best novels the taste and feeling of life itself. His very imperfections seem a merit, for his books are a quest and a groping after truth and he refuses to put down anything he has not seen or felt. Hence the lack of all the usual paraphernalia of plot and dramatic dialogue. A pessimist and materialist on principle, there seeps through his bare style and grey descriptions a sort of lyricism that turns many of his novels, perhaps against his intention, into poetic meditations. We learn from him how little conscious art and contrivance a novelist needs if he has enough sincerity.

The Spanish drama is a special region, very impressive as a whole but without outstanding summits. Its most striking plays, *La Vida es Sueño*, *El Burlador de Sevilla* and *Fuenteovejuna*, owe their greatness to their themes. The first is an allegorical muddle, the second reads as if it had been written in a fortnight, while the third lacks the charm and freshness of many of Lope's pieces. Yet time has made them great. However, in spite of this lack of outstanding plays, the drama is perhaps the most characteristic of Spanish literary forms. The quantity of life, poetry, action and humour poured out in its long stream of productions is without equal in any other literature.

But it is in poetry that we must seek the crown of the Spanish literary achievement. Epic and narrative verse are more or less confined to the medieval period, yet, admirable though these are, they do not compare with the lyric poetry which sprang up when Galicia, Andalusia and Italy joined their currents to the sober Castilian stream. It is precisely this injection of the rich and musical and nostalgic into a graver and more masculine idiom and mode of feeling that gives to Spanish lyric poetry a pre-eminence that only English can contest.

Let us recapitulate the major figures. The Archpriest of Hita, Garcilaso de la Vega and Góngora are three very great poets. San Juan de la Cruz reaches in his brief rocket-like flights a lyric altitude that is scarcely touched by anyone else, while Luis de León, in his more halting way, comes not far behind. Auziàs March, the Marqués de Santillana and Jorge Manrique surpass all the lyric poets of their age except Villon and possibly Lorenzo de' Medici and Politian, while Lope de Vega, Calderon and Quevedo wrote poetry that is, in every sense of the word, great. Nor must we forget the great body of the Galician *cantigas de amigo*, surely the most beautiful song poetry of the Middle Ages, or the *villancicos* of the sixteenth-century *Cancioneros*, which are one of the high-water marks of Spanish literature. I would especially recommend the study of these last to English poets.

To come to the recent period, Rubén Darío and Juan Ramón Jiménez are both in their very different ways poets of outstanding mastery in their art, while Antonio Machado and García Lorca rank in power and genius with the finest poets of this century. But above all these there stands out the great and baffling figure of Góngora. His *Soledades*, though difficult to penetrate, will appear to the reader who has steeped himself in its melodies as one of the most haunting poems ever written. It raises a question of values. In the purely aesthetic sense one can only compare it, in spite of its fundamentally lyric facture, to Vergil and Milton, yet no subject of importance to human life is treated in it. It offers us a nostalgic recollection of the world as it is taken in by the eye of a child, deprived of all moral and causal implications. Thus, as we have seen, its imagery handles the minute drops of water on a woollen garment and the Straits of Tierra del Fuego as though they were objects of the same size and interest. The plaintive or joyful music it gives out reaches us through a filter that deprives it of actuality. Yet, as a man, Góngora was tough, hard-bitten and worldly. He spent his nights at the card table and was one of the most formidable wits who have ever lived. In his two longer poems this experience of the world is shown only in the fineness and maturity of his artistry.

How is it that the lyric, or poem of lyric feeling, has come to be the most successful branch of Spanish literature? One reason, I think, lies in the connection it has had with folk-song. With the exception of Garcilaso de la Vega, Luis de León, Herrera and Calderon, every poet of importance has been influenced by this

perennial poetry. Its existence, still more its growth and development down to modern times, is a mark of how different the Spanish
situation is to the European. It should, however, be borne in
mind that the concept of folk-song is by no means a simple one.
In the first stage to which we can trace these ditties they are the
property of the peasants, who have fitted them to their dances and
courtship ceremonies and given them their peculiar flavour. But
before they are taken over by the professional poets, they have as a
rule been worked up by strolling jongleurs, or by anonymous
song writers, or even by guilds of singers, such as persist today in
the Andalusian *cantaores*, into a form more suited to the sentiments
of townspeople and to instrumental music. That is to say, several
different social and intellectual strata have had a hand in them, so
that almost the only general characteristics they show are a freedom
from the idiosyncrasies of a personal style and a power of catching
popular taste.

The existence of this popular sung poetry, flowing like an underground stream under the surface, has meant that there was always
a source from which the poetry of the learned poets could renew
itself. In England new movements in poetry have frequently gone
back—Donne, Wordsworth, Browning, Eliot—to the rhythms and
language of colloquial speech. This has scarcely ever happened in
Spain. There prose has revitalized itself in this way, but poetry has
fallen back on other poetry—that is, on the popular lyric. It is this
that has sustained the rhythmic vitality of Spanish poetry at a time
when in England it has tended to become progressively flatter.
One has to remember too that behind these popular lyrics there is
a vigorous and animated popular life and culture such as we have
no experience of in this country. If the chief obstacle to the writing
of English poetry lies in the steady desiccation and devitalization of
English life, due to our increasing intellectual and political puritanism, that in Spanish poetry lies in provincialism and in the tendency
of Iberian culture to turn round and round within the same
circle of ideas. That is to say, the English social pattern is flatter
and of lower tension, but open; the Spanish more intense, but
closed.

A feature of Spanish literature that must strike every reader is the lack of letters, diaries, memoirs of a personal kind and biographies. The chief reason for this is the strong convention in Spain which forbids the publication of intimate details about the lives of people whose descendants down to the fifth and sixth generation are still in existence, and which usually leads to their private correspondence being destroyed. If one judged by published records, one might suppose that no Spaniard had ever written a love letter. In this way Spanish literature has been spared that fantastic diversion of interest from the work of writers to their personalities and lives that has taken place in other countries. I am thinking, for example, of the dozen or so books that have been published on Shelley's life and character to the exclusion of any serious examination of his poetry. However, taking it all round, the loss caused to literature by this prudishness has been great. The detailed biography or collection of letters is one of the best aids to the understanding of human nature and is especially revealing in the case of writers, because we already possess in their work a more or less intimate revelation of their inner selves; by contrasting this with the outer features and circumstances of their lives, we are able to get the most complete picture possible of what a human being is like. But this opportunity will be sought for in vain in Spanish literature. The material is not to be found and the biographer's art is in its infancy. The consequence is that, though the Spaniards are a sociable and observant people, greatly given to gossip and scandal, their views on human personality and character lack a finish and subtlety which is taken as a matter of course among intellectuals in other countries. Further, their great writers have not received the attention due to them abroad because their personalities have not been adequately presented. What foreigner, for example, without a biographical study to guide him, can make anything of the work of Valle-Inclán? To get one's bearings in it, one has to have talked to a friend of his.

We are often told that the Spaniards are great individualists and it may be interesting to see what traces there are of this in their literature. Certainly we do not find much development of the personality in their novels or plays. If we exclude Galdós, who saw Spain partly from a foreign angle, the characters in Spanish drama and fiction are for the most part very simple and built up round some predominant trait or feature. Celestina, Don Quixote and Sancho Panza are the only ones to be at all elaborated. On the other hand the sense of the group or family is strong. This agrees, I think, with the picture which any foreigner residing in Spain is likely to form of the country. The pattern of Spanish life is narrow and conventional and fitted to a sort of clan system. The social forces operating on the individual are—or have been till quite recently—powerful. Yet within this framework the Spaniards are a people of great independence and self-assertiveness. It is here that their famous individualism comes in. They do not, they cannot, allow their personalities to grow and flow in the easy way in which we do in England, but rapidly set about building up each one their *yo*, or ego, as a fortress in which they can defend themselves and maintain, at the point of the sword if necessary, their separate uniqueness against their neighbours. The sense of honour, which, it is generally agreed, is one of the most marked of Spanish characteristics, is simply their sense of the respect due to this principle of sublimated egoism. It teaches generosity, nobility, the fine gesture—all those acts by which men rise above the lower forms of selfishness and display to the world at large the proof of their superiority. But it also inclines to pride and touchiness. Thus in their social dealings Spaniards are by turns better and worse than other people.

Of this assertive and sometimes combative individualism we shall find abundant examples in Spanish literature, especially in the seventeenth century, when it reached its height. Perhaps, under the more complex stresses of city life, it is breaking down today. At all events we find in Galdós a whole gallery of characters in whom it has definitely ceased to exist. His observant and sympathetic eye reveals to us the wrecks and failures of the system—the people who, in the arctic climate of the great cities, have been unable to live up to the national tradition and to maintain against the world their high opinion of themselves. Baroja too, from his different angle, shows us the stripped and defenceless man, who is not tough enough to take part in the fierce scrum of modern competitive life. Under the protective covering of the *yo*, which the endemic civil war of Spanish society has produced, there lies, I have no doubt, a great sensitivity and loneliness. And with the decline of religious faith, this loneliness tends to take a political or metaphysical form. For this reason the deepest need in Spain today is for a social and political system which will help to restore the old sense of solidarity and brotherhood which religion and monarchy once gave. For Spanish individualism left to itself is—unlike the English kind—anarchic and disruptive.

Another feature of Spanish literature is its realism. In the Middle Ages this consisted simply in taking a practical, objective view. But with the heightening of religious tension in the sixteenth century, there came to be something more in it than the practice of keeping the eyes skinned. It became purposeful. First in the name of morality and then in that of religion, it undertook the task of showing up the frauds and deceptions of the world. Thus *Lazarillo* is an exposure of the alterable state of society, *Guzmán* of the unalterable conditions which human nature is born to. The pace quickened: very soon Baroque pessimism was in full blast. '*El delito mayor del hombre es haber nacido*', exclaims Segismundo in *La Vida es Sueño*, 'the greatest crime man has committed is having been born', and Gracián echoes him. Realism was the means of proving that this judgment was true. But by this time the taste for actuality had diminished, and it does so in the mask of melodrama and caricature.

Was this pessimism a reflection of the consciousness of national decline and failure? In some writers, perhaps. But it was even more, I think, due to the fact that the prevailing state of religious and nationalist intoxication left nothing to be done that, in such a mood, seemed worth doing. Spain was like a person who, having been to a cocktail party and drunk a good deal, has no better way of spending the evening than to return home to his room.

In more general terms one may say that Spaniards, who have often an excessive vitality when young, grow up to expect a great deal from life. But their country does not offer many openings for ambition, their natural high spirits makes them resent the drudgery of small employments and by the time they are thirty they are apt to feel disillusioned and deceived. The world has not given them what they consider that their merits deserve. The realism of their writers is the expression of this disillusion. And then the Semitic or African bareness of the Spanish mind, its lack of small amenities and interests, of those pleasant zests and hobbies that fill out the Western European's life, leaves them singularly exposed to the sense of purposelessness and boredom. Their religion has of course accentuated and fed upon this. It has sanctified tedium and idleness because they kill the appetite for life and has provided exercises for directing them to spiritual ends. Climate and scenery have had their influence too, creating those sun-drenched *páramos* of the mind in which the middle-aged Spaniard resigns himself like a lizard to hours and days of passivity. Yet religious tedium, stoic resignation, lethargic acceptance of the blessedness of being oneself cannot be the lot of everyone, and so one finds that in most ages the note given out by Spanish literature is that of discontent. Realism is the natural instrument by which this is expressed—not the comfortable, debunking sort mixed with small packets of indignation to which we are accustomed in England, but a painful penetrating sentiment which, in describing the world as it is, has always in mind some utopia.

Everyone will have noted the scarcity of ideas in Spanish literature, at all events down to the beginning of the present century. We feel that Spaniards are mentally as alert as other people, yet in every age of their history there has been a poverty and monotony of thought and an absence of speculation. The principal reason for this, I think, lies in the attitude of the Spanish Church towards thinking on religious and philosophical matters. There were no schoolmen in Spain during the Middle Ages—or rather the Spanish schoolmen were not Catholics, but Jews and Moslems. Down to 1355 there was no chair of theology at any Spanish university. Even then it was badly taught and nominalism was not introduced till 1512, when Cardinal Ximenes brought it to his new University at Alcalá. The sudden enthusiasm for Thomism during the sixteenth century led to no new development—though it produced in Suárez one eminent theologian—because the day of scholasticism was then over. The most valuable thinking of this age followed more practical lines—the writings on international law of Francisco de

Vitoria, the political and sociological treatises of Luis Vives and the works of the Jesuit casuists.

The truth is that religious speculation was alien to the spirit of the Spanish Church. Fray Ambrosio Montesino, the chaplain of Queen Isabella, summed up the general attitude in a verse from his poem on the Blessed Sacrament:

> El callar con el creer
> en cosa tan admirable
> es, según mi parecer,
> la vena del merecer,
> la corona perdurable.

Keeping silent on matters of belief . . . is the way to earn the eternal crown.

Erasmus was, at about this time, dismissing the formalistic religion of the Spaniards as a new Judaism and, had he known Spanish, he might have found some support for this view in the fact that the Spanish word for to pray, *rezar*, is derived from the Latin *recitare* and not from *orare*. The era of the mystics was brief—it is a complete mistake to regard Spain as having a natural leaning to mysticism —and by the middle of the seventeenth century an unthinking loyalty to the letter of the Church had become the sole test of the religious man. As the dramatist Vélez de Guevara wrote:

> Yo bien podré ser también
> mal cristiano, pero buen
> católico ¡vive Dios!

I can well be a bad Christian but a good Catholic.

Spain had, in short, become more Catholic than Christian, more ecclesiastical than spiritual.

The Inquisition had done a great deal to increase the natural bias of the Church against the free use of the intelligence. People think only when their received ideas have been challenged and it was a succession of such challenges that had brought into being the Scholastic philosophy of the Middle Ages. The new ideas then thrown up had had to run the gauntlet of the authorities, had at first been condemned and in the end had prevailed. But what the

463

Spanish Inquisition condemned was condemned for ever, and the general consequence of the terror it set up was to stop people thinking at all. This, according to Saint-Simon, who visited Spain in 1721, was the deliberate intention, and down to the middle of the century it worked well.[1] Even when that institution had ceased to exist, its principles survived and in 1823 we read of the second university in the country publicly dismissing all thinking as 'a dangerous novelty'.

Now writers are not usually philosophers and few of them read many books of metaphysics. Yet in one way or another they are affected and stimulated by the ideas that these books contain. The drying up of the fountain of speculation produces a weakening of the intelligence through the whole body of literature, a short-circuiting of the current of tradition and a loss of direction. This is what happened in Spain in the sixteenth century and what continued until the other day. The present century has, it is true, seen a revival of popular philosophic writing, based on the work of such foreign thinkers as Kant, Kierkegaard and Nietzsche, which proves that Spaniards are by no means badly endowed for this sort of thing. But inevitably it has been just a little provincial and narrow: Spaniards are today so obsessed by the problems of their own country that they have not much to give, in the way of ideas, to the rest of Europe. Perhaps this will change. Or perhaps, on the other hand, we must accept the fact that Spanish culture is, what it has generally been in the past, an inward-looking affair, working out its destiny with some help from outside, but in an idiom that is more or less strange and foreign to the rest of Europe. When, in a liberal mood, one has let one's indignation fly out over some Berber-like obtuseness of this only partly European people, one is pulled up by the thought that perhaps its greatest glory lies in its powers of resistance to foreign influence and to modern civilization, in its determination to preserve pure and unmixed its own highly

---

[1] 'Elle veut une obéissance aveugle sans oser réfléchir ni raisonner sur rien, par conséquent elle abhorre toute lumière, toute science, tout usage de son esprit; elle ne veut que l'ignorance, et l'ignorance la plus grossière; la stupidité dans les chrétiens est sa qualité favorite et celle qu'elle s'applique le plus soigneusement d'établir partout, comme la plus sûre voie du salut, la plus essentielle, parce qu'elle est le fondement le plus solide de son règne et de la tranquillité de sa domination' (*Mémoires du Duc de Saint Simon, ed.* 1875, *tôme* XVIII, p. 179).

original soul. Spain will be the last country in Europe to surrender to cosmopolitanism.

The literature we have been surveying, then, is a narrow literature, following a deeply channelled, well-marked bed. Every fragment of it gives out a special note or flavour that is not in the least like that of any other people. It is concentrated, harsh, bitter, yet also lyrical: the product of a dry, monotonous country, given to bursts of exuberance and to sudden amazing flights. A literature more inclined to action than to thought, to moralizing than to speculation: at once parochial and sophisticated, having its roots in the medieval wisdom of the villages, but flowering in the cities. A literature where tragedy is never far below the surface, where life and death go hand in glove and where the East and the West meet. The English reader who embarks upon it will find a whole world of new experiences awaiting him.

APPENDIX

In December 1948 an article appeared in *Al-Andalus* (vol. XIII, Fasc. 2) by a young Hebrew and Arabic scholar, S. M. Stern, which has revolutionized our knowledge of the origins of Spanish lyric poetry. S. M. Stern discovered, embedded in Spanish-Hebrew *muwassahas*, twenty short verses or stanzas in Romance or early Spanish, nearly all of which can be dated to the eleventh century. These verses are not easy to read because the Hebrew script omits the vowels and sometimes makes mistakes over the consonants: besides, the Romance idiom of this time is imperfectly known and some of the words in these verses are in popular Arabic. However, since Stern's article, two studies have appeared by E. García Gómez in *Al-Andalus* (vol. XIV, Fasc. 2, 1949 and vol. XV, Fasc. 1, 1950) which correct the text and give further elucidations, while another article has been announced which will contain twenty more Romance verses or stanzas, taken this time from Arabic *muwassahas*.

Before looking at these verses, we will consider the *muwassahas* discovered by Stern. The fact that they are in Hebrew will not introduce any complication, because every Hebrew *muwassaha* is a close imitation of an Arabic one. Their form is different from that of the *zéjels* written a few years later by Ibn Guzmán, in the first place because they are written in classical instead of in popular Arabic and secondly because the emphasis falls not on the theme-stanza at the beginning of the poem, but on the verses that rhyme with it at the end. These are known as *jarchas* (the English transcription is *kharja*) and it is they that are sometimes written in Romance. Another peculiarity is that, when the poem is about love, they are put into the mouth of a woman of the lower classes. According to the thirteenth-century Egyptian poet, Ibn Sana al-Mulk, who composed an anthology of Spanish Arabic *muwassahas*, the *jarcha* is a popular verse, written either in Arabic or in Romance, but always in the idiom of the lowest dregs of the populace, and aiming at a searing, penetrating, *cri de cœur* effect which shall deeply stir and move the hearer. That is to say not unlike the effect produced by those brief, three-lined poems, the *soleares*, that are sung in *cante jondo* in Andalusia today. The whole development of a *muwassaha* was designed to lead up to, and explode in, one of these little passionate verses. This seems to accord with the new translation that S. M. Stern gives of the passage in Ibn Bassám where he speaks of the *muwassahas* of Mocádem of Cabra: what Ibn Bassám apparently said was 'Mocádem took expressions in vulgar Arabic or Romance, called them *markaz* and built on them his *muwassahas*'. Stern is of the opinion that these Spanish *markaz* or *jarchas*, as they are best called, formed the metrical basis on which the *muwassaha* was built.

Let us now look at these little verses themselves: here are three examples, which I give in the corrected text offered by F. Cantera and E. García Gómez. The first is from a poem by Yehudá Halevi, which may be dated round 1100, and it is put into the mouth of a girl whose lover is sick.

> Vayse meu corachón de mib.
> ¿Ya, Rab, si se me tornarád?
> ¡Tan mal meu doler li-l-habib!
> Enfermo yed, ¿cuándo sanarád?
> My heart goes out from me.
> O God, will it ever come back?
> Great is my grief for my lover.
> He is sick — when will he be well?

This *jarcha* was used again with slightly modernized spelling by a Jewish poet at the court of Alfonso el Sabio, Todros Abulafia (b. 1247). The verses I will quote now are likewise from him, but since he drew on earlier Jewish poets for his *jarchas* and the form *mibi* is very ancient, one may take it that this *jarcha* is also eleventh century.

> ¿Qué faré yo o qué serád de mibi?
> Habibi,
> non te tolgas de mibi.

> What shall I do? What will become of me?
> My love,
> do not take yourself from me.

Finally here is a *jarcha* by Yosef the Scribe, which can be dated with certainty to some time before 1042.

> Tant' amáre, tant' amáre,
> habib, tant' amáre,
> enfermaron uelios gaios,
> e dolen tan male.

So much loving, so much loving,
dear, so much loving—
Eyes that were once gay are sickened
and ache with pain.

Let us consider certain points about these poems. First the date. The earliest of these *muwassahas* that can be dated was written before 1042: most of the others belong to the second half of the eleventh century. But the *jarchas* they contain must be earlier. Hebrew *muwassahas* were, as we have said, close imitations of Arabic ones and they took over their *jarchas* from them, just as we have seen that a Jewish poet did from Hebrew poems that had been written more than a century and a half before his time. When, too, we examine Castilian *villancicos* of the late Middle Ages we often find that their *estribillos* are written in what was then an archaic language, and the same may be said of the first verses of some of the Galician *cantigas de amigo*. For this reason, as well as for linguistic ones, we may reasonably suppose that a few of these *jarchas* were composed in the tenth century. They provide the earliest examples known to us of the Mozarabic idiom, which was the dialect into which Latin broke down during the Dark Ages throughout the greater part of the Iberian Peninsula. It has strong affinities with Navarro-Leonese and with Aragonese, but contains a large admixture of Arabic words, some of which were absorbed into what, after the Castilian influence had worked upon it, came to be known as Spanish.

We also notice that in these *muwassahas* the *jarcha* is always introduced at the end of the poem. This suggests an affinity with the envoi or *tornada* of Provençal poetry, though the spirit of this is very different. A somewhat closer parallel is found in the French *chansons de toile*, which were written down in the twelfth century. But, to keep to Spain, we may point to at least one fifteenth-century Castilian *villancico* where a popular verse is brought in at the end of each stanza in much the same way as the *jarcha* of a *muwassaha*. This is the famous *villancico* written by the Marqués de Santillana to his three daughters (it is given in the *Oxford Book of Spanish Verse*), and we may be fairly certain that it had popular models. We have therefore to recognize that there were, probably from a very early time, two different kinds of poem, called *zéjels* and *muwassahas*, in one of which the theme-stanza at the beginning of the poem was the controlling feature and in the other the *jarcha* which came with, as we are told, a violent, culminating effect at the end. Of these the first kind is likely to be the more primitive, because it is a verse form associated with a choral dance, whereas the second has every appearance of being more artificial. This may be why it was the first form that lived on in Spanish villages through the Middle Ages, to flower in the court poetry of the fifteenth and sixteenth centuries as the *villancico*.

Finally we come to the *jarchas* themselves. As we have said, they are generally put into the mouth of a woman of the lower classes and they are complaints of love. Their being so often written in Romance may be due to the fact that in Moslem Spain at this time Romance was the woman's language and was usually spoken in the home. In their feminine characterization they resemble the Galician *cantigas de amigo* and (to a lesser degree) the earliest Northern French lyrics, the *chansons de toile*. Only they are much earlier. The further we go back in lyric poetry, the closer we seem to draw to a time when the most current sort of love poetry was a feminine affair. Although, in the age at which we catch them, these poems were usually written by men, that should not blind us to the fact that, in their origins, they are a women's poetry. How far we should have to go to find them both composed and sung by women we cannot say. Martial and Juvenal speak of the *Gaditanae puellae* who learned their art at the temple of Marine Venus at Cadiz and were exported to Rome to titillate the rich with their lascivious dances and songs. In the earliest folk-poetry known to us, the Chinese *Book of Odes*, most of the love poems were put into the mouths of women. Perhaps we may venture on the guess that at some early age the men's love poems were courting poems, that is, poems of flattery and praise, while the women's poems expressed a situation of waiting, of longing, of forlorn or unrequited love. If so, then the women's sort of poem would offer greater possibilities of poetic development and a richer emotional field. For this reason, as society grew less tribal and warlike, men would come to feel its attraction to the point of composing poems for women, or put into the mouths of women, themselves. Not till the great reversal of erotic values that expressed itself in Provençal poetry and in the customs of Chivalry could men write love poems that expressed their own subjection and weakness. I offer this hypothesis with due diffidence, because I am fully aware that in every region things must have developed in a somewhat different way.

But to return to the *jarchas*—what strikes us most forcibly about these little three- or four-lined poems is that they are identical in form and style of phrasing not only with the *estribillos* of the fifteenth and sixteenth century *villancicos*, but with many of those little verses known as *coplas* that are sung all over Spain, and particularly in Andalusia, today. (See pages 365-376 for an account of them.) Through nearly a thousand years of Spanish poetry they keep appearing and disappearing from our sight, sometimes forming the kernel for longer poems by literary poets, at other times sinking into the uncharted regions of folk-song. Their persistence and their recurring influence upon cultured poetry are one of the most surprising things in Spanish literature.

ADDITIONAL NOTE TO PAGE 27

An article by S. M. Stern (*Al-Andalus*, vol. xvi, Fasc. 2, 1951) throws new light on the differences between the *muwassaha* and the *zéjel* and obliges me to modify what I have previously written. The *muwassaha*, it seems, has either five or six stanzas, is written in literary Arabic and has for subject-matter the traditional themes of classical Arabic poetry. Only its *jarcha*, or final verse, is in vulgar Arabic or Romance. The *zéjel*, on the other hand, is written in popular Arabic and on light themes and may have any number of stanzas. Another difference is that, whereas the rhyming scheme of the *muwassaha* (to give its simplest form) runs *A A b b b A A c c c A A*, that of the *zéjel* normally runs *A A b b b A c c c A*.

What are we to conclude from this? Both forms seem to be ultimately derived from the same type of folk-song, but they have been modified, probably even before being taken over by the Arabs, to suit the performances of street singers or jongleurs. The *muwassaha* came in *c.* 900, the *zéjel c.* 1100. These dates seem to mark two separate waves of popular influence upon the educated classes, the first taking its models from the performances of Romance-speaking jongleurs, the second from Arabic-speaking ones. In between them lies the influence of Baghdad and of classical Arabic poetry.

I have made another emendation. According to S. M. Stern, the correct name for the theme-stanza is not, as previous Arabic scholars have supposed, the *markaz*, but the *matla*. The *markaz* is identical with the *jarcha* and comes at the end. I have corrected this error in the text and mention it here merely to prevent confusion in the minds of those who may be familiar with the earlier interpretation.

Appendix

A NOTE ON FRANCISCO DE ALDANA

Francisco de Aldana (1537–78) is an interesting poet whose verses have only recently been rediscovered. He came of a family of soldiers from Estremadura, but was brought up at Florence where his father was a captain in the service of the Medici. After a youth spent in the soft hedonistic atmosphere of that city with its cult of poetry and neo-platonism, he went when he was thirty to Flanders in the train of the Duke of Alba. Here his feelings underwent a change. He threw himself with enthusiasm into that sordid and cruel war and seemed to think that he had found a vocation in a soldier's life. But disillusion followed. He was severely wounded, the Spanish armies suffered a defeat and Alba was recalled to Spain. His thoughts then turned to religion—to that same sort of neo-platonic retreat from the world that was the dream of Luis de León. But fate had other things in store for him. He was now in Spain, almost for the first time, and Philip II sent him on a mission to King Sebastian of Portugal to advise him on his projected invasion of Africa. This led to his accompanying him on that disastrous expedition that ended in the annihilation of the Portuguese army and in his own death. His poems were later published by his brother Cosme, but in such a mangled edition that they were little read.

Aldana's work covers a wide range from love poems to poems on war and on religion. He was a very personal poet, at times a very outspoken one, and while he was in Flanders his feelings fluctuated violently between his love of soldiering, of which he gives some vivid descriptions, and his longing to escape from it to the contemplative life of the hermit. This makes him perhaps the most representative poet of his age. One can read with pleasure his sonnets on war, his *Canción* to the crucified Christ, his *Pocos tercetos* and his *Carta para Galiano*, but incomparably his finest poem is the long *Carta para Arias Montano*, composed just before he sailed for Africa. It is a poem in *terza rima* which begins with a very disillusioned account of his own life and goes on to paint a picture of the *patria verdadera* he is seeking. It is written in a lean, spare style that anticipates Quevedo's *Epístolas*, and in spite of a sense of strain in many passages and a certain repetitiousness, it is a fine and moving poem as well as a most original one.

A SHORT BIBLIOGRAPHY

THIS bibliography is intended to help the general reader to find the best available texts of the writers he may wish to read and the most useful books of a critical and biographical nature that have been written upon them. Whenever possible I have listed editions that are still in print and not too expensive. I have omitted books that are of interest only to the specialist.

ABBREVIATIONS

Bibl. Aut. Esp.	Biblioteca de Autores Españoles
Bibl. Contemp.	Biblioteca Contemporánea, Losada, Buenos Aires
Bibl. Sopena	Biblioteca Sopena, Buenos Aires
Clas. Cast.	Clásicos Castellanos
Col. Aus.	Colección Austral, Buenos Aires
Col. Crisol	Colección Crisol, Aguilar, Madrid

As a rule the best edition in which to read the Spanish classics is that of Clásicos Castellanos (Espasa Calpe, Madrid), with its good print, footnotes and excellent introductions, but when these cannot be obtained one of the cheap Argentine editions, Austral (Espasa Calpe, Buenos Aires) or Contemporánea (Losada, Buenos Aires) will be found useful. A new edition published by Aguilar, Madrid, printed on India paper and relatively expensive, offers the complete works of a number of writers: otherwise one has to fall back on the large, unattractive volumes of the Biblioteca de Autores Españoles, published in the last century by Rivadeneyra, but usually kept in print.

GENERAL

A useful general history of Spanish Literature is *Historia de la literatura Española* by Angel Valbuena Prat, 3 vols., 3rd ed., 1950. The best general anthologies are the *Oxford Book of Spanish Verse*, rev. J. B.

Trend, 1949, and *A Critical Anthology of Spanish Verse* by E. Allison Peers, 1948.

For an account of the rise of the various Latin languages of the Peninsula, see *The Spanish Language* by W. J. Entwistle, 1936, and *El Idioma Español en sus primeros tiempos* by R. Menéndez Pidal, Col. Aus.

M. Menéndez Pelayo's *Historia de las ideas estéticas en España*, 1882–1891, republished in 5 vols. in 1940, is a useful guide to the development of literary taste and dogma.

CHAPTER I

The best edition of Prudentius is in the *Édition 'Les Belles Lettres'* with a French translation opposite the Latin. A Loeb edition has also begun to appear. *Passions des Martyres* by H. Delehaye, Paris, 1921, throws light on the cult of the martyrs, and Gaston Boissier's *Fin du paganisme*, 2 vols., Paris, 1891, gives the general background. See also P. de Labriolle, *Histoire de la Littérature Latine-Chrétienne*, Paris, 1924, which ends in the sixth century.

For Eugenius and the Mozarabic hymns see F. J. E. Raby, *History of Secular Latin Poetry in the Middle Ages*, 2 vols., 1934, and *History of Christian Latin Poetry*, 1927. For Martial, I recommend Gaston Boissier's essay, 'The Poet Martial', contained in *Tacitus and other Roman Studies*, London, 1906.

CHAPTER II

The most discriminating writer on Spanish-Arabic poetry is Emilio García Gómez, whose two principal works, *Poemas Arábigoandaluces*, 1930, and *Cinco Poetas Musulmanes*, 1935, are in Col. Aus. Numerous articles by him have also come out in the review *Al-Andalus*, published twice yearly in Madrid, of which he is director. Among these I would single out 'Un eclipse de la poesía en Sevilla', on the Almoravide epoch, which appeared in 1945. R. Menéndez Pidal's essay on the connection between popular Arabic and popular Castilian poetry, entitled *Poesía Arabe y poesía Europea*, 1938, Col. Aus., is also extremely suggestive. See too A. R. Nykl's anthology, *Hispano-Arabic Poetry*, Baltimore, 1946: Henri Pérès, *La poésie andalouse en arabe classique au XIième siècle*, Paris, 1937, and Émile Dermenghem, 'Thèmes de la poésie amoureuse' in *Le génie d'oc*, Cahiers du Sud, Paris, 1943.

473

Ibn Hazm's treatise on love has been translated by A. R. Nykl under the title of *The Dove's Neck-Ring*, Paris, 1931. A Spanish translation by E. García Gómez entitled *El collar de la paloma* came out in 1952 with a good introduction. Ibn Guzmán's *Cancionero* has been published by A. R. Nykl with the Arabic text in Roman characters and a Spanish translation of some of the songs on another page, Madrid, 1933. Another translation by G. S. Colin and E. Lévi-Provençal will appear shortly. See too an essay by S. M. Stern in *Al-Andalus*, 1951, and a review by E. García Gómez. The latter has also published an essay on Ibn Guzmán in *Cinco Poetas Musulmanes*, Col. Aus., 1945, which largely supersedes Julián Ribera's study, given in his *Discurso de Recepción de la Real Academia Española* in 1912, which first drew attention to this poet. The difficult question of the origins of Arabic and Spanish popular poetry is developing steadily as the texts are more closely studied, and the recent discovery by S. M. Stern of eleventh-century Spanish verses embedded in Hebrew poems (*Al-Andalus*, 1948) has given it a new impetus. See on this E. García Gómez's articles in *Al-Andalus*, 1949 and 1950, and an essay by Dámaso Alonso in the *Revista de Filología Española*, Madrid, 1949. Then, for 24 new *jarchas* in Romance derived from Arabic *muwassahas* see E. García Gómez's article in *Al-Andalus*, vol. XVII, Fasc. 1, 1952.

On Hebrew religious poetry there is a work of the first order, *La Poesía Sagrada Hebráico-española* by José Millás Vallicrosa, 2nd ed., Madrid, 1948.

To get the general background of this period one may read R. Dozy's *Spanish Islam*, first published in 1861 and translated into English in 1913—a book which is still a classic in spite of its over-romantic colouring. More substantial is *La España Musulmana* by C. Sánchez-Albornoz, 2 vols., Buenos Aires, 1946. This is a collection of contemporary extracts from Latin and Arabic sources, some of which throw light on Spanish-Arabic literature. *España en su Historia* by Américo Castro, Buenos Aires, 1948, is an important book on the cultural formation of Spain which gives full weight to the Arabic and Jewish influences.

GENERAL WORKS ON THE MIDDLE AGES

The *opus magnum* on Spanish poetry down to the year 1542 is Menéndez Pelayo's *Antología de Poetas Líricos Castellanos*, left uncompleted on the author's death in 1912. The latest edition of 1944 is in 10 vols. Of these the first three contain critical and biographical studies of the poets; vols. IV and V give an anthology of them; vols. VI and VII discuss the anonymous *romances*; vols. VIII and IX give their texts, and vol. X is devoted to Juan Boscán and to the indexes.

This work, magnificent though it is, needs to be supplemented by R. Menéndez Pidal's studies of popular poetry, which have altered our way of looking at Spanish literature. These studies comprise 'La primitiva poesía lírica española', 1919, republished in *Estudios Literarios*, Col. Aus.; 'Poesía popular y tradicional', 1922, republished in *El Romancero*, ed. Paez, Madrid, 1927; *Poesía juglaresca y juglares*, 1924, republished under the same title but without notes or appendices in Col. Aus.; *Poesía Arabe y poesía Europea*, 1938, also republished in Col. Aus.; and *De primitiva lírica española y antigua épica*, Col. Aus., 1951. Another important aid to the study of medieval Spanish poetry is *La versificación irregular en la poesía castellana* by P. Henríquez Ureña, Madrid, 1920.

A particularly valuable book is the anthology entitled *Poesía de la Edad Media y poesía de tipo tradicional*, selected by Dámaso Alonso and published in Buenos Aires in 1942. It contains 430 pages of lyrical poetry and 106 of ballads, and is especially rich in the *villancicos* found in the song books and in plays down to the time of Lope de Vega. I would also recommend *The Medieval Latin and Romance Lyric* by F. Brittain, Cambridge, 1937. This is an anthology of early medieval poetry in six languages with an admirable introduction, which assists one to study the poetry of this international age in a comparative way.

CHAPTER III

The *Poema de Mio Cid* is best read in the Clas. Cast. edition, with a preface and notes by Menéndez Pidal. His *España del Cid*, 2 vols., 1929 (4th revised ed., 1947), published in English in one vol. as *The Cid and his Spain*, London, 1934, gives the historical background. Dámaso Alonso's essay, 'Estilo y creación en el poema del Cid', published in *Ensayos sobre Poesía Española*, Revista de Occidente, Buenos Aires, 1944, gives a critical appreciation. What I have said of the origins of the *Chanson de Roland* is based chiefly on J. Bédier's *Légendes Épiques*, 1926. Those who wish to explore further the subject of Spanish epic poetry should read R. Menéndez Pidal, *Reliquias de la Poesía Epica Española*, 1951.

A good selection of Galician-Portuguese poetry will be found in the *Oxford Book of Portuguese Verse*, ed. Aubrey Bell, 1925. Only scholars will wish to consult the three bulky *Cancioneiros* from which it is taken, but there is a complete edition of the *Cantigas de amigo* in 3 vols., with a critical introduction by J. J. Nunes, Coimbra, 1916-28. See too *Cantigas d'el-Rei D. Dinis*, 1942, with notes and glossary, Livraria Clássica Editora, Lisbon.

The most authoritative writer on this poetry is M. Rodrigues Lapa: *Das origens da poesia lírica em Portugal na Idade-Média*, Lisbon, 1929 and *Lições de Literatura Portuguesa. Época Medieval*, Coimbra, 1942. Menéndez Pidal's *Poesía juglaresca y juglares*, Col. Aus., also covers this field and a good summary will be found in Aubrey Bell's *Portuguese Literature*, Oxford, 1922.

The *Cantigas de Santa Maria* by Alfonso X of Castile were published in an illustrated *édition de luxe* by the Academia Española in 1889. Eleven of these poems are included in the *Oxford Book of Portuguese Verse* and there is a complete edition, ed. M. Rodrigues Lapa, Lisbon, 1933. A facsimile edition of the *codice princeps* in several volumes with the music is now in course of publication in Madrid. For a general study of the literary work of this king see J. B. Trend, *Alfonso the Sage and other essays*, London, 1926.

Gonzalo de Berceo's complete works are in Bibl. Aut. Esp. *Los Milagros de Nuestra Señora* are in Clas. Cast. with a good introduction. All his other poems are in the Clásicos Bouret, Paris, with a glossary. *Los Milagros, Sancto Domingo* and *Sancta Oria* occupy 2 vols. in Col. Aus. On his poetry see a pamphlet by J. B. Trend, *Berceo*, Cambridge, 1952.

Selections from the *Libro de Apolonio* and the *Libro de Alexandre* are given in Dámaso Alonso's medieval anthology. The full text is in Bibl. Aut. Esp., vol. LVII. A good collection of the anonymous poetry of this century, but excluding the above mentioned *Libros*, is given in the pocket Saturnino Calleja edition of the *Poema de Mio Cid*; this includes the oldest of Spanish dramatic pieces, the *Auto de los Reyes Magos*. See too Menéndez Pidal, *Tres poetas primitivos*, Col. Aus.

For a discussion of the versification of this period, see Menéndez Pelayo, *Antología de Poetas Líricos*, vol. I, and P. Henríquez Ureña, *La versificación irregular en la poesía castellana*, Madrid, 1920.

CHAPTER IV

The Archpriest of Hita should be read in Clas. Cast., 2 vols. For further information on him consult Menéndez Pelayo, *Antología de Poetas Líricos*, vol. I, and Menéndez Pidal's valuable essay on him, contained in *Poesía Arabe y poesía Europea*, Col. Aus.

Bibliography

CHAPTER V

The poets of this age are most easily studied in Menéndez Pelayo, *Antología de Poetas Líricos*, vols. I and II for information and vols. IV and V for the text. (Vol. II has been published in Col. Aus. with the title of *Poetas de la Corte de Don Juan II.*) R. Foulché-Delbosc's *Cancionero Castellano del siglo XV*, 2 vols., 1912-15, gives a larger selection. See also Pierre le Gentil, *La poésie lyrique espagnole et portugaise à la fin du moyen âge*, Rennes, 1949. Juan de Mena's principal poem, *El Laberinto de Fortuna*, is in Clas. Cast. See on him a large work by María Rosa Lida de Malkiel: *Juan de Mena, poeta del prerenacimiento español*, Mexico, 1950.

There is no satisfactory edition of the lyric poetry of the Marqués de Santillana. The Clas. Cast. edition omits two of the best *serranillas* and the attractive Dolphin Bookshop edition, ed. J. B. Trend, *Marqués de Santillana, Prose and Verse*, Oxford, 1940, omits all the *canciones* and *decires*, though it gives some of his sonnets, his very interesting *prohemios* or introductions, and the collection he made of *refranes* or proverbs. His complete poetical works are in Foulché-Delbosc's *Cancionero*. For Jorge Manrique see P. Salinas, *Jorge Manrique o tradición y originalidad*, Buenos Aires, 1947.

For Sem Tob see *Santob de Carrion, Proverbios morales*, ed. I. González Llubera, Cambridge, 1947. Pero López de Ayala's poem, *Rimado de Palacio*, is in Bibl. Aut. Esp., vol. LVII. A complete edition of his poetry was published in 1920 by the Hispanic Society of America, New York.

The Chronicles of the Castilian kings up to the Reyes Católicos are in Bibl. Aut. Esp., vols. LXVI, LXVIII and LXX. They include the Chronicles of Don Pedro and Don Enrique by Pero López de Ayala. Prosper Mérimée's admirable *Histoire de Don Pèdre I^{ier}*, Paris, 1848, is mainly founded on them. Don Juan Manuel's *Conde Lucanor* is in Clas. Cast. So are Pérez de Guzmán's *Generaciones y Semblanzas* and Hernando del Pulgar's *Claros varones de Castilla*.

E. Allison Peers has translated five of the books of Ramon Llull: *Blanquerna, The Book of the Beasts, The Book of the Lover and the Beloved, The Art of Contemplation* and *The Tree of Love*, and has also written his life, *Ramon Llull: a biography*, 1929. The Catalan texts of three of Llull's works are in the edition Els Nostres Clàssics, Barcelona.

The critical edition of Auziàs March, ed. Amadée Pagès, a large work in 2 vols., Barcelona, 1912 and 1914, is the only one in which

477

the text is not hopelessly corrupt. See too Pagès, *Commentaire des Poésies d'Auziàs March*, Paris, 1925.

Muntaner's *Chronicle* has been translated into English, 2 vols., 1920-1. For Jaume Roig, *Llibre de les dones*, and Bernat Metge, *Lo Somni*, see Els Nostres Clàssics edition, Barcelona. Jordi de Sant Jordi's poetry has not been reprinted since 1902. The best anthology of Catalan poetry is that published by the Dolphin Book Co., Oxford, ed. Joan Triadú, 1951. The best history of Catalan literature is that of Jordi Rubió, contained in *Historia General de las Literaturas Hispánicas*, published under the direction of G. Díaz-Plaja. Only vol. I has appeared so far (Barcelona, 1949), but vol. II is due to come out shortly.

CHAPTER VI

The Court poets of this age are best read and studied in Menéndez Pelayo, *Antología de Poetas Líricos*, vols III and V. Fray Ambrosio Montesino is well represented.

A good selection of the anonymous *villancicos* is to be found in Dámaso Alonso's anthology, *Poesía de la Edad Media*. For further examples see Ansejo Barbieri, *Cancionero musical de los siglos XV y XVI*, Madrid, 1890 (a book hard to obtain), and Santiago Magariños, *Canciones populares de la Edad de Oro*, Barcelona, 1944. The latter contains a large collection of songs from seventeenth-century plays. The best of the song-books to have been republished in recent times is the short *Cancionero de Uppsala*, ed. R. Mitjana, under the title of *Cincuenta y cuatro canciones Españolas del siglo XVI*, Uppsala, 1909, and republished with its musical settings in Mexico, 1944.

The best edition in which to read the *romances* is Menéndez Pelayo, *Antología de Poetas Líricos*, vols. VIII and IX. This consists of the collection made by F. J. Wolf and C. Hofmann, first published in Berlin in 1856 under the title of *Primavera y Flor de Romances*, followed (vol. IX) by an appendix containing additional material. The *Romancero General* by Agustín Durán, 2 vols., Bibl. Aut. Esp., 1877 and 1882, offers a much larger collection, partly because it includes *romances* by known poets such as Lope de Vega and Góngora down to 1700. A good short edition is *Spanish Ballads*, chosen by Guy le Strange, Cambridge, 1920. Another is *Flor Nueva de Romances Viejos*, selected by Menéndez Pidal, 1938, Col. Aus. This contains some fine ballads not published elsewhere, and useful notes. See too J. M. de Cossío, *Romances de tradición oral*, Col. Aus.

Bibliography

A full discussion of the romances will be found in vols. vi and vii of Menéndez Pelayo, *Antología de Poetas Líricos*, but this needs to be supplemented by Menéndez Pidal's volume, *El Romancero*, which contains in the essay 'Poesía popular y tradicional' a most important contribution not only to the study of Spanish *romances*, but to that of ballads in general. One may also consult W. J. Entwistle, *European Balladry*, 1939.

La Celestina is best read in Clas. Cast., 2 vols. An admirable translation by James Mabbe came out in 1631 and was republished in 1923 in the Broadway Translations. See too Ramiro de Maetzu, *Don Quijote, Don Juan y la Celestina*, Col. Aus., and Menéndez Pelayo, *La Celestina*, Col. Aus.

There is a large collection of Juan del Encina's poems and eclogues in Menéndez Pelayo, *Antología de Poetas Líricos*, vol. v. A facsimile of the 1514 edition of *Farsas y Eglogas* by Lucas Fernández was published by the Academia Española in 1929. It includes the *Auto de la Pasión*. For Torres Naharro, see *Propalladia and other works...*, 2 vols., Bryn Mawr, Pennsylvania, 1943-6. See too *Colección de Autos, Farsas y Coloquios del siglo XVI*, 4 vols., ed. Leo Rouanet, and published by the Hispanic Society of America, Macon, 1901-2.

Gil Vicente's complete works may be read in *Obras Completas*, 6 vols., in the *Collecção de Clássicos Sá da Costa*, Lisbon, ed. with introduction and notes by Marques Braga. A new edition, reproducing the text of the first edition of 1562, was prepared at Coimbra, but only the first volume, containing 15 *autos* and two other pieces with notes by Braga, has yet come out: *Obras Completas, I, Obras de Devaçam*, 1933. Besides this there are *Four Plays by Gil Vicente*, Cambridge, 1920, with an introduction by Aubrey Bell and an English verse translation facing the text, and *Teatro y Poesía*, giving Spanish texts only, Col. Crisol. Dámaso Alonso brought out an admirable edition of the *Tragicomedia de Don Duardos* with notes and introduction in 1942. For the lyrics from his plays see *Líricas de Gil Vicente*, Lisbon, 1943 and *Poesías de Gil Vicente*, ed. Dámaso Alonso, Madrid, 1934.

CHAPTER VII

For Boscán and the Italian hendecasyllable, see Menéndez Pelayo, *Antología de Poetas Líricos*, vol. x. Garcilaso de la Vega is best read in Clas. Cast. There is a study of his life and work by H. Keniston, Hispanic Society of America, New York, 1922. See also Rafael Lapesa, *La trayectoria poética de Garcilaso*, 1948.

Luis de León's poetry may be read either in Col. Crisol, or else in *Poesías Originales de Luis de León*, ed. J. R. Sánchez, 2nd ed., Madrid, 1942. His life has been written by Aubrey Bell, Oxford, 1925. San Juan de la Cruz's complete works are most easily read in the Editorial Seneca edition, one vol., Mexico, 1942. The verse, with extracts from the prose, is in Col. Aus. For an analysis of his poetry see Dámaso Alonso, *La poesía de San Juan de la Cruz*, 1942, and two studies by myself in *Horizon*, May and June, 1947. The first of these contains an account of his life. The poems of Fernando de Herrera published by himself are in Clas. Cast. Others left in MSS. have been published by J. M. Blecua, *Rimas inéditas*, 1948. A complete edition of Herrera by J. M. Blecua is appearing shortly. Those of Baltasar del Alcázar, edited by Rodríguez Marín, were published in Madrid in 1910. They are also in Bibl. Aut. Esp., vols. XXXII and XLII. Cristóbal de Castillejo's poetry is in Clas. Cast., 4 vols., and also in Bibl. Aut. Esp., vol. XXXII.

The prose works of this century are either in Clas. Cast. or in Bibl. Aut. Esp. The best edition of Santa Teresa is that of P. Silverio de Santa Teresa, 9 vols., Burgos, 1922, but her complete works are also in the Aguilar edition, Madrid. Isolated books are in Clas. Cast. and Col. Aus. There is a complete translation of her work by E. Allison Peers and her life has been written by, among other people, Mrs Cunninghame Graham. There is an interesting study of *Guzmán de Alfarache* by E. Moreno Báez, Madrid, 1948.

Here are a few outstanding translations:

Amadis of Gaul, trans. Robert Southey, 1803, republ. 1872.

The Dial of Princes, by Antonio de Guevara, trans. Sir Thomas North, 1557, republ. in selections, London, 1919.

Lazarillo de Tormes, trans. David Rowland of Anglesey, 1576, republ. Oxford, 1924.

Guzmán de Alfarache, trans. James Mabbe, 1622, and into French by Le Sage. Mabbe's translation has been reprinted in the Tudor Translations, 4 vols., London, New York, 1924.

The Discovery and Conquest of New Spain, by Bernal Díaz del Castillo, trans. A. P. Maudslay, Broadway Travellers, 1928.

There is no translation of *Tirant lo Blanc* into English. A French translation came out *c.* 1737 and was republished in 1775. The Catalan text in 5 vols. may be read in the Els Nostres Clàssics edition, Barcelona.

Bibliography

CHAPTER VIII

The best complete edition of Cervantes is that of R. Schevill and A. Bonilla, 19 vols., Madrid, 1914-41. There is also an edition in one vol. by Aguilar, Madrid. But *Don Quijote* and the *Novelas exemplares* are most easily read in Clas. Cast. The best short introduction to him is *Cervantes* by W. J. Entwistle, Oxford, 1940: a good biography is that by J. Fitzmaurice-Kelly, Oxford, 1917. Menéndez Pidal, *De Cervantes y Lope de Vega*, Col. Aus., throws light on certain questions and S. de Madariaga, *Don Quixote*, London, 1934, offers illuminating criticism. See too Américo Castro, *El Pensamiento de Cervantes*, 1925, and J. Casalduero, *Sentido y forma de las Novelas Ejemplares*, 1946: *Sentido y forma del Quijote*, 1949.

CHAPTER IX

For the Spanish stage see: J. P. W. Crawford, *Spanish Drama before Lope de Vega*, Philadelphia, London, 1937; H. A. Rennert, *The Spanish Stage in the time of Lope de Vega*, Hispanic Society of America, New York, 1909; A. Morel-Fatio, *La Comédie espagnole du xviiième siècle*, Paris, 1885; H. J. Chaytor, *Dramatic Theory in Spain*, Cambridge, 1925.

There is a selection of Lope de Rueda's short dramatic pieces both in Clas. Cast. and in Col. Aus., as well as a complete edition by the Academia Española, 2 vols., 1908, and an edition of the *pasos* in Col. Crisol.

Lope de Vega's complete works have appeared in the vast edition of the Academia Española, containing some 500 plays and *autos*, preceded by a biography and containing critical introductions to vols. ii-xiii by Menéndez Pelayo. There is also a large selection in 2 vols. in the Aguilar edition. An older collection is that of the Bibl. Aut. Esp. in 4 vols., containing some 120 plays. Selected plays have also come out in Clas. Cast. and Col. Aus., and there is an edition in 4 vols. published by Garnier, Paris. Separate plays, among them *Peribáñez*, have come out in the *Teatro Antiguo Español* series with admirable introductions by José F. Montesinos. The lyric poems are in Clas. Cast., 2 vols, and in Col. Aus. For his biography see H. Rennert and A. Castro, *Vida de Lope de Vega*, 1919.

Of the many books on his writings I would recommend J. Fitzmaurice-Kelly, *Lope de Vega and Spanish Drama*, 1902; Menéndez Pidal, *De Cervantes y Lope de Vega*, Col. Aus.; Karl Vossler, *Lope de Vega y su tiempo*, Madrid, 1940 and, especially, José F. Montesinos, *Estudios sobre*

Lope, Mexico, 1951. For further information see Menéndez Pelayo, *Estudios sobre el Teatro de Lope de Vega*, 6 vols., 1949.

The complete works of Tirso de Molina are coming out for the first time in the Aguilar edition. The Bibl. Aut. Esp. contains 36 of his *comedias*, but none of his religious plays. Select plays are to be found in Clas. Cast., Col. Aus. and Bibl. Sopena. For an appreciation of Tirso's *Don Juan*, see Ramiro de Maetzu, *Don Quijote, Don Juan y la Celestina*, Col. Aus., and *Tirso de Molina, Studies in Dramatic Realism*, by I. L. McClelland, Liverpool, 1948.

The complete works of Ruiz de Alarcón are in Bibl. Aut. Esp., and three of his plays are in Clas. Cast. and Col. Aus. Mira de Amescua may be read in Clas. Cast., 2 vols. In the same edition there are two plays by Vélez de Guevara. The other dramatists must be read in Bibl. Aut. Esp., vols. LXIII and LXV. There is a collection of short dramatic pieces, ed. E. Cotarelo y Mori, entitled *Colección de Entremeses, Loas, Bailes, Jácaras y Mojigangas desde fines del siglo XVI a mediados del XVIII*, 2 vols., Madrid, 1911.

CHAPTER X

The standard edition of Góngora, from which all other editions derive, is *Obras Poéticas*, ed. R. Foulché-Delbosc, 3 vols., Hispanic Society of America, New York, 1921. As this is out of print, one must choose between the Losada edition in 2 vols., and the Aguilar edition, which includes his letters, in one. Two attractive editions are *Romances de Góngora*, ed. J. M. de Cossío, 1927, and *Soledades de Góngora*, ed. Dámaso Alonso, 1927, reprinted 1935. Both were published by the Revista de Occidente, Madrid, and the latter volume contains a prose translation which is very helpful. There is also a selection of Góngora in Col. Aus., and another made by the poet Alberti in the Edición Pleamar, Buenos Aires. There is an English translation of the *Soledades* by E. M. Wilson, Cambridge, 1931, which will be found useful in interpreting the Spanish.

Dámaso Alonso's three essays on Góngora in *Ensayos sobre Poesía Española*, Revista de Occidente, Buenos Aires, 1944, are very valuable. There is a short but suggestive essay in *La Poesía de la Soledad en España* by Karl Vossler, Editorial Losada, 1946. The only biography of Góngora is that by Miguel Artigas, Madrid, 1925. See too E. Churton, *Góngora: A Historical and Critical Essay on the Times of Philip III and IV*, 2 vols., London, 1862.

Bibliography

There is a short but interesting anthology of the poets who followed Góngora entitled *Antología poética en honor de Góngora*, ed. Gerardo Diego, Revista de Occidente, 1927. A selection from Pedro Espinosa's famous anthology, *Flores de poetas ilustres de España* (1605), is contained in Bibl. Aut. Esp., vol. XLII. His works were edited by Rodríguez Marín in 2 vols., Madrid, 1907-9. Francisco de Rioja's poems are in Bibl. Aut. Esp., vol. XXXII. An edition of Juan de Tarsis, Conde de Villamediana, came out in Madrid in 1944; Juan de Jáuregui's *Orfeo* in 1948. Josef de Valdivielso's shorter poems appeared in 1880, ed. P. Mir, under the title of *Romancero Espiritual*. His *autos* are in Bibl. Aut. Esp., vol. LVIII. For the popular religious poetry of this and the previous century, see Bibl. Aut. Esp., vol. XXXV.

For studies of Francisco de Rioja and Pedro Espinosa, see two essays by Audrey Lumsden in *Spanish Golden Age Poetry and Drama*, II, Institute of Hispanic Studies, Liverpool, 1946. There is a biography of Pedro Espinosa by Rodríguez Marín, Madrid, 1907.

CHAPTER XI

The complete works of Quevedo are published in *Obras Completas*, ed. L. Astrana Marín, 2 vols. (4000 pp.), Madrid, 1932. His prose works are more easily read in Clas. Cast.; *Los Sueños*, 2 vols.; *El Buscón*, 1 vol., *Obras satíricas y festivas*, 1 vol. *La Política de Dios* is in Col. Aus., and so is an anthology of his poetry.

On Quevedo's life and background one may read E. Mérimée, *Essai sur la vie et les œuvres de don Francisco de Quevedo*, Paris, 1886, and René Bouvier, *L'Espagne de Quevedo*, Paris, 1936. There is a rather free translation of Quevedo's satirical works, made by various seventeenth and eighteenth century writers and edited by Charles Duff, in the Broadway Translations.

Gracián's complete works have come out in the Aguilar edition, one vol., 1944. There is a magnificent edition of *El Criticón* in 3 vols., ed. M. Romera-Navarro, Philadelphia, London, 1938-40. *El Criticón* and three of his shorter works are in Col. Aus. There is no modern English translation.

CHAPTER XII

The complete edition of Calderon's *Comedias* is contained in 4 vols. of Bibl. Aut. Esp. The last complete edition of the *Autos Sacramentales* came out in 6 vols. in 1759-60. There is a complete edition of his

Dramas, ed. Astrana Marín, in Aguilar, to be followed shortly by a volume of *Comedias* and another of *Autos Sacramentales*. There are also 2 vols. of *autos* and 1 vol. of *comedias* in Clas. Cast. Copies of *Teatro Selecto de Calderón*, 4 vols., Madrid, 1827, and of London and Paris editions of the same period, may often be picked up second-hand.

There are two excellent recent studies on Calderon's work: *The Allegorical Drama of Calderon*, by A. A. Parker, Dolphin Book Co., Oxford, 1943, dealing with the *autos*: and an essay in the *Modern Language Review*, vol. XXXI, 1936, by E. M. Wilson, dealing with his imagery. See also: *Calderón, su personalidad, su arte dramático, su estilo y sus obras*, by A. Valbuena Prat, Madrid, 1941; 'Three Studies in Golden Age Drama', by Kathleen Gouldson, in *Spanish Golden Age Poetry and Drama*, 1, Institute of Hispanic Studies, Liverpool, 1946; *Ensayo sobre la vida y obras de D. Pedro Calderón*, by E. Cotarelo y Mori, Madrid, 1924, and *Historia de la Zarzuela*, vol. 1, 1934, by the same author. For a different view of Calderon's tragedies on jealousy see E. M. Wilson, *La discreción de don Lope de Almeida* in *Clavileño*, May-June, 1951.

Rojas Zorrilla is found complete in Bibl. Aut. Esp., but his two best plays are in Clas. Cast. This is also the case with Moreto. Bances Candamo's *Obras Lyricas* were republished in 1949. There is no modern edition of his plays.

CHAPTER XIII

Feijóo may be read in selections in Bibl. Aut. Esp. and in Clas. Cast. The only edition of Luzán since 1789 is that by J. Cano, Toronto, 1928. Torres Villarroel is in Clas. Cast. Padre Isla is in Bibl. Aut. Esp.

The complete works of Leandro Fernández de Moratín came out in 4 vols. in 1830-1. His plays are in one vol. in Col. Crisol. His *Obras póstumas* came out in 3 vols. in 1867-8. They include a biography by M. Silvela.

Ramón de la Cruz's *Sainetes* are in Col. Crisol. A selection of Meléndez Valdés' poetry is in Clas. Cast.

CHAPTER XIV

Espronceda's complete poetical works are in Bibl. Sopena and Aguilar. There is also a selection in Clas. Cast., together with two of his plays. Selections of the poetry of the Duque de Rivas, Zorrilla and Campoamor will be found in Clas. Cast. and in Col. Aus. The complete works of these three are in Aguilar.

For both the prose and poetry of this period, see *The Romantics of Spain* by E. Piñeyro, translated by E. Allison Peers, 1934. A fuller work is *A History of the Romantic Movement in Spain* by E. Allison Peers, 2 vols., Cambridge, 1940. See too G. Díaz-Plaja, *Romanticismo Español*, 1936.

Bécquer's complete works, both verse and prose, are in the Aguilar edition. His poems with some of his prose *Rimas y Leyendas*, are in Col. Aus. There is a good discussion of his poetry by Dámaso Alonso in *Ensayos sobre Poesía Española*, Revista de Occidente, Buenos Aires, 1944.

The complete works of Rosalía Castro, verse and prose, with a biography by Garcia Marti, are in the Aguilar edition. It contains a glossary. There is also a good selection in Col. Aus. Pondal's verse has not been republished since his death. There is a selection of Gabriel y Galán in Col. Aus. and his complete works are in Bibl. Sopena and in Aguilar.

The principal collection of Spanish *coplas* is that brought out by Rodríguez Marín, *Cantos populares españoles*, 5 vols., Seville, 1882-3 and since reprinted. The various collections made by G. M. Vergara and Dámaso Ledesma of Castilian *cantares* or *coplas* have more folk-loric than literary merit. The *Cancionero musical de la lírica Asturiana* by E. Martínez Torner, Madrid, 1920, contains some fine poetry, but is difficult to read because this is printed with the music. Various other short collections by E. M. Torner, covering every region of Spain, allow the verse to be easily read: *Cuarenta canciones españolas*, Madrid, 1924; *Cancionero musical*, Bibl. del Estudiante, Madrid; *Canción tradicional española*, Madrid, 1931; *Cancionero musical español*, London, 1948. For Galician *coplas*, see J. Pérez Ballesteros, *Cancionero popular gallego*, 2 vols., Buenos Aires, 1942.

For collections of popular poetry in earlier centuries, see the bibliography to chapter VI. The standard work on popular song music, in which the words are printed with the music, is F. Pedrell, *Cancionero musical popular español*, 4 vols., 1918-22.

An essay on the poetry of the *copla* will be found in S. de Madariaga, *Shelley and Calderon and other essays*, London, 1920. See too, on the origins of this poetry, A. González Palencia and E. Mele, *La Maya*, Madrid, 1944.

Bibliography

Chapter XV

The best of Larra's articles are in 3 vols. in Clas. Cast. Mesonero Romanos and Estébanez Calderón are in Col. Aus.; so are the two best novels of Fernán Caballero.

Of the six novels by Juan Valera which I have mentioned, five are in Bibl. Sopena. For *Las ilusiones del Doctor Faustino* one must consult on. of the early editions, or else the large Aguilar edition of Valera's complete works in 3 vols. Translations of *Pepita Jiménez, Doña Luz* and *El Comendador Mendoza* appeared in New York and London in 1891-3 under the same titles.

The *Episodios Nacionales* of Pérez Galdós are published in 23 vols., Madrid, and also in Aguilar. All his novels of contemporary life are in Bibl. Contemp. For a good account of his life and work, see Joaquín Casalduero, *Vida y obra de Galdos*, 1943, in the same edition.

The novels of Pereda and of P. A. de Alarcón are in both Bibl. Sopena and Col. Aus. *Los Pazos de Ulloa*, by the Condesa de Pardo Bazán is in Col. Crisol. *La Regenta* by Leopoldo Alas has been republished in Buenos Aires, 1946. The best novels of Palacio Valdés are in Col. Aus.

All the novels of Blasco Ibáñez which I have mentioned are in Col. Aus., except *Flor de Mayo*, which has not been reprinted except in his complete works, 3 vols., Aguilar edition. On his life, see C. Pitollet, 1921 and R. Martínez de la Riva, 1929. *La Barraca, Flor de Mayo* and *Cañas y Barro* were translated as *The Cabin, Mayflower* and *Reeds and Mud*, London, 1919, 1922 and 1928.

There is a complete edition of Menéndez Pelayo's work in 49 vols. Madrid, 1940-5.

Chapter XVI

Ganivet's *Idearium español* is in Col. Aus. So are most of Ortega y Gasset's books. Unamuno's *Ensayos* are best read in the attractive edition of the Residencia de Estudiantes in which they first appeared in 7 vols. in 1916–18. If this is unobtainable, they may be read in Aguilar. His other books, including a selection of his poems, have been republished in Col. Aus. On his philosophy see Julián Marías, *Miguel de Unamuno*, Col. Aus.

Rubén Darío's poems have been published in 6 vols. in Col. Aus. The best are *Prosas profanas, Cantos de vida y esperanza, Poema del otoño* and *El canto errante*. His *Poesías Completas* are in Aguilar. On his work there is Pedro Salinas' *La poesía de Rubén Darío*, Buenos Aires, 1948.

The most attractive edition in which to read Antonio Machado is that of Espasa Calpe: *Poesías completas*, Madrid, 1936. This includes two chapters of criticism taken from his two prose works (see below), but not his war poems. The latter are contained in the Bibl. Contemp. edition of 1943, which contains all his verse but omits the prose. Bibl. Contemp. also publishes his prose works, *Abel Martín*, 1 vol. and *Juan de Mairena*, 2 vols. There is further a complete edition of prose and verse printed on India paper, Mexico, 1940. There is a selection of the poetry of his brother, Manuel Machado, in Col. Aus.

The bibliography of Juan Ramón Jiménez is complicated. To compress it, *Segunda Antolojía poética*, first published in 1922 and reprinted in Bibl. Contemp., contains the final versions of what he regarded as his best poetry between 1898 and 1918. Since then have appeared *Poesía* and *Belleza*, both in Bibl. Contemp., containing his verse written between 1918 and 1923, *La estación total, con las Canciones de la nueva luz* (1923-1936), Editorial Losada. The Dolphin Book Co. has brought out an edition of fifty of Jiménez's poems, with translations by J. B. Trend opposite the text and a bibliography, Oxford, 1950. There is an interesting discussion of his work by the poet, E. Díez Canedo, *Juan Ramón Jiménez y su obra*, Mexico, 1944.

Moreno Villa's poetry has come out in *La música que llevaba*. *Antología poética* (1913-1947), Buenos Aires, 1949. There is a selection of it in the excellent anthology made by Pedro Salinas with English translations by Eleanor Turnbull opposite: *Contemporary Spanish Poetry*, Baltimore, 1945. See, too, for all these poets Gerardo Diego's excellent anthology, *Poesía Española*, Madrid, 1934.

There is a selection of Gómez de la Serna's *Greguerías* in Col. Aus. and a complete collection in *Greguerías Completas*, Barcelona, 1947. Most of Valle-Inclán's books are either in Col. Aus. or in Bibl. Contemp. There is a selection of his poetry in Col. Aus., which also publishes a study of his work and character by Gómez de la Serna.

Some sixteen of Baroja's novels are in Col. Aus. The complete edition of S. and J. Álvarez Quintero's plays is in 6 vols., Madrid, 1947-9. Four of them are in Col. Aus. and two in Bibl. Contemp. There are fourteen plays by Benavente in Col. Aus., and ten by Grau in Bibl. Contemp. Three by Martínez Sierra are in the Col. Crisol, Madrid.

Pérez de Ayala's novels and 'Azorín's' essays are in either Col. Aus. or Bibl. Contemp. *El Conde-Duque de Olivares* by G. Marañón is in

Bibliography

Col. Aus. Juan Belmonte's autobiography (out of print in Spanish) was translated into English by Leslie Charteris as *The autobiography of a matador*, London, 1937.

For an excellent critical study of the principal writers covered by this chapter see César Barja, *Libros y autores contemporáneos*, Madrid, 1935. It deals with Ganivet, Unamuno, Ortega y Gasset, 'Azorín', Baroja, Valle-Inclán, A. Machado, Pérez de Ayala.

Chapter XVII

On the character of Spanish literature as a whole it is difficult to quote precise works, because most writing on this subject is contained in essays. Two outstanding books however are Karl Vossler, *Algunos caracteres de la cultura española*, 1942, Col. Aus., and *La poesía de la Soledad en España*, 1946, Editorial Losada, Buenos Aires. 'Azorín' and Unamuno devote a number of essays to Castilian culture. S. de Madariaga has written on the Spanish character in *Ingleses, franceses, españoles*, 6th ed., Buenos Aires, 1946. Another useful book is L. Pfandl, *Cultura y costumbres del pueblo español de los siglos XVI y XVII*, Barcelona, 1929.

Of the many critics and scholars whose studies on Spanish literature are valuable, but whose essays I have not already mentioned, one may select these names: M. Milá y Fontanals, J. Fitzmaurice-Kelly, A. Morel-Fatio, R. Foulché-Delbosc, A. Coster, A. Reyes, A. Castro, P. Henríquez Ureña, K. Vossler; and on poetry, Pedro Salinas, Dámaso Alonso and G. Díaz-Plaja. Finally Menéndez Pelayo's *Estudios y discursos de Crítica Histórica y literaria*, 7 vols., Madrid, 1941, and his rather too discursive *Orígenes de la novela*, 4 vols., 1943, are books to be dipped into. A book which has just appeared, *Poesía Española*, by Dámaso Alonso, Madrid, 1950, contains studies of a rather technical nature upon the poetry of the six principal poets of the Spanish Golden Age.

Appendix

Francisco de Aldana's complete works were published in Madrid in 1953, edited by M. Moragón. A selection of his poems came out in Clas. Cast. in 1957, edited by Elias L. Rivers.

A GLOSSARY OF
MEDIEVAL VERSE FORMS

arte mayor: stanzas of eight lines written in a twelve-syllabled metre. It superseded *cuaderna vía* at the end of the fourteenth century. See pp. 89-91.

cantar de gesta: chanson de geste, or epic poem.

cantigas de amigo: Galician-Portuguese love songs, in which the speaker is a woman. Date, thirteenth century.

cossante: the form in which many of the *cantigas de amigo* were written. It consists of couplets employing alternate assonances in *i* and *a* and divided by a refrain. These pairs of couplets are parallelistic—that is, each *a* couplet repeats each *i* couplet in slightly different words—while the poem develops by means of a device known as *leixa-pren.* See p. 54.

cuaderna vía: stanzas of four lines, all having the same rhyme and written in a fourteen-syllabled metre, the alexandrine. This was a learned form, practised by the school of clerical poets known as *mester de clerecía.* It came in from France about 1200 and lasted for two centuries.

estribillo: the theme-verse or stanza (of from two to four lines) of a *villancico.* We first meet it in the eleventh century in the form of the Romance *jarcha* of a Hebrew poem and, after *villancicos* ceased to be written, it developed a new lease of life as the popular *copla* of modern times. That is to say, the *estribillo* is the continuous or basic element in Spanish popular lyric poetry. See *villancico.*

estribote: an old name for the *villancico,* which went out of use about 1400.

jarcha: a popular verse or stanza (also known as a *markaz*) which comes at the end of a Spanish-Arabic or Hebrew *muwassaha.* It is often written in Spanish. See pp. 466f. One may compare its function in one of these poems to that of the *estribillos* in the Marqués de Santillana's *villancico* to his three daughters. (See the *Oxford Book of Spanish Verse,* p. 35.)

matla: the theme-verse, usually of two or three lines, which comes at the beginning of an Arabic *muwassaha* or *zéjel.*

mester de clerecía: the school of clerical poets who wrote in *cuaderna vía.* Also applied to the type of poetry they wrote.

muwassaha: a form resembling that of the *zéjel,* but written in classical Arabic or Hebrew. Every *muwassaha* ends with a verse of three or four lines called the *jarcha,* which is written in popular Arabic or Romance and constitutes the culminating point of the poem. Probably it was sung by a singing-girl. See note on p. 470.

romance: a ballad.

villancico: the form of a popular dance-song, in which a theme-verse or stanza, known as an *estribillo,* is developed in a succession of longer stanzas, each of which ends with a repetition of part of the theme-stanza. This form is identical to that of the Spanish-Arabic *zéjel.* For an early example see the Archpriest of Hita's *trova cazurra* (*Oxford Book of Spanish Verse,* p. 8). At the end of the Middle Ages the *villancico* was taken up by courtly poets and, with a change in the musical settings, underwent a transformation. See for this pp. 119-25. It retained its old form only in Christmas carols.

The word *villancico* is also applied by some writers to the *estribillo,* or theme-stanza, with which the song begins. See p. 119n.

zéjel: a Spanish-Arab popular or semi-popular song, in which a theme-verse or stanza, known as a *matla,* is developed in a succession of longer stanzas, each of which ends with a repetition of the rhyme of the theme-stanza. See p. 470. This form is identical with that of the *villancico.*

For further information consult the index.

INDEX

Numbers in bold type are main references

Index

Index

Index

494

Index

Index

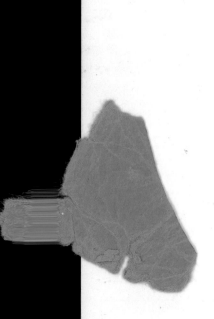